The Economic Impacts of Terrorist Attacks

The Economic Impacts of Terrorist Attacks

Edited by

Harry W. Richardson

The James Irvine Chair of Urban and Regional Planning, School of Policy, Planning and Development and Department of Economics, University of Southern California, USA

Peter Gordon

School of Policy, Planning and Development and Department of Economics, University of Southern California, USA

James E. Moore II

Department of Industrial and Systems Engineering and Department of Civil Engineering and School of Policy, Planning and Development, University of Southern California, USA

Edward Elgar

Cheltenham, UK • Northampton, MA, USA

Published by
Edward Elgar Publishing Limited
Glensanda House
Montpellier Parade
Cheltenham
Glos GL50 1UA
UK

Edward Elgar Publishing, Inc.
136 West Street
Suite 202
Northampton
Massachusetts 01060
USA

A catalogue record for this book
is available from the British Library

Library of Congress Cataloguing in Publication Data

The economic impacts of terrorist attacks / edited by Harry W. Richardson, Peter Gordon, James E. Moore II.
p. cm.
Based on a conference held in Aug. 2004 at the Center for Risk and Economic Analysis of Terrorism Events, University of Southern California.
Includes bibliographical references and index.
1. Terrorism—Economic aspects—United States—Congresses. 2. Infrastructure (Economics)—United States—Congresses. 3. Transportation—Effect of terrorism on—United States—Congresses. 4. Harbors—Security measures—United States—Congresses. 5. Terrorism—United States—Prevention—Congresses. I. Richardson, Harry Ward. II. Gordon, Peter, 1943– III. Moore, James Elliott.

HV6432. E36 2005
338.4′336332′0973—dc22 2005047800

ISBN 1 84542 301 1 (cased)

Printed and bound in Great Britain by MPG Books Ltd, Bodmin, Cornwall

Contents

Contributors

Clark C. Abt, Abt Associates Inc., Cambridge, MA, US, clarkabt@aol.com.

Jay Apt, Department of Engineering and Public Policy, Carnegie Mellon University, US.

Chang-Hee Christine Bae, Department of Urban Design and Planning, University of Washington, US.

Alon Bassok, Department of Urban Design and Planning, University of Washington, US.

Richard L. Bernknopf, US Geological Survey.

Larry Blain, Puget Sound Regional Council, Seattle, US.

David S. Brookshire, Department of Economics, University of New Mexico, US.

Stephanie E. Chang, School of Community and Regional Planning, University of British Columbia, Canada.

Walter Enders, Bidgood Chair of Economics, Department of Economics, Finance, and Legal Studies, University of Alabama, Tuscaloosa, AL 35487, US, wenders@cba.ua.edu.

Alex Farrell, Energy and Resources Group, University of California, Berkeley, US.

Philip T. Ganderton, Department of Economics, University of New Mexico, US.

Peter Gordon, School of Policy, Planning, and Development and Department of Economics, University of Southern California, US.

Daniel G. Hallstrom, Faculty Research Associate CEnREP, US.

Jon D. Haveman, Director, Economy Program, and Research Fellow, Public Policy Institute of California, 500 Washington St, Suite 800, San Francisco, CA 94111, US, haveman@ppic.org.

Geoffrey Heal, Graduate School of Business, Columbia University, New York, NY 10027, US, gmh1@columbia.edu.

Howard Kunreuther, Center for Risk Management and Decision Processes, Wharton School, University of Pennsylvania, Philadelphia, PA 19104, US, kunreuther@wharton.upenn.edu.

Lester B. Lave, Tepper School of Business, Carnegie Mellon University, US.

Timothy L. McDaniels, School of Community and Regional Planning, University of British Columbia, Canada.

Susan E. Martonosi, Massachusetts Institute of Technology, US.

James E. Moore II, Department of Industrial and Systems Engineering and Department of Civil Engineering and School of Policy, Planning and Development, University of Southern California, US.

M. Granger Morgan, Department of Electrical and Computer Engineering, Carnegie Mellon University, US.

David S. Ortiz, RAND Corporation, 201 North Craig Street, Suite 202, Pittsburgh, Pennsylvania, US.

Qisheng Pan, Texas Southern University, Houston, US.

Christian L. Redfearn, School of Policy, Planning, and Development, University of Southern California, Los Angeles, California 90089-0626, redfearn@usc.edu.

Dorothy Reed, Department of Civil and Environmental Engineering, University of Washington, US.

Harry W. Richardson, The James Irvine Chair of Urban and Regional Planning, School of Policy, Planning and Development, University of Southern California, US, hrichard@usc.edu.

Adam Rose, Professor of Energy, Environment and Regional Economics, Department of Geography, The Pennsylvania State University, University Park, PA 16802, US.

Todd Sandler, Robert R. and Katheryn A. Dockson Professor of International Relations and Economics, University of Southern California, Von Kleinsmid Center 330, Los Angeles, CA 90089-0043, US, tsandler@usc.edu.

Richard E. Schuler, Professor of Economics, Professor of Civil and Environmental Engineering, Cornell University, 422 Hollister Hall, Ithaca, NY 14853-3501, US, res1@cornell.edu.

Howard J. Shatz, Research Fellow, Public Policy Institute of California, 500 Washington St, Suite 800, San Francisco, CA 94111, US, shatz@ppic.org.

V. Kerry Smith, University Distinguished Professor, North Carolina State University and Resources for the Future University Fellow, US.

Ernesto I. Vilchis, Graduate Student, Woodrow Wilson School of Public and International Affairs, Princeton University, US.

Henry H. Willis, RAND Corporation, 201 North Craig Street, Suite 202, Pittsburgh, Pennsylvania, US, hwillis@rand.org.

Preface and acknowledgments

In 2004 the US Department of Homeland Security established the first of a series of research centers at US universities studying terrorism and counter-terrorism at the University of Southern California (USC). The center, CREATE (Center for Risk and Economic Analysis of Terrorism Events), focuses on two major issues, risk analysis and economic impacts. Subsequent research centers have different research agendas. CREATE is primarily a combination of researchers in two schools at USC, the Viterbi School of Engineering and the School of Policy, Planning and Development under the co-directorship of Professors Randolph W. Hall and Detlof Winterfeldt. Researchers at other universities are also involved as part of a consortium; some of them are chapter authors in this book. This book is one of the early products from CREATE initially under the Co-Directors. Now Professor Detlof Winterfeldt is the sole Director because of Professor Randolph W. Hall's transfer to a Vice-Provost position.

Although the research in this book was supported by the United States Department of Homeland Security through the Center for Risk and Economic Analysis of Terrorism Events (CREATE), grant number EMW-2004-GR-0112, any opinions, findings and conclusions or recommendations in the book are those of the authors and do not necessarily reflect views of the US Department of Homeland Security.

1. Introduction

Harry W. Richardson, Peter Gordon and James E. Moore II

Since 9/11 there has been considerable speculation and research about future potential terrorist attacks on the United States. Interestingly, and perhaps predictably, much of this research has focused on the cost of human lives and psychological effects rather than more direct economic impacts. Yet there is little doubt that both the economic costs of protection and the potential economic damage from certain types of terrorist attacks could be substantial. This book focuses on some of these issues. It is the result of one of the first activities of CREATE (the Center for Risk and Economic Analysis of Terrorism Events) established at the University of Southern California by the US Department of Homeland Security. This was a conference held in August 2004 that brought together economists and planners from around the country who have developed research interests in terrorism and its economic impacts.

There was a spate of studies after 9/11 (for example, Glaeser and Shapiro, 2001) that considered the problem of whether the attack would lead to a reassessment of corporate location decisions with firms choosing sites less visible than downtown (or midtown) Manhattan. It did not happen, mainly because of a widespread and probably justified belief that future terrorist attacks would diversify rather than repeat the same kind of targets.

'Extreme events' are characterized by non-linear responses, low probabilities, high consequences and the potential for systems interaction that may lead to catastrophic losses. Terrorist acts are probably the most serious of these events because they are done deliberately. However, as suggested in several chapters of this book, the research methodologies previously applied to 'natural' extreme events, such as earthquakes and hurricanes, can be helpful. Several scholars have been studying the economics of natural disasters for some time. Economists interested in understanding and achieving the benefits of mitigation are playing a disaster mitigation game against nature. Although the factors leading to natural disasters remain poorly characterized, the parameters are relatively stable. However it makes sense to improve our understanding of natural hazards. The information acquired will be useful in both natural disaster and terrorism research.

On the other hand, when the source of disaster is cognitive, the process generating adverse events is no longer stationary and the events have minimal predictability. This is why game theory in combination with more, possibly new, analytical tools is so important. But the issues have not yet been resolved and the origins of this book represent only an exploratory, but worthwhile effort.

Also, new approaches may be needed to analyze the often subtle differences between natural and manmade events. For example terrorist attacks are much less predictable in terms of time, place and type of event than natural disasters. Also, even with multiple simultaneous attacks, it is difficult for terrorism to replicate the number of locations that might be impacted by a severe hurricane. On the other hand, certain types of terrorism (for example, the spatial diffusion of epidemics) can affect a larger geographical area and impact many more people.

There may also be many inexpensive cost-effective policies which help to combat terrorism, but also have beneficial societal impacts. A few examples are mentioned in this book, but there must be scores of others. The ones mentioned include: battery-operated traffic signals (Lave et al.; Chapter 4); the wider use of surveillance cameras, especially near bridges and other components of critical infrastructure (Richardson et al.; Chapter 14); and the general public health benefits of bioterrorism defenses (Abt, Chapter 7). The point is that an integrated approach to homeland security issues is required, as well as a public explanation of the more general social benefits, including policies that they come from what appears to be totally unrelated fields.

There is also a strategy and a minimal risk in our endeavors. We recognize that by publishing our views of these problems, we are to some degree providing potential information to knowledgeable terrorists. The risk is minimal because there is almost no specific information in the book that provides significant value added to what is already widely in the public domain. It is to our net benefit to inform each other about the issues and to collaborate on developing our best analytical tools. Advertising the state of information about targets and their vulnerability yields little, because once we recognize our vulnerabilities there will be policies planned and/or implemented to remedy them. In the words of the 9/11 Commission (US National Commission, 2004, p. 391): 'In measuring effectiveness, perfection is unattainable. But terrorists should perceive that potential targets are defended. They may be deterred by a significant chance of failure.'

This book is intended as a good first step. Scenario building will remain fundamental to the problem of anticipating and responding to terrorist threats. Effective protection against terrorist threats is going to take something more, something new. We cannot afford to pick courses of action by exhaustively evaluating every feasible alternative and comparing each one to find the preferred option. We need to be mathematically more sophisticated. We need approaches that allow us to make choices without explicit enumeration of alternatives. It will always be necessary to evaluate some alternatives in detail, and the lessons learned from our research to date will continue to pay off in this dimension. However we need to learn to couple the techniques we have developed with a means to identify third-best alternatives that do not merit intensive evaluation. Becoming systematic about identifying and evaluating scenarios is merely a first step. Also it is important to stress mitigation and recovery because 100 per cent prevention is a fruitless goal.

The chapters employ a wide range of analytical techniques used in other fields of economics and planning. These include cost–benefit analysis, game theory, experimental economics, hedonic pricing models, input–output/transportation network and computable general equilibrium models. Cost–benefit analysis, which features – not unexpectedly – in many chapters, presents especially difficult problems in the field of terrorism because of the extreme uncertainty of the benefits.

What follows is a summary of what we have learned from this experience. Certainly, as Sandler and Enders point out in Chapter 2, both theoretical and empirical techniques can be used to put modern-day terrorism into perspective. Their chapter surveys past contributions, presents updated empirical findings and suggests new directions for research. Because of strategic interactions among terrorists and targeted governments, game theory and economic methods play an important role in identifying novel policy recommendations and behavioral insights. Transnational terrorism and efforts to curtail it involve externalities and market failures. The chapter analyzes how terrorists alter tactics in reaction to government policies and how a no-negotiation hostage policy is difficult to institute in practice.

Heal and Kunreuther explore the problem of interdependent security among agents in Chapter 3. In an interdependent world the risks faced by any one agent depend not only on its choices but also on those of all others. Expectations about others' choices will influence investments in risk management, and the outcome can easily be suboptimal for all. They model this as a Nash equilibrium game and give conditions for a suboptimal equilibrium to be tipped to an optimal one. They also investigate the smallest coalition to tip an equilibrium (the minimum critical coalition) and show that this is also the cheapest critical coalition to move the system from the suboptimal to the optimal equilibrium. The results are examined for a few case studies: airline security, the control of infectious diseases via vaccination, and investment in research and development.

Several of the chapters deal with the consequences of power failures. In Chapter 4 Lave, Apt, Farrell and Morgan point out that energy, transportation, telecommunications and water infrastructures are potentially attractive targets, because it is impossible to protect some elements of these complex systems, and disruptions could impose large costs and possibly result in thousands of deaths. The electric power system is an especially attractive target because of its ubiquitous importance in both the economy and our personal lives, from heating and cooling, access to drinking water, sewage disposal, access to media outlets, traffic lights – without which emergency services would be paralysed – to most economic production, including the entire information technology sector. Their chapter discusses these issues and recommends changes to lower the number of blackouts, reduce the vulnerability of the system to terrorists, and decrease the social costs of blackouts when they occur.

These problems are similar to those discussed in Chapter 5 by Chang, McDaniels and Reed. Infrastructure service outages can cause broad-ranging disruptions across all sectors of an economy. The problem of infrastructure failure interactions (IFIs) is particularly important. The objectives of the chapter are to characterize IFIs and to identify promising mitigation strategies for effectively containing them. The conceptual base of the chapter includes a new framework for characterizing and identifying important IFIs, as well as approaches for evaluating strategies to mitigate their effects. A case study involves a preliminary assessment of IFIs that occurred in a 63-hour storm beginning on 20 January 1993 in the Pacific Northwest. Although this was a natural event (as are multiple references to earthquakes in the chapter), many of the findings apply to man-made events, especially terrorism.

Schuler in Chapter 6, examines some of the features of the bulk power system that might enhance its capacity to recover from a breakdown. In general it is characterized by robustness because power could be restored quickly even after a major terrorist attack. The only way to avoid this would be a highly coordinated attack on multiple regional facilities, although restocking and repair of equipment might increase delays. Collateral damage may be more of a problem, especially if the attack was in the winter in the north. Low-voltage distribution outages may also be irritating because repair crews have to proceed step by step (compare the bulk power failure in the Northeast in August 2003 and the low-voltage distribution failures of the Florida hurricanes in the late summer of 2004).

In discussing the question of the design and coordination of the bulk power system, Schuler adopts a simulation approach that examines the number of agents and whether they act collectively or individually in response to external random shocks. His results suggest three general conclusions. First, it is desirable to have a larger group size as the frequency of potential external shocks increases to facilitate the impact on only a subgroup. Second, risking collapse of the whole system may be worthwhile if restoration can be speeded up. Third, a 'hotchpotch' system may have benefits provided that there is coordination.

In Chapter 7, Abt makes three key points: (1) under current conditions of inadequate US biodefenses, a single catastrophic bioterrorist attack can kill more people than any single nuclear terrorist attack; (2) catastrophic bioterrorism attacks are difficult to deter or defend against, but their risks of massive potential fatalities can be prevented and mitigated by scientifically feasible, economically affordable and politically acceptable means; and (3) cost–benefit assessment of improved biodefenses reap a dual net benefit of at least an order-of-magnitude reduction in deaths and damages and additional peacetime public health benefits to protect against natural deadly epidemics, for an annual investment of less than the $10 billion. This compares with the amount currently invested in ballistic missile defense, a much smaller and less likely threat.

Cost–benefit assessments are considered for improved biodefenses against three catastrophic bioterrorist attacks on the most valuable and vulnerable urban transport centers (New York, Washington, DC and Los Angeles). Potential economic and loss-of-life costs of the three most catastrophic types of bioterrorist attacks (smallpox, plague and anthrax) are estimated from realistic scenarios for current and near-future improved biodefenses. Deaths from a current potential mass bioattack on US cities range from 500 000 to 30 million people; economic damage ranges from $200 billion into trillions. The median and the range of deaths and damages of a catastrophic bioterrorist attack on any large city exceed those from a single nuclear terrorist attack.

Ganderton, Brookshire and Bernknopf report in Chapter 8 on the application of an innovative web-based tool to investigate aspects of the Homeland Security Advisory System (HSAS). The system's high profile has attracted serious criticism for failure to provide relevant threat information, in particular the nature, location and timing of the threat. Their experiments provide a mechanism for analyzing the current system's weaknesses and should aid in the search to improve its value as a risk communication mechanism. Employing the interactive and graphical features of the Internet, experiments are conducted in which subjects faced with potential security threats can purchase more detailed (more spatially accurate) alert information and concurrently choose appropriate preparation and response actions. Empirical analysis of the responses suggest that more geographically detailed threat warnings have value that increases with the level of the threat, and that people base their intended responses on the information and the level of the threat. This research supports the case for more spatially detailed terrorist threat information, made easier with the use of maps. The methodology relies heavily on the principles of experimental economics, a now widely accepted approach, but still controversial (especially with human subjects).

Redfearn's Chapter 9 addresses the market's perception of risk from terrorism by examining the prices of single-family homes before and after the 9/11 terrorist attacks. In the wake of the attacks, government officials responded by raising security at sites considered to be likely targets of future attacks. In the greater Los Angeles metropolitan area, these included the ports of Long Beach and Los Angeles, Los Angeles International Airport and several local civic centers, among others. The skyscrapers of downtown Los Angeles were also thought to be potential targets. It is clear that some markets internalized these actions as representative of the real risk of repeat attacks (for example a pronounced increase in terrorism insurance premiums for commercial properties and 'trophy' properties). It is not clear however that the consumers have similarly altered their behavior. Where surveys indicate that terrorism is seen as a genuine risk, the actions of home buyers in the LA Basin indicate otherwise: the effects of 9/11 on residential markets have been insignificant in the areas surrounding potential targets. Of course many houses sold are too far away from potential targets at least for certain types of attack (for example conventional bombs), because of natural barriers around certain types of facility (for example the ports and the airports). Nevertheless results suggest that the perceived risk of harm from terrorism is in fact unchanged since 9/11.

The purpose of Smith and Hallstrom's Chapter 10 is to outline most of the major methodological and empirical issues associated with developing cost–benefit analyses for homeland security policies. Their starting point is that the post-9/11 environment is irreversible, so that the net benefits of these policies should not be treated as an effort to restore a pre-9/11 baseline. They also suggest that in discussing the links between policies and risk reductions, the limited information base relating to national security implies drawing from the research on large-scale natural hazards would be helpful, especially in the context of individual responses. Hence they refer to research results relating to Hurricane Andrew, using home sales in Lee County, Florida (which Hurricane Andrew narrowly missed) to estimate how new information about the risk of severe storms is capitalized in housing prices for areas recognized to have potential for damage. Lee County residents in flood hazard areas with significant risk of damage from future storms received new information about the severity of these storms but no actual damage. The results confirmed the a priori hypothesis, in that the risk information conveyed by Hurricane Andrew reduced the property values for homes in the area prone to coastal hazards. The measured effects of the information conveyed by Andrew implied a 19 per cent reduction in the rate of change of the property values. Smith and Hallstram conclude with an important implication for cost–benefit analysis: the strategic induced responses to terrorist (or natural disaster) risks convert the standard aggregate cost–benefit analysis into a type of general equilibrium problem that needs to be addressed in future research.

To estimate the economic losses from terrorism, Rose argues in Chapter 11 that it is necessary to deploy a comprehensive and sophisticated model. Faced with two alternative strategies, one approach is to adapt existing models from related areas such as impact analysis and the economics of natural hazards. The other approach is to begin from square one and develop an entirely new modeling approach for the purpose at hand. Rose suggests that the best strategy would be to enhance the existing approach of computable general equilibrium (CGE) analysis, which has proven successful in recent applications to related areas. At the same time, there is an acknowledgement of limitations of the approach, although most of them are not insurmountable.

The purpose of the chapter is to assess the capability of CGE analysis to estimate the production-related losses of a terrorist attack. The assessment includes a discussion of advantages and disadvantages of CGE in general and in the context of the economics of terrorism. It also deals with attempts to overcome CGE model limitations with respect to disequilibria, parameter specifications and behavior. It further emphasizes the ability of CGE modeling to address two aspects of loss estimation that have typically been neglected (at least quantitatively) in almost all studies of disasters, both man-made and natural. The first of these is the full range of indirect or general equilibrium impacts, which have the potential to increase substantially the size of loss estimates. The second is individual business and market resilience, or the inherent ability of businesses and markets to cushion themselves against shocks, which have the potential to lower these loss estimates.

Martonosi, Ortiz and Willis in Chapter 12 use the example of port container scrutiny to suggest that the goal of transportation security initiatives be cost-effective risk reduction and to argue that all policies should be subject to rigorous cost–benefit analysis. The chapter provides a case study for a specific proposal: 100 per cent inspection of containers at US ports. Container scanning and inspection is a key element in ensuring a secure containerized shipping system. Complete primary inspection is not wholly infeasible, although the percentage of containers currently scanned remains very low. The chapter presents a cost–benefit analysis of implementing a policy of scanning 100 per cent (or less) of incoming containers at US ports, exploring issues of technological improvement, the impacts of different scanning rates (which could vary from port to port) on cost and effectiveness, the uncertainty of the consequences, and the probabilities of an attack.

A policy of 100 per cent scanning is not feasible with current technology and constraints relating to personnel and port space. A $10 billion event would make 100 per cent scanning cost-effective, leaving aside the personnel and land constraints. A $1 billion event would not justify 100 per cent scanning unless its probability was very high (say 80 per cent per year). Improved scanning technology and more resources (both human and non-human) could increase cost-effectiveness, especially if it reduced the false positive rate and had a deterrent effect (on both terrorists and smugglers). Making do with less than 100 per cent scanning would require a targeting strategy superior to random selection.

In Chapter 13 Haveman, Shatz and Vilchis take a somewhat broader look at maritime security than container screening. Despite the rapid speed of passage for the Maritime Transportation Security Act (MTSA), the legislation lacks a comprehensive view of maritime security issues, especially the maritime transportation supply chain. The CBP (US Customs and Border Patrol), via its initiatives – Customs–Trade Partnership against Terrorism (C-TPAT) and the Container Security Initiative (CSI) – is in the process of shifting the security of container protection from foreign to domestic shores and in encouraging maritime shipping participants to develop their own security plans. However the resources to implement federally mandated measures are not yet in place and there are gaps in the coverage of some programs (such as the lack of inspectors in some ports and concerns about the effectiveness and continuing implementation of supply chain security plans). Until these gaps are remedied, the maritime transportation network remains vulnerable to a terrorist event and the capacity to respond to it.

Chapter 14 by Gordon, Moore, Richardson and Pan examines the impact of an attack on the twin ports of Los Angeles and Long Beach via radiological bombs supplemented by the destruction of overpasses on access freeways. They distinguish between 'local effects' (that is shutting down port and port-related activities in the vicinity of the ports) and 'regional effects' (more accurately, including national and international consequences) associated with the interruption of international trade. Their estimates cover a wide range, depending on whether the ports are shut down by very small bombs alone for 15 days, or whether the access bridges are also taken out which would imply a minimum of 120 days to rebuild. In the minimum case, the direct, indirect and induced damages would only be $138.5m of output and 1258 person-years of employment, with two-thirds of the impacts confined within the region. In the 120-day case, the damages could rise to more than $34 billion of output and 212 165 person-years of employment, with two-thirds of the impacts felt outside the region. These impacts might be modified by deferred purchases, diversion of trade to other ports (probably minimal), and more use of the newly built separated rail line (the Alameda Corridor, although this is also subject to terrorist attack).

Bae, Blain and Bassok in Chapter 15 also address a transportation network problem in their assessment of what might happen if terrorists blew up to the bridges across Lake Washington in the Seattle region that link downtown with the edge cities on the Eastside; in addition, scenarios are examined where a bomb cuts the critical I-5 Interstate North–South link by blowing up the area under the Convention Center. The lake, the hills and other aspects of the unusual topography plus the chronic underinvestment in highways make the Seattle recovery model problematic. Currently there is no model in Seattle with the capacity to evaluate the economic impacts (the well-known UrbanSim model is much more oriented to land-use impacts), so the results of this study are confined to transportation impacts. Because commuters (and others) would have to go around the lake by relatively narrow surface roads, trip times could almost triple and total regional travel times (by hours and value, for both commuting and freight) could increase by up to 16 per cent. Temporary or partial bridge restoration costs would probably be about $200 million. These consequences might be moderated by trip deterrence, and the provision of more and superior bus services, especially if the circumstances could induce an even temporary two-thirds increase in the transit share.

This book does not pretend to offer a comprehensive approach to all the issues relating to the economic consequences of terrorist attacks. That would take many books. To take merely a few examples, there are no chapters relating to airports (other than airline baggage-checking security), tourism, attacks on nuclear power stations, border controls or protecting US homeland security abroad. To briefly mention the first, it would not be very difficult to explode a moderately sized conventional bomb in the pre-security area of an airline terminal in a large airport at a busy time of day. This raises a more conceptual issue that has been addressed in the economics of crime literature, the so-called 'displacement effect'. There are always too many targets that need protecting, and terrorists (and other criminals) can always seek out those unprotected or very lightly protected. An exploded bomb in a busy terminal could do at least as much damage as on a plane in flight. However the purpose of this Introduction is to discuss the current book, not a menu for future research.

REFERENCES

Glaeser, E.L. and J.M. Shapiro (2001), 'Cities and Warfare: The Impact of Terrorism on Urban Form', paper prepared for the *Journal of Urban Economics* Symposium on Terrorism and the Future of Cities.

US National Commission on Terrorist Attacks upon the United States (2004), *The 9/11 Commission Report*, New York: W.W. Norton & Co.

2. Transnational terrorism: an economic analysis*

Todd Sandler and Walter Enders

INTRODUCTION

On 11 September 2001 (henceforth, 9/11), the world watched aghast as two commercial airliners toppled the twin towers of the World Trade Center (WTC) and a third plowed into the Pentagon. Yet a fourth hijacked plane landed short of its intended Washington, DC target as passengers took matters into their own hands. Economic methods – both theoretical and empirical – have been applied by a small and growing group of economists to understand a host of issues associated with such terrorist events. These issues concern the policy effectiveness of alternative responses (for example toughening punishments, retaliatory raids and installing technological barriers), negotiation responses in hostage incidents, the terrorists' choice of target, the economic impacts of terrorism, the provision of terrorism insurance, the curbing of interdependent risk, and others.

Terrorism is the premeditated use, or threat of use, of a high level of violence by an individual or a subnational group to obtain a political objective through intimidation or fear directed at a large audience usually beyond the immediate victims. An essential aspect of this definition concerns the presence of a political objective (for example getting the United States out of the Persian Gulf states) that the terrorist acts or campaigns are designed to achieve. Incidents that have no specific political demands are criminal rather than terrorist acts – for example extortion for profit. Another crucial ingredient is the use of extranormal violence or brutality to capture news headlines. As the public becomes numb to their acts of violence, terrorists respond with more heinous actions to recapture media attention. Thus the escalation experienced on 9/11 was part of an ongoing process. Terrorists often direct their violence and threats toward a vulnerable target group, not immediately involved with the political decision-making process that they seek to influence. The two planes that crashed into the WTC fit this pattern, but the other two planes were targeted against decision makers. In a deliberate attempt to create a general atmosphere of fear, terrorists strike at a variety of targets with alternative modes of operations (for example assassinations, bombings and kidnappings), thus making it difficult for the authorities to anticipate the venue of the next incident. Such actions make attacks appear to be random, so that a targeted society must expend large amounts of resources to protect a wide range of vulnerabilities. This simulated randomness provides terrorists with a cost advantage over the stronger authorities who must defend against the threat that they pose. Because people tend to over-respond to unlikely catastrophic events while ignoring more likely daily dangers (for example dying in a car accident), terrorists succeed in achieving society-wide anxiety with minimal resources.

When a terrorist incident in one country involves victims, targets, institutions, governments, or citizens of another country, terrorism assumes a transnational character. In the WTC tragedy, citizens from over 80 countries lost their lives at the hands of foreign terrorists who crossed into the United States from abroad. Obviously the four hijackings on 9/11 constitute transnational terrorist attacks. Transnational terrorist incidents are transboundary externalities insofar as actions conducted by terrorists or authorities in one country may impose uncompensated costs or benefits on people or property of another country. As such, myriad market failures are associated with collective actions to curb international terrorism.

Economic methodology is particularly well suited to provide insights in studying terrorism. Economic analysis can account for the strategic interactions among opposing interests – for example among rival terrorists, the terrorists and the authorities, and among targeted countries. Rational-choice models, based on microeconomic principles, can be applied to ascertain how terrorists are apt to respond to policy-induced changes to their constraints. The same methods can be used to analyze how governments react to terrorist-induced changes to their policy-making environment. Altruistic-based intergenerational rewards can even be shown to motivate the growing use of suicide bombings (Azam, forthcoming). Additionally, the theory of market failures can underscore how agents' independent optimization may be at odds with socially efficient outcomes, so that governmental failures may result from well-intentioned policies. In addition, various economic empirical methods can be applied to evaluate theoretical predictions and policy recommendations. Empirical techniques can evaluate the economic consequences of terrorism – for example the impact of terrorism on tourism (Enders et al., 1992), foreign direct investment (Enders and Sandler, 1996) and per capita GDP (Abadie and Gardeazabal, 2003).

The primary purpose of this chapter is to survey some crucial insights gained from applying an economic perspective to the study of terrorism. A second purpose is to present an updated analysis of trends and cycles, policy-induced externalities, collective action responses and hostage negotiation strategy. A third purpose is to identify some future research directions.

A LOOK AT THE DATA

To provide a perspective on the nature of the transnational terrorist threat, we compile Table 2.1 based on data from the US Department of State (1988–2004). This table indicates the annual number of transnational terrorist events, the associated deaths, the number of wounded and the number of attacks against US people and/or property for 1968–2003. During these 36 years there were 14 857 transnational terrorist incidents in which 14 807 people (including those on 9/11) died. On average there were 411 fatalities per year which is relatively few, especially compared with the 41 000 or so people killed annually on US highways. Each terrorist incident kills on average about one person. The casualties on 9/11 represent a clear outlier with deaths on this single day approximately equal to all transnational terrorist-related deaths recorded during the entire 1988–2000 period.

An examination of Table 2.1 suggests that transnational terrorism follows a cyclical pattern with much of the 1990s being relatively calm compared to the earlier two decades. Transnational terrorism is particularly low during 2002–2003, with incidents on par in number to that of 1969 at the start of the era of transnational terrorism. Something that cannot be seen from Table 2.1 is that a high proportion of total casualties for a given year is typically associated with a couple of 'spectacular' events – for example the simultaneous bombings of the US embassies in Nairobi, Kenya and Dar es Salaam, Tanzania accounted for 291 deaths and almost 5000 injuries in 1998 (US Department of State, 1999). The right-hand column of Table 2.1 indicates that approximately 40 per cent of all transnational terrorist attacks are against US interests. This is especially noteworthy from an externality viewpoint, because relatively few incidents take place on US soil – that is, during 1998–2003, only six incidents (including the four skyjackings on 9/11) occurred in the United States (US Department of State, 2004).

By having relatively secure borders, the United States must rely on foreign governments to protect US citizens and property while abroad. Terrorists that target US interests – for example Revolutionary Organization 17 November in Greece (known as 17 November) – may operate with impunity if the risks to foreigners are of little concern to the local government. This leads to underdeterrence of terrorism from a multi-country viewpoint (Lee, 1998). Until the summer of 2002 when a 17 November terrorist injured himself in an attempted bombing, the group had engaged

Table 2.1 Transnational terrorism: events 1968–2003

Year	Number of events	Deaths	Wounded	Attacks on US interests
2003	208	625	3646	84
2002	202	725	2013	77
2001	355	3296	2283	219
2000	426	405	791	200
1999	395	233	706	169
1998	274	741	5952	111
1997	304	221	693	123
1996	296	314	2652	73
1995	440	163	6291	90
1994	322	314	663	66
1993	431	109	1393	88
1992	363	93	636	142
1991	565	102	233	308
1990	437	200	675	197
1989	375	193	397	193
1988	605	407	1131	185
1987	665	612	2272	149
1986	612	604	1717	204
1985	635	825	1217	170
1984	565	312	967	133
1983	497	637	1267	199
1982	487	128	755	208
1981	489	168	804	159
1980	499	507	1062	169
1979	434	697	542	157
1978	530	435	629	215
1977	419	230	404	158
1976	457	409	806	164
1975	382	266	516	139
1974	394	311	879	151
1973	345	121	199	152
1972	558	151	390	177
1971	264	36	225	190
1970	309	127	209	202
1969	193	56	190	110
1968	125	34	207	57

Source: US Department of State (1988–2004) and tables provided to Todd Sandler in 1988 by the US Department of State, Office of the Ambassador at Large for Counterterrorism.

in over 140 attacks and 22 assassinations since 1973 with no arrests (Wilkinson, 2001, p. 54). If instead much of the threat is to a host country's interests, then overdeterrence may result as the country does not account for the transference externality of causing the terrorists to switch their attacks to another less-protected country. In the overdeterrence scenario, each country engages in a Prisoners' Dilemma 'arms race' to deflect the common terrorist threat to an alternative venue (Arce and Sandler, 2004; Sandler and Lapan, 1988; Sandler and Siqueira, 2003). Unless such actions decrease the overall level of attacks, each country expends resources without securing their citizens' safety, which is particularly relevant when these citizens are targeted in other countries. This is a real concern for the United States, which has deflected almost all attacks on its interests to foreign soil.

Data

Except for some annual totals, government-collected data sets have not been made available to researchers. Mickolus (1982) developed a data set, International Terrorism: Attributes of Terrorist Events (ITERATE) for 1968–77. This event-based data set was extended to cover 1978–2003 by Mickolus et al. (2004). ITERATE uses a host of sources for its information, including the Associated Press, United Press International, Reuters tickers, the Foreign Broadcast Information Service (FBIS) Daily Reports, and major US newspapers (for example the *Washington Post* and the *New York Times*).

ITERATE poses a number of shortcomings that researchers must take into account when testing theories. By relying on newspaper accounts, ITERATE is better at chronicling the actions of terrorists (for example number of terrorists in a hit squad or terrorists' actions during negotiations) than in recording those of the authorities (for example how many commandos were used to free a hostage). In select instances, government strategy is revealed by newspapers and is coded by ITERATE. Because ITERATE is an events data-set, researchers must rely on event counts rather than on continuous measures of intensity unless casualty counts are used (Enders and Sandler, 2000, 2002). ITERATE picks up newsworthy transnational terrorist incidents, so that there is some bias, which must be recognized. The bias has worsened since mid-1996 when the FBIS Daily Reports were no longer available to ITERATE coders.

Despite these difficulties, ITERATE is suited to a wide range of empirical tasks. For example it can display trends and cycles for events for forecasting purposes (for example Cauley and Im, 1988; Enders, Parise and Sandler, 1992). The data have even been used to investigate terrorist and government bargaining behavior in hostage-taking events – that is, kidnapping, skyjackings and takeover of facilities (barricade and hostage-taking events) – by Atkinson et al. (1987). This latter study applied a time-to-failure model, where the length of an incident is related to choice variables of the adversaries – for example sequential release of hostages, allowing deadlines to pass uneventfully and the number of hostages secured.

If the time series for all transnational incidents and bombings are displayed with ITERATE data, there is a marked downturn in transnational terrorism due, in large part, to fewer states sponsoring terrorism in the post-Cold War era (Enders and Sandler, 1999). When the time series for all events and bombings are placed on the same diagram, the bombing series comprises about half of the all-events series. Moreover the bombing series imparts its shape to the all-incident series. Time series for all events, bombings, assassinations and hostage-taking incidents display peaks and toughs. The assassination and hostage-taking time series include far fewer incidents per quarter than the bombing series. If terrorists are rational actors, as we suppose, then they should respond to risk and engage less frequently in those events that are more risky and logistically complex, such as assassinations and hostage taking (Sandler et al., 1983). Assassinations and hostage missions fell just prior to 9/11 and have not returned to their old levels. There are probably three explanations for these drops. First, today's terrorists are more interested in greater carnage than an assassinated individual. Second, extra precautions at airports have reduced skyjackings – one kind of hostage-taking mission. Third, the war on terror has compromised al-Qaida's leadership and its ability to execute logistically complex and costly attacks.

Terrorist experts have documented a change in the make-up and motivation of the general perpetrators of terrorism since the takeover of the US Embassy in Tehran in November 1979 (Hoffman, 1998). From the late 1960s until the latter 1980s, transnational terrorism has been primarily motivated by nationalism, separatism, Marxist ideology and nihilism (Wilkinson, 1986). In the 1990s, the motivation of terrorism changed with 'the emergence of either obscure, idiosyncratic millennium movements' or religious-based fundamentalist groups (Hoffman, 1997, p. 2). Since the beginning of 1980, the number of religious-based groups has increased as a proportion of the active terrorist groups: 2 of 64 groups in 1980, 11 of 48 groups in 1992, 16 of 49 groups in 1994, and 25 of 58 groups in 1995 (Hoffman, 1997, p. 3). With the earlier prevalence of leftist-based organizations that wanted to win the hearts and minds of the people, such terrorist groups avoided casualties except of individuals characterizing the establishment or the 'enemy'. Today fundamentalist terrorist groups purposely seek out mass casualties, viewing anyone not with them as a legitimate target, as 9/11 showed. Enders and Sandler (2000) show that a significant rise in casualties from transnational incidents can be traced back to the takeover of the US Embassy in Tehran. In recent years, an incident is almost 17 percentage points more likely to result in death or injury compared with the earlier eras of leftist terrorism. Since 9/11, transnational terrorisms have decreased the proportion of hostage events and greatly increased the proportion of bombings. This pattern is consistent with today's fundamentalist terrorists going for greater carnage and avoiding costly and risky hostage events.

Trends and Cycles

Judging by the public's and media's reaction to 9/11, one might conclude that international terrorism is on the rise, which is not the case. This misperception may be due to the increasing likelihood of an incident resulting in casualties, making incidents on average more newsworthy. The standard procedure for ascertaining the form of a deterministic trend is by fitting a polynomial in time (t), where additional trend terms (that is, t, t^2, t^3) are added until the associated coefficient is no longer statistically significant. For 1968–2003 we investigate trends for six time series extracted from ITERATE: hostage taking, bombings (of all types), threats and hoaxes (that is, threatened future incidents or a false claim for a concurrent incident – a bomb aboard a plane, when there is no bomb), assassinations, incidents with casualties, and all transnational terrorist incidents. Table 2.2 indicates the polynomial trend estimates for these six series (where time $= t$), all of which are characterized by a non-linear trend. The t-ratios associated with the coefficient estimates are indicated in parentheses beneath the constant and the time trend terms. Five of the six series are represented by a quadratic trend with a negative coefficient for the squared time term. This characterization reflects the fact that series tended to rise in the late 1960s and to decline in the late 1990s. Only the threats and hoaxes series is represented by a more complicated cubic trend; nevertheless this series also displays a similar inverted U-shaped pattern.

In Table 2.2, the next-to-last column on the right reports the F-statistics and their 'prob' values in brackets, representing the statistical significance of the overall regression. These significance levels are all zero to three digits, which are strongly supportive of the fitted non-linear trend equations. Such fitted trends are not useful for very long-term forecasting, because there is little reason to believe that the number of incidents will continue to decline. Instead, the fit of the non-linear trend cautions against simple statements about a decidedly upward or downward trend to any form of international terrorism. Such proclamations are common in the media.

Table 2.2 Trend and other statistical properties of transnational terrorist incidents, 1968–2003

Incident type	Constant[a]	Time	(Time)^2	(Time)^3	*F*-Stat[b]	Variance	Percent[c]
Hostage taking	2.926	0.244	−0.002		13.83	31.837	0.311
	(2.009)	(5.120)	(−4.839)		[0.000]		
Bombings	37.710	0.954	−0.008		30.296	624.310	0.241
	(5.916)	(4.637)	(−6.040)		[0.000]		
Threats and hoaxes	6.024	−0.061	0.006	−0.000	15.011	79.431	0.263
	(1.940)	(−0.326)	(1.811)	(−2.854)	[0.000]		
Assassinations	−1.069	0.397	−0.003		65.367	18.126	0.393
	(−0.976)	(10.716)	(−11.371)		[0.000]		
Casualties	5.112	0.810	−0.006		58.444	86.454	0.391
	(2.138)	(10.494)	(−10.811)		[0.000]		
All events	43.075	2.293	−0.018		44.240	1256.651	0.222
	(4.725)	(7.790)	(−8.855)		[0.000]		

Notes:
[a] *t*-ratios are in parentheses.
[b] Prob values are in brackets under the *F*-statistics.
[c] Proportion of variance of the detrended, fitted-polynomial series that is accounted for by the lowest 15 per cent of the frequencies (that is the longest cycles).

The trend analysis suggests that there is persistence in each of the incident series – high and low levels of terrorism come in waves or cycles. Shocks to any incident series are not permanent, so that there is a reversion toward a long-run mean.

Cycles in terrorism data have been attributable to a number of factors. Alexander and Pluchinsky (1992) explain fluctuations in terrorism using demonstration and copycat effects. Heightened public sensitivity following a successful terrorist attack induces other terrorists to strike when media reaction is likely to be great. The anthrax attacks following the events of 9/11 appear to correspond to this pattern. Economies of scale in planning terrorist incidents by terrorist groups or networks may also lead to the bunching of attacks. Cycles may also stem from the attack–counterattack process between the terrorists and the authorities (Faria, 2003). Public opinion following a spate of attacks can prompt governments' periodic crackdowns that temporarily create a lull in transnational terrorism. These downturns are subsequently followed by countermeasures and recruitment by the terrorists as they prepare for a new offensive. Chalk (1995) indicates that cycles based on public-opinion pressure swings are in the three- to five-year range, insofar as time is required for the public to unite and successfully make their demands on officials to do something – a prediction borne out by time series investigations (Enders and Sandler, 1999).

In our past work, we find that each type of terrorist series has its own characteristic cycle that hinges on the logistical complexity of the attack mode. Enders and Sandler (1999) and Enders et al. (1992) argue that logistically complex events such as skyjackings, large suicide car bombings and assassinations will have longer cycles than less sophisticated events as the attack–counterattack interaction among adversaries takes longer. Such complex missions utilize relatively large amounts of resources as compared to small explosive bombings, threats and hoaxes. Given their resource constraints, terrorists can more easily gear up for a campaign dominated by small bombs than one relying on more resource-intensive events.

The theory of Fourier series allows a wide class of functions to be expressed in terms of sine and cosine components. To uncover the underlying cycles in a series, a researcher must regress the detrended values of a series on all frequencies in the interval $[1, T/2]$, where T is the number of observations. The frequency of a series indicates how fast the underlying cycle is completed – a low (high) frequency implies a long (short) cycle. A graphical depiction of the proportionate variation explained by each frequency (called the periodogram) has large peaks representing the crucial underlying frequencies. Some series with obvious cycles, like sunspots or average daily temperatures, will display a periodogram with a single focal frequency. Given the stochastic behavior of terrorists and the measures applied to curb terrorism, there is unlikely to be one deterministic frequency that dominates the periodicity for any of the six series. Thus we use a different approach than trying to identify one particular frequency. Series with long periods will have most of their variance explained by the low frequencies, whereas series with short periods will have most of their variance explained by high frequencies.

In accordance with spectral analysis, we detrended each series using the fitted polynomial trends in Table 2.2. The last two columns of Table 2.2 report the total variance of each series and the proportion of this variance accounted for by the lowest 15 per cent of the frequencies. In particular, we report the proportion of the variance explained by the frequencies in the interval $[1, 0.15 \times T/2]$. We anticipate that the logistically complex incidents types will have relatively large amounts of this proportion attributable to the low frequencies. The all-events series has a large variance of 1256.651 with just 22.2 per cent corresponding to the relatively low frequencies. In marked contrast and in accordance with our assumptions, the more complex events of assassinations and those involving casualties have smaller variances with more of this variance (39.3 and 39.1 per cent, respectively) attributed to low frequencies. As predicted, threats and hoaxes of bombings display the greatest evidence of short cycles with approximately 25 per cent of their variance explained by the longest cycles. Hostage taking is in the intermediate range with 31.1 per cent of the variance explained by the low frequencies. Some hostage-taking events (for example skyjackings) are complex, while others (for example kidnapping) are not so complex; hence this intermediate finding for all hostage-taking missions is sensible.

GAME THEORY AND HOSTAGE TAKING

Despite the events of 9/11, hostage taking may still involve negotiations, because most such missions involve kidnappings, where the terrorists are not suicidal. Skyjackings in Turkey and Cuba during March 2003 demonstrate that not all such events include terrorists bent on mass destruction. Nevertheless suicide skyjackings and the responses of desperate passengers to fight back must be analyzed in the future along with a government's decision to destroy a hijacked plane.

To date there have been seven economic analyses of hostage-taking events – that is, Atkinson et al. (1987), Lapan and Sandler (1988), Selten (1988), Islam and Shahin (1989), Sandler and Scott (1987), Scott (1991) and Shahin and Islam (1992). The first three studies stress game-theoretic aspects, while the latter four studies do not. We focus our remarks around the Lapan and Sandler (1988) study, which is the most general of these three game-theoretic studies. The question posed by their investigation is whether or not a stated policy by which a government pre-commits never to negotiate with hostage takers will have the intended consequence of keeping terrorists from ever taking hostages. The conventional wisdom states that if terrorists know ahead of time that they have nothing to gain, they will never abduct hostages. This belief has become one of the four pillars of US policy with respect to addressing transnational terrorism – that is, 'make no concessions to terrorists and strike no deals' (US Department of State, 2001, p. iii).

The underlying game tree is displayed in Figure 2.1, where the government goes first and chooses a level of deterrence, D, which then determines the likelihood, θ, of a logistical failure (that is, failure to secure hostages). Because deterrence expenditure (equivalent to D) must be paid by the government in all states of the world, it is analogous to an insurance premium and is hence part of the cost to the government's pay-off, listed above that of the terrorists, at the four endpoints to this simple game in Figure 2.1. More risk-averse governments choose higher deterrence levels and experience less hostage taking at home. Once deterrence is decided, the terrorists must then choose whether or not to attack. The probability of an attack, Ω, depends on whether the terrorists' expected pay-offs from a hostage-taking attack are positive. If $c < c^* = [(1-\theta)/\theta] \times [pm + (1-p)\tilde{m}]$, then the terrorists are better off attacking even though they receive $-c\theta$ for a logistical failure and $(1-\theta)[pm+(1-p)\tilde{m}]$ for a logistical success. We have $c < c^*$ when the expected pay-off from a logistical success, which accounts for negotiation success or failure, exceeds the expected pay-off from a logistical failure. In Figure 2.1, Ω corresponds to $\int_0^{c^*} f(c)\,dc$, where $f(c)$ is the probability density for c which reflects the unknown resolve of the terrorists.

If hostages are apprehended (that is, logistical success occurs), then the government must decide whether or not to capitulate to terrorists' demands, where p is the likelihood of government capitulation. The probability of a hostage-taking incident increases with the likelihood of a logistical success, the probability of a government capitulation (if hostages are secured), and the benefit of a successful operation, m. In contrast, the

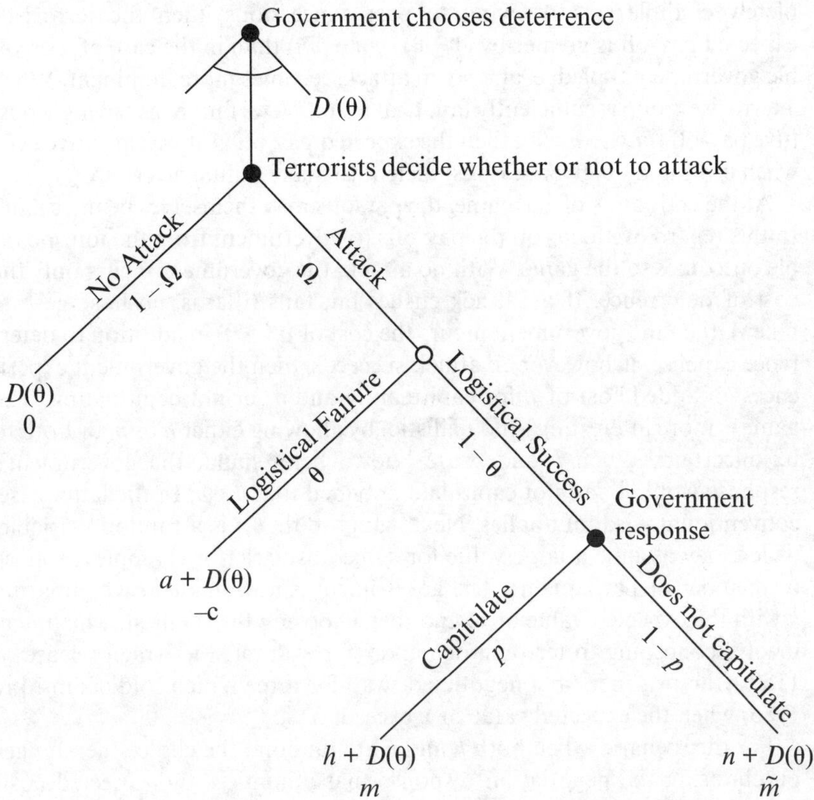

Figure 2.1 Game theory for hostage event

likelihood of an attack decreases with smaller terrorist pay-offs associated with logistical and negotiating failures – that is, smaller $|c|$ and $\tilde{m}$.

The conventional wisdom for the never-to-capitulate policy hinges on at least four implicit assumptions: (1) the government's deterrence is sufficient to stop all attacks; (2) the government's pledge is fully credible to all would-be hostage takers; (3) the terrorists' gains from hostage taking only derive from the fulfillment of their demands; and (4) there is no uncertainty concerning the pay-offs. Each of these assumptions may not hold in practice. Deterrence will not stop all attacks if the terrorists perceive that there is a positive expected pay-off from taking hostages – that $(1-\theta)\times[pm+(1-p)\tilde{m}]-\theta c>0$. Even if the government's pledge is believed by the terrorists ($p=0$), conditions on $\tilde{m}$ exist $[(1-\theta)\,\tilde{m}>c\theta]$, so that the terrorists can derive a positive gain from securing hostages when getting no concessions. This may arise when media exposure from holding the hostages is sufficient reward in itself. If however the government's pledge is not completely credible ($p>0$) owing to past concessions, then the terrorists' expected pay-off is greater by $(1-\theta)\,(pm-p\tilde{m})$ than in the case of a credible governmental pledge, and so an attack becomes more imminent. When a terrorist group is sufficiently fanatical that it views failure as having a positive pay-off ($\tilde{m}>-c>0$), then the expected pay-off is always positive even when $\theta=1$ and deterrence is insufficient to make failure a certainty.

At the endpoints of the game, the pay-offs may themselves be uncertain. In this regard, we focus on the pay-offs to government from the four possible outcomes to the game. With no attack, the government incurs only the cost of deterrence. If an attack ensues but fails (that is, no hostages are taken), then the government incurs the cost of a (>0) in addition to deterrence expense; if however an attack succeeds, then the government experiences an added cost of h for capitulating and n for not capitulating. The game is more interesting (and realistic) by allowing either h or n, or both to be uncertain. When h and n are known beforehand, the government's response would be to not capitulate provided that $h>n$. In the latter case, conventional wisdom applies. Next, suppose that n is a random variable, which may assume a large value for some hostages (for example a soldier or member of parliament). The government is now guided by comparing h with the expected value of n, and then choosing the smallest, which may involve conceding to terrorist demands (for example the Israeli release of 1150 Arab prisoners in a negotiated swap for three Israeli soldiers in May 1985) when the expected value of n exceeds h.

For the scenario when both h and n are random, the choice then hinges on choosing the negotiation response that minimizes the expected cost. A pre-commitment strategy to never concede to hostage takers' demands may be time inconsistent when a government later discovers that the cost of holding firm is too high owing to cost randomness. Although the government has every intention to fulfill its pledge, its inability to deter all incidents and the terrorists' ability to capture the 'right' hostage means that a government may, at times, renege on its pledge.

The game representation can be made more realistic by allowing multiple periods and reputation costs. A government concession in one period to hostage takers makes terrorists raise their belief about future concessions. As p increases for future periods, more hostages will be taken, so that there is an added cost to conceding in any period. This cost is denoted by R for loss of reputation, and results in capitulation costs to the government, becoming $h + R + D(\theta)$ in Figure 2.1. Even when reputation cost is included, conceding may not be eliminated unless $h + R$ exceeds n for all its realizations. Such a scenario may be achieved through rules – for example a constitutional amendment that imposes sufficiently severe punishment to eliminate any discretion of government negotiators.

The game can be made still more realistic by including additional sources of uncertainty in terms of the terrorists' pay-offs. Hostage-taking incidents involve asymmetric information and uncertainty on the part of both terrorists and governments (Lapan and Sandler, 1993; Overgaard, 1994). The beauty of game theory is that it permits the evaluation of policies while accounting for uncertainty and strategic interactions of opposing interests. In so doing, easy fixes may not be so straightforward.

GAME THEORY AND GOVERNMENTAL RESPONSES

We have already discussed the transference externality when terrorists target two or more countries and each independently chooses a level of deterrence that fails to account for associated external costs or benefits. External costs are present when deterrence at home displaces the attack abroad, while external benefits are relevant when deterrence at home either protects foreigners or reduces the level of attacks globally. Depending on the opposing external effects – and there may be others not listed – there may result too much or too little deterrence (Sandler and Arce, 2003; Sandler and Lapan, 1988; Sandler and Siqueira, 2003). The overdeterrence–underdeterrence problem is heightened when a terrorist network (for example al-Qaida) operates in upwards of 60 countries and stages its attacks worldwide (US Department of State, 2001). Underdeterrence is particularly acute in countries sympathetic to a group's grievances when the group focuses their attack on foreigners. As the number of potential targets increases, transference efforts may be especially large. By forming a global network, terrorists limit the effectiveness of countries' efforts to thwart terrorism as externalities are maximized through countries' uncoordinated decisions. Terrorists will naturally seek out the weakest link – that is, the country with the least security – for the venue for their next attack. To address these weaknesses, prime targets such as the United States have instituted programs to assist such weakest-link countries in bolstering their counterterrorist capabilities. In fact this assistance is another of the four pillars of US antiterrorism policy (US Department of State, 2001). Ironically US efforts to induce other countries to secure their airports and public places make the United States a more attractive target, as 9/11 sadly demonstrated.

If the terrorist networking advantage is to be countered, then targeted nations must learn to coordinate their own efforts at counterterrorism. This poses a special problem because nations resist sacrificing their autonomy over security matters to a supranational collective. With this in mind, terrorist experts have often called for piecemeal policy where intelligence is shared but not deterrence decisions (for example Kupperman, 1987, p. 577). Such piecemeal responses may be inadvisable when the strategic incentives are taken into account. Suppose that a terrorist network targets three countries, each of which are engaged in overdeterrence to transfer the attack abroad. Further suppose that intelligence allows the targeted countries to better judge the marginal effectiveness of diverting attacks by revealing the terrorists' preference for alternative targets. As these nations acquire this information, they become better adept at diverting attacks, thereby augmenting the negative transference externality. The net impact of this information sharing may be to heighten the transference race without providing more security, so that the added deterrence cost simply makes the three countries worse off. This results in a second-best outcome in which the change in one policy parameter (increased information sharing) which would under full cooperation improve efficiency, may worsen inefficiency when a second policy (coordination of deterrence) is not chosen optimally. A similar second-best scenario may characterize other partial responses – for example greater actions to apprehend terrorists without coordinating efforts to increase punishments. The failure to coordinate retaliatory responses until 7 October 2001 is another piecemeal response that may have led to inefficiencies. Thus the application of game theory again raises policy concerns previously ignored in the literature.

FIGHTING TERRORISTS AND THEIR SPONSORS

Although governments are often confronted by the same terrorists who will target the countries' assets and people at home and abroad, countries nevertheless find it difficult to form coalitions to attack the terrorists or their sponsors directly. Actions to coordinate retaliation against terrorist camps are typically characterized as a Prisoners' Dilemma (Lee, 1988; Sandler, 1997; Sandler and Arce, 2003) where the dominant strategy, giving the greatest reward regardless of the other countries' action, is to do nothing. This representation follows because a country's own cost of attacking exceed its perceived benefits. Terrorists locate in out-of-the-way places that give them a strategic and cost advantage – for example al-Qaida located in the caves and mountains of Afghanistan. This locational advantage raises a retaliator's costs, thus limiting a nation's desire to assume this role. Perceived retaliation cost may also be high relative to derived benefits, because the retaliator often attracts subsequent terrorist attacks as a protest to its action (Brophy-Baermann and Conybeare, 1994; Enders and Sandler, 1993). Any retaliatory action however yields purely public benefits – non-excludable and non-rival – to all potential target countries. For example suppose that three countries confront a common terrorist threat. Further suppose that unilateral action by any nation costs it 6 but confers benefits of 4 on each of the targeted nations. Thus the retaliator nets −2, while the other nations receive a free-rider benefit of 4. From a social viewpoint, each retaliator gives more total benefits to society than its individual costs; however from the nation's perspective, costs exceed benefits and it will do nothing.

Action may however occur if some nation is the prime target so that its actions provide more benefits to it than to other countries. When these nation-specific benefits begin to outweigh the associated costs, a prime-target nation acts and 'privileges' other less-preferred targets with a free ride (Arce and Sandler, 2004; Sandler, forthcoming). After 9/11, the two countries – the United States and the United Kingdom – that lost the most were the main two participants in the attack of the Taliban and al-Qaida in Afghanistan. These targeted countries had to be seen by their people to be doing something to protect lives and property against another devastating attack. Without action, the ruling government would lose legitimacy. This need to maintain legitimacy in the aftermath of 9/11 raised the benefits of retaliatory action sufficiently to warrant acting alone if required. This was particularly true for the United States.

A number of lessons in building a coalition to weaken a terrorist threat can be gleaned from the aftermath of 9/11. Asymmetric targets foster action. If some countries are the choice targets, then they may be sufficiently motivated to act. In addition, the terrorists encourage this coalition building by concentrating their attacks on relatively few nations and escalating the magnitude of spectacular attacks. If they were to spread their attacks more evenly over nations, no nation may derive sufficient benefits to privilege the rest of the group with a free ride from a retaliatory action. Terrorists will concentrate their attacks to satisfy a constituency. Terrorists' desire to capture the attention of the media means that they must kill lots of people with some attacks. As death tolls mount, nations become motivated to act as benefits start to outweigh costs.

RATIONAL-CHOICE REPRESENTATIONS OF TERRORISTS

Beginning with the Landes (1978) study of skyjackings, economists characterize terrorists as rational actors who maximize expected utility or net payoffs subject to constraints. Arguments in these constraints may consist of terrorists' resource endowments or actions taken by the authorities to thwart terrorism. In the Landes (1978) model, potential hijackers engage in a hijacking provided that the associated expected utility exceeds other non-skyjacking means of furthering their goals. Based on this utility comparison, Landes (1978) specifies an offense (that is, number of skyjackings) function, whose independent variables include the hijackers' subjective estimate of the likelihood of apprehension, their estimate of the conditional probability of imprisonment (if apprehended), and other actions by the authorities (for example the presence of US sky marshals on flights). Using data on US hijackings for 1961–76, Landes demonstrates that greater prison sentences and enhanced likelihood of apprehension are significant deterrents. He also indicates that the installation of metal detectors on 5 January 1973 led to between 41 and 50 fewer hijackings in the United States during 1973–76.

In a subsequent analysis, Enders and Sandler (1993) examine a wide range of policy interventions, including metal detectors, fortification of embassies, retaliatory raids and the Reagan 'get-tough-on-terrorists' laws. The theoretical model for the terrorists that underlies their study is analogous to the consumer-choice model. Terrorists maximize utility or expected utility derived from the consumption of basic commodities, produced from terrorist and non-terrorist activities. For example al-Qaida terrorists may gain utility from a reduced political resolve on the part of the United States to remain in the Persian Gulf as Americans lose their lives in terrorist attacks (for example the destruction of the Al Khubar Towers housing US airmen and others on 25 June 1996 near Dhahran, Saudi Arabia). This weakening of US resolve is the basic commodity that can be produced with a number of alternative attack modes. Substitution possibilities among terrorist tactics arise when alternative modes of operations produce the same basic commodities (for example political instability or media attention) in varying amounts. Substitution is enhanced when attack modes possess closely related outcomes and are logistically similar. This is clearly the case for hijackings and other kinds of hostage events. Complementarity results when combinations of attack modes are required to produce one or more basic commodities. When threats follow real attacks, both actions assume a heightened effectiveness and are thus complementary.

To produce these basic commodities, a terrorist group must choose between non-terrorist and terrorist activities, while being constrained by resources. In the latter choice, terrorists must further choose between different modes of terrorist attacks based on the perceived 'prices' associated with alternative operations. Choices are many and include the intended lethality of the act, its country of location, and whom or what to target. The expenditure on any activity consists of its per-unit price times the activity's level. Each mode of operation has a per-unit price that includes the value of time and resources, and anticipated risk to accomplish the act. The securing and maintenance of a kidnapping victim in a hidden location is logistically more complex and requires more resources than leaving a small bomb in a trash bin in a railroad station, so that the former has a greater per-unit price. In choosing a venue, the price differs based on security measures taken by the authorities; a country with more porous borders will be the staging ground for attacks against targets from other more secure countries. The prices confronting the terrorists for each tactic are determined in large part by the government's allocation of resources to thwart various acts of terrorism. If for example embassies are fortified, then attacks against embassy personnel and property within the mission's ground become more costly for the terrorists – that is, there is a rise in the relative price of such attacks. Similarly metal detectors in airports increase the relative price of skyjackings as compared with other kinds of terrorist acts, including kidnappings.

Government policies aimed at a single type of terrorist event (for example the installation of bomb-sniffing equipment in airports) adversely changes its relative price and results in a substitution into now less expensive modes of attack. Thus Landes's (1978) measure of the success of metal detectors, in terms of fewer skyjackings, does not go far enough because the application of this technology may have induced a large number of other kinds of events. Similarly, to judge the success of embassy fortification a researcher must also examine assassinations and other attacks against embassy personnel once outside of the compound.

To account for these substitutions Enders and Sandler (1993) apply vector autoregression (VAR) analysis to allow for the potential interactions among various terrorist time series (for example skyjackings and other hostage events) in response to government policies. They find that metal detectors decreased skyjackings and threats, but increased other kinds of hostage incidents, not protected by detectors. The trade-off between events was about one for one (also see Enders et al., 1990; Im et al., 1987). Both substitutions and complementarities are uncovered. Fortification of US embassies and missions reduced attacks against such installations, but were tied to a disturbing increase in assassinations of officials and military personnel outside of protected compounds. In addition Enders and Sandler (1993) establish that the US retaliatory raid against Libya on April 1986 (for its suspected involvement in La Belle Discothèque in West Berlin on 4 April 1986) was associated with an immediate increase in terrorist attacks against US and UK interests. This increase was shortly followed by a temporary lull as terrorists built up depleted resources. Apparently the raid caused terrorists to intertemporally substitute attacks planned for the future into the present to protest the retaliation. Within a relatively few quarters, terrorist attacks resumed the same mean number of events.

There are a number of ways to institute antiterrorist policies that address these likely substitutions and complementarities. First, the government must make the terrorists substitute into less harmful events. Second, the government must go after the terrorists' resource endowment (its finances, its leadership and its membership) if an overall decrease in terrorism is to follow. Efforts to infiltrate groups or to freeze terrorists' finances have this consequence. Third, the government must simultaneously target a wide range of terrorist attack modes, so that the overall rise in the prices of terrorist attacks becomes analogous to a decrease in resources. Success in raising the price of all modes of terrorist attacks would induce terrorists to shift into legal protests and other non-terrorist actions to air grievances. Based on the above, we can conclude that a reliance on technological barriers merely causes a substitution into other attack modes in the short run. In the long term, terrorists will develop ingenuous countermeasures (that is, plastic guns, bottles of flammable liquid) to circumvent the technology. This terrorist response is an innovation effect, which gives rise to a dynamic strategic interaction. Consequently, authorities must be ever vigilant to improve the technology by anticipating terrorists' ways of circumventing such barriers. This vigilance must lead to periodic upgrades in the technology prior to the terrorists exposing the technology's weakness through a successful attack. Unfortunately authorities have been reactive by only responding after a technological barrier's weakness has been exploited, so that the public remains vulnerable until a new technological fix is found and installed.

Other Kinds of Substitutions

Substitution effects abound in the study of terrorism and involve not only actions of the terrorists, as described above, but also actions of the targets.

For targets, the economic literature addresses two kinds of substitutions. First, there are studies that examine the tourists' choice of vacation spot based on the perceived threat of terrorism and other costs. An alteration in travel risks, arising from increased terrorist incidents in a country, raises the price of a holiday there in comparison to other vacation venues not confronted with terrorism. In a study of Spain, Enders and Sandler (1991) employ VAR analysis to demonstrate that a typical transnational terrorist incident is estimated as scaring away just over 140 000 tourists when all monthly impacts are combined. Companion studies by Enders, Sandler and Parise (1992) and Drakos and Kutan (2003) establish and quantify terrorism-induced substitutions in tourism for Greece, Austria, Italy, Turkey, Israel and other terrorism-ridden countries. Countries like Greece that have not addressed transnational terrorist attacks directed at foreigners lose significant foreign-exchange earnings as a consequence. The cost of terrorism comes in many forms.

Second, target-based substitutions involve foreign direct investment (FDI). Investors decide where to invest based on their perceived economic risks, political risks and monetary returns. An increase in transnational terrorism directed at FDI – for example attacks by Euskadi ta Askatasuna, (ETA), in the Basque region of Spain – is sure to divert such investment. Enders and Sandler (1996) show that an 'average' year's worth of terrorism reduced net FDI in Spain by 13.5 per cent annually, and it reduced net FDI in Greece by 11.9 per cent annually. These reductions translated into declines in real net FDI of $488.9 million and $383.5 million, respectively, or the equivalent of 7.6 per cent and 34.8 per cent of annual gross fixed capital formation in Spain and Greece. Transnational terrorism displayed a significant economic cost, not counting the billions spent on barriers and deterrence. In a more recent study of the Basque region, Abadie and Gardeazal (2003) establish that terrorism reduced per capita GDP by ten percentage points in relation to the terrorism-free synthetic control region.

Studies of Risks

After 9/11, there is greater interest in applying economic methods to study antiterrorism policy choices. One useful line of study examines interdependent security (IDS) risks where the effectiveness of the protective actions by one agent is highly dependent on those of other agents (Heal and Kunreuther, 2004; Kunreuther and Heal, 2003). If for example luggage in the cargo hold of a commercial plane is not rechecked during transfer, then airlines' incentives to invest in screening their own luggage are diminished because the safety of the flight is dependent on exogenous factors. These authors show that a variety of game forms may apply. They also make policy recommendations to create tipping and cascading equilibriums, whereby firms become more motivated to augment their own security as transferred luggage of key carriers (that is, those with the greatest number of feeder flights) become safely screened. To achieve these equilibriums, government must target airline subsidies to key carriers. There are many IDS concerns associated with protective measures against terrorist attacks in a globalized world.

Economists are also interested in the insurance implications of terrorism, since extreme events such as 9/11 are very costly – about $90 billion in losses (Kunreuther et al., 2003) – and virtually impossible to predict. Following 9/11, most insurers dropped their terrorism coverage or made it prohibitively expensive. Terrorism coverage raises public policy issues – for example should the government provide coverage, and if so, how should public and private coverage interface? Clearly, economics can fruitfully be applied to such problems.

TOWARD A COST–BENEFIT ANALYSIS OF TERRORIST-THWARTING POLICIES

As a future research project, economists should assess the benefits and costs of specific policies to thwart terrorism. Such an exercise has not been adequately done and poses some real challenges. Costs are fairly straightforward since figures are available in, say, the United States as to what is paid to fortify embassies and missions, or to guard US airports. Consider the cost associated with airport security. The value of lost time as travelers are screened must be added to the cost of guards and screening equipment.

On the benefit side, calculations are less transparent. One way to estimate a portion of this benefit would be to compute the reduced loss of life attributable to airport security measures – that is, fewer people killed in skyjackings. If the net number of such lives saved, after adjusting for substitutions into other life-threatening terrorist actions, can be measured, then the average 'value of a statistical life' can be applied to translate these lives into a monetary figure. To this figure a researcher must also compute and add the reduced losses in property values (that is, from destroyed planes) attributable to the fewer hijackings. In addition, a portion of the value of net air travel revenues must be considered as a benefit arising from a heightened sense of security stemming from security upgrades. The events of 9/11 clearly underscore that there is a cost to a breach in airport security as the public loses its confidence in air travel. Any of these components are fraught with measurement difficulties, because there may be intervening factors at work – for example air travel was already in a slump prior to 9/11.

Every policy to thwart terrorism would entail its own stream of benefits and costs. Invariably the benefit calculations are problematic. The US-led retaliation against al-Qaida and the Taliban in Afghanistan has well-defined costs in terms of deployed soldiers, ordnance, diplomacy and side payments to 'allies'. But the true savings or benefits from fewer future acts of terrorism, in terms of lives and property saved, is so much more difficult to calculate as they require counterfactual information. Time-series techniques, engineered by Enders and Sandler (1991, 1996) to measure losses to tourism or to FDI from terrorism, can be utilized following the retaliation to roughly estimate the decline in terrorist incidents and their economic value.

CONCLUDING REMARKS

Although economic methods have enlightened the public on a number of issues concerning transnational terrorism, there are many other issues to analyse. For instance there is a need for applying more dynamic game methods – that is, differential game theory – if the waxing and waning of terrorist organizations (for example Red Brigades and Red Army Faction) are to be understood. Clearly, past successes and failures determine the size of these groups over time. The terrorists try to increase their organization's size through enhanced resources, successful operations and recruitment, while the government tries to limit the group's size through raids, intelligence, group infiltration and actions to thwart successes. This dynamic strategic interaction needs to be modeled and empirically tested. In addition, researchers must better assess the role of information and intelligence on behalf of the terrorists and the authorities. Given how little governments really know about the strength of the terrorists that they confront – for example the US government had almost no clue about the size of al-Qaida (US Department of State, 2001, p. 69) prior to 9/11 – asymmetric information characterizes efforts to thwart terrorism. Similarly the terrorists are ill-informed about the resolve of the government and the amount of resources that it is willing to assign to curbing terrorism. Additionally, there is a need to model terrorist campaigns – that is, the choice of the sequence and composition of attacks used by terrorists. As researchers better understand these choices, more effective policy responses can be devised that adjust for the strategic interaction. Another unresearched issue is the optimal choice between proactive and defensive antiterrorism policies. Arce and Sandler (2004) show that governments have a proclivity to favor defensive policies when confronting transnational terrorism, but these authors do not indicate the optimal mix.

NOTES

* This chapter is an extended, updated, and modified version of 'An economic perspective on transnational terrorism', which appeared in 2004 in the *European Journal of Political Economy*, **20** (2), 301–16. Portions of this article are being republished with the kind permission of Elsevier B.V. The Center for International Studies (CIS) at the University of Southern California supported the updating of the terrorism data for 2003.

BIBLIOGRAPHY

Abadie, Alberto and Javier Gardeazabal (2003), 'The economic costs of conflict: a case study of the Basque Country', *American Economic Review*, **93** (1), 113–32.

Alexander, Yonah and Dennis Pluchinsky (1992), *Europe's Red Terrorists: The Fighting Communist Organizations*, London: Frank Cass.

Arce, M., Daniel G. and Todd Sandler (2004), 'Counterterrorism: a game-theoretic analysis', Los Angeles, CA: School of International Relations, University of Southern California (unpublished manuscript).

Atkinson, Scott E., Todd Sandler and John T. Tschirhart (1987), 'Terrorism in a bargaining framework', *Journal of Law and Economics*, **30** (1), 1–21.

Azam, Jean-Paul (forthcoming), 'Suicide-bombing as inter-generational investment', *Public Choice*.

Brophy-Baermann, Brian and John A.C. Conybeare (1994), 'Retaliating against terrorism: rational expectations and the optimality of rules versus discretion', *American Journal of Political Science*, **38** (1), 196–210.

Cauley, Jon and Eric I. Im (1988), 'Intervention policy analysis of skyjackings and other terrorist incidents', *American Economic Review*, **78** (2), 27–31.

Chalk, Peter (1995), 'The liberal democratic response to terrorism', *Terrorism and Political Violence*, **7** (4), 10–44.

Drakos, Kostas and Ali M. Kutan (2003), 'Regional effects of terrorism on tourism: evidence from three Mediterranean countries', *Journal of Conflict Resolution*, **47** (5), 621–41.

Enders, Walter, Gerald F. Parise and Todd Sandler (1992), 'A time-series analysis of transnational terrorism: trends and cycles', *Defence Economics*, **3** (4), 305–20.

Enders, Walter and Todd Sandler (1991), 'Causality between transnational terrorism and tourism: the case of Spain', *Terrorism*, **14** (1), 49–58.

Enders, Walter and Todd Sandler (1993), 'The effectiveness of anti-terrorism policies: vector-autoregression intervention analysis', *American Political Science Review*, **87** (4), 829–44.

Enders, Walter and Todd Sandler (1996), 'Terrorism and foreign direct investment in Spain and Greece', *Kyklos*, **49** (3), 331–52.

Enders, Walter and Todd Sandler (1999), 'Transnational terrorism in the post-Cold War era', *International Studies Quarterly*, **43** (1), 145–67.

Enders, Walter and Todd Sandler (2000), 'Is transnational terrorism becoming more threatening?' *Journal of Conflict Resolution*, **44** (3), 307–32.

Enders, Walter and Todd Sandler (2002), 'Patterns of transnational terrorism 1970–99: alternative time series estimates', *International Studies Quarterly*, **46** (2), 145–65.

Enders, Walter, Todd Sandler and Jon Cauley (1990), 'UN conventions, technology and retaliation in the fight against terrorism: an econometric evaluation', *Terrorism and Political Violence*, **2** (1), 83–105.

Enders, Walter, Todd Sandler and Gerald F. Parise (1992), 'An econometric analysis of the impact of terrorism on tourism', *Kyklos*, **45** (4), 531–54.

Faria, João (2003), 'Terror cycles', *Studies in Nonlinear Dynamics and Econometrics*, **7**, Article 3, http://www.bepress.com/snde.

Heal, Geoffrey and Howard Kunreuther (2004), 'IDS models and airline security', New York: Graduate School of Business, Columbia University (unpublished manuscript).

Hoffman, Bruce (1997), 'The confluence of international and domestic trends in terrorism', *Terrorism and Political Violence*, **9** (2), 1–15.

Hoffman, Bruce (1998), *Inside Terrorism*, New York: Columbia University Press.

Im, Eric I., Jon Cauley and Todd Sandler (1987), 'Cycles and substitutions in terrorist activities: a spectral approach', *Kyklos*, **40** (2), 238–55.

Islam, Muhammad Q. and Wassim N. Shahin (1989), 'Economic methodology applied to political hostage-taking in light of the Iran-Contra affair', *Southern Economic Journal*, **55** (4), 1019–24.

Kunreuther, Howard and Geoffrey Heal (2003), 'Interdependent security', *Journal of Risk and Uncertainty*, **26** (2–3), 231–49.

Kunreuther, Howard, Erwann Michel-Kerjan and Beverly Porter (2003), 'Assessing, managing and financing extreme events: dealing with terrorism', Working Paper No. 10179, National Bureau of Economic Research, Cambridge, MA.

Kupperman, Richard N. (1987), 'Vulnerable America', in Paul Wilkinson and A.M. Stewart (eds), *Contemporary Research on Terrorism*. Aberdeen: University of Aberdeen Press, pp. 570–80.

Landes, William M. (1978), 'An economic study of US aircraft hijackings, 1961–1976', *Journal of Law and Economics*, **21** (1), 1–31.

Lapan, Harvey E. and Todd Sandler (1988), 'To bargain or not to bargain: that is the question', *American Economic Review*, **78** (2), 16–20.

Lapan, Harvey E. and Todd Sandler (1993), 'Terrorism and signalling', *European Journal of Political Economy*, **9** (3), 383–97.

Lee, Dwight R. (1988), 'Free riding and paid riding in the fight against terrorism', *American Economic Review*, **78** (2), 22–6.

Mickolus, Edward F. (1982), *International Terrorism: Attributes of Terrorist Events, 1968–1977* (ITERATE 2), Ann Arbor, MI: Inter-University Consortium for Political and Social Research.

Mickolus, Edward F., Todd Sandler, Jean M. Murdock and Peter Flemming (2004), *International Terrorism: Attributes of Terrorist Events, 1968–2003* (ITERATE 5), Dunn Loring, VA: Vinyard Software.

Overgaard, Per B. (1994), 'Terrorist attacks as a signal of resources', *Journal of Conflict Resolution*, **38** (3), 452–78.

Sandler, Todd (1997), *Global Challenges*, Cambridge: Cambridge University Press.

Sandler, Todd (forthcoming), 'Collective versus unilateral responses to terrorism', *Public Choice*.

Sandler, Todd, G. Daniel and M. Arce (2003), 'Terrorism and game theory', *Simulation and Gaming*, **34** (3), 319–37.

Sandler, Todd and Harvey E. Lapan (1988), 'The calculus of dissent: an analysis of terrorists' choice of targets', *Synthèse*, **76** (2), 245–61.

Sandler, Todd and John L. Scott (1987), 'Terrorist success in hostage-taking incidents', *Journal of Conflict Resolution*, **31** (1), 35–53.

Sandler, Todd and Kevin Siqueira (2003), 'Global terrorism: deterrence versus preemption', Los Angeles, CA: School of International Relations, University of Southern California (unpublished manuscript).

Sandler, Todd, John T. Tschirhart and Jon Cauley (1983), 'A theoretical analysis of transnational terrorism', *American Political Science Review*, **77** (1), 36–54.

Scott, John L. (1991), 'Reputation building in hostage incidents', *Defence Economics*, **2** (3), 209–18.

Selten, Reinhard (1988), 'A simple game model of kidnappings', in Reinhard Selten (ed.), *Models of Strategic Rationality*, Boston, MA: Kluwer Academic, pp. 77–93.

Shahin, Wassim N. and Muhammad Q. Islam (1992), 'Combating political hostage-taking: an alternative approach', *Defence Economics*, **3** (4), 321–7.

United States Department of State (1988–2004), *Patterns of Global Terrorism*, Washington, DC: US Department of State.

Wilkinson, Paul (1986), *Terrorism and the Liberal State*, rev. edn, London: Macmillan.

Wilkinson, Paul (2001), *Terrorism versus Democracy: The Liberal State Response*, London: Frank Cass.

3. You can only die once: interdependent security in an uncertain world*

Geoffrey Heal and Howard Kunreuther

INTRODUCTION

There are certain bad events that can only occur once. Death is the obvious example: an individual's death is irreversible and unrepeatable. More mundane examples are bankruptcy, being struck off a professional register, and other discrete events. In addition there are other events that can in principle occur twice but that are so unlikely and/or so dreadful that one occurrence is all that can reasonably be considered. The events of 11 September 2001 are perhaps of this type. A nuclear meltdown in a highly populated region is another. The fact that such events are typically probabilistic, taken together with the fact that the risk that one agent faces is often determined in part by the behavior of others, gives a unique and hitherto unnoticed structure to the incentives that agents face to reduce their exposures to these risks.

The key point is that the incentive that any agent has to invest in risk-reduction measures depends on how he expects the others to behave in this respect. If he thinks that they will not invest in security, then this reduces the incentive for him to do so. On the other hand should he believe that they will invest in security, then it may be best for him to do so too. So there may be an equilibrium where no one invests in protection, even though all would be better off if they had incurred this cost. Yet this situation does not have the structure of a prisoners' dilemma game, even though it has some similarities.

The fundamental question that motivates our research is: 'Do organizations, such as airline companies and computer network managers, invest in security to a degree that is adequate from either a private or social perspective?' In general the answer is no. The natural next question is of course: 'So what should we do about this?'

Common Features of the Problem

There are several different versions of this problem and all have certain features in common. We have already indicated one of these: a pay-off that is discrete. A bad event either occurs or does not, and that is the full range of possibilities. You die or you live. A firm is bankrupt or not. A lawyer is disqualified or not. A plane crashes or not. It is not useful in these examples to differentiate the outcomes more finely.

Another feature common to the problems that we consider is that the risk faced by one agent depends on the actions taken by others – there are externalities. The risk of an airline's plane being blown up by a bomb depends on the thoroughness with which other airlines inspect bags that they transfer to this plane. The risk that a corporate divisional manager faces that his company will be sent into bankruptcy depends not only on how he manages his divisional risks but also on how other division heads behave.

Finally, there is a stochastic element in all of these situations. In contrast to the standard prisoners' dilemma paradigm where the outcomes are specified with certainty, the interdependent security problem involves chance events. The question addressed is whether to invest in security when there is some probability, often a very small one, that there will be a catastrophic event that could be prevented or mitigated. The risk depends in part on the behavior of others. The unfavorable outcome is discrete in that it either happens or does not.

Importance of Problem Structure

These three factors – non-additivity of damages, dependence of risks on the actions of others, and uncertainty – are as we shall see sufficient to ensure that there can be equilibria at which there is underinvestment in risk-prevention measures. The precise degree of underinvestment depends on the nature of the problem. We focus on the two extremes that span the spectrum of possibilities. These are the security of airlines and computer networks. If an airline accepts baggage that contains a bomb, this need not damage one of its own planes: it may be transferred to another airline before it explodes. So in this framework one agent may transfer a risk fully to another. It may of course also receive a risk from another. There is a game of 'pass the parcel' here. The music stops when the bomb explodes. It can only explode once, so only one plane will be destroyed.

The structure of this game is quite different in the case of computer networks. Here it is commonly the case that if a virus (or hacker) enters the network through one weak point, it (or he) then has relatively easy access to the rest of the network and can damage all other computers as well as the entry machine (Kearns, 2005). In this case the bad outcome has a characteristic similar to a public good: its consumption is non-rivalrous. Its capacity to damage is not exhausted after it has inflicted damage once. A bomb, in contrast, has a limited capacity to inflict damage, and this capacity is exhausted after one incident.

In both cases the incentives depend on what others do. Suppose that there are a large number of agents in the system. In Kunreuther and Heal (2003) we show that in the computer security problem, if none of the other machines are protected against viruses or hackers then the incentive for any agent to invest in protection approaches zero. For airline security, if no other airline has invested in baggage checking systems and there is a high probability that bags will be transferred from one airline to another, the expected benefits to any airline from this investment approaches 63 per cent of what it would have been in the absence of contagion from others.

This structure is common to a wide range of problems with discrete and interdependent risks that may not involve security issues. In 1995 Barings was destroyed by the actions of a single trader in its Singapore branch. In 2002 Arthur Anderson was sent into bankruptcy by its Houston branch. In each case we had multi-unit organizations in which the risk of bankruptcy faced by any unit was affected by its own choices and by the choices made by other units. In such a situation the incentive that any unit has to reduce bankruptcy risks is reduced by the knowledge that others are not doing so. A culture of risk-taking can spread through the organization because knowledge that a few groups are taking risks reduces the incentives that others have to manage them carefully (Kunreuther and Heal, forthcoming).

As we will show below, there can be a stable equilibrium where all agents choose not to invest in risk reduction measures, even though all would be better off if they did invest. An interesting property of some of these equilibria is the possibility of 'tipping' as described by Schelling (1978). How can we ensure that enough agents will invest in security that all the others will follow suit? In some cases there may be one firm occupying such a strategic position that if it changes from not investing to investing in protection, then all others will find it in their interests to do the same. And even if there is no single firm that can exert such leverage, there may be a small group. We show when this can happen and how to characterize the agents with great leverage. Obviously this finding has significant implications for policy-making. It suggests that there are some key players whom it is particularly important to persuade to manage risks carefully. Working with them may be a substitute for working with the population as a whole.

CHARACTERIZING THE PROBLEM: TWO-AGENT PROBLEM

In this section we set out formally the framework within which we study interdependent security (henceforth denoted IDS) and contrast this with other problems that have a prisoners' dilemma (henceforth PD) structure. We will utilize airline security to illustrate the IDS problem and protecting against terrorist attacks to illustrate a PD problem.

Airline Baggage Screening: An IDS Problem[1]

Consider two identical airlines A_1 and A_2, each having to choose whether or not to invest in a baggage screening system. Each faces a risk of a bomb exploding on its plane, causing a loss of L. There are two possible ways in which damage can occur: a bomb can explode either in a bag initially checked onto the airline's own plane or in a bag transferred from the other airline. The probability of a bomb exploding in luggage initially checked onto a plane of an airline that has not invested in security is p. The expected loss from this event is pL. If the airline has invested in security precautions then this risk is assumed to be zero.

Even if an airline has invested in a baggage screening system, there is still an additional risk of loss due to contagion from the other airline if it has not invested in security. The probability of a dangerous bag being accepted by one airline and then being transferred to the other is denoted by q. With respect to the chances of contagion, q is the likelihood that on any trip a dangerous bag is loaded onto the plane of one airline and is then transferred to another airline where it explodes. We assume that there is not enough time for an airline to examine the bags from another airline's plane before they are loaded onto its own plane.

These probabilities are interpreted as follows. On any given trip there is a probability p that an airline without a security system loads a bomb that explodes on one of its own planes. For the airline scenario, thorough scanning of baggage that an airline checks onto its own plane will prevent damage from these bags, but there could still be an explosive in a bag transferred from another airline. There is thus an additional risk of loss due to contagion from another agent who has not invested in loss prevention, denoted by q. If there are $n \geq 2$ airlines, the probability per trip that this bag will be transferred from airline i to airline j is $q/(n-1)$. Note that the probability per trip that a bag placed on an airline without a security system will explode in the air is $p+q$.

We assume throughout that the damage that results from multiple security failures is no more severe than that resulting from a single failure.

In other words, damage is not additive. In the airline baggage scenario, this amounts to an assumption that one act of terrorism is as serious as several. In reality, having two bombs explode on a plane is no more damaging than just one. The key issue is whether or not there is a failure, not how many failures there are. Indeed as the probabilities are so low, single occurrences are all that one can reasonably consider. One could think of the definition of a catastrophe as being an event so serious that it is difficult to imagine an alternative event with greater consequences. We focus first on the case of two airlines, each of which is denoted as an agent. This example presents the basic intuitions in a simple framework. We then turn to the multi-agent case.

To illustrate the framework in the context of a real-world event consider the destruction of Pan Am flight 103 in 1988. In Malta, terrorists checked a bag containing a bomb onto Malta Airlines, which had minimal security procedures. The bag was transferred at Frankfurt to a Pan Am feeder line and then loaded onto Pan Am 103 in London's Heathrow Airport. The transferred piece of luggage was not inspected at either Frankfurt or London, the assumption in each airport being that it was inspected at the point of origin. The bomb was designed to explode above 28 000 feet, a height normally first attained on this route over the Atlantic Ocean. Failures in a peripheral part of the airline network, Malta, compromised the security of a flight leaving from a core hub, London.

Assume that each airline has two choices: to invest in baggage screening, S, or not to do so, N. Table 3.1 shows the pay-offs to the agents for the four possible outcomes.

Here Y is the income of each airline before any expenditure on security or any losses from the risks faced. The cost of investing in security is c. The rationale for these pay-offs is straightforward. If both airlines invest in security, then each incurs a cost of c and faces no losses from damage so that their net incomes are $Y-c$. If A_1 invests and A_2 does not (top right entry) then A_1 incurs an investment cost of c and also runs the risk of a loss from damage emanating from A_2. The probability of A_2 contaminating A_1

Table 3.1 Expected costs associated with investing and not investing in airline security

		Airline 2 (A_2)	
		S	***N***
	S	$Y-c,\ Y-c$	$Y-c-qL,\ Y-pL$
Airline 1 (A_1)	***N***	$Y-pL,\ Y-c-qL$	$Y-[pL+(1-p)\,qL]$, $Y-[pL+(1-p)qL]$

is q, so that A_1's expected loss from damage originating elsewhere is qL. This cost represents the negative externality imposed by A_2 on A_1. In this case A_2 incurs no investment costs and faces no risk of contagion but does face the risk of damage originating at home, pL. The lower left pay-offs are just the mirror image of these.

If neither airline invests, then both have an expected payoff of $Y-pL-(1-p)qL$. The term pL here reflects the risk of damage originating at one's own airline. The term qL, showing the expected loss from damage originating at the other airline, is multiplied by $(1-p)$ to reflect the assumption that the damage can only occur once. So the risk of contagion only matters to an airline when that airline does not suffer damage originating at home.

The conditions for investing in security to be a dominant strategy are that $c<pL$ and $c<p(1-q)L$. The first constraint is exactly what one would expect if there were only a single airline: the cost of investing in security must be less than the expected loss. Adding a second airline tightens the constraint by reflecting the possibility of contagion. This possibility reduces the incentive to invest in security. Why? Because in isolation, investment in security buys the airline complete freedom from risk. With the possibility of contagion it does not. Even after investment there remains a risk of damage emanating from the other airline. Investing in security buys you less when there is the possibility of contagion from others.

This solution concept is illustrated below with a numerical example. Suppose that $p=0.2$, $q=0.1$, $L=1000$ and $c=185$. The matrix in Table 3.1 is now represented as Table 3.2.

One can see that if A_2 has protection (S), then it is worthwhile for A_1 to also invest in security since its expected losses will be reduced by $pL=200$ and it will only have to spend 185 on the security measure. However if A_2 does not invest in security (N), then there is still a chance that A_1 will incur a loss. Hence the benefits of security to A_1 will only be $pL(1-q)=180$ which is less than the cost of the protective measure. So A_1 will not want to invest in protection. In other words, either both airlines invest in security

Table 3.2 Expected costs associated with investing and not investing in airline security for illustrative example

		Airline 2 (A_2)	
		S	***N***
Airline 1 (A_1)	***S***	$Y-185$, $Y-185$	$Y-285$, $Y-200$
	N	$Y-200$, $Y-285$	$Y-280$, $Y-280$

or neither of them does so. These are the two Nash equilibria for this problem.

Protecting Against Terrorist Attacks: A PD Problem

As a contrast to the airline security problem, consider two neighboring countries, each of whom wants to determine whether or not to invest c dollars to prevent the occurrence of a terrorist attack in their region of the world. If one country invests in security (S) but the other country does not (N) then there is a probability (p) of a terrorist attack on their region of the world with a loss to each country of L. If neither country invests in security then the probability of a terrorist attack is $p' > p$ and the loss is $L' > L$. We thus have the pay-off matrix shown in Table 3.3.

If $c > pL$ and $c > p'L' - pL$ then each country's dominant strategy is not to invest in security and the expected losses to both of them will be $p'L'$. Whenever $pL < c < p'L'$ it would be in the interest of both countries to invest in security, although they will not do so voluntarily. When this condition holds we have the structure of a PD game.

There is a key difference between the IDS and PD problems described above. In the terrorist attack problem the behavior of the other country does not affect the incentive to invest in protection. In the baggage security problem the behavior of the other airline does affect the incentive to invest in baggage security. More generally, in the terrorist attack problem there is an increase in both the probability of an attack and the magnitude of the losses if both countries do not invest in security. In the airline security problem, an explosion from the transfer of a contaminated bag leads to incremental losses conditional on not having a dangerous bag on your plane already. You can only die once!

To illustrate the difference between the airline security problem and the terrorist attack problem consider the illustrative example in Table 3.1, except that we make the extreme assumption that it is certain that the terrorists will attack Country i if Country j has not invested in security.

Table 3.3 Expected pay-offs to investing and not investing in security against a terrorist attack

		Country 2 (C_2)	
		S	***N***
Country 1 (C_1)	***S***	$Y-c,\ Y-c$	$Y-c-pL,\ Y-pL$
	N	$Y-pL,\ Y-c-pL$	$Y-p'L',\ Y-p'L'$

Table 3.4 Pay-offs to investing and not investing in security against a terrorist attack for illustrative example

		Country 2 (C_2)	
		S	N
Country 1 (C_1)	S	$Y-c,\ Y-c$	$Y-c-100,\ Y-100$
	N	$Y-100,\ Y-c-100$	$Y-300,\ Y-300$

We leave c unspecified and specify $p=0.1$ $p'=0.2$ $L=1000$ and $L'=1500$ The relevant pay-offs are depicted in Table 3.4.

Whenever $c>200$ then a dominant solution is for neither country to invest in protection against a terrorist attack. However if $200<c<300$ each would be better off if both had invested in security.

Meltdown of a Nuclear Reactor: An IDS Problem

Consider now a change in the specification of this problem so that the issue is not a terrorist attack but the meltdown of a nuclear reactor. Assume that each country has one nuclear reactor and that if it invests in a set of safeguards the chances of an accident from the power plant is reduced to zero. We imagine a group of small adjacent countries (for example Belgium, Holland and Luxembourg or Latvia, Lithuania and Estonia) so that a meltdown in any one will lead to massive radioactive contamination in all of them. Then it is reasonable to assume that the loss to any country from a meltdown is catastrophic and would not be worsened by an additional nuclear reactor accident. In this case Table 3.5 gives the pay-offs.

Now we have a structure similar to that of the IDS problem depicted in Table 3.1 with p replacing q since the chances of contaminating another country are the same as the chances of contaminating one's own country. Investment in security will be a dominant strategy if $c<p(1-p)L$. The presence of another country that has not invested in reactor safeguards

Table 3.5 Pay-offs to investing and not investing in nuclear reactor safeguards

		Country 2 (C_2)	
		S	N
Country 1 (C_1)	S	$Y-c,\ Y-c$	$Y-c-pL,\ Y-pL$
	N	$Y-pL,\ Y-c-pL$	$Y-pL-(1-p)pL,$ $Y-pL-(1-p)pL$

Table 3.6 Pay-offs to investing and not investing in nuclear reactor safeguards illustrative example p = *0.1* L = *1000*

		Country 2 (C_2)	
		S	***N***
Country 1 (C_1)	***S***	$Y-c$, $Y-c$	$Y-c-100$, $Y-100$
	N	$Y-100$, $Y-c-100$	$Y-190$, $Y-190$

reduces the incentive to protect one's own reactor. The reason should be clear from the characterization of the problem: a meltdown elsewhere can damage a country as much as a meltdown at home. However this is only relevant if the country does not suffer a loss as a result of its own reactor's failure. By investing in protection a country reduces the risk it faces domestically but increases the chance of damage originating elsewhere from countries that have not invested in reactor safeguards.

Table 3.6 characterizes the outcomes for this problem for the two country case using $p = 0.1$ and $L = 1000$ but leaving c unspecified so it can be contrasted with the terrorist attack problem.

Whenever $c < 100$ Country 1 will invest in reactor safeguards if it knows that it will not be contaminated by Country 2. However if Country 2 does not invest in protection, then for Country 1 to invest in reactor safeguards it is necessary that $c < 90$. The decision rule for Country 2 is identical to that of Country 1. In contrast to the terrorist attack problem, there is a range for c where one country will want to invest in protective measures if the other country also does, but will not incur this cost if the other country doesn't (that is, $90 < c < 100$). In other words, there are two Nash equilibria. Within this range both countries will be better off by investing in protection than not investing, just as was the case in the terrorist attack problem. A key difference between these two problems is that by inducing one country to invest in nuclear reactor safeguards the other country will find it optimal to also invest. In the terrorist attack problem if one country invests in security the other country will not want to incur this cost.

THE MULTI-AGENT IDS CASE

We have set out our framework now for the two-agent case: this is, of course, the simplest and most intuitive case. The results carry over to the most general settings with some increase in complexity. In this section we review briefly the main features of the general cases, without providing detailed proofs of the results. These can be found in Kunreuther and Heal (2003).

There are two key points that emerge from the discussion of the general case with respect to the IDS problem. One is that the main feature of the two-agent case carries over to n agents: the incentive that any agent faces to invest in security depends on how many other agents there are and on whether or not they are investing. Other agents who do not invest reduce the expected benefits from one's own protective actions and hence reduce an agent's incentive to invest.

Secondly there is a new possibility that emerges from the multi-agent case. There is the possibility of a 'tipping' phenomenon.[2] In some cases there may be one firm occupying such a strategic position that if it changes from not investing to investing in protection, then all others will find it in their interests to follow suit. And even if there is no single firm that can exert such leverage, there may be a small group. We show when this can happen and how to characterize the agents with great leverage. Obviously this point has considerable importance for policy-making. It suggests that there are some key players whom one needs to persuade to manage risks carefully.

Characterization of Solutions

In the multi-agent case we can see clearly the difference between two classes of IDS problems discussed in the introduction: the airline security problem in which a bomb can damage only one airline, as opposed to the virus or hacker problem in which all agents in a computer network can be compromised by the same intruder. In this latter case, as we noted, the damage has a public good aspect to it and the capacity to inflict damage is not exhausted after one hit.

Airline security

Consider first n identical airlines. Each has a probability p of loading a bomb that explodes on one of its planes if it does not invest in security systems; this probability is zero if it invests. Each also has a probability q of loading a bomb and transferring it unexploded to another airline. We assume that the probability of any one airline receiving this unexploded bomb is $q/(n-1)$. Let c and L be the cost of investing and the loss in the event of damage, respectively. We denote by $X(n,0)$ the total expected cost imposed on an airline which has invested in security when none of the other $n-1$ agents have taken this step. In other words, $X(n,0)$ is the expected negative externality imposed on a protected airline when all the others are unprotected.[3] We show that the limit of this expression for large values of n is $(1-e^{-q})L$.

The externality is largest when there is only one other airline and decreases to $(1-e^{-q})L$ as the number of airlines rises. There is an obvious intuition here: as the number of airlines increases, the chance of a transferred bag reaching any particular airline falls. If there is a positive expected loss from other airlines not investing even if airline j invests itself, then its incentive to invest is reduced.

The externality is also affected by the likelihood of contagion by another airline. If $q=0$ then $X(n,0)=0$ indicating that if there are no bags transferred from one airline to another there are no negative externalities. We show that $X(n,0)$ increases monotonically in q reaching its largest value of $0.63L$ when $q=1$. If bags are transferred to other airlines with probability 1 then the expected negative externality to any airline is 63 per cent of the possible loss. The total expected loss to any airline is thus $[p+0.63(1-p)]L$.

Computer security

When a virus infects computer j on a network, it is passed on to all other computers in the system with probability q. When none of the other $n-1$ computers invest in security then the negative externalities to a computer that has installed protection can be shown to be $X(n,0)=L$ as n gets very large.[4] In this case the expected loss to any computer j approaches L as a result of contamination from all the other unprotected computers on the network. In this situation there is no cost incentive to invest in protecting any machine against viruses or hackers.

Kearns (2005) considers a computer network with many workstations sharing commonly owned network resources. The IDS problem arises because a hacker or a virus can access the common network resources through security weaknesses in any of the workstations and damage the common resources to the detriment of all workstations. Thus even if one agent takes full precautions to secure his or her workstation against viruses or hackers, he or she can still be damaged because of a failure on the part of another workstation user to do the same. So the incentive that any agent has to invest in security is undermined by failures on the part of others who share the system with him. This is a variant of the IDS problem as it arises with airline security and according to Kearns is a central problem in computer network security. Like the airline problem, the situation becomes worse as the number of agents increases and if there is a purposive agent who is looking for weak links, as would be true of cyberterrorists.

Tipping

Now consider the tipping problem. For this it is essential that the agents differ in either their costs and/or the nature of the risks they face. We can rank firms by the total expected loss that they inflict on all others by not investing. Suppose there are n firms that can contaminate each other. If firm j changes from investing to not investing when no other firms are investing, then it creates a set of negative externalities that increases the expected losses of all other firms, which we denote by $E_j\,(n,0)$.

We can characterize the agents who can lead to tipping in a rather intuitive manner when the probability of being contaminated by agent j is the same for all agents i. In the airline security example this means that an agent is equally likely to transfer a bag to any other agent. We rank agents by $E_j\,(n,0)$. If there is a single individual who can cause all agents to invest in security, it will be the one for whom this value is largest. If tipping can be caused by a group of say K agents then this group will contain the top K agents ranked by total expected cost imposed on others by not investing.

Consider the baggage security problem. The ranking has the intuitive property that the airline that has the highest value of $E_j\,(n,0)$ is the one that should be encouraged to adopt a security measure because it has the best chance of tipping a situation from one where no airline has adopted protection to one where every airline wants to invest in baggage security.

To be more precise, suppose that there is a Nash equilibrium at which no agent invests. Then if there is one agent k, with the property that if starting from this equilibrium k changes strategy and invests in security, then all others also do the same, then this agent must be the one for which $E_j(n,0)$ is greatest. For the other agents their best response if k invests in security is to also invest in security. In Heal and Kunreuther (2004) we give sufficient conditions for such a tipping agent and equilibrium to exist.

Societal Costs

Up until now the focus of our discussion has been on the costs of contagion to the individual agents rather than to society as a whole. From a risk management perspective one has to consider the impact that investing in security will have on the affected public.

In the airline security case the societal costs depend on three elements: (1) how many airlines invest in baggage security systems: (2) the probability (p) of a bomb being loaded onto an airline without a baggage checking system and exploding on one of its own planes; and (3) the probability (q) that such a bag will be loaded and transferred to a plane from another airline before it explodes. Suppose there are n identical airlines, none of whom invest in security. Let $S(n)$ represent the societal cost when there is a loss L from any bomb explosion. For any probabilities p and q then

$$S(n) = npL + n(1-p)\ \{1 - [1 - q/(n-1)]^{n-1}\}\ L.$$

For the illustrative example used above where $p=0.2$, $q=0.1$ and $L=1000$, when $n=2$ then $S(2)=560$. If the number of airlines increases to $n=20$, then $S(20)=5526$.

A simple example may help to clarify the central issues in determining social costs. Suppose $p+q=1$ so that it is certain that a bomb will explode on either your own airline or another one. Let $p=q=1/2$ and assume that there are two airlines 1 and 2. We now have four possible cases:

- Case 1: Both airlines 1 and 2 load bombs that explode on their planes. In this case the loss is $2L$.
- Case 2: Each airline loads a bomb and transfers it to the other airline. The loss is again $2L$.
- Case 3: Airlines 1 and 2 load bombs with 1 transferring its bomb to 2 and 2 not transferring its bomb to 1. The loss is now L as only airline 2 takes on a bomb that explodes.
- Case 4: The reverse of *case* 2. The loss is L as only airline 1 takes on a bomb that explodes.

Since each of these four cases has an equal chance of occurring the expected social loss is $1.5L$.

Turning to the computer security problem, the societal losses depend on the number of computers n in the network. Define $S(n)$ as the societal cost if none of the computers have security systems. Then for any probabilities p and q:

$$S(n) = npL + n(1-p)\{1-(1-q)^{n-1}\}\ L$$

For the illustrative example where $p=0.2$, $q=0.1$ and $L=1000$ for n=2 $S(2)=560$. As n gets very large then $S(n)$ approaches $nL=1000n$. If there are enough computers on any network it is almost certain that each machine will experience a loss.

Note that the expected societal cost for IDS problems is larger than for PD problems for the same parameters, simply because the chances that any agent will suffer a loss is greater than p because of the possibility of contagion from others. (that is, $q>0$). For computer network-like problems this probability approaches 1 as n gets large. Hence there is a strong need for developing risk management strategies for reducing these costs.

PROPOSED RISK MANAGEMENT SOLUTIONS TO THE IDS PROBLEM

How can we overcome the impact of contagion on an agent's investments in security? Below we examine a set of different measures ranging from private market mechanisms to regulations to collective choice that may internalize the externalities associated with protective measures where there are interdependencies between agents. We use the airline security problem to illustrate the role of different policy tools, but they can be applied to any IDS problem.

Insurance

Insurance appears to be a logical way of encouraging security since it rewards those who adopt protective measures by reducing their premium to reflect the lower risk. However in order to deal with the externalities created by others who do not invest in protection, the agent causing the damage must be forced to pay for the losses. For example if a bag transferred from Airline 1 to Airline 2 exploded, Airline 1's insurer would have to pay for the cost of the damage to Airline 2. This is not how current insurance practice operates. An insurer who provides protection to A_i is responsible for losses incurred by agent *i* no matter who caused them.[5] One reason for this contractual arrangement between the insurer and insured is the difficulty in assigning causality for a particular event.[6]

Interestingly enough, social insurance programs have the advantage over a competitive insurance market in encouraging investment in security. If the government were to insure all the airlines, then it would want to internalize the externalities associated with contaminated baggage transferred between airlines. Each airline investing in a screening system would be given premium reductions not only for the reduced losses to its own planes but also for the reduction in losses to all the others. Under such a program as long as $c < pL$, there would be an incentive for all airlines to invest in baggage security.

Liability

If an airline that caused damage to other airlines by not adopting a protective measure were held liable for these losses, then the legal system would offer another way to internalize the externalities due to IDS. However we know of no cases in which an agent has been held liable for the damages to others because it did not invest in protection. In the case of an aircraft explosion, it would be difficult to know whether a bag from another airline was the cause or whether it was one of the airline's own bags. The Pan Am crash in 1988 illustrates this difficulty. The bag that destroyed the plane was in a container of transferred bags and it took considerable detective work to determine which one actually caused the crash.

Taxation

A more direct way of encouraging greater security is to levy a tax of t dollars on any airline that does not invest in baggage security. The magnitude of the tax depends on the number of agents and the cost of protection, c. Kunreuther and Heal (2003) show that for identical airlines, any firm will want to invest in protection when no one else does, if the tax t is greater than $c - p[L - \mathrm{X}(n,0)]$. This implies that as the negative externalities $[X(n,0)]$ increase, the tax also increases.[7] Note that a subsidy on protective measures plays an identical role in inducing agents to invest in security. The cost c is reduced due to the subsidy, so that the protective measure is more attractive to the agent.

Regulations and Third-Party Inspections

The possibility of contagion from other units provides a rationale for well-enforced regulations that require individuals and firms to adopt cost-effective protective mechanisms when they would not do so voluntarily. In the identical n-agent example, a regulation would be viewed as desirable from both private and social welfare perspectives under the following conditions:

- there are two stable Nash equilibria $(S, S, \ldots S)$ and $(N, N \ldots N)$;
- the equilibrium $(S, S \ldots S)$ yields higher profits for all agents than $(N, N \ldots N)$;
- none of the agents voluntarily adopted protective measures because they believed others would not do so.

One would thus want to consider a regulation whenever $p[L - X(n,0)] < c < pL$. Each agent would be better off if it was forced to invest in security, knowing that all the other agents were required to do the same. In this case regulation solves the coordination problem. There may also be a need for well-enforced regulations if there were externalities to other parties in addition to the contagion effects between the agents. For example when a building collapses it may create externalities in the form of economic dislocations and other social costs that are beyond the economic losses suffered by the owners. These may not be taken into account when the owners or developers evaluate the importance of adopting a specific mitigation measure and hence may justify the need for building codes (Cohen and Noll, 1981; Kleindorfer and Kunreuther, 1999).

One way for the government to enforce its regulations is to turn to the private sector for assistance. More specifically, third-party inspections coupled with insurance protection can encourage divisions in firms to reduce their risks from accidents and disasters. Such a management-based regulatory strategy shifts the locus of decision making from the regulator to firms who are now required to do their own planning as to how they will meet a set of standards or regulations (Coglianese and Lazer, 2003).

Coordinating Mechanisms

Rather than relying on government regulations, one could turn to the private sector to coordinate decisions through industry associations. In the context of the illustrative example of airline security, the International Air Transport Association (IATA), the official airline association, could have made the case to all the airlines that they would be better off if each one of them utilized internal baggage checking so that the government would not have had to require them to do so.

An association can play a coordinating role by stipulating that any member has to follow certain rules and regulations, including the adoption of security measures, and has the right of refusal should they be asked to do business with an agent that is not a member of the association and/or has not subscribed to the ruling. IATA could require all bags to be reviewed carefully and each airline could indicate that it would not accept in-transit bags from airlines that did not adhere to this regulation. By receiving a seal of approval from IATA, the airline would also increase its business since passengers would shun airlines that were not part of the agreement.[8]

Another solution would be for airlines that had invested in security to announce publicly that they will not accept passengers and hence baggage from any airline that doesn't have security. They would then publicly announce to all prospective passengers which airlines fell in this category. This tactic may encourage the unprotected airlines to invest in security because of their fear of losing customers in the future.

The possibility of contagion by other units provides a rationale for well-enforced regulations and standards requiring individuals and firms to adopt protective mechanisms. The need for baggage review systems took on greater importance after the 9/11 tragedies and has led the government to require their use by the airlines. The US Congress now requires airlines to have a checked baggage security program to screen all bags for bombs (*NY Times*, 2002).

EXTENDING THE ANALYSIS

The choice of whether to protect against events where there is interdependence between your actions and those of others raises a number of interesting theoretical and empirical questions. We mention some of these in this section.

Differential Costs and Risks

The nature of Nash equilibria for the problems considered above and the types of policy recommendations may change as one introduces differential costs across the agents who are considering whether or not to invest in security.

Consider each airline deciding whether to invest in a baggage security system. In Heal and Kunreuther (2004) we have shown that if there are differential costs and/or risks between companies, we would expect to find some airlines investing in baggage security systems and others who would not. Furthermore, as we discussed above, the airline which creates the largest negative externalities for others should be encouraged to invest in protective behavior not only to reduce these losses but also to make it profitable for other airlines to follow suit, thus inducing tipping behavior.

Multi-Period and Dynamic Models

Deciding whether to invest in security normally involves multi-period considerations since there is an upfront investment cost that needs to be compared with the benefits over the life of the protective measure. An airline that invests in a baggage security system knows that this measure promises to offer benefits for a number of years. Hence one needs to discount these positive returns by an appropriate interest rate and specify the relevant time interval in determining whether or not to invest in these actions. There may be some uncertainty with respect to both of these parameters.

From the point of view of dynamics, the decision to invest depends on how many others have taken similar actions. How do you get the process of investing in security started? Should one subsidize or provide extra benefits to those willing to be innovators in this regard to encourage others to take similar actions?

Behavioral Considerations

The models discussed above all assumed that individuals made their decisions by comparing their expected benefits with and without protection to the costs of investing in security. This is a rational model of behavior. There is a growing literature in behavioral economics that suggests that individuals make choices in ways that differ from the rational model of choice (Kahneman and Tversky, 2000).

With respect to protective measures there is evidence from controlled field studies and laboratory experiments that many individuals are not willing to invest in security for a number of reasons that include myopia, high discount rates and budget constraints. (Kunreuther et al., 1998). In the models considered above there were also no internal positive effects associated with protective measures. Many individuals invest in security to relieve anxiety and worry about what they perceive might happen to them or to others so as to gain peace of mind (Baron et al., 2000).[9]

A more realistic model of interdependent security that incorporated these behavioral factors as well as people's misperceptions of the risk may suggest a different set of policy recommendations than a rational model of choice. For example if agents were reluctant to invest in protection because they were myopic, then some type of loan may enable them to discern the long-term benefits of the protective measure. A long-term loan would also help relieve budget constraints that may deter some individuals or firms from incurring the upfront costs of the risk-reducing measure.

FUTURE RESEARCH ON RISK MANAGEMENT STRATEGIES FOR IDS PROBLEMS

We conclude by suggesting a set of problems that involve interdependent security and suggesting the types of risk management strategies that could be explored for addressing them.

Types of Problems

The common features of IDS problems are the possibility that other agents can contaminate you, and your inability to reduce this type of contagion through investing in security. You are thus discouraged from adopting protective measures when you know others have decided not to take this step.

Here are some problems that fit into this category, some of which have been discussed in this chapter:

- Investing in airline security.
- Protecting against chemical and nuclear reactor accidents.
- Making buildings more secure against attacks.
- Investing in sprinkler systems to reduce the chance of a fire in one's apartment.
- Avoiding gambles by divisions in a firm that could bring the entire firm into bankruptcy.Two recent examples come to mind: (1) Nick Leeson operating in the Singapore futures market division causing the collapse of Baring's Bank, and (2) Arthur Anderson being brought into bankruptcy by the actions of its Houston branch.
- Making computer systems more secure against terrorist attacks.
- Investing in protective measures for each part of an interconnected infrastructure system such as electricity, water or gas so that services can be provided to victims of a disaster

In each of these examples there are incentives for individual units or agents not to take protective measures, but there are large potential losses to the organization and to society. Furthermore the losses are sufficiently high that they are non-additive. An airplane can only be destroyed once; a building can only collapse once; one can only be bankrupt once; an interconnected system is only as good as its weakest link. You can only die once!

These IDS problems can be contrasted with others that do not have these features. Two that are discussed in more detail in Kunreuther and Heal (2003) are theft protection and vaccination. In the case of theft protection if you install an alarm system that you announce publicly with a sign, the burglar will look for greener pastures to invade. With respect to vaccines, if you knew everyone else has been vaccinated, then there would be no point in getting vaccinated since you cannot catch the disease.

Risk Management Strategies

For each IDS problem there is a range of risk management strategies that can be pursued by the private and public sectors for encouraging agents to invest in cost-effective protective measures.

- Collecting information on the risk and costs (for example constructing a scenario so that one can estimate p, q, L and c with greater accuracy).

- Developing more accurate catastrophe models for examining the risk of terrorist attacks and other large-scale disasters.[10]
- Designing incentive systems (for example subsidies or taxes) to encourage investment by agents in protective measures.
- Developing insurance programs for encouraging investment in protective measures when firms are faced with contagion.
- Structuring the liability system to deal with the contagion effects of IDS.
- Carefully designed standards (for example building codes for high-rises to withstand future terrorist attacks) that are well enforced through mechanisms such as third-party inspections.
- Introducing federal reinsurance or state-operated pools to provide protection against future losses from terrorist attacks to supplement private terrorist insurance.

It may be desirable to integrate several of these measures through public–private risk management partnerships. For example banks and financial institutions could require that firms adopt security measures as a condition for a loan or mortgage. To ensure that these measures are adopted there may be a need for third-party inspections or audits by the private sector. Firms who reduce their risks can be rewarded through lower insurance premiums. If there are federal or state reinsurance pools at reasonable prices to cover large losses from a future terrorist attack, then private insurers may be able to provide terrorist coverage at affordable premiums.

NOTES

* This a revised version of a paper originally prepared for the Columbia-Wharton/Penn Roundtable on 'Risk Management Strategies in an Uncertain World' (April 2002). Financial support from the Columbia University Earth Institute, the Wharton Risk Management and Decision Processes Center and Radiant Trust, Lockheed Martin.

1. The material in this subsection is based on Kunreuther and Heal (2003).
2. See Schelling (1978) for a characterization of a number of tipping problems.
3. We show in Kunreuther and Heal (2003) that

$$X(n,0) = [q/(n-1)]\sum_{t=0}^{n-2}[[1-q/(n-1)]^t]L = \{1-[1-q/(n-1)]^{n-1}\}L$$

4. In general we show in Kunreuther and Heal (2003) that

$$X(n,0) = qL\sum_{t=0}^{\infty}[(1-q)^t] = [1-(1-q)^{n-1}]L$$

5. If the damage from an insured risk is due to negligence or intentional behavior then there are normally clauses in the insurance policy that indicate that losses are not covered (for example a fire caused by arson).

6. With respect to fire damage, a classic case is H.R. Moch Co., Inc. v Rensselaer Water Co. 247N.Y.160, 159 N.E. 896 which ruled that: 'A wrongdoer who by negligence sets fire to a building is liable in damages to the owner where the fire has its origin, but not to other owners who are injured when it spreads.' We are indebted to Victor Goldberg who provided us with this case.
7. Note that if $c \leq p(L - X(n,0))$ then there is no need to impose any tax on an agent for it to want to invest in protection on its own because the internal benefits from protection exceed the cost of protection even if the airline faces negative externalities from transferred bags.
8. On a more informal level it might be possible to establish social norms that generate pressure to invest in protection. See Sunstein (1996) for a more detailed discussion of social norms. Ostrom (1990, Chapter 6) deals with the conditions under which norms evolve governing the use of common property resources.
9. Of course if these individuals become aware that substantial losses may be imposed on them or their firm from others who are unprotected, then this new knowledge may increase their anxiety by showing that investing in these protective measures has more limited benefits than they had initially assumed it would.
10. For more details on the challenges in developing catastrophe models and appropriate strategies for dealing with them see Posner (2005) and Grossi and Kunreuther (2005).

REFERENCES

Baron, Jonathan, John Hershey and Howard Kunreuther (2000), 'Determinants of priority for risk reduction: the role of worry', *Risk Analysis*, **20**, 413–27.

Coglianese, Cary and David Lazer (2003), 'Management-based regulation: prescribing private management to achieve public goals', *Law & Society Review*, **37**, 691–730.

Cohen, Linda and Roger Noll (1981), 'The economics of building codes to resist seismic shocks', *Public Policy*, Winter, 1–29.

Grossi, Patricia and Howard Kunreuther (eds) (2005), *Catastrophe Modeling: A New Approach to Managing Risk*, New York: Springer.

Heal, Geoffrey and Howard Kunreuther (2004), 'Interdependent security: a general model', NBER Working Paper #10706.

Kahneman, Daniel and Amos Tversky (2000), *Choices, Values and Frames*, New York: Cambridge University Press.

Kearns, Michael (2005), 'Economics, computer science and policy', *Issues in Science and Technology*, Winter 37–47.

Kleindorfer, Paul and Howard Kunreuther (1999), 'The complementary roles of mitigation and insurance in managing catastrophic risks', *Risk Analysis*, **19**, 727–38.

Kunreuther, Howard and Geoffrey Heal (2003), 'Interdependent security', *Journal of Risk and Uncertainty, Special Issue on Terrorist Risks*, **26**, 231–49.

Kunreuther, Howard and Geoffrey Heal (forthcoming), 'Interdependencies within an organization', in B. Hutter and M. Powers (eds), *Organizational Encounters with Risk*, New York: Cambridge University Press.

Kunreuther, Howard, Ayse Onculer and Paul Slovic (1998), 'Time insensitivity for protective measures', *Journal of Risk and Uncertainty*, **16**, 279–99.

NY Times (2002), 'Airlines scramble to meet new bag check deadline', 14 January.

Ostrom, Elinor (1990), *Governing the Commons: The Evolution of Institutions for Collective Action*, Cambridge: Cambridge University Press.

Posner, Richard (2005), *Catastrophes*, New York: Oxford University Press.
Schelling, Thomas (1978), *Micromotives and Macrobehavior*, New York: Norton.
Sunstein, Cass (1996), 'Social norms and social roles', *Columbia Law Review*, **96**, 903–68.

4. Increasing the security and reliability of the US electricity system

Lester B. Lave, Jay Apt, Alex Farrell and M. Granger Morgan

INTRODUCTION

The 2001 terrorist attacks showed that our airliners, tall buildings, water and even our mail are potential targets. What will actually be attacked depends on the terrorists' goals, the damage that could be done, and our ability to protect each one. Terrorists attack highly visible, symbolic targets in order to make each of us fear that 'this could happen to me'. However although it is impossible to prevent terrorists from causing disruptions in a free society, much can be done to limit their ability to spread panic.

Energy, transportation, telecommunication and water infrastructures are potentially attractive targets, because some elements of these complex systems are nearly impossible to protect and disruptions could impose large costs, threaten our well-being, and possibly cause thousands of deaths. The electric power system is an especially attractive target since virtually every aspect of our economy and personal lives requires electricity to function. Without electricity, we cannot heat or cool our buildings, get drinking water or dispose of sewage, have television or radio, run our computers and financial systems, or produce the goods and services that make up almost all of GDP. If a terrorist attack blacked out any of our large cities, the traffic signals would cease to function, resulting almost immediately in gridlock that prevented police, fire or paramedic vehicles from moving. In the wake of 11 September 2001, the electric power system in particular faces a number of important challenges – challenges that will require greater government involvement than has previously existed.

We discuss each of these issues and recommend changes to lower the number of blackouts, reduce the vulnerability of the system to terrorists and decrease the social costs of blackouts when they occur.

BLACKOUTS DUE TO NATURAL HAZARDS

The need to protect the electricity system against ice storms, earthquakes, hurricanes, tornadoes and other natural disasters has created a set of institutions and a physical system that can handle a wide range of physical insults. For example a 1998 ice storm brought down 800 transmission towers in Quebec and New York; we cannot imagine terrorists causing such extensive physical damage. Except for a few highly vulnerable structures, the current US electric power system could likely handle all but the largest, best-organized physical attacks by terrorists.

Blackouts occur more frequently than often assumed. About every four months, a major blackout affects 1 million or more people. Smaller blackouts, ones in the local distribution rather than transmission system, occur much more frequently. As noted above, natural hazards, equipment failure and operator mistakes create many blackouts and the current system has been designed to handle them. Terrorism could add little to the annual number of blackouts, but might result in a large event. Quite apart from the threat of terrorism, the United States would benefit from greater attention to the blackouts caused by 'natural' and accidental events. This point is magnified by the fact that the system will be highly vulnerable to terrorism for some years.

The local distribution system is the source of most outages; these affect relatively small numbers of people. The bulk power (generation and transmission) system causes only a few outages each year. In a recent report on failures in this part of the electric power system, the North American Electricity Reliability Council (NERC) identified 58 'Interruptions, Unusual Occurrences, Demand and Voltage Reductions, and Public Appeals' in 2000. Of these events, almost half (26) were due to weather, mostly thunderstorms. Operator or maintenance errors accounted for 12 events, another 12 were due to faulty equipment and 2 (including the largest single event) were due to forest fires. Six outages occurred simply due to failure to have sufficient power to meet demand. Not all of these 58 events caused the lights to go out, but when they did, many customers were affected. Even so, recovery was typically swift. The largest single outage in 2000 affected more than 660 000 customers in New Mexico, but lasted for less than four hours.

Natural challenges of even larger scale have been met. For example in January 1998 an ice storm struck Southern Canada and New York State, felling 800 transmission towers and 30 000 distribution poles while sending thousands of tree branches into power lines. This event left 1.6 million people without power, some for more than a month. Almost 250 000 people were forced to leave their homes. Insurance claims reached about $1 billion

(Canadian). This event was disruptive and costly, but it did not create terror or significant loss of life.

PUBLIC REACTIONS TO BLACKOUTS

Many terrorism scenarios involve disruption of electric services. Whether this would allow terrorists to create widespread fear and panic is open to question. In the United States, households lose power for an average of 90 minutes per year. For the most part, individuals and society cope with these outages well, and power companies respond rapidly to restore service. Facilities that have special needs for reliability, such as hospitals and airports, typically have back-up generators.

There is more to be learned from studying past outages. Contingency planning, spare equipment pre-placement, emergency preparedness training and temporary personnel transfers have all been key. Power companies often loan trained workers in emergencies under fairly informal arrangements, knowing that some day they would likely need to make similar requests. NERC has highlighted several aspects of successful management of electric system outages: planning, training, analysis and communications (NERC, 2001). Communication during and after an event might be difficult, especially if the attack is not on the physical part of the electric power system but on its computer and telecommunications components.

The Great Northeastern Blackout of 1965 shut down New York, as well as much of Ontario and New England, after an equipment failure. New York City was blacked out for an entire night, and about 30 million people were directly affected. The National Opinion Research Center studied this event and found that 'an outstanding aspect of public response to the blackout was the absence of widespread fear, panic, or disorder. There is probably little question that this absence is largely due to the ability of individuals to interpret their initial encounter with power loss as an ordinary event . . . Of equal importance in maintaining order was the rapid dissemination of information about the blackout.'

A second, less-widespread outage in New York City in July 1977 was far more troubling, because looting, arson and other crime became widespread. Although there was no outright panic, the blackout was frightening and shocking in ways that ordinary electricity outages are not.

The largest blackout in the United States occurred on 14 August 2003. In contrast to 1977, New York City residents were calm and helped each other. A repeat of the 1977 behavior would have resulted in social costs far higher than the costs caused directly by the blackout. These examples suggest that if terrorists do manage to cause a significant blackout, government and industry leadership will have key roles to play in curbing unrest and criminal activities that could induce widespread fear.

The intent to cause harm may not be a sufficient condition to create terror. The power sector handles several deliberate physical attacks each year, but these have generally been aimed at harming the local utility company and not capturing headlines. Eco-terrorists have also attacked the electricity system, but without much success.

HIGH-HAZARD FACILITIES

Much less massive damage than downing 800 transmission towers could blackout the system. Critical points exist in the electricity infrastructure where attacks could result in more damage. Well-organized terrorists (no longer an oxymoron) could damage these choke points because they are designed only to withstand natural hazards.

Parts of the current system are especially vulnerable to physical attack. Large transformers and substations constitute the bulk of these vulnerabilities, according to a 1990 Office of Technology Assessment report. These facilities are fenced off, but typically are not armored or actively guarded. Some relatively low-cost security enhancements could help, from using bulletproof encasements to standardizing and stocking replacement parts (which today are rare and typically custom-made, especially for higher-voltage equipment).

Recent experience suggests that the existing system would respond well to an assault. An equipment failure-caused fire in 2000 destroyed much of Dominion Virginia Power's Ox Substation and knocked the entire facility out of service. Despite the critical location of the facility, the fire had a relatively small impact on the system; service was restored to all customers within one hour, and the substation was restored to full service (and improved) within a month.

Some parts of the electric power system are especially tempting targets for terrorists, such as nuclear power sites, certain locks and dams, and fossil fuel storage locations. If terrorists could secure access to these facilities, they could use explosives to scatter radioactive material or breech a dam such as Hoover, causing vast destruction downstream. In addition, cooling towers in urban areas might be used to disseminate a chemical or biological agent into the atmosphere. These attacks could cause panic, deaths or extensive property damage. Further, many of these facilities may tempt terrorists for their symbolic value.

Nuclear reactor containment buildings are massive structures designed to withstand significant impacts. There is at least some data suggesting that they and the reactor vessels they house could withstand a direct hit by a jumbo jet. Far more vulnerable are the buildings that house spent reactor fuel, which is currently stored in water-filled pools or above-ground containers at all operating reactor sites. These 'temporary' facilities have grown because of the failure to develop a permanent high-level nuclear waste disposal site. The Bush administration has taken some steps to resolve this problem, but legal battles are expected to continue for some time. Even after the issue of secure long-term waste storage is resolved, it will still take a decade or more to complete the facility and move the waste into it, during which time the terrorist threat will remain.

Security programs in place around nuclear power plants frequently test them against simulated commando assaults. However a 1999 Nuclear Regulatory Commission (NRC) review found 'significant weaknesses' in 27 of the 57 plants that were evaluated. Despite this poor performance, the nuclear energy industry has long sought reduced federal oversight of security planning and had planned to move toward a self-regulation model starting in mid-September 2002. The terrorist attacks have halted these plans temporarily, and the NRC and other federal organizations have ordered increases in security.

As the owners of high-hazard electricity facilities have begun to face competition and the bottom line has become more important, security costs have received greater scrutiny. Adequate institutions for the protection of high-hazard electricity facilities in the new competitive industry have yet to be developed.

BARRIERS TO PREVENTING BLACKOUTS

The robustness of the US electric power system and its ability to restore power quickly is no accident. Both government regulatory bodies and private institutions have been established to promote reliability. Most important have been voluntary industry actions: industry has taken seriously the 'duty to serve' that comes with its monopoly franchise (bolstered by the threat of further regulation). But restructuring is undoing the monopoly franchise system, raising serious questions as to whether private approaches will be adequate. In addition, because reliability and security are not equivalent, it is not clear whether the existing reliability institutions would be able to provide adequate electricity system security. Reliability and security are both crucial public goods, implying that there are few incentives for private companies to invest in them, and government will have to become more involved.

The oldest reliability institutions in the United States are state-level public utility commissions. In regulating the utility monopolies, these commissions sought to ensure an efficient and reliable electric service for all customers. Restructuring of the electricity industry is dismantling this system by placing major portions of the electricity system beyond the scope of the commissions. It is also creating major uncertainties about who will eventually own transmission systems and how owners will be allowed to recover costs and earn returns. This has greatly reduced investment in the transmission system, and its safety margins are shrinking.

The radical restructuring now taking place in the electric power system because of 'deregulation' (more accurately, changes in regulation) also threatens the system's robustness. Competitive markets will force the adoption of low-cost solutions to providing electricity under the stipulated rules. If security is not an attractive investment above a minimal level, companies will not be able to make investments. Because security is a classic public good, our expectation is that it will not be an attractive investment. Thus it is up to government to answer questions concerning how much the nation is willing to pay for additional security, what organizations will be charged with ensuring it and who should pay for it. Currently, many different organizations inside and outside of government, at both the state and national levels, envision themselves as holding the primary authority and responsibility for governance over electric power system security. Congress needs to resolve this issue, but to do so carefully, as there are many trade-offs to be balanced. It needs to decide both what institutional arrangements need to be created and how to pay for improvements.

Competition in electricity generation has increased demands on the transmission system, because the generators are located in places their owners find convenient, not in places that are necessarily convenient for transmission. Public objections often make building new transmission lines difficult or impossible. In many cases expanded capacity could be achieved if advanced transmission technologies were used to increase the reliability and capacity of the existing system. But again, the lack of economic incentives is inhibiting investment. Thus the transmission system provides the most immediate institutional challenge for improving the security of the electric power system.

Deregulation has increased uncertainty about the expected returns from investments in the industry. As a result, companies have had a difficult time raising funds for investments. In some places it has been all but impossible to find funds for investments in transmission because the return on these investments, if any, is uncertain. Deregulation will fail unless we can find ways to reduce uncertainties and attract investors at reasonable rates of return.

In addition to the difficulty of investing in new capacity and system upgrades, the industry has been doing so little R&D that many promising technologies have not been developed. Federally funded energy R&D spending dropped by about 40 per cent between 1980 and 1995, and industry spending on R&D has dropped to 0.2 per cent of sales, a level that is completely inappropriate for an industry that should be experiencing rapid technological change.

The state regulators and voluntary reliability organization have done a good job of developing a power system that is highly resistant to natural threats. It is not clear however that such voluntary, cooperative organizations can continue to function adequately in a competitive environment. In other industries, such as transportation, the United States relies upon government safety regulators, and companies tend to invest in more proprietary research. Further, standards designed to promote reliability in the face of weather and accidental equipment failures are not likely to be adequate in the face of well-organized assaults. Currently it is unclear who has the responsibility and authority for restructuring. Several agencies argue that they have an important role to play: the Department of Energy, the Federal Bureau of Investigation (and of course the Department of Homeland Security), the Federal Energy Regulatory Commission, and the many state-level energy and law-enforcement bodies. Until this important institutional issue is resolved, it will be impossible for the industry to develop a rational response.

After the Great Northeastern Blackout of 1965, there were calls to increase the federal role in the electricity industry, both by strengthening regulations and by expanding funding of federally controlled research. The industry responded by quickly creating a system of voluntary, regional reliability organizations, loosely organized under NERC and dedicated to promoting the reliability of bulk electric supply in North America. NERC operates by developing reliability planning and operating standards. Traditionally the industry has complied with these standards on a voluntary basis, with the only monitoring occurring in regional councils in which peer pressure can be applied. Recently however, Congress has been considering legislation to establish a mandatory 'electricity reliability organization' that would make mandatory what NERC has tried to establish voluntarily.

In short, one of the key future challenges is ensuring that institutional solutions to emerging security problems are created for whatever new structure the electricity industry takes. This includes looking at threats that go beyond those considered in traditional contingency planning.

NEW VULNERABILITIES

In contrast to the issues of physical security, electricity system planners have given less attention to cyber attacks on their real-time supervisory control and data acquisition (SCADA) systems that provide system status information and control its operation. SCADA technologies were originally designed as proprietary, stand-alone systems, and often the specific technologies vary from company to company. Until several years ago, almost all of these functions were carried out with entirely private and highly secure communication links. More recently, dial-up modems have been installed in some systems for remote monitoring and, in a few cases, for control. Greater interaction between public and secure communication networks occurs in a few systems; fiber-optic capacity may be leased out or the Internet may be used for communication or control. The widespread use of networking technologies has begun to transform SCADA systems; Internet-based applications are being used for SCADA and other functions, such as energy management. To further complicate matters, these systems are becoming open to more users as more companies participate in regional electricity markets and transmission system operation.

This evolution has produced a troubling combination of older secure systems with insecure uses for what were once stand-alone systems, and wide-open Internet-based systems. Preparation for the successful Y2K rollover led to some improvements and upgrades, and provided a model for dealing with cyber threats in the electricity industry. However private security consultants and the Department of Defense both report successfully penetrating electric power control systems. Some security policies at electricity industry companies are inadequate, including computer systems that allow for blank passwords. Again, because of unclear responsibilities and inadequate incentives, no adequate, systematic approach is being taken to address this problem.

In addition to the conventional modes of attack, some exotic scenarios also warrant consideration. For example relatively simple, inexpensive devices that can deliver a very fast rise-time electromagnetic pulse (EMP) have been designed and tested by the United States and other nations. An EMP can induce instantaneous voltages of thousands of kV in conductors, irreversibly damaging electrical and electronic devices. EMP has long been understood as an area-wide risk from nuclear weapons. Smaller, non-nuclear EMP weapons might be used on a much more localized scale to attack critical electric power system components, networked computers and telecommunication systems, without physically penetrating facility perimeters. It is not clear how vulnerable the current system is to such an assault. Nor do we know what could be done to defend against them. More research is clearly needed.

During the past few years we have also begun to understand that the physical electric power system is just one part of a complex, adaptive system that has strong interactive effects. Other parts include the SCADA systems that control the physical power system, the market data systems that plan its short-term operation, and the fuel delivery systems that keep it running. The tightness of these couplings, the specific mechanisms by which different networks are interdependent, and the ways in which these mechanisms can transmit faults from one network to another can vary greatly. For example the fact that there is little electricity storage means that power could be cut off at any time, disrupting communications, gas line compressors and other systems that depend on electricity. Lack of power could also cause traffic signals to go out, slowing the arrival of emergency service vehicles. In contrast, the coupling between a coal-fired power plant and its fuel supply system is fairly loose, because there are generally several weeks of fuel on site and multiple routes for obtaining additional fuel.

The increasing reliance on natural gas for electricity generation is increasing dependence on the gas transmission system. Fortunately the gas system is harder to attack and more robust than the electric system, largely because it is buried underground and because gas can be stored in the transmission system and at relatively secure locations close to demand, such as in depleted oil and gas underground formations. And like the electricity industry, gas companies have long recognized and effectively planned for contingencies designed to mitigate terrorism. Spare parts are generally kept on hand to effect quick repairs. However problems in gas system maintenance were recently highlighted when internal corrosion caused a 30-inch gas pipe near Carlsbad, New Mexico, to rupture and explode in August 2000, killing 12 people. The explosion led to significant increases in gas prices in California, exacerbating the electricity crisis there. The National Transportation Safety Board subsequently determined that decades of inadequate testing and maintenance by the pipeline company caused the accident. This example shows that the interdependent systems that support the supply of electricity to the United States are not perfect, and that institutional mechanisms to support reliability and security may need to be strengthened.

Only recently have analysts at DOE, the national laboratories, and EPRI (Electric Power Research Institute) begun to examine infrastructure interdependencies. Several of the strategic planning documents produced by the government during the past few years have pointed to this issue as one in particular need of fundamental and applied research.

POTENTIAL SOLUTIONS: ACHIEVING SYSTEM SURVIVABILITY

In recent years, the concept of 'survivability' has emerged as a result of research and practice at the Software Engineering Institute at Carnegie Mellon University to counter Internet security threats. Survivability is the ability of a system to fulfill its mission in a timely manner, despite attacks, failures or accidents, in contrast to the current fortress model of security. No one can prevent a terrorist from taking down a transmission tower. However the system can be configured so that, although the failure of single elements may lead to discomfort, the electric power system will still be able to fulfill its mission. The electric power industry must move toward a survivability approach to security.

A fundamental assumption of survivability analysis and design is that no individual component of a system is immune from attacks, accidents or design errors. Thus, a survivable system must be created out of inherently vulnerable sub-units, making survivability an emergent property of the system rather than a design feature for individual components.

Survivability resembles a quasi-biological model and has three components: resistance, recognition and recovery. In unbounded systems, it is difficult to recognize attacks until there is extensive damage. Thus ways must be found to recognize attack early and to protect the system without taking the time to discover the cause of the attack. Survivable systems must be able to maintain or restore essential services during an attack and to recover full service after the attack. In essence, the system must fail gracefully, shedding low-priority tasks and then adding tasks in order of priority during recovery. The current system for electric power supply and use generally does not use this approach, with a few exceptions, such as plants for systematic emergency load shedding and critical facilities such as hospitals that choose to invest in back-up generators.

A simple example concerns traffic signals. In most cities, the same circuits that provide service to much less critical buildings and billboards also power traffic signals. During the rolling blackouts in California in 2000, one of the major causes of injury and property loss were crashes due to blank traffic signals. Worsening the problem, blackouts results in gridlock that prevents police and fire vehicles, as well as emergency response crews, from reaching their destinations. Fortress-type thinking creates a system in which blackouts are never supposed to occur, but when they do, the consequences are severe. In contrast, a system designed with survivability concepts might use commercially available low-power LED traffic signals with uninterruptible power (such as trickle charge batteries) to ensure that a blackout does not interrupt traffic flow. Replacing the incandescent bulbs with LEDs would save so much energy that the systems are attractive investments. In addition, adding the battery back-up would ensure that traffic continued to flow in a blackout, whether caused by a natural disaster or by terrorists.

One relatively straightforward solution to some security concerns would be to eliminate high-hazard facilities, such as on-site storage of spent nuclear fuel. This is feasible for a few potential targets but would require time to implement and is likely to make electricity much more expensive, because nuclear and hydro power make up about 30 per cent of the nation's electricity supply. Some selective retrofitting makes sense, and certainly devoting greater consideration to vulnerabilities to terrorism is imperative for new investments. However progress in reducing overall vulnerability will clearly be slow.

Another helpful step would be more thorough training for workers. System operators are like air traffic controllers and pilots: years of boredom punctuated with an occasional crisis. Better operator training is needed, especially on simulators that can mimic the full range of operations problems. Better monitoring is needed to ascertain the state of the system at each moment, and better control over load could allow operators to shed load and avoid a blackout.

A key to avoiding future cascading blackouts is to be able to shed load when the system becomes overloaded. At present this can only be done at the substation level. However the costs to the economy and society would be much lower if marginal kilowatts, low value energy, could be shed.

DISTRIBUTED GENERATION

The current electricity system with its large central generators and long transmission and distribution lines is inherently vulnerable. In contrast, a system with many small generators located at large customers or in neighborhoods would be made much less vulnerable. These systems would still be grid-connected, but could operate when the grid went down. A variety of existing and emerging technologies make it possible to design power systems based on distributed generation (DG). DG units are attractive for two reasons: they produce electric power on-site to supplement or serve the grid and they recover waste heat for use onsite, making them more efficient than central station generation which dumps waste heat. Small-scale renewable forms of energy such as wind and solar may also hold promise, because they eliminate the need for fuel. However solar-electric technologies are still expensive; not all locations have a good renewable resource base, and even those with an adequate base face intermittent supply problems, because the wind does not always blow nor does the sun always shine.

Fossil-fueled DG is no longer a fringe idea. Equipment manufactures such as ABB and Capstone are building business plans around these technologies. In some countries, the installed capacity of DG is extensive. For example in the Netherlands distributed generation units constitute about 30 per cent of installed electrical capacity.

In the United States, many electricity providers have opposed DG, believing that it undermines their large investments in central generation and transmission facilities and threatens their core competencies in these areas. Despite laws requiring easy DG interconnection, a number of regulatory and commercial barriers have been used to block proposed DG installations. A major reason for the success of DG in the Netherlands was the break-up of vertically integrated power providers, which barred distribution companies from owning large-scale generation but allowed them to participate in DG. This is another example in which institutional and regulatory choices will be critical to the feasibility of technical solutions to the problems of electric power system security.

CONCLUSION

The United States electricity system has been constructed to resist natural hazards, such as ice storms, hurricanes and earthquakes. These natural hazards pose such a difficult challenge to the physical infrastructure that perhaps 90 per cent of the physical challenge from terrorists has already been addressed. The new challenges posed by terrorists in the energy sector are attacks on nuclear power plants and their spent fuel and the SCADA systems. Responding to these challenges and making needed investments is hampered by the deregulation wave. These actions are difficult to take because of the reluctance of state regulators to approve expenditures that will increase electricity prices, and even more by the inability of deregulated companies to attract capital for the investments and the need to keep their costs low to compete. Since 2000, actions have been taken to reduce the physical and cyber vulnerability of the electricity system, but the pace is slow. Eliminating even the greatest vulnerabilities is likely to take a decade or more. In the meantime, system survivability should be the primary focus of both government and private efforts.

BIBLIOGRAPHY

Lipson, H. and D. Fischer, (1999), *Survivability: A New Technical and Business Perspective on Security*, Proceedings of the New Security Paradigms Workshop, Caledon Hills, ON: ACM.

Morgan, M.G. and S.F. Tierney (1998), 'Research support for the power industry', *Issues in Science and Technology*, Fall, 81–7.

Rinaldi, S.M., J.P. Perenboom and T.K. Kelly (2001), 'Critical infrastructure interdependencies', *IEEE Control Systems*, 11–25.

US–Canada Power System Outage Task Force (2003), *Interim Report: Causes of the August 14th Blackout in the United States and Canada*, November, available at https://reports.energy.gov/

Zerriffi, H., H. Dowlatabadi and N.D. Strachan (2005), 'Electricity and conflict: the robustness of distributed generation', *Electricity Journal*.

5. Mitigation of extreme event risks: electric power outage and infrastructure failure interactions

Stephanie E. Chang, Timothy L. McDaniels and Dorothy Reed*

INTRODUCTION

Terrorist acts are perhaps the most dreaded and distressing of the set of calamities referred to by researchers as 'extreme events'. Of course terrorism may be inherently more frightening and disturbing than other (more natural) kinds of extreme events (such as earthquakes or the impacts of extreme weather) because it is done deliberately. From a structural point of view, the effect of a terrorist attack on the electric power delivery system is most similar to a shallow-focus seismic event. In this type of event, substations for high-voltage transmission or low-voltage distribution systems may be severely damaged. Component replacement for these substations is neither inexpensive nor rapid. If winter storm weather accompanied by snow and ice is combined with a seismic (or terrorist) event, the duration of the outage would be much longer than for a single event. Strengthening the structural delivery or generation system for one hazard often increases its reliability (or safety) for another. Therefore to focus on one particular type of event is not the most cost-effective approach.

As defined by the National Science Foundation, extreme events are characterized by non-linear responses, low probabilities, high consequences and the potential for systems interaction that leads to catastrophic losses (Stewart and Bostrom, 2002). Managing extreme event risks requires new approaches including performance metrics for engineered systems and their impacts, methods for addressing multiple hazards and strategies for urban risk management (Kunreuther and Lerner-Lam, 2002).

When researchers examine the consequences of extreme events such as terrorism, whether in economic terms or other metrics, one motivation is to help provide guidance for investment decisions to address and perhaps mitigate their adverse consequences. In the research project introduced in this chapter, we address a particular kind of investment decision for managing the consequences of extreme events. We discuss an approach to setting broad priorities for mitigating the adverse effects of power outages in terms of mitigating potential interactions that could cause the failure of other kinds of key societal infrastructures because of a power failure.

Electrical Interdependencies

Critical infrastructure systems provide vital services for societal functions. Consequently, their loss in disasters – whether natural or human-induced in origin – can potentially result in widespread, catastrophic disruptions. In the case of electric power, the risk of large-scale failures from cascading events is increasing because economic and regulatory influences have resulted in power systems operating increasingly closer to their capacity limits (ARI, 2001). The high-voltage transmission grid has expanded very slowly, in part because of environmental regulations. Structural changes in the industry have led to competitive energy markets, in which growing amounts of bulk power are being transported across long distances in response to market prices. Deregulation has transformed vertically integrated utilities into independent companies for power generation, transmission and distribution. Hence issues of electrical reliability have become more salient sources of concern in North America because of limits on expansion of and structural changes within the electrical sector.

The electrical system is important to study within the context of extreme events for another reason: failures in electrical supply can lead to failures in other infrastructure systems that rely on the power system, thus potentially widening and deepening the consequences of a power outage.

Structure and Specific Objectives

As noted earlier, our overall research objective is to develop an approach for setting broad priorities for mitigation investments. Our emphasis is on reducing the potential for failure of other kinds of key societal infrastructures because of a power failure. The power failure could be caused either by an extreme event (such as terrorism) or by conditions and component failures within the electrical system.

This chapter has sub-objectives that relate to this overall objective. One specific objective, discussed in the next section, is to present our conceptual framework for examining interdependent infrastructure failures, which we distinguish from interdependent infrastructure systems. In the third section, we outline the conceptual framework for comparing and evaluating mitigation options to reduce the consequences of interdependent infrastructure failures. We outline the conceptual and applied basis for a broad screening approach, using concepts from the risk ranking and the risk priority-setting literature. We further summarize our research design and study components. The fourth section outlines the interdependent infrastructure failures that occurred during a severe storm in the Pacific Northwest in 1993. Historically, this particular event has been the 'worst-case scenario' in terms of outage durations for the Pacific Northwest utility. The final section includes some discussion and conclusions.

Infrastructure Failure Interdependencies: A Conceptual Framework

One goal of this study is to identify the most important channels by which electric power outages impact other infrastructure systems and thereby disrupt cities, their populations and their economies. Despite growing recognition of the importance of infrastructure failure interdependencies, very few studies have examined this issue from either an empirical or a methodological standpoint. We first discuss the concept of 'infrastructure interdependencies' (sometimes referred to as 'lifeline interactions') and briefly survey the relevant literature. We then make a distinction between 'infrastructure interdependencies' and 'infrastructure failure interactions' (for which we coin the acronym 'IFIs') and propose a conceptual framework for studying the latter.

The Issue of Infrastructure Interdependencies

Infrastructure interdependencies have been a growing concern in both the natural hazards field and the area of infrastructure security. In an important conceptual paper, Rinaldi et al. (2001, p. 14) define a critical infrastructure interdependency as a 'bidirectional relationship between two infrastructures through which the state of each infrastructure influences or is correlated to the state of the other'. Such interdependencies are often referred to as 'lifeline interactions' in the natural hazards field, particularly in earthquake engineering.

Perhaps the most instructive and dramatic example of infrastructure interdependencies in natural disasters is the 1995 Hyogoken-Nanbu earthquake ($M_w = 6.9$) that struck the Kobe region of Japan. This disaster was the world's first experience of a catastrophic urban earthquake in a developed country. The catastrophic dimensions of this event derived not only from the extent of damage but also from the spillover impacts from one infrastructure system to another (Nojima and Kameda, 1996). For example electric power outage was widespread, affecting some 2.6 million households and lasting in some areas for nearly a week. The power outage disabled about 3000 traffic signals in the affected region, snarling traffic and impeding emergency response. The satellite-based prefectural emergency communications system, which could withstand telephone outages, was disabled for six hours because of power loss and inadequate battery backup. The power outage also disrupted telecommunications, hospitals, water systems, high-rise buildings, disaster response and emergency sheltering. Electric power sparks in the presence of natural gas leakage ignited fires. Table 5.1 summarizes those interactions that derived from electric power outage specifically.

As noted previously, the Kobe event illustrates many of the aspects of a terrorist attack on electric utility delivery systems: no immediate warning of its occurrence, an impact-type loading to the structural delivery system, confusion created by the secondary failure of communication facilities, and so on. One major difference was the prevalent attitude that an earthquake had occurred: there was no confusion (or panic) as to whether a terrorist attack had created the ground-shaking and related lifeline failures.

Another example of interdependent effects is the prolonged electric power crisis that affected California in 2001 (Rinaldi et al., 2001). This disaster arose from a very different set of circumstances, including deregulation, substantial load growth, inadequate investment in new capacity, infrastructure deterioration, high natural gas prices, a drought in the Pacific Northwest, volatility in the spot market and regulatory constraints. Nevertheless the electric power disruptions caused significant interdependent failures in other systems, such as oil and natural gas (production, refineries, pipeline transport) and long-distance water transport for crop irrigation.

Interdependent infrastructure failures are of great concern in the Pacific Northwest, which is the primary area of interest in our research. In June 2002 the Pacific Northwest Economic Region (PNWER) conducted a tabletop exercise that focused on infrastructure interdependencies (http://www.pnwer.org/pris/CascadesReport.htm). Co-sponsored by the Federal Emergency Management Agency (FEMA) and its Canadian counterpart (Office of Critical Infrastructure Protection and Emergency Preparedness), the exercise brought together over 70 public and private organizations. The exercise involved a terrorism scenario that began with targeted disruption of the region's electric power and spread to many western states, as well as other sectors such as transportation and emergency services. One of its key findings was the need for improved understanding of regional infrastructure interdependencies.

Table 5.1 Interdependent effects of electric power outage in the 1995 Kobe earthquake

Dependent infrastructure system	Type of interaction	Description of interaction
Transportation	Functional damage propagation	Malfunction of traffic signals due to power outage
Telecommunications	Functional damage propagation	Loss of satellite communications for emergency communications, due to power loss at prefectural control centre
Telecommunications	Functional damage propagation	Malfunction of 285 000 telephone subscribers' lines due to loss of power at telephone exchange centres
Telecommunications	Functional damage propagation	Unavailability of public emergency phone system, which relies on electric power to read telephone cards
Hospitals	Functional damage propagation	Blackout due to loss of power supply and failure of emergency generators from lack of coolant
Water	Functional damage propagation	Loss of filtration plants and pump stations due to power loss
High-rise buildings	Functional damage propagation	Loss of elevators and pumps to move water to roof tanks
Disaster response	Recovery interruption	Inability to mobilize rapidly due to transportation disruption (indirectly due to electric power outages)
Natural gas	Compound damage propagation	Fire ignitions due to natural gas leakage and electric power sparks
Emergency shelters	Compound damage propagation	Lack of heating due to power loss

Source: After Nojima and Kameda (1996).

In terms of modeling, recent studies of infrastructure performance in disasters have made major advances in evaluating the impacts of infrastructure disruption on urban and regional economies. However these have focused on single infrastructure systems such as electric power (Rose et al., 1997), transportation (Cho et al., 2001) or water (Chang et al., 2002). Studies that have modeled interactions between electric power and water systems have focused on engineering aspects of the problem (for example Shinozuka et al., 2004).

Beyond the natural hazards arena, infrastructure interdependencies have been gaining substantial policy and research attention from the perspective of infrastructure security. The importance of this issue for public policy was raised by a report from President Clinton's Commission on Critical Infrastructure Protection (PCCIP, 1997). This report led to the issue of Presidential Directive 63 on Critical Infrastructure Protection in 1998, which was superseded in 2003 under the Bush administration by a directive on Critical Infrastructure Identification, Prioritization, and Protection (Hspd-7). A report by the North American Electric Reliability Council (NERC) identified infrastructure interdependencies as one of four areas of greatest concern for infrastructure protection in the electricity sector (NERC, 2001).

The issue of infrastructure interdependencies is also attracting substantial research attention. While some and perhaps even most of this work is classified, it is clear from documents in the public domain that major research efforts are under way in this area. Haimes and Jiang (2001) provide a stylized methodology for evaluating risk in complex interconnected infrastructures. In 1998 the Electric Power Research Institute and the Department of Defense jointly funded a five-year, $30 million research effort, the Complex Interactive Networks/Systems Initiative (CIN/SI). This initiative involved researchers at 26 US universities. It developed basic knowledge and new tools for modeling, measuring and managing complex infrastructure systems (Amin, 2000; Amin, 2004). Researchers at the National Laboratories have developed several models related to infrastructure interdependencies. For example one model that simulates outage duration times takes into account escalating failures because of infrastructure interdependencies (Peerenboom et al., 2001). More recently, in 2003 a major effort was initiated at three of the National Laboratories (Argonne, Los Alamos and Sandia) to develop a Critical Infrastructure Protection/Decision Support System (CIP/DSS). At the center of this effort is a large-scale model of 14 types of critical infrastructure and their primary interdependencies at both the urban and national scales. Energy, including electric power, is one of these 14 infrastructures (CIP/DSS Overview, 2004).

Conceptual Frameworks

Rinaldi et al. (2001) offer an important conceptual framework for understanding infrastructure interdependencies. They suggest that interdependencies can be classified into six dimensions: type of interdependency (physical, cyber, logical, geographic); environment (economic/business, public policy, legal/regulatory, health/safety, technical/security, social/political); coupling and response behaviour (degree of coupling, coupling order, linear/complex, adaptive/inflexible); infrastructure characteristics (spatial, temporal, operational, organizational); type of failure (cascading, escalating, common cause); and state of operation (normal, stressed/disrupted, repair/restoration).

While such a framework is valuable for studying interdependencies, it does not provide a sufficient basis for conceptualizing interdependent failures. Interdependencies are linkages between systems; interdependent failures are a manifestation of these linkages in which disruption in one system leads to disruption in another. The distinction is subtle but important for several reasons. First, for failures the specific context is important. Earthquakes should be distinguished from grid control problems. Second, the societal impact is important for failures. We want to distinguish events that lead to hundreds of deaths from those that result in minor inconvenience. Of course the context is important in the definition of societal impact as population densities vary throughout the world. Third, failures may reveal unintentional interdependencies that are not part of normal infrastructure operations and are hence often overlooked in emergency preparedness planning (Robert et al., 2003). Finally, failures may be studied from an empirical perspective, even without a complete understanding or ability to model the mechanisms of interdependence.

Nojima and Kameda (1996) provide a conceptual framework for interdependent failures in their study of the Kobe earthquake. They identify six forms of lifeline interactions observed in the Kobe disaster: physical damage propagation; functional damage propagation; recovery interruption; back-up functions of substitutive systems; compound damage propagation; and end users' inconvenience. While this framework is also insightful and useful, it does not provide an adequate basis for systematically identifying which interdependent failures are most important (from a societal standpoint).

We therefore propose a conceptual framework for IFIs (infrastructure failure interactions). We draw some key concepts from the Rinaldi et al. and the Nojima and Kameda frameworks. However, our framework is designed specifically to provide a typology of IFIs that will help in systematically gathering, structuring and analyzing data from actual outage events. It is intended to help answer two questions:

- What are the channels by which electric power outages cause failures in other infrastructure systems?
- Which of these channels are the most important?

The basis for this framework is the observation that any given IFI arises from a particular electric power outage event that impacts a particular dependent infrastructure system, leading to certain societal consequences. It is therefore useful to classify IFIs according to characteristics of the outage event, electric power interactions with the impacted system and the consequences to society. Table 5.2 summarizes the framework.

Table 5.2 Conceptual framework for infrastructure failure interdependencies

IFI dimension	Characteristic	Example values
OUTAGE	Initiating event	Internal to electric power system External
	Spatial extent	Local Regional National International
	Duration	Minutes Hours Days Weeks
	Weather	Moderate Extreme
	Temperature	Cold Mild Hot
INTERACTIONS	Type of dependency	Physical Geographic
	Type of interdependent failure	Cascading Escalating Restoration Compound

Table 5.2 (continued)

IFI dimension	Characteristic	Example values
		damage propagation Substitutive
	Order	Direct Second Higher
	Complexity	Linear Complex
	Feedback to electric power	Yes No
	Operational state of dependent system	At capacity at time of event Near capacity Below capacity
	Potential for adaptive response	High Low
	Restart time for dependent system	Minutes Hours Days Weeks
CONSEQUENCE	Severity of impact	Minor inconvenience Moderate disruption Major disruption
	Type of impact	Economic Environmental Health Safety Social
	Spatial extent of impact	Local Regional National International
	Number of people impacted in spatial extent	Few Many Most
	Duration of impact	Minutes Hours Days Weeks

This framework for characterizing IFIs provides a basis for further stages of our research. Ultimately we intend to characterize disruption values and identify promising mitigation strategies through an expert-based ranking exercise.

COMPONENTS OF ANALYSIS FOR MITIGATION RANKING EXERCISES

This section discusses concepts and practical approaches that could help guide efforts to compare and rank mitigation investment opportunities to reduce the risks of or consequences from interdependent infrastructure failures stemming from power outages. First, we discuss an overview of the analytical tasks involved, then some key assumptions needed to help simplify and guide the tasks, and finally, the components of our approach to be applied over the course of our research project.

In broadest terms, we can think of a set *A* of possible mitigation options to reduce the potential for independent infrastructure failures stemming from an electrical outage. Given this set of alternatives, the broad policy analysis task is to compare, evaluate and rank these mitigation options, based on a set of societal values, which we denote as *V*. The basic question is then: which of the alternatives in *A* are more attractive and thus good mitigation investment prospects given their estimated consequences *C* and our representative set of societal values *V*?

Based on subjective expected utility theory, what information is needed as a basis for comparing such alternatives to make a decision on their ranking and merits? We would need to develop performance indices to characterize the technical performance or consequences *C* of the alternatives in *A*. In other words, what are the consequences of the alternatives in terms of important societal objectives such as cost, avoidance of adverse health, social, environmental effects? Then we need a value function *V* to compare these diverse kinds and levels of impacts into an overall assessment of merit or aggregate net benefit. Hence we need to make use of well-informed and well-structured judgements about the technical impacts and about the values associated with a choice among the alternatives (Keeney, 1992).

Within the welfare economics paradigm, all impacts are valued in dollar terms, based on willingness-to-pay for opportunities created and willingness-to-sell for opportunities foregone within a specific reference group. The approach we outline here is a broader version, which could have some impacts valued in dollar terms and others in non-monetary units (for example years of life lost, years of morbidity, stress or worry). It is a multi-attribute approach to valuing the pros and cons of public policy alternatives (Keeney, 1992).

Assumptions Guiding the Analysis

One major limitation on using the expected utility paradigm as a basis for these comparative rankings is the profound uncertainties regarding the frequency of extreme events that may affect the power system and thus other infrastructure systems. These are, by definition, low-probability, high-consequence events, for which we have little or no data to model probabilities. One might rely on informed judgements elicited from experts about the probabilities of these extreme events (Keeney and von Winterfeldt, 1999; Morgan and Henrion, 1990).

Instead we have adopted a different analytical strategy as one conceptual basis for the analysis, as articulated by Haimes (1998) for analyzing and managing the consequences of extreme events. Haimes argues that *ex ante* expected value or expected utility analysis can undervalue the benefits of avoiding adverse extreme events, given an *ex post* perspective after the event occurs. He suggests analysis based on what he terms the conditional partitioned-set expected value or, in other words, the consequences of the alternatives, conditional on the assumption that one or more extreme event occurs. So for power outages this approach to analysis is not based on estimating the probability of major outages occurring and then the probability-weighted *ex ante* net benefits of a mitigation option. Instead the task is to assume that major outages will occur and then estimate the potential *ex post* net benefits of a mitigation option, given a major outage has occurred (Haimes, 1998).

A second conceptual basis recognizes the advantages of structured but largely qualitative and exploratory approaches to characterizing complex systems, based on both influence diagrams (Clemen, 1997) and scenarios. A third conceptual basis relies on experts to make judgement-based comparisons about ranking of risk management options, based on preliminary information across a wide range of alternatives (Florig et al., 2001; Morgan et al., 2001). A fourth conceptual basis recognizes the crucial role of values in defining what is important for mitigation decisions. It uses those values as a basis for structuring that analysis and for creating more attractive and widely supported alternatives (Keeney, 1992).

Research Design and Study Components

Our research project focuses on the Pacific Northwest as a regional case study. For present purposes, the Pacific Northwest is defined to include

Oregon, Washington and British Columbia (a portion of the territory covered by the Western Electric Coordinating Council). The effort will concentrate on hazards that are most relevant to this region, including earthquakes and winter storms. Other hazards such as floods, drought and terrorism will also be considered.

The methodological approach consists of three closely linked tasks that all relate to the Pacific Northwest case study. The tasks will investigate respectively: the interdependent effects of electric power outage on critical infrastructure systems; associated scenarios of extreme events; and strategies for mitigation.

The first task will focus on identifying and characterizing the interdependent effects of electric power disruption on critical infrastructure systems. Attention will be paid to telecommunications (including the Internet), transportation, water, wastewater, hospitals and financial institutions. This task seeks to identify the specific and most important mechanisms by which electric power outages cause failures in other critical infrastructure systems. A framework to facilitate empirical data collection as part of this process was presented above.

Data will be gathered on historic power outages in the Pacific Northwest and supplemented by interviews with technical and managerial staff in various infrastructure agencies. Major events such as the 1993 winter storm (discussed further below) will be used as focal points in the investigation. Data will also be sought from experiences and sources outside the Pacific Northwest; for example, the 14 August 2003 severe power outages in eastern Canada and the northeast US.

Further efforts will include the development of influence diagrams. Influence diagrams are an approach in decision analysis that can be used to characterize and communicate conditional probabilistic relationships among variables, as a basis for model structuring, qualitative understanding or for conducting quantitative analysis (Clemen, 1997). Figure 5.1 is an example of an influence diagram developed in a previous study of reliability for BC Hydro, the electric utility serving British Columbia, Canada. In contrast to Figure 5.1, the outcomes of this study will focus on interdependent failures between electric power and other systems. To the extent possible, quantitative models such as fragility curves will be developed of the interactions identified in the influence diagrams.

The primary outcome of the empirically derived models will be to characterize and, in some cases, quantify the influence of power outages on the performance of dependent systems. In this process, possible engineering design solutions should become apparent. For example it may be preferable for some systems to design structural components for ease of repair rather than for ultimate strength. Engineering design approaches to mitigation

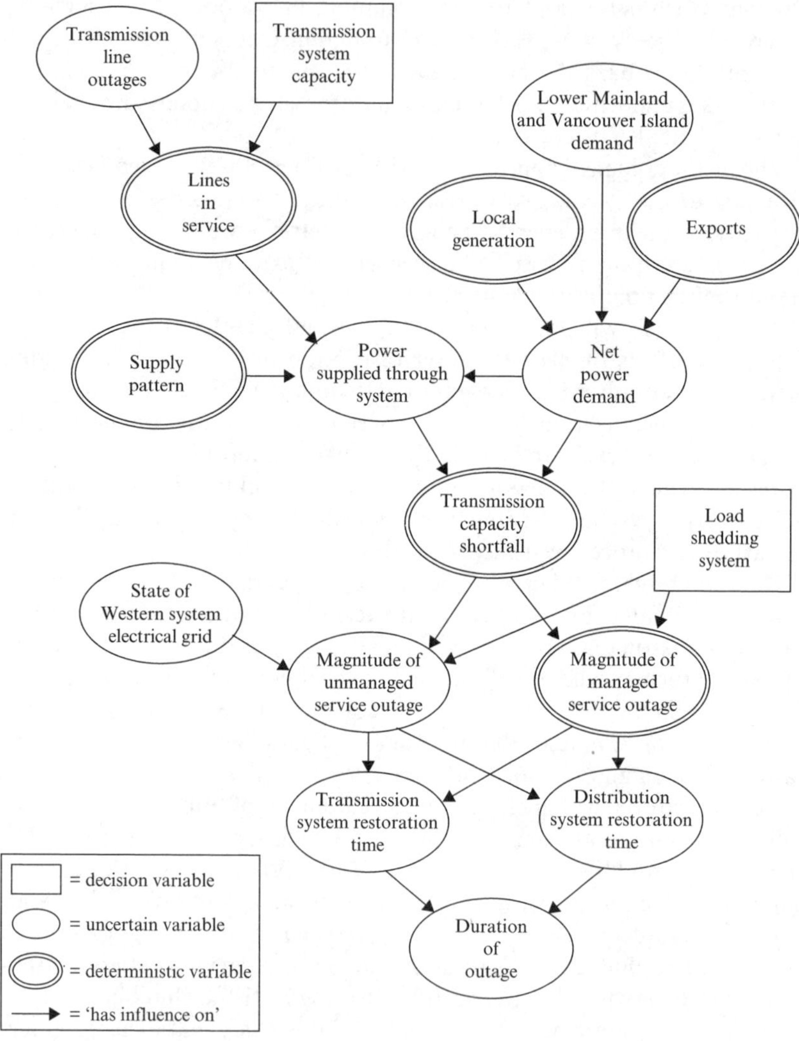

Source: Keeney et al. (1995)

Figure 5.1 Example influence diagram of electric power reliability

will provide an input to the mitigation evaluations to be performed later in this study.

The second task will characterize infrastructure failure interdependencies within the context of specific hazards. It seeks to identify the types of extreme events in which power outage would cause significant interdependent failures in other infrastructure systems and to identify the interdependent failures that are common to many types of hazards. These questions will be approached through the development of a series of realistic scenarios of extreme events.

A range of different hazard events will be considered. This will include both the major natural hazards in the Pacific Northwest – earthquake, flood and winter storm – as well as other influences such as drought, environmental regulation and increasing power demands from urban and economic growth. Terrorism events will also be considered. It is important to examine the range of relevant hazards because IFIs will differ significantly in these scenarios. For example a major earthquake would damage regional transportation networks that would then impede electric power restoration and prolong outages. Severe windstorms would affect collocated infrastructures because overhead power distribution lines are located on poles that are also used for cable, telephone and Internet connections. These compounding effects would not be present in a terrorism event that targeted a critical power generation facility. Approximately 65 per cent of electricity generated in the area is through hydropower. The safety of the extensive dam facilities in the region is therefore crucial.

Detailed modeling of IFI effects is not possible because of the substantial uncertainty and lack of data regarding extreme event disasters. However scenarios provide an effective means for summarizing what is known through developing 'snapshots' of extreme events. In the disaster management field, complex computer models of disasters (for example the FEMA-sponsored HAZUS loss-estimation model) are a recent development, enabled by the accumulation of knowledge and techniques related to disaster loss estimation. Previously there had been a long tradition of using static 'paper' scenarios to portray potential disasters and support mitigation and preparedness planning.

Specific scenarios will be developed to trace through the potential for cascading effects. An example might be a magnitude 6.7 earthquake on the Seattle Fault. Data for the scenarios will be gathered from interviews with experts, including scientists, engineers and technical and managerial staff with infrastructure organizations. As noted earlier, the latter will include organizations ranging from water to transportation and finance. The scenarios will be computer based for visualization of interdependent infrastructure failures as they take place over space and time.

The third task synthesizes findings by seeking to identify the values that can be associated with avoiding disruptions and the strategic interventions that can most effectively address the effects of power disruption in extreme events. Many modeling studies of disaster impacts have encountered empirical challenges with quantifying impacts because of lack of appropriate data, in particular on business revenue losses. Here an alternative approach is explored, that of developing data on those values decision makers attach to mitigation and loss avoidance.

The approach will involve judgements about: (1) what matters in making decisions about mitigation options; and (2) the relative performance of an array of mitigation options. To address the first question, methods of value-focused thinking (Keeney, 1992) will be applied to structure a set of objectives relevant for evaluating mitigation options, based on interviews with technical experts and decision makers. To address the second question, judgement-based rating approaches will be developed that involve technical experts considering the relative performance of these mitigation methods, based on simple indicators for the broader set of objectives.

Data to implement these approaches will be obtained through interviews with and a workshop involving technical and managerial staff at infrastructure agencies. The interviews and workshop will refer specifically to the scenarios developed in the second task. Values will be elicited with respect to avoiding disruptions. Particularly critical points of systems interaction and potential mitigation strategies will be identified. For example in many situations one IFI of electricity outage would be loss of power to traffic signals. The ensuing traffic disruptions would have far-reaching effects, not least upon the ability of repair crews to rapidly restore electric power. In this case an effective mitigation strategy may be the installation of batteries for back-up power in traffic signals at key intersections.

The intent of these efforts is not to create the final list of ranked mitigation alternatives for the Pacific Northwest. Rather, the intent is to conduct preliminary screening based on limited current information. The resulting priority areas could then be further analyzed and civic society groups could be involved in providing their advice about these priorities. At that point, more refined analysis would be conducted. Hence this study is a first step in an iterative analysis.

INFRASTRUCTURE FAILURE INTERDEPENDENCIES IN RECENT DISASTERS

To illustrate our approach to analyzing infrastructure failure interdependencies, we first explore the case of one of the most severe power outage events recently experienced in the Pacific Northwest. On 20 January 1993, a major winter windstorm struck the Pacific Northwest. Lasting 63 hours, the storm caused massive power outages that lasted up to 84 hours in some areas. The storm primarily caused extensive damage to trees and aboveground power distribution lines. In contrast to major transmission system

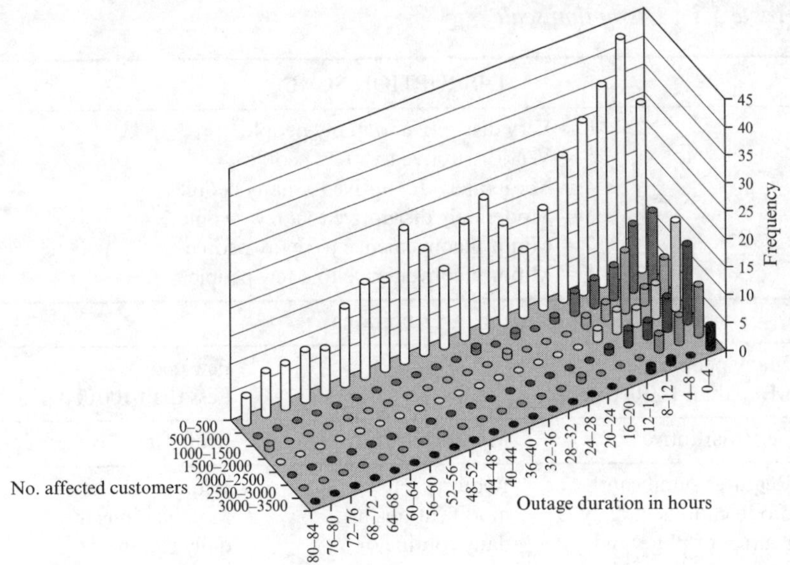

Figure 5.2 Frequency count of outage events in 1993 Inauguration Day windstorm

failures in which a single blackout can cover a very wide area, this pattern of distribution system damage led to some 554 distinct, local power outage events. These events affected some 286 000 customers (accounts) and resulted in a total of 2.5 million customer-hours of power outage. Figure 5.2 shows the distribution of these local outage events by duration and size (in terms of number of affected customers). Some 40 per cent of the local outage events lasted over 24 hours, although each of these events affected less than 500 customers.

Loss of electric power caused widespread disruption to other critical infrastructure systems. For purposes of this preliminary analysis, we use the disruption scale shown in Table 5.3, where impacts are defined on the basis of severity of disruption to normal activities as well as population affected. The impact of the IFIs range from 'minor inconvenience to a few people' (score = 1) to 'very disruptive to many people' (score = 6).

Figure 5.3 describes some of the IFIs that resulted from the storm. Circles in the figure denote major classes of infrastructures that were affected by the power outages. Rectangles indicate the type of IFI that was experienced, shaded according to severity of impact. Only IFIs at the upper end of our impact scale (scores of 4–6) are shown in the figure. For example in the building-support category of infrastructure, power

Table 5.3 Disruption scale

DISRUPTION SCALE		
6 = Very disruptive to many people 5 = Very disruptive to a few people 4 = Moderately disruptive to many people 3 = Moderately disruptive to a few people 2 = Minor inconvenience to many people 1 = Minor inconvenience to a few people		
Definitions		
Many people More than 100 000 people		Few people Less than 100 000 people
Very disruptive	Moderately disruptive	Minor inconvenience
Requires significant modifications in daily routine or plans and causes considerable hardship to the person or entity	Requires a few modifications in daily routine or plans and causes some hardship to the person or entity	Requires minor modifications in daily routine or plans and causes negligible hardship to the person or entity

outage caused elevator problems in high-rise buildings that were, according to our impact scale, 'very disruptive to few people'. The most severe impacts – those that were 'very disruptive to many people' – were experienced in the utilities sector, where power outage caused a failure of the wastewater system and led to raw sewage being dumped into Elliott Bay; in the health sector, where downed power lines posed a public safety threat throughout the region; and in the government sector, where emergency school closures occurred during the day. This last problem, compounded by impassable roads and congestion, caused widespread confusion and disruption as parents attempted to bring their children home from school; many children ended up staying overnight at school. This impact illustrates the compounding effects of second-order and higher-order interdependent failures (in this case, between failures in both transportation and schools that were caused by power outage) as indicated in the figure by dotted lines.

Table 5.3 and Figure 5.3 illustrate several aspects of our framework and point toward fruitful ways for working on other examples of power outage disasters. First, a systematic assessment of power outage impacts on

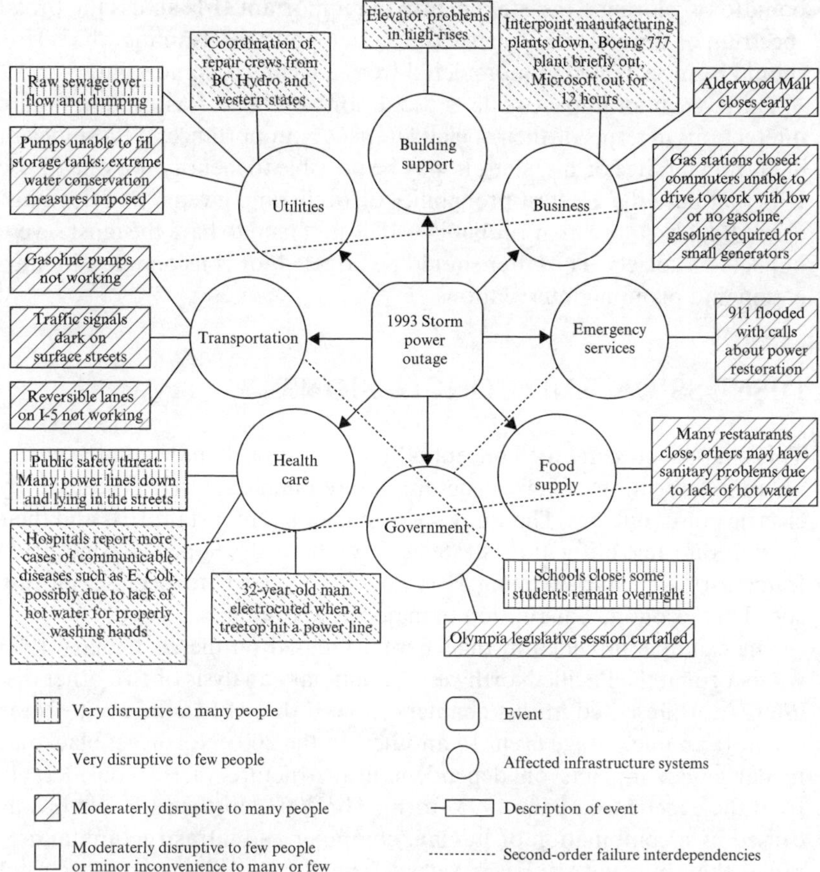

Figure 5.3 Infrastructure failure interactions in the 20 January 1993 windstorm

dependent infrastructure systems, if performed across a meaningful sample of outage disasters, can help identify critical infrastructures (for example transportation and hospitals) that are most frequently disrupted when electric power systems fail. A sufficiently large sample of disasters or disaster-impacted communities may provide a basis for estimating IFI occurrence in probabilistic terms.

Second, an impact scale similar to that in Table 5.3 can be used to mine a broad range of data sources. For example newspaper articles provide a readily accessible source of secondary data on major outage events and their local societally significant impacts. They represent a natural entry point for exploring a disaster, identifying important IFIs across the broad spectrum of dependent infrastructure systems and determining which IFIs should be investigated in more detail from a technical standpoint.

Third, such an impact scale is useful for ranking infrastructure failure interactions in terms of their societal impact or importance. With sufficient data from a range of disasters, it may be possible to identify not only those IFIs that have the greatest probability of occurring, given a power outage event, but also those high-probability IFIs that tend to have the most severe impacts on society. The latter should be targeted for consideration in mitigation and planning interventions.

DISCUSSION AND CONCLUSIONS

This chapter presents the conceptual basis, approach and initial progress on an investigation of infrastructure failure interactions (IFIs) caused by electric power outages. The study seeks to identify important IFIs and their most promising mitigation strategies. We have developed a conceptual framework for characterizing IFIs and have used it to begin exploring social and economic disruption in major power outages.

The example provided in this chapter focused on the 20 January 1993 windstorm in the Pacific Northwest. Preliminary analysis of two other disasters (not presented in this chapter) showed that IFIs will vary to some extent from one outage event to another. In the 2003 Northeast blackout, in particular, impacts on dependent infrastructure varied considerably from the experience of the 1993 storm. The 2003 Northeast blackout was caused by a combination of human, computer and infrastructure failures rather than by a natural hazard event. Therefore power outages occurred in the absence of other direct damage (for example localized flooding) that is characteristic of natural disasters. Moreover the 2003 blackout was caused by failures in the interregional power transmission network rather than in local distribution systems. Duration of outage is another key difference which remains to be further explored; IFIs are expected to exhibit non-linear and threshold effects in relation to power outage duration. However preliminary analysis indicates that impacts on transportation tend to be severe and widespread across most outage events, suggesting a potentially important system to target for mitigation. Further data collection and analysis across a broader range of disasters and disaster-impacted communities will help to develop more robust findings.

The framework outlined here should be useful for both conceptual and applied analysis of infrastructure interdependencies and, specifically, of infrastructure failure interdependencies in extreme event disasters. It will also be useful for helping to address issues of how to design and rank alternatives for mitigation. This kind of analysis can lead to the development of more disaster-resilient communities – communities that are better able to withstand both natural hazards and human-induced threats.

NOTE

* This research was supported by the National Science Foundation under grant number CMS-0332002. We thank Krista Peterson for her assistance with preparing the figures and tables for this document.

REFERENCES

Alexandria Research Institute (ARI) (2001), 'Mitigating the vulnerability of critical infrastructures to catastrophic failures', introduction to CRIS/DRM/ IIIT/ NSF Workshop on Mitigating the Vulnerability of Critical Infrastructures to Catastrophic Failures, Alexandria, VA, 10–11 September (www.ari.vt.edu/workshop).

Amin, Massoud (2000), 'National infrastructures as complex interactive networks', in Tariq Samad and John Weyrauch (eds), *Automation, Control, and Complexity: An Integrated Approach*, Chichester, UK and New York: John Wiley and Sons, pp. 263–86.

Amin, Massoud (2004), 'North American electricity infrastructure: system security, quality, reliability, availability, and efficiency challenges and their societal impacts', in National Science Foundation, *Continuing Crises in National Transmission Infrastructure: Impacts and Options for Modernization*, Washington, DC: National Science Foundation.

Chang, S.E., W.D. Svekla and M. Shinozuka (2002), 'Linking infrastructure and urban economy: simulation of water disruption impacts in earthquakes', *Environment and Planning B*, **29** (2), 281–301.

Cho, S., P. Gordon, J.E. Moore II, H.W. Richardson, M. Shinozuka and S.E. Chang (2001), 'Integrating transportation network and regional economic models to estimate the costs of a large urban earthquake', *Journal of Regional Science*, **41** (1), 39–65.

Clemen, Robert T. (1997), *Making Hard Decisions: An Introduction to Decisions Analysis*, 2nd edn, Duxbury, MA: Duxbury Press.

CIP/DSS Overview (2004), 'Critical Infrastructure Protection Decision Support System (CIP/DSS) project overview', Argonne, Los Alamos and Sandia National Laboratories.

Florig, H. Keith, M.G. Morgan, K.M. Morgan, K.E. Jenni, B. Fischhoff, P.S. Fischbeck and M.L. DeKay (2001), 'A deliberative method for ranking risks (I): overview and test bed development', *Risk Analysis*, **21** (5), 913–22.

Haimes, Yacov Y. (1998), *Risk Modeling, Assessment and Management*, New York: John Wiley & Sons.

Haimes, Y.Y. and P. Jiang (2001), 'Leontief-based model of risk in complex interconnected infrastructures', *Journal of Infrastructure Systems*, **7** (1), 1–12.

Keeney, Ralph L. (1992), *Value-Focused Thinking*, Cambridge, MA: Harvard University Press.

Keeney, R.L., T.L. McDaniels and C. Swoveland (1995), 'Evaluating improvements in electric utility reliability at British Columbia Hydro', *Operations Research*, **43** (6), 933–47.

Keeney, R. and D. von Winterfeldt (1999), 'Eliciting probabilities from experts in complex technical problems', *IEEE Transactions on Engineering Management*, **38**, 191–201.

Kunreuther, H. and A. Lerner-Lam (2002), 'Risk assessment and risk management strategies in an uncertain world', executive summary of workshop on Risk Management Strategies in an Uncertain World, 12–13 April (www.ldeo.columbia.edu/CHRR/Roundtable).

Morgan, K.M., M.L. DeKay, P.S. Fischbeck, M.G. Morgan, B. Fischhoff and H.K. Florig (2001), 'A deliberative method for ranking risks (II): evaluation of validity and agreement among risk managers', *Risk Analysis*, **21** (5), 923–38.

Morgan, M. Granger and Max Henrion (1990), *Uncertainty: A Guide to Dealing with Uncertainty in Quantitative Risk and Policy Analysis*, Cambridge: Cambridge University Press.

Nojima, Nobuoto and Hiroyuki Kameda (1996), 'Lifeline interactions in the Hanshin-Awaji earthquake disaster', in Committee of Earthquake Engineering, *The 1995 Hyogoken-Nanbu Earthquake: Investigation into Damage to Civil Engineering Structures*, Tokyo: Japan Society of Civil Engineers, pp. 253–64.

North American Electric Reliability Council (NERC) (2001), *An Approach to Action for the Electricity Sector*, Princeton, NJ: Working Group Forum on Critical Infrastructure Protection.

Peerenboom, J., R. Fisher and R. Whitfield (2001), 'Recovering from disruptions of interdependent critical infrastructures', paper prepared for CRIS/DRM/IIIT/NSF Workshop on Mitigating the Vulnerability of Critical Infrastructures to Catastrophic Failures, Alexandria, VA, 10–11 September.

President's Commission on Critical Infrastructure Protection (PCCIP) (1997), *Critical Foundations: Protecting America's Infrastructures*, Washington, DC.

Rinaldi, S.M., J.P. Peerenboom and T.K. Kelly (2001), 'Identifying, understanding, and analyzing critical infrastructure interdependencies', *IEEE Control Systems Magazine*, **21** (6), 11–25.

Robert, Benoît, Marie-Hélène Senay, Marie-Ève P. Plamondon and Jean-Pierre Sabourin (2003), *Characterization and Ranking of Links Connecting Life Support Networks*, Ottawa, Canada: Public Safety and Emergency Preparedness Canada.

Rose, A., J. Benavides, S.E. Chang, P. Szczesniak and D. Lim (1997), 'The regional economic impact of an earthquake: direct and indirect effects of electricity lifeline disruptions', *Journal of Regional Science*, **37** (3), 437–58.

Shinozuka, M., S.E. Chang, T.C. Cheng, M. Feng, T.D. O'Rourke, M.A. Saadeghvaziri, X. Dong, X. Jin, Y. Wang and P. Shi (2004), 'Resilience of integrated power and water systems', in *Research Progress and Accomplishments 2003–2004*, Buffalo, NY: Multidisciplinary Center for Earthquake Engineering Research (MCEER), pp. 65–86.

Stewart, T.R. and A. Bostrom (2002), workshop report 'Extreme Event Decision-Making', Albany, NY: Center for Policy Research, Rockefeller College of Public Affairs and Policy, University at Albany (www.albany.edu/cpr/xedm).

6. Float together/sink together? The effect of connectivity on power systems

Richard E. Schuler

INTRODUCTION

The recent mantra for reorganizing power systems in the US has been to extend the geographic scope of control centers to span several states, utilities and/or grid operators, initially for the purpose of expanding the range of economic transfers and more recently to improve operational reliability, in both cases through the reduction of 'seams' at the borders of control areas. In the early days of electric deregulation this push for coordination was in the guise of forming four to five Regional Transmission Organizations (RTO), combining existing power pools and Independent System Operators (ISO), that might dispatch power at least cost over wide regions of the country. The Federal Energy Regulatory Commission (FERC) also proposed a standard market design (SMD) for all control areas so that neighboring entities could exchange power more effectively, but this initiative has fallen victim to massive states' rights battles (Whatever happened to the Commerce Clause of the US Constitution?). Following the 14 August 2003 Northeast blackout, similar calls for far greater regional coordination have been based upon the perceived benefits in terms of greater reliability and reduced susceptibility to cascading disturbances across control area borders.

Currently the power system(s) in the US is a hodge-podge – institutionally, economically, physically and in terms of regulatory oversight. It is the epitome of nationwide decentralized decision making about a set of systems that are nevertheless highly centralized locally. This analysis reviews these seeming inconsistencies and examines the likely consequences for reliability. Conceptually, it compares strongly coordinated network systems vs. decentralized loosely coupled systems as applied to the vulnerability of power grids to catastrophic collapse. As an example, would the Northeast blackout of 14 August 2003 have been limited or more widespread (and therefore tougher to restore) had the PJM and New England ISOs not separated from New York prior to New York's protection system isolating it from Ontario? How does this experience affect the way we design future systems to improve their sustainability in the face of both natural and terrorist threats? How might that prospect affect the terrorists' targeting?

From the perspective of critical infrastructure, none seems as essential for the working of modern societies as the electricity grid. While the telecom, transportation, water and sewer and financial networks are highly interdependent with the electrical network, on a first principles basis the others cannot be sustained for a long period without reliable electricity supplies. As an example, following the 14 August blackout, several cities lacked water supply until the electric service was restored. And in New York City following the 11 September 2001 attack on the World Trade Center, water was available to fight the fires only because diesel-powered fireboats pumping water from adjacent rivers were pressed into service. Telecom service in NYC was also rapidly restored in large part because of diesel-powered emergency generators, but with prolonged outages of the electricity grid, how is the fuel to get in without the signals, powered by electricity, to unsnarl traffic? With such an ill-coordinated electricity system across geographic and institutional boundaries, it would appear at first glance that this is by far our most critically vulnerable system. While that is true for local pockets of customers, the good news is that on a wide geographic scale, hodge-podge and loose coupling may be beneficial! Short of all-out, ongoing warfare, it is difficult for even a coordinated terrorist action to bring large contiguous sections of the power grid down for more than a day or two. Hurricanes seem to do a much better job than can malevolent people.

After reviewing the design and operating practices for electricity systems throughout the US, simple agent-based simulations are used to illustrate essential principles about the relationship between the size of an organization (for example the number of local activities or control areas that agree to coordinate their actions and/or are spanned by an ISO/RTO) and the number of external connections (for example interconnections with other entities whose objectives are autonomous, like other ISOs) where individual local control areas 'learn' how best to respond to system insults. Overall the greater the number of non-cooperating external pathways, the larger the organization should become in order to enhance reliability (performance). However the outcome hinges in part upon the expected duration of the threatening environment. For short time horizons, it is useful to build large interconnected entities so a larger number of experiences can be shared, but as the planning horizons is extended, the optimally-sized organization grows smaller, even in the face of many potential external insults, as the improvement of performance of individual agents outweighs the 'confusion' created by too many tightly linked partners.

PRIMER ON ELECTRICITY SYSTEMS

Most major electricity systems use alternating current (AC) because that is essential for transforming voltages (the energy potential) from one level to another, and high voltages in turn are required for the economical hauling of electricity over long distances (with low losses). But AC systems cannot modulate the flow of electric energy over particular paths, unlike water and natural gas flows that can be adjusted by turning valves; instead the flows between generators and users and the paths selected are governed by the laws of physics (Kirchhoff's Law). Furthermore since economical generation methods are usually very large in scale, the suppliers are concentrated at particular points (frequently near fuel supplies or where environmental impacts are minimal, and always near water), and multiple transmission lines are erected to provide alternative paths that enhance the reliability of connecting those low-cost generators with concentrations of customers in urban areas.

An illustrative schematic diagram of a bulk power system is shown in Figure 6.1. Here transformers step the voltage of power produced by

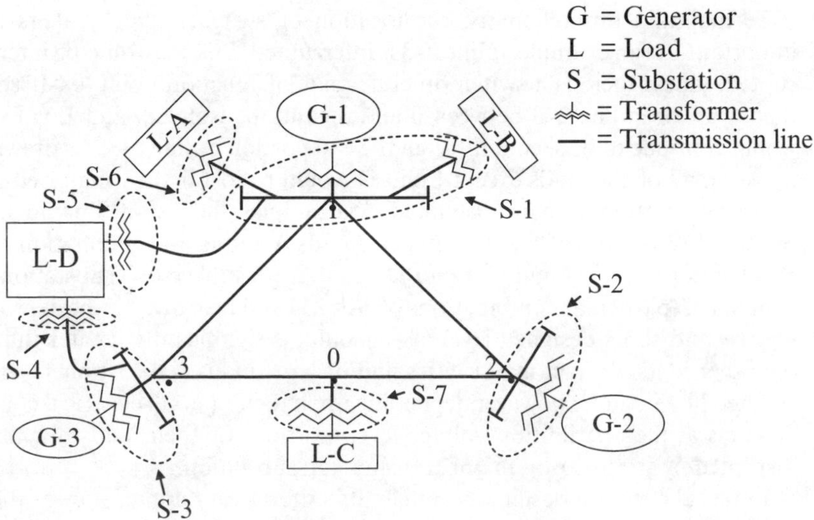

Figure 6.1 Schematic diagram of bulk power delivery system

generators up to higher levels in preparation for long-distance hauling over transmission lines (the solid lines). Similarly, step-down transformers reduce the voltage in preparation for delivery to the local distribution system. Frequently these transformers are located together with switches and connecting facilities called busses in substations (encircled with dashed lines in Figure 6.1). These transformers are large and are located on the ground or underneath in vaults, but the connecting busses are usually located overhead on a steel superstructure. There are also many switches located in each substation that can connect or disconnect the various transformers and lines at each of the junction points, and some of them operate automatically when a problem is 'sensed' on the system, much like the circuit breakers in the switch box in every home. However since this is an AC system, those switches are either entirely open or closed, and the apportionment of power flow among those lines when there are parallel paths is governed entirely by Kirchhoff's Laws.

This simple system is constructed so that it satisfies the single contingency design criterion for bulk power system in the US, that is, the system can withstand the interruption of any single transmission line or generator and still be capable of delivering power. In fact, in the hypothetical system illustrated in Figure 6.1, every load center can continue to be served despite the loss of any single generator (if those generators are each sized with sufficient excess capacity, all loads might also be met with the loss of any two generators), and the same is true with the loss of any one of the three major transmission lines (those connecting 1–2, 2–3 or 2–3).

To maintain this reliability, the location of switches and breakers is important. As an example, if line 2–3 is interrupted, Load C would be interrupted, unless there is a switch on either side of junction point '0'. If so, then a break in line 2–3 between 0 and 3 could be isolated, and Load C would continue to be served through the 3–0 portion of line 2–3. As drawn however, all of the loads except Load D would be lost if their major connecting substation were incapacitated. As examples: the loss of S-6 knocks out Load A, the loss of S-1 disconnects Loads A and B, and elimination of S-7 denies power to Load C. Load D however must have two substations eliminated (particular combinations of S-1, 3, 4 and 5) in order to be denied service, and so its designed level of reliability is significantly greater than the other loads. In fact major cities and/or large industrial customers are situated like Load D; however depending upon their internal electrical connections at the distribution voltage level, portions of their loads may be disrupted by the loss of a major transmission substation.

In fact the system design and reliability criteria vary appreciably at the distribution voltage level from that at the bulk power system level. With the exception of large, high-density urban areas like NYC (New York City), the lower voltage distribution system (the load side of substations in Figure 6.1) is routinely laid out with radial feeds to customers from the substation. These are the lines on the cross-arms of poles that line highways and city streets or are underground adjacent to them. Because of the radial configuration, when a distribution line is interrupted, all customers along it are without service. However if these lines are skillfully configured spatially so that the ends of two lines are in close proximity, some customers may be reconnected to the system before the original cause of the line outage is repaired, simply by opening and closing switches along these lines, and back-feeding those customers beyond the short-circuit on the interrupted line.

Nevertheless, because the distribution system is usually exposed to many more insults as a result of its ubiquitous presence along nearly every street and highway (the exception is in major cities where the distribution system is configured differently as an underground network), and because of its radial configuration without instantaneous alternative paths of supply, approximately 80 per cent of all power disruptions in the US are caused by distribution system failures. The remaining 20 per cent are attributable to failures in the bulk power system illustrated in Figure 6.1. However since all major regional blackouts are failures of the bulk power system (far more than a single contingency is experienced simultaneously), studies of catastrophic failures focus on the bulk power system. Only in the case of widespread natural catastrophes like hurricanes or ice storms are the sources of disruption usually at both the distribution and bulk power levels. In these cases however, the bulk power system is usually restored to full service in a day or two, primarily because of its network configuration with parallel paths, and the prolonged customer outages of more than a week are usually the result of the multiplicity of distribution failures that must be repaired one by one until all customers can be restored to service.

The exception is in large cities like New York where because of the spatial density of demand and of the distribution pathways along the local streets, not only are all distribution facilities placed underground where they are less exposed physically, they are configured in a grid as a tightly coupled set of networks with many parallel paths and multiple sources of bulk power supply. Under this distribution configuration, the loss of any one or two lines results in hardly a blip in the service to any customer, and this reliability is accomplished automatically without dispatching operators to open and close switches, as is the case with radial distribution systems. Obviously the cost of providing electric service is also much greater when this underground network configuration is used, but the extra cost is proportionately lower as the spatial concentration of demand increases, as in megalopolises like New York.

REGULATORY AND INSTITUTIONAL STRUCTURE

So who is in charge of this complex system? The answer is: lots of entities and institutions, and therefore in effect, no one! Although the various private and public facility owners and operating entities (privately owned utilities, municipal electric companies, state and federal power agencies and rural coops), the coordinating power pools, Independent System Operators (ISO) and Regional Transmission Organizations (RTO), and the state PUCs and PSCs (regulatory bodies), as well as the Federal Energy Regulatory Commission (FERC) all have a role to play, none of these entities has clear overall authority to provide (or order to be provided) the necessary facilities, connections and coordination that would enhance overall system reliability or lead to regional economy of service. That is why after the 1965 Northeast blackout the National Electric Reliability Council (NERC) was formed, together with its regional councils, but the operating and design guidelines and recommendations of NERC are voluntary because it is a voluntary industry-formed organization. The major push for the deregulation of exchanges of bulk power supplies that occurred in the 1990s was motivated by attempts to achieve more economical regional costs of bulk power supplies through market incentives, but many regions of the country are still balking at the introduction of systematic (and uniform) exchange mechanisms.

So while FERC can nudge the creation of ISOs and RTOs (both organizations are agents of FERC) to create larger market areas and to operate the transmission systems that undergird these market areas reliably, so far they have been unable to withstand the political backlash of ordering their formation. Particularly vehement has been the local differential reaction to imposing a uniform structure to these markets (FERC has outlined a Standard Market Design (SMD) in very broad, flexible terms, but even that has drawn severe derision from some regions of the US) so that exchanges can be made efficiently and reliably across the borders of the control areas. Furthermore FERC has recently been rebuffed in its attempts to order (provide incentives for) the construction of transmission links that might actually allow the power to flow physically across these borders.

Similarly, in the area of establishing and maintaining reliability standards, NERC is toothless and therefore unable to mandate and enforce compliance with its issued guidelines. And so despite an heroic analysis of the causes and faults of the 14 August 2003 blackout in which NERC identified many instances of non-compliance with its rules, it has no authority to impose sanctions. This leaves FERC searching for threads whereby it might impose sanctions on hardware owners and operators for non-compliance, and many knowledgeable and concerned professionals around the nation calling for federal legislation that would make compliance with NERC standards and guidelines mandatory. In fact most state public service commissions do have the authority to impose mandatory performance guidelines on the utilities that they regulate, and to back them up with penalty actions in subsequent rate proceeding if there is inadequate compliance. In most instances they can also authorize the construction of needed new facilities. The problem with each state's authority however (which may not be uniform across states), is that it cannot reach beyond its limited political borders, and as the 14 August 2003 blackout demonstrated, many of these events are multi-state, requiring regional solutions.

OPERATION, CONTROL AND RELIABILITY PHILOSOPHY

Operational control of these complex systems is currently in the hands of a system operator who together with his or her staff oversees the operation and dispatching of power within her control area (power pool, ISO or RTO). In addition each of these regional control centers will call upon operators at smaller area control centers that are staffed by individual utilities and/or at individual generating stations to carry out orders to open or close switches and to increase or decrease the supply from any particular generating unit. Usually this dispatch is designed to minimize the total cost of supplying all power demanded by customers, subject to the available generation capacity, flow limits on individual transmission lines, and maintaining adequate service quality (frequency at 60 cycles and design voltage levels); otherwise the performance of users' and generators' equipment, indeed its survival, might be compromised. This constrained optimization is so complex that it must be solved by a computerized routine, usually every 15, but increasingly every five minutes. The costs of generation for each unit and their available capacities are furnished by the suppliers in a regulated utility power pool framework or by price–quantity offer schedules from potential suppliers in a market context. In either case, excess generation (above the power demanded) that is equal to the size of the single largest generator then operating is always kept running so that the system's load can be matched should that largest unit fail, with a lag of no longer than five minutes (operating reserves).

In planning and ordering these dispatches, the system operator must know what units are available to be called upon in an emergency and which lines are out of service, so that if any contingency occurs on the bulk power system, he or she can immediately have a revised optimal dispatch computed. Because of Kirchhoff's Laws, an operator cannot dictate over which line an ordered increase in generation will flow. As an example, if there is increased load at L-B in Figure 6.1, and it is scheduled to be served by the next highest cost producer at G-2 over transmission line 2–1, in fact the increased generation at G-2 will most likely flow over both parallel paths, 2–1 and 2–3–1. If the capacity limits are being reached on line 3–1, the amount of generation reaching L-B from G-2 may be limited, even if line 2–1 has spare capacity. Kirchhoff's Law of equalizing voltage drops across parallel paths will prevail. In this example, the only way the operator can guarantee that the power might flow over line 2–1 is to open the switches at both ends of line 3–2; thereby taking that line out of service. The flow on any individual line in this network of parallel paths cannot be modulated without the addition of expensive new technology. And, having parallel (redundant) paths is essential for maintaining the reliability of the bulk power system.

This example also illustrates how crucial it is for the system operator to have accurate up-to-date information about the operation and condition of all equipment, including which lines are or will be out of service. Where control areas are interconnected (as they are across ISOs and RTOs in the Northeast), the informational needs are more extensive, and it is equally important to know what is happening in neighboring control areas as well. That was not the case on 14 August 2003.

In addition, many things that happen within these power systems are too fast for human intervention (they may be too fast for centralized computerized analysis and response as well). Thus an automated back-up protection system is in place, triggered by sensing devices at particular locations in the grid that send signals through relays causing circuit-breakers (automated switches) to open and close. Although these 'trip-signals' are planned and simulated on a system-wide basis ahead of actual events, once the devices are set, they operate autonomously on a totally decentralized basis. As an example, were a transmission tower on line 1–3 in Figure 6.1 to collapse, the resulting short circuit would cause sensing devices to 'see' an inrush of electric current from both points 1 and 3, and the associated relays most probably would be set to open the breakers on the busses at points 1 and 3 that feed line 1–3, thereby isolating the problem. In this case, because of the redundant configuration of the bulk power system all loads would continue to have service following this contingency.

If instead a hot air balloon were to land by accident on a transmission bus at point 0, providing a path for electricity to flow to ground, sensors at points 2 and 3 might signal associated relays to trigger the breakers to open at points 2 and 3 on line 2–3, once again isolating the problem. But in this case load L-C would be disconnected from the system, since no redundant path is available to serve it. However because it is probable that a hot air balloon falling on the bus at point 0 might eventually slide off the facility (or burn up because of the heat generated by the electricity flowing through it to ground), the short circuit might last for only a few seconds, or even a fraction of a second. In that case, it would be unfortunate for customers at L-C to be out of service for an extended period of time, waiting until a crew could be dispatched to inspect the source of the problem at point 0, and if cleared without any further structural damage, to reclose the breaker. That is why circuit-breakers are installed in many locations with automatic reclosing features. Frequently, the breakers are set to test the line twice after opening automatically the first time. With a short delay, the breaker closes automatically after a preset interval (one or two seconds, as an example) and then opens again if the short circuit is still detected. In some cases the breaker is programmed to try to close a second or third time after successively longer waits, but usually on the third try, it is locked open waiting human intervention. In this way, failures that might be transitory, like lightning strikes or tree limbs blown against a line, are interrupted but then restored automatically and quickly if the original insult has moved on without causing permanent damage.

Human judgement and decision making determines the nature of detection devices and relays that are installed and where and under which measurable conditions the breaker will open (for example massive change in current flow, impedance on the line, voltage, and so on, since the sensors cannot actually 'see' a short circuit). Human design also determines how rapidly the breaker should open after detecting an abnormal condition. A fast response reduces the chances of damage to facilities or people along the line, but it also increases the chances that customers will be interrupted if the phenomenon measured was only transitory, or worse, a false signal. As long as the breaker remains closed following a persistent assault on the line, the system will continue to feed tremendous amounts of energy into the short circuit with a consequent increased probability of destroying not only the object that interfered with the line, but also the line itself and its supporting structures. Erring on the side of a very rapid response minimizes the chance of damage to facilities, but it increases the probability that many customers will be inconvenienced at very high costs to them, even when the source of the breaker operation was transitory.

The trade-off is between trying to maintain the integrity of the entire system by keeping the breaker closed or keeping the potential physical damage to the system to a minimum by interrupting the power flow rapidly. This is a precise example of a trade-off in protection philosophy: how long do we keep all of the lifeboats lashed together, even though several have holes in their hulls, so that everyone might survive, versus when do we cut those damaged boats loose so we all don't sink together?

There are further ramifications to this choice of breaker setting on overall system reliability, when the subsequent speeds of likely service restoration are factored into the choice. A system that separates prematurely because of extremely sensitive breaker response settings may nevertheless experience a much higher overall level of reliability compared to a system with very slow response times. Customers in the second system will experience many fewer, annoying, light-flickering outages, but when a permanent short circuit occurs, the chances are much greater that severe damage will have been inflicted upon power supply equipment, that may in turn result in a very lengthy outage until the facilities can be replaced or repaired. By comparison, customers in the first system will experience many more annoying bumps in their computers, but few truly prolonged service interruptions, since even with a solid short circuit, the line will be interrupted before truly catastrophic damage will have occurred, and therefore the repair time should be much shorter. This trade-off is exacerbated if the failure affects and damages a transformer like the one in substation S-7 in Figure 6.1, and that transformer is unique with no spares in inventory (a very costly proposition, since many substation transformers are nearly one of a kind because of non-standardization of power system electrical design across the US).

These sensors and relays are distributed throughout the system, and some are designed to sense voltage, others to detect frequency, as well as those that measure the direction and amount of power flow and line impedance. Maintaining voltage in a close band around its design level is important, because low voltage will tend to increase the current flow which overheats devices and, as an example, can cause motors to burn out. By comparison, too high voltage causes electric arcs between adjacent conductors which again can destroy anything in its path. Overfrequency causes motors and generators to spin too rapidly, and that can lead to the destruction of that equipment through centrifugal force. So all of these relays, one way or another, detect and respond to potential threats to equipment; and it is equipment that they protect directly. Indirectly, people may be helped if they face lower repair costs and more rapid system restoration.

POSSIBLE TERRORIST ASSAULTS

As with the study of most infrastructure systems from the perspective of strategies to withstand and/or rebound from a malevolent human assault, this analysis of the electricity network begins and is greatly informed by existing designs and procedures for dealing with natural events. Thus to understand the consequences of a terrorist assault, we merely need to substitute a conscious physical assault for a lightning strike or a falling tree limb. And we see that the bulk power system is designed to withstand any single such event and to maintain service to all customers without any interruption; in many cases two or three such simultaneous events might be of little notice to virtually all customers. Even if such multiple assaults were to bring down the bulk power system, in most cases the automatic, decentralized protection devices are designed to protect the equipment so that the bulk power system can be restored as rapidly as possible following an outage. And while it is much easier to attack isolated portions of the low-voltage electric distribution system, this will in most instances cause only localized harm and discomfort, but not result in the widespread regional blackout about which most people are concerned. That would require an assault on the high-voltage, bulk power system, which because of its inherent redundancy would also require coordinated simultaneous assaults on multiple facilities over a wide area. That type of attack borders on all-out warfare, but if conceivable, it needs to be examined in the context of overall system design philosophy.

While it may be much easier for terrorists to destroy key isolated portions of the low-voltage electric distribution system, particularly where facilities are above ground, the resulting service interruptions, while prolonged, would most likely be limited both in their geographic scope and in the number of customers affected. Furthermore the speed of restoration would be inversely related to the number of simultaneous, geographically related hits, since the limiting factor for restoration is the number of trained line crews that are (and that can be made) available in the area of assault. For this purpose it would be prudent to station crews in a dispersed geographic pattern.

In large metropolitan areas where the distribution system is usually underground and frequently configured as a network rather than a radial system, the considerations might be more similar to the subsequent analysis of the high-voltage bulk power system. And because redundancy and alternative paths are built into those low-voltage distribution networks, the impact of simultaneous distributed assaults would probably be far less severe than on an overhead radial system. Bringing an entire local network down (there are 21 separate such networks serving New York City) would require a coordinated simultaneous assault on separate feeds (there may be up to 20 such separate feeds into a single NYC network). Usually these networks are designed to withstand a loss of 20 per cent of their feeds at peak load periods, but in fact during the 1999 blackout of the Washington Heights neighborhood in NYC (US Department of Energy, 2000) that occurred during a prolonged August heatwave, half of the feeds into that network were lost, yet all customers were still being served, before the operators elected to disconnect the remaining feeds and place the customers out of service. This eventual neighborhood blackout was selected in order to protect the remaining facilities from damage due to overload. Because of this decision, the service was restored within two days, probably far faster than would have been the case had the remaining facilities remained at risk, requiring a much greater number of repairs.

The remaining focus of this analysis therefore will be on the tightly coupled high-voltage bulk power system, and how the possible number of assaults might affect the system design and desired interconnectedness. Furthermore this problem can be thought of in a hierarchical manner. As an example, how many utilities with their own separate area control centers should be tightly connected with each other and have their operations coordinated and controlled by a power pool operator or an ISO/RTO? The answer hinges in normal times, in part, on how many other neighboring ISOs and internal actions can assault that ISO and affect its stability. At a higher level of analysis, given recent economic pressures plus the fallout from the 14 August 2003 blackout to forge larger coordinated region-wide virtual RTOs by tightly coupling neighboring ISOs, the question remains: how many ISOs should be grouped together, and how big is too big in terms of maintaining system reliability? This question of how large is too large is being asked increasingly about the ever-expanding PJM RTO, even in the absence of consideration of possible terrorist activity. Furthermore, as electricity control areas grow ever larger, is the proper operating and reliability philosophy still to float together or sink together? Under what circumstances should the components be separated so that pieces might be saved in order to reassemble the entire system more rapidly, and how do those guidelines change as systems grow larger?

A strategic response cannot be to rely solely on hardening each of the constituent parts of the system in order to improve the average survivability of the aggregate system, if this is a tightly coupled complex system involving many agents. As an example, Wang and Thorp (2001) have shown through many numerical simulations of a bulk power system that the probability of a cascading failure leading to a blackout remains at about once every 35 years, even if the reliability of individual components is improved. It is the degree of interconnectedness of the system that can dominate the expected frequency of catastrophic events and not just the reliability of individual pieces, even though increasing the reliability of those components, including the weakest link, will improve the average reliability of the entire system.

INSIGHTS THROUGH NUMERICAL SIMULATION

Conceptual insights to possible approaches to these questions can be gleaned from earlier analyses by Levitan et al. (2002) on ways in which organizational performance and stability vary with the size and connectedness of organizations in a stochastic environment. This analysis explores a very simple question: what is the optimal number of similar agents to have working together (behaving under a set of coordinated rules) where each is engaged in the same activity, but when they are jolted periodically by some external force that is not subject to the group's rules? So the example could be how many area control centers are coordinated by an ISO/RTO, or how many ISOs are linked together formally by an overarching set of coordinating rules? These models presume that the individual operators (agents) are periodically given the opportunity to try to improve their performance (for example learning is included explicitly in these simulations), and each agent precisely sees one period ahead to know whether the available change will improve or decrease their individual performance. Therefore each agent also has the freedom to accept or reject the available change. Alternatively, these simulations can be thought of as a set of trial and error experiments where the random change is forced upon the individual agent (and the group), but they can always return to their prior state if that turns out to have been better.

When several agents are combined in a group, having one participant change their mode of operation affects the performance of all other members of the group. Therefore it is best for the group to agree upon a commonly applied acceptance rule, namely each member of the group will adopt an available change only if it improves the overall group performance (even when the individual performance of the deciding agent might decline). Obviously, in order to make such rules palatable to individual performers, each agent must share a portion of the group's improved performance, even when their own individual contribution declines while that of their colleagues' increases. Otherwise how could the agent be induced to behave in the interest of the entire group? One simple pay-off rule is to share the group's performance equally, under all circumstances, with all members. In fact if the performance criterion is the reliability of the bulk power electricity system, this egalitarian 'sharing' formula for the group's performance is realistic since all local control areas in a pool experience a similar level of reliability in terms of avoiding a major blackout. In this example then, each agent is randomly assigned a sequence of random shocks, at which point the agent must decide to accept or reject the change, according to the group's predetermined criterion. In these generalized simulations, any bias is removed from the choice by also assigning the performance value associated with each change randomly.

Thus depending upon the individual agent's original contribution to group performance, in combination with all group members' performances, a chance to change the way a single agent performs will depend upon not only how that agent's performance would change, but also the effect of that change on how all other members in the group would perform, where these performance values are randomly assigned. Typically, the number of performance states for each agent is limited, and in most of the exercises reviewed here, that number of states will be limited to two (for example a switch is either open or closed, a generator is on or off). Nevertheless since the performance of each agent hinges on the states of all of the other agents in the group, even with only two members, each with only two states, the entire group has available to it four possible combinations of states, and therefore four potential different pay-off values. With only two states, but three participants in the group, the number of possible different performance levels is eight, so where S equals the number of states and L equals group size, the number of possible combinations of states, and therefore of group performance values, is equal to S^L.

Therefore the process of finding the highest possible level of performance can be viewed as a random search over a landscape, where the landscape is comprised of all possible combinations of states as vertices. One final determinant of the outcome is the process used for searching for improvements. What has been described previously is the mechanism by which a potential improvement is selected or rejected by an individual participant. Which participant's turn it is to choose is selected randomly, and only one participant gets to choose at a time. This last point is important, because this type of incremental search can result in a group becoming stuck at a local optimum and never reaching its highest possible level of performance; nevertheless most changes in organizations are incremental, unless subjected to a cataclysmic disruption.

A Model of Organizational Performance

An example of this search is illustrated in Figure 6.2 for a group of two participants, each with two possible states. In the example, the binary states are represented by [0;1], and each participant's performance, in combination with its partner's performance, is selected randomly over the unit interval (as an example from the uniform probability distribution). Through a monotonic transformation, this performance level could be transformed into any measure the group valued (for example proportion of maximum profit, sales, and so on or 'fitness' in a biological context), but since the purpose here is to explore system reliability, the outcomes should be scaled to the unit interval, although perhaps not linearly.

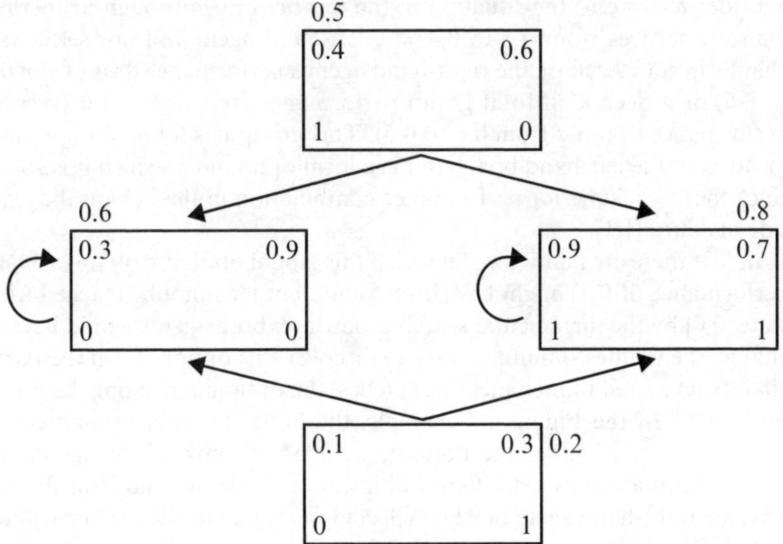

Note: The two columns of decimal numbers inside each box denote the pay-offs to agents 1 and 2 under the given configuration; the decimal number outside each box denotes the group's average pay-off. The arrows indicate state transitions that increase average group pay-off.

Figure 6.2 Possible pay-offs for a group of size L = 2 with S = 2 and J = 0

In this illustration in Figure 6.2, suppose we begin in the states [0;1] represented by the bottom box with a total group performance of 0.4 (average per agent of 0.2). Suppose the right-hand agent is selected randomly to consider changing his or her state to a 1, so the group situation is now [0;0] as shown in the left-hand box. In this case, the right-hand agent would accept this change, not just because his or her own performance increased from 0.3 to 0.9, but also because the group's total performance improved to 1.2 (a group average of 0.6). If at the next random shock, the right-hand agent were again selected randomly to consider a change of state, the only option available is to choose state 1, and since his or her partner is still in state 0, he or she would have to consider returning to the bottom box. This the agent will not do because that move represents a reversion to the previous lower level of average group performance of 0.2; therefore the right-hand agent (and the group, by its rules) will choose to remain in the left-hand box in state [0;0]. If at some still later time, the left-hand agent were randomly selected to consider a change, he would have the opportunity to choose state 1 which would imply the opportunity to consider moving to the situation in the top box. Even though his performance improves from 0.3 to 0.4, the left-hand agent will not select this change in state because the right-hand agent's performance drops from 0.9 to 0.6, or a decline in total group performance from 1.2 to 1.0 (average performance declines from 0.6 to 0.5). This group has found an optimum location in the left-hand box, but it is a local optimum at which it is stuck, since there is a superior performance combination in the box on the right side at states [1;1].

In fact there are many ways in which this global optimum of 1.6 (average performance of 0.8) might have been found, but it cannot be reached from state [0;0] by the incremental search procedure; both agents would have to change their states simultaneously to discover this option. With the participants restricted to incremental searches, the optimum can only be found by chance. In the Figure 6.2 example, the initial random assignment of states must be in either the bottom, right or top box (if the agents are assigned initial states [0;0], they will always stay there), and if in the top box, the right-hand agent must be selected randomly to choose first (otherwise, if the left-hand agent is selected first, he or she will choose to move to the left, suboptimal box, and the group will be stuck there). Similarly, if the initial state assignment is [0;1] (the bottom box), the left-hand agent must be randomly selected to consider the first change: otherwise if the right-hand agent is picked first, she will opt to move to the left side box [0;0] which again is suboptimal. Of course, any group lucky enough to be assigned states [1;1] in the first place will choose to remain there throughout all subsequent trials.

Although it may seem unreasonable for a group's final performance to hinge so crucially on the luck of the initial draw of positions, and also on the subsequent random selection of the sequence in which the agents get to try different states in combination with the others in their group, these simulations are repeated many times (500 times per treatment) with random (and therefore usually different) assignments of initial positions and choice sequences. In this way it is difficult to attribute any conclusion to the arbitrary initial assignment of states or of sequence of choice. The results that are reported are averaged over these 500 repetitions.

The objective of these simulations is to observe regularities in the relative performance between groups of different sizes. But as the size of each group increases, so does the complexity of possible combinations of states, so another experimental design issue is how long to run the simulation (how many random shocks?) The simulations reported are continued until the group's performance stabilizes at a particular value, usually far less than 2000 iterations in the cases investigated here. Outcomes for group sizes ranging from one to as large as 11 entities are simulated, but over this range the overall group performance reaches a maximum and stabilizes before the 2000 iterations are completed.

Modeling the Effect of Externally Transmitted Shocks

An important additional complication, particularly for analyzing the effect on electricity system performance of shocks precipitated by neighboring ISOs or terrorist activity, needs to be included in these simulations. So far the shocks imposed on the system are completely random, and they might be due to weather and natural events, technological innovation and/or changing customer patterns, but they are not related to the conscious choice by some other group. Therefore in these simulations that may have anywhere from 9 to 100 other groups acting autonomously, the possibility of having the actions in one group affect the performance of another is added. The variable J reflects the number of connections each group has to other external groups (the identities of these connections are selected randomly), and what is different about J, as compared to the relationship among agents within a group, L, is that given a chance to select another state, any agent only considers the effect upon members of its own group, and not upon the J interconnected groups that also will have their performance influenced by the choice. This is an externality in economic terms, and it realistically represents the possible interactions between neighboring ISOs when their activities are not tightly coordinated.

These J relationships are also used to illustrate the possible consequences of terrorist activities; although in that case the parallel may not be as strong. In many instances agents in the malevolent group will base their selection of an alternative state based upon how well it satisfies their own performance goals, but these are measured in part by how badly it affects the neighboring group. In short, the terrorist may consider intergroup effects explicitly in deciding to accept a possibility. However in the context of this existing model by Levitan et. al. (2002), since the terrorists' objectives (for example headlines, and/or body count), may not be the same as that of the other groups that represent neighboring power systems (who are trying to improve their own reliability), a decline in one may not be directly proportional to an increase in the malevolent group's satisfaction. Thus the more 'neutral' connectivity represented by these simulations may nevertheless be illustrative of the relative effects that these external connections might have on the qualitative relationship between the optimal size of the power system and the number of external influences. The key here is that those external impacts on the power system would fluctuate in response to activity by members of those external groups trying to improve their own performance, in isolation from the objective of the agents in the power system.

Results of Numerical Simulations

In the first instance, think of a generic organization trying to estimate what its optimal group size should be. Figures 6.3a and 6.3b illustrate the performances of a variety of group sizes over both time, and for different numbers of connections with external groups. What is true in all of these simulations (there are always 100 agents in each simulation, so where $L=1$, there are 100 different 'groups', and where $L=11$ there are only nine groups) is that for only a few trials (called 'generations' which crudely represents elapsed time if the random shocks hit the agents at a constant rate) larger groups perform better. But as shown in Figure 6.3a, after approximately 15 periods the performance of smaller groups begins to eclipse that of the larger ones, and in this case where there are no external connections between different groups, by the time the performance stabilizes at about 300 generations, agents acting alone pull ahead of the groups of 11.

What is going on? In this first set of simulations with $J=0$, we can think of each group as searching for the largest of the group's feasible number of 'order' statistics. As an example, with $L=1$ and each individual allowed only two states, each group (here an individual agent) is searching for the largest of two order statistics. When the performances are drawn randomly from the uniform density, the expected value in this case is 0.67, $n/(n+1)$, and Figure 6.3a shows that after about 300 generations all 100 agents have been selected randomly to try a different state, and they have, on average achieved that expected highest level of performance, 0.67. But why then doesn't the group of size 11 outperform these individuals acting alone, since the expected value of the largest of 11 order statistics is 0.91? Two factors interfere with these larger groups reaching this isolated ideal. The first cause is a statistical phenomenon. As group size increases, the group pay-off becomes the sum of the random draws from a uniform probability distribution, and the probability of that sum is no longer uniform. It becomes a truncated Beta probability distribution, and as an example for groups of two, the sum follows a triangular distribution. In fact as L increases, the central limit theorem applies and the distribution of the pay-offs approaches a normal probability distribution. So counteracting the search for an ever-greater available order statistic as group size increases is the fact that the probability mass is concentrating around the mean and away from that highest order statistic.

However there is a second factor, the search process itself, that is muting, on average the attainment of the highest conceivable performance. As illustrated in Figure 6.2, there is a possibility for any group larger than one of getting stuck at a local optimum that is less in value than the greatest possible pay-off. In fact that possibility of getting stuck at suboptimal levels of

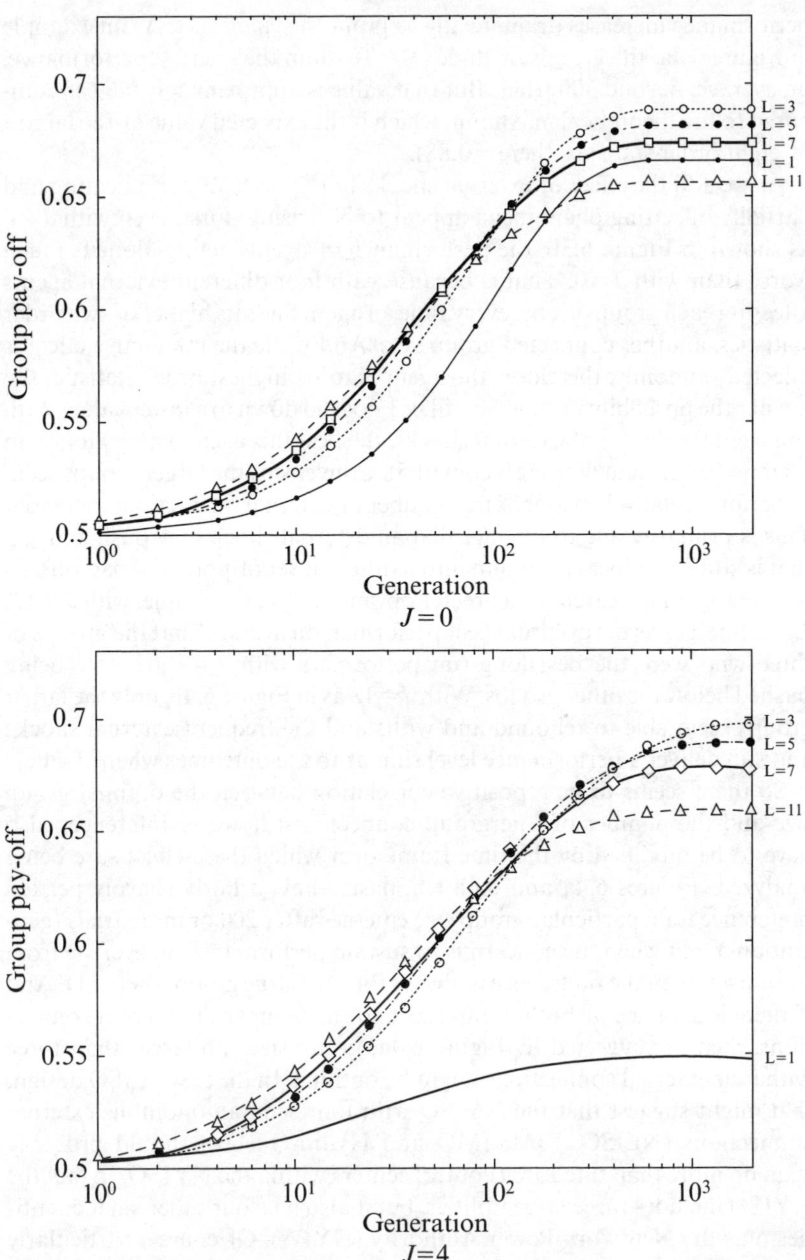

Figure 6.3 Average group pay-off over time (generations) for different group sizes, L, and two different levels of externalities, J = 0 and 4

performance increases dramatically as group size increases. As an example in Figure 6.3a, the groups of three ($L=3$) attain the greatest performance, on average, beyond 300 trials. But that value is approximately 0.69 as compared to the theoretical maximum which is the expected value of the largest of eight order statistics (here $=0.88$).

As we add the effect of external shocks in Figure 6.3b, complicating and partially offsetting phenomena appear to be arising. First, even with $J=4$ as shown in Figure 6.3b, the performance of agents acting alone is much worse than with $J=0$. That is because with four different external agents affecting each group of one, every time an agent finds its higher of two order statistics, another connected group acts. And while the interactive effect is selected randomly, the closer the agent is to its highest order statistic, the greater the probability is that he will be knocked down to a lower value. With sufficient frequency of external shocks, the best this agent acting alone can do is no better than flipping a coin (0.5). Conversely, the larger groups seem to perform relatively better as the number of external interactions increases. This is primarily due to the fact that an external shock may push a group that is stuck at a local optimum into a different set of potential pay-offs, so it is free again to search for a greater optimum. As an example, with $J=12$, $L=5$ emerges as the eventual best performer, on average, and the groups of three who were the best long-run performers with $J=4$ are now being pushed below the other groups. With $J=18$ as in Figure 6.4b, only the larger groups seem able to rebound and withstand the frequent external shocks and still deliver a performance level similar to the outcomes where $J=0$.

So there seems to be a positive correlation between the optimal group size and the number of intergroup connections; however inferences also have to be modified by the time frame over which these effects are being analyzed. Figures 6.4a and 6.4b emphasize how a fairly sharply peaked preference for a particular group size emerges after 200 or more trials (generations), but when the concern is to sustain performance on average from the outset, then the preference is always for very large groups (here 11). And if there is a choice of both group size and the number of external connections, then as suggested by Figure 6.4a, group sizes no larger than three with four external connections might be optimal. In the case of ISO design, that might suggest that the NYISO with four semi-autonomous external connections (NEISO, PJM, IMO and Hydro-Quebec) should probably span no more than three area control centers within the NYISO. In fact the NYISO includes three large utilities, but it also has four other smaller entities plus the New York Power Authority (NYPA). Of course, particularly with its recent expansion to include AEP and the MISO, the PJM RTO encompasses a far greater number of area control centers, but as its geographic scope increases, so too does the number of external connections.

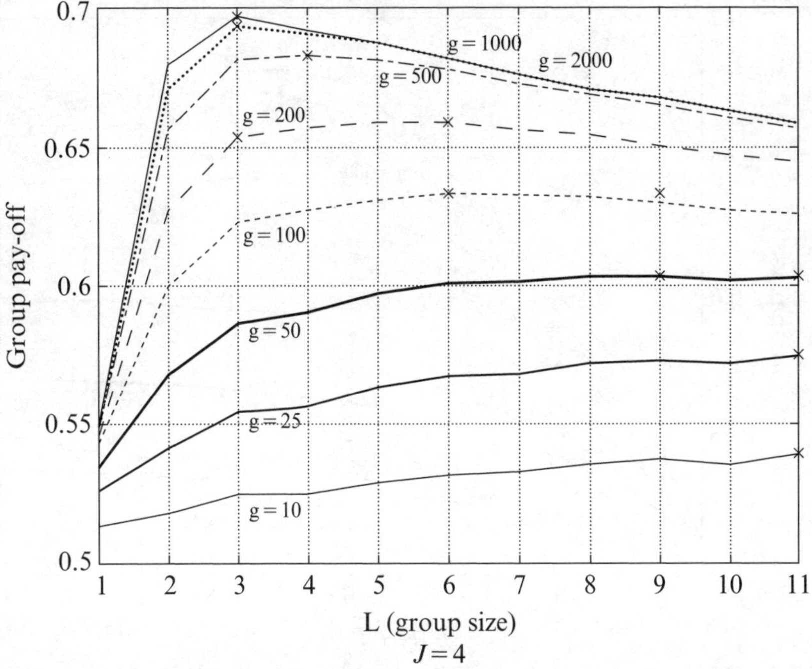

Figure 6.4a Average group pay-off per group size (L) for varying generations (g) and two different levels of externalities J = 4 and 18

Figure 6.5 illustrates how for longer time horizons (generations in excess of 100), a ridge of optimal performance begins to emerge suggesting that as *J* increases, so should *L*, the desired group size. This suggests that in response to increased dispersed terrorist activity (greater *J*?) recovery and overall performance might be greater with ever larger-sized coordinated units. But Figure 6.5 also suggests there is a price to be paid by getting bigger and more coordinated, not only in terms of those costs of coordination, but also in terms of reduced performance because of performance failures, particularly in the long run. As emphasized in Figure 6.5, once a system has attained the optimal group size for any particular *J*, increasing *L* even further results in an average loss of performance. Nevertheless the general rule is the larger the number of external effects that are expected, the larger the number of members that should be included in the internal group.

Not only is the average performance of each group affected by the combination of external connections and group size, so too is the stability of the outcome, as illustrated in Figure 6.6. This diagram shows one measure

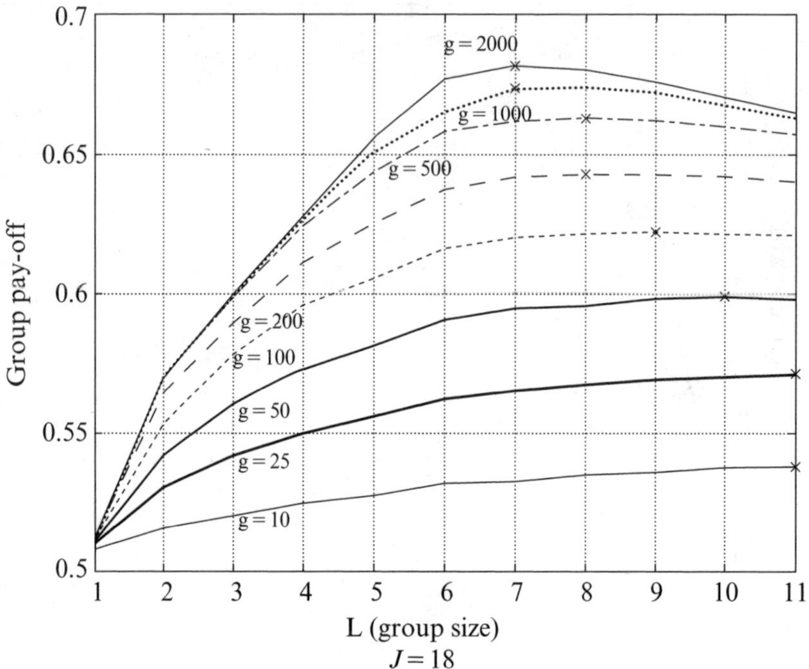

Figure 6.4b Average group pay-off per group size (L) for varying generations (g) and two different levels of externalities J = 4 and 18

of the extent to which each agent is selecting new states after a particular period of time has elapsed. As an example, Figure 6.6 shows that even after 2000 generations, agents acting alone ($L = 1$) but with five to ten external connections, are still moving to other states in more than 40 per cent of the randomly selected opportunities to choose (in this case generated mostly by changes in states by externally connected agents). With $L = 1$, every time an agent finds the largest of their two order statistics, a change in state by some externally connected agent alters the performance values of all states for agents with which they are linked, thereby setting in motion an additional set of possible choices.

A consistent pattern that seems to emerge by comparing Figures 6.5 and 6.6 for identical durations (generations) is that there is also a positive relationship between group size, L, and the number of external connections per group, J, that leads to higher flip rates, and therefore greater instability, that parallels the combinations that lead to optimal performance (for example system reliability). As an example, in Figure 6.6, for any particular J, the

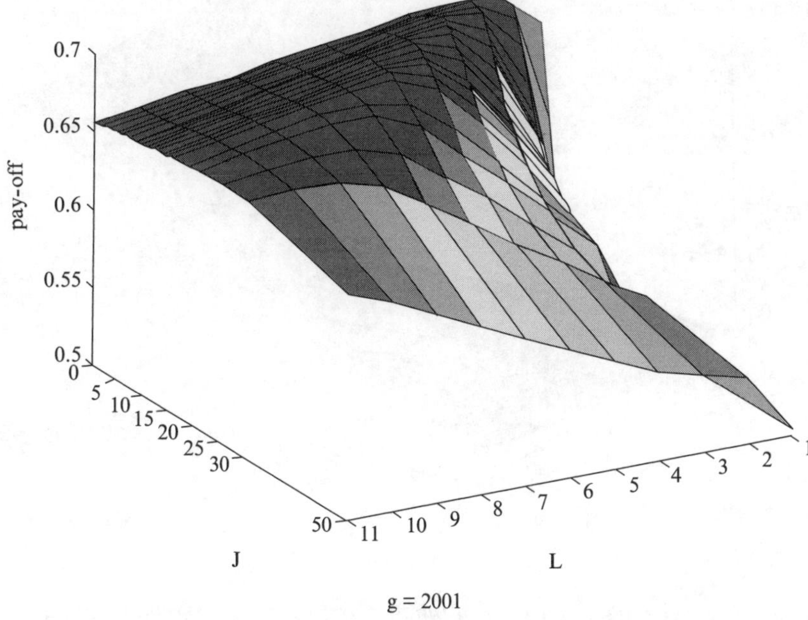

Figure 6.5 Average group pay-off as a function of group size, L, and level of externalities, J, after 2001 generations

flip rates settle down to extremely low levels by 2000 generations for a sufficiently high *L* (large group size). As however the number of external connections continue to increase for any given size group, the flip rates begin to increase rapidly, indicating a region of instability. Furthermore, in comparing the ridge of optimal performance in Figure 6.5 with the regions of instability in Figure 6.6, those flip rates begin to rise as the number of external connections rises above the level that yields the best performance. The message seems to be that optimal system performance borders a region of instability. So not only is it desirable to get the right group size in relation to the anticipated number of externally imposed shocks in order to maximize the system reliability, it is extremely important to err on the side of having groups that are larger than optimal in order to avoid being driven into a region of instability should the frequency of those external shocks increase. In this instance, that unstable region with higher flip rates might be representative of more frequent extensive blackouts, even though the average performance level does not fall precipitously until *J* becomes significantly larger, because the higher flip rate implies groups being knocked off their locally optimal states more frequently and therefore searching continuously for better outcomes.

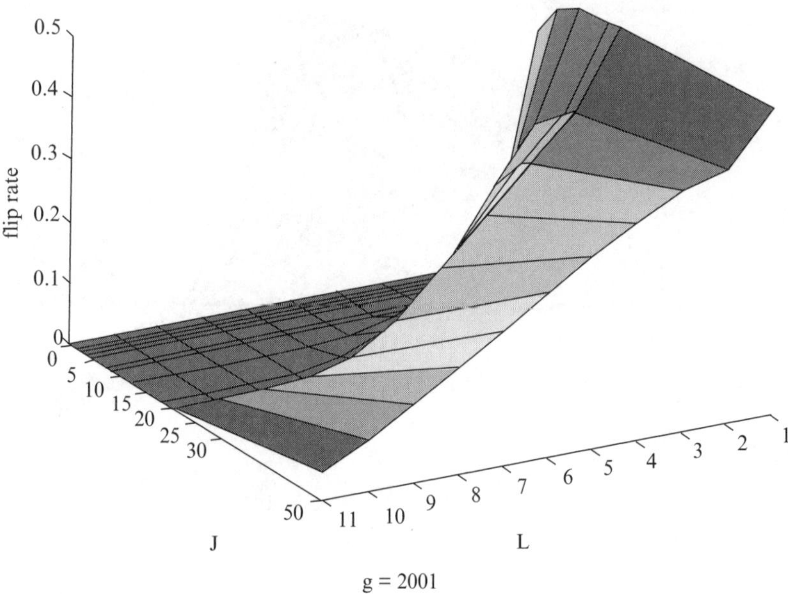

Figure 6.6 Average flip rate as a function of group size, L, and magnitude of externalities, J, for 2001 generations. (See main text for definition of 'flip rate')

POTENTIAL INFERENCES

Although this discussion emphasizes the robustness of the high-voltage bulk power system in the US, precisely because of its decentralized nature, some principles to guide improvement do emerge. First, because of the network configuration of the transmission grid, plus the settings on the automatic decentralized protection equipment that are biased to preserve the hardware, even if an extensive blackout were to occur, many areas may be restored to service quite rapidly, usually within a day or two. In order for an assault on the bulk power system to result in a prolonged region-wide outage, a massive region-wide coordinated attack on multiple key facilities would be required. However in that instance, one aspect of the 'hodge-podge' nature of multiple, non-standardized, ill-coordinated electric systems could create difficulties. To the extent that key equipment is not standardized electrically, (for example voltage, phase configuration and so on) across control areas or individual utilities, spare equipment may not be available in inventory. To the further extent that an increasing portion of that equipment is being manufactured abroad, the lag in securing replacements may be prolonged (or worse, if under the control of an ally of the inflictor of the original trauma) with attendant delays in restoring total service to everyone. However most surrounding regions would be patched back into service rapidly, awaiting the replacement of the damaged equipment. In all cases the potential for long-lasting trauma to the US would also depend on the extent of collateral damage that resulted from the original power outage, and that in turn would hinge upon the timing (associated weather) or social conditions that were coincident with the triggering electrical event. One example would be a prolonged power outage in the north during an extended period of subzero weather. In that event, many automated space heating systems would be interrupted, risking the freezing and bursting of water pipes, and thereby causing enormous widespread distributed damage to many customers.

In the case of the power grid therefore, while a 'signature' event capable of garnering widespread publicity, like a major regional blackout, is possible, the actual damage is likely to be relatively small in most instances. The regional blackout is a failure of the bulk power system that because of redundancies can be re-established rapidly in most instances. By comparison it is widespread failures of the low-voltage distribution system that leads to prolonged (up to a week or more) outages of many customers, primarily because repair crews must attend to nearly every customer before all service is restored. Evidence of this comparison in terms of natural events is the Northeast blackout of 14 August 2003 (a bulk power system failure) that is estimated to have cost society $7 billion but where most service was restored by the next day, as compared to the consequences of the hurricane season in Florida in August and September 2004 (largely widespread failures of the low-voltage distribution system) in which many customers were out of service for more than a week. Florida Power and Light co. incurred out-of-pocket costs of $890 million for labor, supplies and infrastructure repair, but the societal costs were probably even greater than those incurred in the 2003 Northeast blackout.

So with respect to designing and coordinating the bulk power system, in addition to the question posed at the beginning – 'Float together or sink together?' – the question must be added that if they sink, how rapidly can the lifeboats be refloated or replaced? Current operating practice seems to err on the side of ensuring rapid restoration by shutting off early and protecting equipment against catastrophic damage. The remaining set of questions relates to the scope of coordination among operating entities.

How many utilities and/or area control centers should be coordinated through a single ISO, and how many neighboring ISOs should be combined into a single virtual RTO? In using the numerical analysis of Levitan et al. (2002) the answer in part depends upon how tightly coupled the agents and group become. If individual agents, or groups acting as a single agent, are each subject to individual choices (shocks) but agree to select alternatives based upon the collective rather than individual good, then as the number of connections to external institutions or activities increases, so too should the number of cooperating entities increase. This increased group size with increased external interactions should not only improve average group performance above what it might otherwise be, it should also reduce the chances of non-stable behavior in the face of shocks. By comparison, if the agents within a group are so tightly coupled that a shock to one seems like a shock to all, and the response by one is a response by all, then in terms of this analytic paradigm all such tightly coupled groups are merely behaving like individual agents, and the proper analogy is the case where $L=1$. In virtually all cases, this is shown to yield inferior performance, in terms of learning, average reliability and stability of results, particularly as the number of connections with other external groups increases.

In the cases of loosely coupled but coordinated groups, the general guideline is to have the size of these groups – whose choices of state are determined by overall group performance, not just by that of individual members – increase as the degree of external connectedness increases. A somewhat different relationship between optimal L in response to the anticipated J is obtained depending upon over what duration of shocks the performance is to be gauged. After 2000 generations, the number of random shocks experienced by each group will have increased 20 times on average, as compared to 100 generations. In each case, this number of cumulative shocks experienced, and therefore the number of state changes evaluated, will increase also as the number of external connections, J, increases. This offers one heuristic explanation of why, for optimal average performance, group size should increase as J increases; the number of random choices to be evaluated within the group keeps pace with the frequency of externally inflicted possible state changes.

But how does this relate to optimal configurations of bulk power control areas for electricity supply? We have previously suggested that for dealing with random natural shocks, where $0<J<5$, $L=3$ is the optimal group size. This implies that the NYISO, as an example, with four external ISOs on its borders capable of transmitting shocks, should be comprised of at least three semi-autonomous internal area control centers, each of which acts however according to some well-agreed-upon group enhancing criterion. In fact the NYISO consists of seven utilities plus the New York Power Authority, perhaps too many to achieve optimal average performance, but sufficiently large to withstand additional external shocks (added J) from malevolent agents. And the slightly larger than optimal L does provide some assurance of not drifting into the unstable regions highlighted in Figure 6.6.

Similarly, early proposals to group three of the first ISOs (NEISO, NYISO and PJM) together into a large regional RTO satisfied this internal group size criterion of $L = 3$, except that as the geographic area covered by the coordinated unit increases, so too does the number of interconnected but non-coordinated groups on the border (in this case nine or ten), so that the optimum group size should also be increased (which might further increase the size of J). So if grouping is done by contiguous units geographically, a key concern about enlarging L is that J may grow by a larger proportion, thus increasing the chances that the group will be driven into an unstable region. It is that region of high flip rate that indicates more frequent collapses into low performance states following an external shock that might be representative of a major blackout.

Conversely, a propensity to separate into semi-autonomous, self-sufficient units in the face of external shocks may reduce the extent of shock transmission through cooperating units, but again it is the ratio of J/L that is important, and an examination of Figures 6.5 and 6.6 shows that for $L = 1$, fairly high levels of average reliability are available so long as J remains very small, but if the frequency of assaults increases even marginally, the performance drops precipitously and the instability soars.

Before concluding precisely what the optimal set of connections should be of neighboring power control areas however, refined calibrations and some rearrangement of interconnections, in these illustrative simulations, need to be performed. In particular the impact of a shock from an externally connected group is drawn randomly in these simulations. That means the consequence could be positive as well as the negative effect desired by a terrorist, as an example (note however that in the simulations described here, as average group performance increases with increased iterations (generations), the results of a randomly drawn new pay-off following an external shock are more likely to be smaller rather than larger). Another realistic modification would be to explore the effects of smaller group sizes for malevolent actors, as compared to the electricity control units; in these simulations, all groups are of the same size.

Nevertheless several general observations can be drawn from this discussion. First, while it pays to have group size increase as the frequency and number of sources of potential externally imposed shocks increases, it pays to do so in a loosely coupled way where each shock hits a subset of the overall group, even though the response is coordinated for the average benefit of the entire group, and not for the initially impacted sub-group alone. Second, it may be all right to risk the collapse of the entire system, if in doing so, equipment is spared so the restoration can be rapid. And third, 'hotchpotch' can be beneficial, so long as there is an agreed upon, coordinating objective.

NOTE

In addition to the specific support for preparing this chapter from the US Department of Homeland Security through New York University the Center for Risk and Economic Analysis of Terrorism Events (CREATE) at USC, the analysis summarized here has evolved over many years and benefited immensely from the collaboration with participants in and the generous support from the Power Systems Engineering Research Center (PSERC), supported by its industrial members together with the National Science Foundation's Industry/ University Cooperative Research Program under grant NSF EEC-0118300, from the Consortium for Electricity Reliability Technology Solutions (CERTS), supported by the United States Department of Energy, from the Santa Fe Institute and from BIOS, Inc. (especially Stuart Kauffman).

REFERENCES

Levitan, B., J. Lobo, R. Schuler and S. Kauffman (2002), 'Evolution of organizational performance and stability in a stochastic environment', *Computational and Mathematical Organization Theory*, **8**, 281–313.

US Department of Energy (2000), 'Report of the US Department of Energy's power outage study team', Washington, DC, Interim Report, January and Final Report, March.

Wang, H. and J. Thorp (2001), 'Optimal locations for protection system enhancement: a simulation of cascading outages', *IEEE Transactions on Power Delivery*, **16** (4), 528–33.

7. Current and improved biodefense cost–benefit assessment

Clark C. Abt

INTRODUCTION

This chapter makes three essential points: (1) under current conditions of inadequate US biodefenses, a single catastrophic bioterrorist attack can kill more people than any single nuclear terrorist attack; (2) catastrophic bioterrorist attacks are difficult to deter or defend against, but their risks of massive potential fatalities can be prevented and mitigated by scientifically feasible, economically affordable, and politically acceptable means; and (3) cost–benefit assessment of improved biodefenses as described show a dual net benefit of at least an order-of-magnitude reduction in deaths and damages and additional peacetime public health benefits to protect against natural deadly epidemics for an annual investment of less than the $10 billion. This compares with the amount currently invested in ballistic missile defense, a much smaller and less likely threat.

Cost–benefit assessments are considered for improved biodefenses against three catastrophic bioterrorist attacks on the most valuable and vulnerable urban transport centers (New York, Washington, DC and Los Angeles). Potential economic and loss of life costs of the three most catastrophic types of bioterrorist attacks (smallpox, plague and anthrax) are estimated from realistic scenarios for current and near-future improved biodefenses. Deaths from a current potential mass bioattack on US cities range from 500 000 to 30 million people; economic damage ranges from $200 billion into trillions. The median and the range of deaths and damages of a catastrophic bioterrorist attack on any large city exceed those from a single nuclear terrorist attack.

Five essential elements of an effective biodefense are described and assessed for their current capabilities and potential for significant improvement in terms of reducing deaths and economic damage. They are:

1. Bioattack early warning and agent identification by biodetectors at potential major target cities, especially New York and Washington.

2. Prompt (48-hour) initiation of exposure tracking, advance preparation and distribution of agent-specific vaccines/antidotes/prophylactic treatments for all exposed.
3. Timely (within the incubation period) prophylactic or isolation treatment of all exposed to infection, together with survivable logistic support.
4. First responders' interoperable communications and logistic support linking warning, diagnostics, treatment functions, and uncontaminated substitute isolation and quarantine facilities.
5. Public and professional education to teach productive responses and to minimize both panic and dysfunctional responses to bioattack and biodefenses.

Several improved alternative biodefense strategies and programs are also described, with potential benefits and costs in reduced deaths and damage. Additional national costs of now feasible biodefense improvements range from under $1 billion to $10 billion per year. The least-cost option for greatly reduced deaths and damages to a single city is under $100 million. Collateral benefits to peacetime public health of improved biodefenses are also described. The 2004–2005 benefits of biodefense improvements, in terms of a worst-case bioattack (costs avoided or reduced), range from one to tens of millions of lives saved, and hundreds of billions of reduced damage costs, yielding benefit–cost ratios in the 10:1 to 100:1 range.

EFFECTIVENESS VS. EFFICIENCY

The primary question for biodefense or any kind of defense policy, program, strategy, tactic or system is that of effectiveness. As a country we are inclined to be much more concerned with defense effectiveness than with defense efficiency, because survival is the most important. But when the government faces the competition for resources, efficiency becomes important in allocating resources. Mathematically, the optimal allocation of resources among competing claims is proportional to their marginal utilities, or relative efficiency or productivity for achieving a particular objective (for example the objective function of an optimization model).

For biodefense optimization, the objective function might be to minimize the expected loss of life and/or to minimize economic losses. These losses can be made commensurate by monetizing the value of lives lost (for example $3.5 million per life), or less commonly, measuring economic losses in terms of the lives lost because of the lack of investment, for example in vaccine development and distribution. The resource allocation decision problems for biodefense are similar to the old defense economics questions: How much is needed to provide an effective defense against a given threat? At what cost? What are the benefits? To what should they be compared?

There are many illustrative analogies between the cost-effectiveness and efficiency issues that faced defense analysts in the 1940s to the 1960s with air defense, and since then (much less successfully) with ballistic missile defense and counter-insurgency defense. Former defense policy analysts began to apply cost–benefit analysis to other policy issues, such as law enforcement, the environment, education, public health and medical problems in the 1960s and 1970s, with some notable progress particularly in health and medicine (for example Bunker et al., 1976). As in national defense, the willingness of the public to spend on healthcare is very high, in fact it is two to three times what we spend on peacetime defense, close to 15 per cent of GNP (vs. about 5 per cent on defense). In times of war of course, the defense-to-health expenditure ratio is more than reversed. In the Second World War, we spent 42 per cent of the US GNP on defense in peak years, or about ten times what we spend now, while healthcare absorbed less than half the percentage of GNP of what it does today. Fortunately today the overlap between military defense and biodefense offers many opportunities for mobilizing public support and funds for the dual benefits of biodefense for both public health and national and international security goals and programs.

ACTIVE VS. PASSIVE DEFENSE

Continuing the analogies between the design of air and missile and biodefenses via cost-effectiveness analysis, several rules of thumb were developed in the air defense evaluations of the 1950s and 1960s. A defense is only as strong as its weakest link. An effective defense depends on the best possible understanding of the threat. There is little argument now about al-Qaida's threats but there remains some dispute about its capacity. It is unclear whether the strategy of inexpensive biodefenses means an imbalance between defense effectiveness and keeping the costs down. In the air defense area, deterrence was enhanced by effective defense, while effective defense against the worst threats was improved by the constraints of retaliatory deterrence (Schelling, 1960), hardly an opportunity for biodefense strategy. Active defense by interception of attacks was made more focused and efficient by combining it with the passive defenses of hardening, hiding and dispersal of targeted defenses and a survivable retaliatory deterrent (Kahn, 1960).

At the tactical level, the main issue for air defense was the best balance of investment in active and passive defense, and within active defense the best balance between alternative missile approaches and an integrated system heavily relying on command-and-control and intelligence. Within each of these broad categories, there were choices of weapon systems and tactics to be made via simulating war games, operational testing and cost-effectiveness evaluation. Answers were found to the key questions of how much was enough to counter an estimated threat and how air defense resources could be most productively allocated. It has hitherto been difficult to achieve the same in the biodefense field.

Nevertheless in biodefense there are functional analogies to the active vs. passive approaches in air defense.

PASSIVE DEFENSES

- 'Hardening' the target population with vaccines providing immunity to deadly contagious diseases.
- Prepositioning of vaccines and antibiotics in population centers and neighborhood pharmacies.
- Provision of dispersed isolation and quarantine sites to limit contagion if prior or prompt vaccination fails to protect against unanticipated genetically engineered pathogens.
- Major facilities and buildings reducing access to heating, ventilating and air conditioning intake ducts and providing them with filters.
- Ultraviolet lights in subways and indoor transport terminals to kill pathogens.

ACTIVE DEFENSES

- Strategic warning with international biological warning intelligence collection.
- Tactical early warning with biodetectors at transport terminals and other concentrated population targets.
- Attack warning, plume tracking and exposure estimation with biodetector networks.
- Area and point target interception, via prophylactic vaccination or antibiotic treatment of targeted and exposed people and by isolation and/or quarantine against communicable disease threats.
- Response and damage control by medical treatment, clean-up and recovery of contaminated areas, and by the substitution of uncontaminated facilities and/or unaffected personnel for those killed or disabled.

- Command-and-control communications for integrating all these essential biodefense elements in both pre- and post-attack phases.
- Public education to maximize cooperative behavior (for example the comparison with civilian air raid wardens and shelter preparation and management in air defense).

In biodefense the functional analogies to (or often identities with) public health and medical defenses against disease are the passive defenses of disease surveillance, hygienic prevention, sound nutrition and clean water supply and sanitation, vaccination and health education. The active public health and medical defenses are prompt diagnosis, appropriate treatment and quarantine.

COST–BENEFIT ASSESSMENT: GENERAL

Proceeding to a preliminary cost–benefit assessment of the current state of our biodefenses, from threat definition and assessment to current biodefense capabilities, the picture is very mixed and quite troubling. We focus on a very rough cost-effectiveness estimation of the five essential elements of biodefense we have identified, under both currently inadequate and near future improved biodefense conditions.

1. Early warning and agent identification by biodetectors at probable and high-value and vulnerable targets, for example urban transport centers. Tens of millions have been spent on R&D and Initial Operational Capability, but full production and deployment costing about $5 billion with much greater savings in human life and economic benefits have not been undertaken.
2. Prompt mobilization of exposure/plume tracking and agent-specific antidote/prophylactic treatment resources. Many millions of dollars have already been spent on vaccine and antibiotic stockpiles, but distribution logistics costing much less have not been put in place, risking the entire system's effectiveness.
3. Actual prompt prophylactic vaccination or antibiotic treatment and/or isolation of all exposed, including the trans-attack and post-attack logistic arrangements that must survive the disruptive effects of the attack. Tens to hundreds of millions of dollars have been spent on preparing first responders, but the planning of timely in-crisis distribution and assurance of communications among all key units and personnel are still very incomplete.

4. Trans- and post-attack logistic support for key functions, including organization of substitute uncontaminated transport facilities, equipment and personnel for public surface and air transport disabled or contaminated by the bioattack. Less than $100 million have been spent, while the potential cost of filling the gap in biodefense effectiveness could run to hundreds of billions of dollars.
5. Pre-, trans- and post-bioattack public and professional education to facilitate productive responses and minimize panic or dysfunctional responses. Perhaps tens of millions of dollars have been spent on planning, but no effective policies or practices have yet been tested or implemented. If training simulation exercises such as TOPOFF (Top Officials Exercise of Response to Terrorist Attack) I and II are appropriately considered part of public and professional education, some $23 million were spent on TOPOFF II with negligible useful results. One-shot exercises with partial geographical coverage are ineffective. Israeli Ministry of Defense preparations for bioattack response offer a better example of preparation and public education.

RESOURCE ALLOCATION COMPARISONS

To judge the proposed expenditures on biodefense, they can be placed in a comparative context. Here are a few examples.

- The current $10 billion per year spent on anti-ballistic missile defense can be compared with $10 billion spent on biodefense vaccine development, in terms of overall cost-effectiveness vs. known threats.
- The less than $100 million spent on biodetector R&D may be contrasted with the many billions of dollars spent on vaccine and antibiotic development in terms of relative and combined cost-effectiveness, a strong case for spending more on the former.
- Billions of dollars are spent on commercial advertising media, and hundreds of millions are spent on army recruiting advertisements, and these can be compared with less than $100 million spent on public education about biothreats and biodefenses.
- Billions of dollars are spent annually in California for earthquake mitigation (including more expensive construction costs, as insurance against a rare major earthquake) compared with the small fraction spent in California on the more likely major biological attack.

COST–BENEFIT ASSESSMENT: SPECIFIC

There is much more cost–benefit analysis to be done before we can answer the key questions definitively. We present here a rough cut cost–benefit assessment of the 2004 state of the nation's biodefenses against two major bioterrorist threats in three of the largest and most vulnerable urban targets, plus what might be feasible in the next few years (2006–2008).

The most deadly and most damaging threats are the outdoor or indoor mass release of weaponized anthrax and the indoor mass release of smallpox and/or pneumonic plague. The most valuable (from a terrorist's perspective) and vulnerable city targets include: New York City and the ports of New York and New Jersey; Washington, DC (especially the yacht basin, many sites inside the Beltway, and Dulles Airport); Los Angeles; Chicago; San Francisco and the Bay Area; Boston; Seattle-Tacoma, Miami; New Orleans; and San Diego.

These ten top American urban population centers are all air–sea–rail–road transport hubs, and centers of commerce, industry and finance. Most of them have subways with major airport, railroad and bus terminal interconnections, making them ideal communicable disease biothreat targets. Because of their national and international air and ocean transport connections, a deadly epidemic created by a clandestine mass release of a deadly contagious agent at any one of them would be almost impossible to contain without early warning to initiate prophylactic vaccination of those exposed provided by biodetectors deployed at transport terminals.

COSTS OF ATTACKS

The costs of current domestic (non-Department of Defense) biodefenses, including R&D and production of biodetectors, vaccines, antibiotics, first responder equipping and training, public education, C3I (Command, Control, Communications and Intelligence), and planning, testing and evaluation are probably in the range of $15–20 billion per year, with vaccine development being the largest and probably most adequately funded share at some $10 billion. Those regarding the risk of mass bioattack as low might find even this amount excessive, palliated perhaps by the dual benefit of vaccine development for public health defenses against emerging diseases. Others may find the amount disproportionately small when compared to the risk and costs of a massive bioattack in the hundreds of billions of dollars (Tables 7.1 and 7.2).

Direct and indirect damage costs do not include costs of lives lost (the EPA estimate is $3.5 million per person), but do include the economic costs

Table 7.1 Costs and potential benefits from biodefenses from anthrax (full implementation, 2004–2005 and 2006–2008)

	Deaths	Damages
Port of New York–NJ		
Costs of attack	1 m.	$500 b.
With 2004–2005 biodefenses	10 000	$100 b.
2004–05 savings	990 000	$400 b.
With 2006–2008 biodefenses	100	$50 b.
Washington–Baltimore		
Costs of attack	1 m.	$200 b.
With 2004–2005 biodefenses	1000	$50 b.
2004–2005 savings	999 000	$150 b.
With 2006–2008 biodefenses	100	$50 b.
Port of Los Angeles		
Costs of attack	500 000	$400 b.
With 2004–2005 biodefenses	3000	$100 b.
2004–2005 savings	497 000	$300 b.
With 2006–2008 biodefenses	100	$50 b.

Notes:
1. The estimates assume biodetectors in DC Metro.
2. m = millions, b = billions.

of domestic and international trade losses from the denial of facilities, vehicles and operating personnel at the cities struck and their global communication hubs (Abt Associates, 2003). The 2002 Los Angeles port strike resulted in losses estimated at $5–10 billion per week from ocean trade disruption (the analysis in Chapter 14 suggests that these estimates were too high). Massive (say 100 pound) anthrax attacks are estimated to deny contaminated buildings, facilities and equipment to unvaccinated personnel for a minimum of three months and a maximum of a year or more during fumigant clean-up and recovery operations. The Capitol Hill clean-up of the very small 2001 anthrax attack (a few ounces) cost $28 million (direct costs only) in three months.

The risk probability of a small anthrax attack is 1.0 because it has already happened (in 2001). However there is also a strong probability of a mass anthrax attack because of the stated intentions from al-Qaida and the likely terrorist capacity of making and delivering weapons-grade anthrax.

The risk probabilities of a mass smallpox attack are controversial. While terrorist intentions to cause maximum deaths and economic destruction are clear, the capacity to make an aerosolized smallpox agent and deliver

Table 7.2 Costs and potential benefits from biodefenses from smallpox (full implementation, 2004–2005 and 2006–2008)

	Dealth	Damages
Port of New York–NJ		
Costs of attack	3–30 m.	$1 tr.
With 2004–2005 biodefenses	1–3 m.	$500 b.
2004–2005 savings	2–27 m.	$500 b.
With 2006–2008 biodefenses	100	$10 b.
Washington–Baltimore		
Costs of attack	1–3 m.	$1 tr.
With 2004–2005 biodefenses	10 000	$100 b.
2004–2005 savings	990 000–2.99 m.	$900 b.
With 2006–2008 biodefenses	100	$10 b.
Port of Los Angeles		
Costs of Attack	1–30 m.	$1 tr.
With 2004–2005 biodefenses	1–2 m.	$400 b.
2004–2005 savings	28–29 m.	$600 b.
With 2006–2008 biodefenses	100	$10 b.

Notes:
1. The estimates assume biodetectors in DC Metro and a 300 million supply of vaccine.
2. m = millions, b = billions, tr = trillions.

it in massive amounts (for example briefcases full of modified spray cans of aerosolized smallpox delivered clandestinely by vaccinated bioterrorists to crowded indoor transport terminals in major transportation hub cities) are not.

The two known repositories of live smallpox virus are in the United States and Russia. Given the insecure storage of nuclear weapons and fissile materials in Russia and the risk of terrorist theft or purchase, it is difficult to feel confident that the risk of bioterrorist purchase or theft of smallpox from the Russian stockpile is low (Alibek and Handelman, 2002). However the risk is lower than for anthrax. But even a 10 per cent per year probability of acquisition accumulates to 100 per cent in only seven years. We estimate a risk probability of 0.7 over the next few years, much too high for comfort.

BENEFITS OF BIODEFENSE EFFORTS

The benefits of the cumulative national biodefense effort, including Biowatch and Biosense and many other federal programs, are best expressed in terms of the estimated reduction in risk and cost of the most deadly mass bioterrorist attacks on the most vulnerable and valuable city targets (Tables 7.1 and 7.2).

We have only begun to develop, deploy and operate the best possible available biodefenses, although considerable progress has been made since 9/11 and even current biodefenses can save many lives.

The biodefenses for 2006–2008 assume the following:

1. At least hundreds of operational biodetectors with high sensitivity and very low false alarm rates to Class A biothreats, deployed in major transport terminals, including subways.
2. C3 (Command, Control and Communications) real-time linking of deployed biodetectors to public health and other first responders, at all levels nationally and internationally.
3. Prompt prophylactic vaccination or antibiotic treatment of exposed/infected population (within three days of agent release detection).
4. Attack-survivable logistic support for first and last responders and preparation of alternative transport facilities during a three-month clean-up period.
5. Timely, accurate, authoritative, effective public education of all language population groups by all media.

This is all attainable for an approximate $10 billion annual budget, yielding probable cost–benefit ratios within the range of 10:1 to 100:1.

ALTERNATIVE SHORT-TERM STRATEGIES

Several improved alternative biodefense strategies and programs to those considered in this chapter are feasible. They may have additional potential benefits and/or reduced costs. Additional national costs of now feasible biodefense improvements range from under $1 billion to $10 billion per year. The least-cost option for greatly reduced deaths and damages in a single city is less than $100 million. Collateral benefits in terms of public health could be significant (see Appendix). Under the proposed 2006–2008 benefits of biodefense improvements examined here, the worst-case bioattack costs reduced range from one to tens of millions of lives saved and hundreds of billions of dollars of reduced damage costs. However perhaps we could do even better? We also need to consider the distributional impact of benefits and costs of alternatives.

A few alternative biodefense strategies, with their estimated benefits and costs, may be identified:

1. Vaccinate/inoculate the entire urban population of the United States, say 240 million, against smallpox, plague and anthrax, at an average cost of $100 per person for each of the three diseases, or $300 × 240 million, or $72 billion. This implies a massive benefit, eliminating the risk of massive bioattacks over the next few years, but at a greatly increased cost and effective only for a few years.
2. Organize and operate a massive public education campaign, preparing people to store at least three weeks' food supply in their homes to self-quarantine themselves at home if a smallpox or plague or anthrax attack is detected. This would be of limited effectiveness without biodetectors providing an early warning. Combined with the early warning of biodetectors in at least ten major target transport hub cities, it should cost less than $1 billion.
3. Significantly increase the local public health staff, facilities and equipment of probable target states and cities, improving their ability to promptly detect and identify a bioattack, distribute the appropriate vaccines and antibiotics, and provide isolation and quarantine for those exposed and infected (but without prophylactic action). This approach would have significant dual benefits for containing natural epidemics such as SARS, flu and the West Nile virus, among others.

CONCLUSIONS

This chapter has presented a cost–benefit assessment of defense strategies against biological attacks, using analogies based on defense strategies during the Cold War. The estimates of benefits are inevitably highly speculative, but they demonstrate beyond doubt a high pay-off from expenditures in the $1 billion to $10 billion range. The results also imply that the almost obsessive preoccupation with airline and airport security represent a misallocation of scarce resources, because the costs of any kind of terrorist attack in that sector are almost negligible compared with the potential catastrophe from an undefended biological attack.

APPENDIX : COLLATERAL 2004–2008 PUBLIC HEALTH BENEFITS OF IMPROVED BIODEFENSES

Overview of the benefits of enhanced response elements in the absence of a biological attack

Intervention being evaluated	Possible dual-use application	Nature of benefits created
Prophylactic treatment on a 'warning' of bio-attack (including augmented capacity of bio-assay labs, stockpiles of drugs, expansion of isolation wards, healthcare communications infrastructure, etc).	• Improved health system infrastructure to support peak load isolation and critical care capacities. • Added laboratory bio-assay capacity. • Better communication 'connections' with the populace, among first responders, health providers and better inter-laboratory communication.	• These resource readiness and capacity building activities would be useful for any disaster (natural, accident, or war related) and prevent unnecessary morbidity and death.
Widespread installation of air quality monitoring devices (BAWS) in indoor public places like public buildings, subways, sports arenas, transport terminals.	• Dual use design of monitors would permit real time testing for specific pathogens related to communicable diseases beyond those agents used by terrorists (e.g. specific flu strains, SARS). Devices would need to be built to have modular capability so that particular worrisome disease modules could be inserted as required by public health authorities (e.g. today we	• Early identification of cases of specific communicable diseases for which vaccine prophylactic treatment would be beneficial in slowing disease incidence (e.g. knowing which type of flu strain is present in the city's population would allow a more accurate vaccine mix to be used). Benefits would accrue to early notice of dozens of disease epidemics and prevent morbidity and death.* • Prevention of morbidity and mortality from better local reporting of air quality

	would be adding a SARS module, next summer we would start to look for early signs of flu types). ● More precise environmental monitoring and reporting at small area levels using modules designed for this purpose. ● Visible presence of air monitoring devices may improve public confidence in bio-security and ease stress about using public facilities.	risk in large cities and heightened public awareness of air quality issues, which may stiffen support for tighter public health and environmental air quality regulations. ● Prevention of morbidity and economic losses associated with mass stress about bio security risks.
Improved bio-attack awareness and readiness of the personnel from ports, transportation workers, health facilities and public health officials (through training, bio-attack response drills, and adequate follow-up resources to remedy deficiencies in training or systems, etc).	● Generally improved readiness, applicable to many circumstances like natural or accident disasters. ● Improved communication between health and other professional groups about health issues that will aid disease surveillance and enable symptom reporting for early identification of communicable diseases.	● Prevent unnecessary morbidity and mortality from natural, environmental, and accidental disasters. ● Enable public health surveillance to be extended to port and transport workers and systems to prevent morbidity and death.
Training port personnel in working in contaminated environments Disaster response training of port personnel.	● Improved response to industrial accidents that are likely to occur near ports (release of hazardous material, for example).	● Ports will not be shut down while decontamination is in progress, economic losses secondary to the accident will be dramatically curtailed.

Note: *Flu alone offers a huge potential area of dual use benefits. Should BAWS (Biological Attack Warning System) be able to identify the strains of flu early in season, then vaccines could be made to include the exact strains present in the population. This would increase the effectives of the vaccine, and likely increase the numbers of persons receiving the vaccine. About 0.5–1.0 million people die each year from the flu globally (Layne, 2001).

BIBLIOGRAPHY

Abt Associates (2003), *The Economic Impact of Bioterrorist Attacks on the Freight Transport System in an Age of Seaport Vulnerability*, Cambridge, MA.

Alibek, K. and S. Handelman (2002), *Biohazard*, New York: Random House.

Bunker, J.P., B.A Barnes and F. Mosteller (eds) (1997), *Costs, Risks, and Benefits of Surgery*, New York: Oxford University press.

Cirincione, J. with J.B. Wolfsthal and M. Rajkumar (2002), *Deadly Arsenals, Tracking Weapons of Mass Destruction*, Washington, DC: Carnegie Endowment for International Peace.

Henderson, D.A., T.V. Inglesby and T. O'Toole (eds), (2002), *Bioterrorism: Guidelines for Medical and Public Health Management*, JAMA & Archives Journals, Chicago, IL: American Medical Association Press.

Kahn, H. (1960), *On Thermonuclear War*, Princeton, NJ: Princeton University Press.

Layne, S. (2001), *Firepower in the Lab*, Washington, DC: Joseph Henry Press.

Lederberg, J. (ed.) (1999), *Biological Weapons: Limiting the Threat*, Cambridge, MA: MIT Press.

Miller, J., S. Engelberg and W. Broad (2001), *Germs: Biological Weapons and America's Secret War*, New York: Simon & Schuster and the Rockefeller Foundation.

Schelling, T.C. (1960), *Strategy of Conflict*, Cambridge, MA: Harvard University Press.

Tierno Jr., P.M. (2002), *Protect Yourself Against Bioterrorism: Everything You Need to Know about Anthrax, Plague, Botulism, Smallpox, Encephalitis, Cholera, Hemorrhagic Fevers, Ricin, and More*, New York: Pocket Book.

8. Improving the Homeland Security Advisory System: an experimental analysis of threat communication for national security*

Philip T. Ganderton, David S. Brookshire and Richard L. Bernknopf

INTRODUCTION

On 1 August 2004, Department of Homeland Security Secretary Tom Ridge raised the Homeland Security Advisory System (HSAS) threat level from yellow to orange for the sixth time since its inception in March 2002 (Ridge, 2004.)[1] While the system has five threat levels, ranging from (1) green – low condition through (3) yellow – elevated condition to (5) red – severe condition, it has only ever been set to two of those levels – yellow by default and orange for short periods of time. When established, the system was intended 'to provide a comprehensive and effective means to disseminate information regarding the risk of terrorist acts to Federal, State and local authorities and to the American people' (Bush, 2002).

The system has become a key element of the government's campaign against terrorism through the role it plays in Homeland Security. The threat level is prominently displayed on government websites, especially the Department of Homeland Security website, but also on those of many private agencies, including the Red Cross. The current HSAS threat level has been continuously displayed on the CNN/Headline News banner that shows at the bottom of the television screen. The system is not only intended to communicate timely and relevant information about security risks and terrorist threats it also contains information about precautions that agencies, businesses and members of the public can take against the threat. For fiscal year 2005, the administration is requesting an appropriation of $10 million to support the HSAS under a program of continual modification and improvement, while maintaining it as a fundamentally sound component of homeland security.

Having such a high profile opens the HSAS up to severe scrutiny, which it has received, and of which more is detailed below. To many critics it falls short as a risk communication mechanism, and may actually contribute to the general level of fear, uncertainty, distrust and complacency in the nation (Pena, 2002). This chapter reports on a research project designed to analyse important characteristics and elements of the system to both model its weaknesses and identify opportunities to strengthen it. We have created a set of web-based instruments capable of studying various elements of a security threat warning system, and have obtained an initial set of data from these instruments. Set up as experimental scenarios, subjects are placed in a risky situation and required to respond to threat warnings. Initially the experiments concentrate on the geographic or spatial detail of threat warnings, but subsequently we will be investigating warning content, timing and audience. Our research plan allows us to study the following dimensions of an Alert System:

1. What kind of threat and risk information can be derived from intelligence, and how much detail should be communicated?
2. When is threat information disclosed and to whom?
3. Should warnings indicate the level of confidence the DHS has in the intelligence?
4. What geographical (spatial) detail should be provided?
5. What temporal detail should warnings contain, both in terms of when and what duration to expect for the identified threat?
6. How much uncertainty is associated with the spatial and temporal dimensions of the warning, and how is this communicated?
7. Should warnings be tailored to audiences and to multiple methods of dissemination?
8. How should threat levels be linked to response?

Because our experiments place subjects in situations where they respond to threats and warnings, we can observe the response to warnings and address the following behavioral questions:

9. What kind of threat/risk information do people value more highly and how does their response vary with the kind of information?
10. Are people more sensitive to changes in the threat level than the actual current level?
11. Are people's preferred responses consistent with the HSAS advised responses?
12. What do the respondents believe they are protecting when they receive a change in threat level?

In the sections to follow we provide an overview of the HSAS, focusing on the limitations of the system that have been identified to date, and then describe the experiments that will be used to investigate some of the suggested and possible modifications to the system. This is followed by a discussion of the initial data gathered and analyses that are made possible by the experimental design, and then we conclude with a plan for continued development of this line of research.

BACKGROUND

Since its formation by Homeland Security Presidential Directive 3 in March 2002, the HSAS has remained on a default level of yellow (level 3 of 5.) This threat level is officially described as:

> 3. Elevated Condition (Yellow). An Elevated Condition is declared when there is a significant risk of terrorist attacks. In addition to the Protective Measures taken in the previous Threat Conditions, Federal departments and agencies should consider the following general measures in addition to the Protective Measures that they will develop and implement:
> a) Increasing surveillance of critical locations;
> b) Coordinating emergency plans as appropriate with nearby jurisdictions;
> c) Assessing whether the precise characteristics of the threat require the further refinement of preplanned Protective Measures; and
> d) Implementing, as appropriate, contingency and emergency response plans. (Bush, 2003)

There is little in the way of risk information in this definition, yet it has become the baseline for homeland security since early 2002. In fact the threat levels contain so little risk information that the only value of the system may arise when the threat level definitions is changed, since this is usually accompanied by a statement from the Secretary of Homeland Security. Including the recent rise on 1 August 2004, the threat level has been increased to orange six times for a total of approximately 100 days. In his statement announcing the increase in threat level from yellow to orange on 1 August Secretary Ridge stated:

> Now this afternoon, we do have new and unusually specific information about where al-Qaeda would like to attack. And as a result, today, the United States Government is raising the threat level to Code Orange for the financial services sector in New York City, Northern New Jersey and Washington, DC.
>
> This will allow us to increase protection in and around those buildings that require it, and also raise awareness for employees, and residents, and customers, and visitors. We know, and we know from experience, that increased physical

> protection and added vigilance from citizens can thwart a terrorist attack. And that is our goal.
>
> Now this is the first time we have chosen to use the Homeland Security Advisory System in such a targeted way. Compared to previous threat reporting, these intelligence reports have provided a level of detail that is very specific. The quality of this intelligence, based on multiple reporting streams in multiple locations, is rarely seen and it is alarming in both the amount and specificity of the information. (Ridge, 2004)

Even though this warning contains specific types of targets (financial services) and specific geographical locations (New York City, Northern New Jersey and Washington, DC) there is no information as to the type of terrorist activity, the risk to property and life, and the timing of the possible attacks. Criticism was quick to emerge:

> On Sunday, the Bush administration won praise for a warning much more precise than those in the past – limited to financial service institutions in New York, New Jersey and Washington – then drew skepticism when law enforcement officials let it be known later that much of the information that led to the alert may have been newly discovered in Pakistan, but was three or four years old. (Purdum, 2004)

Despite the calls for threat level announcements to contain substantially more detail, the system contributes to the overall status of awareness, preparedness, mitigation and response to terrorist threats in the country. Unfortunately the HSAS is not the only risk and threat warning system, nor is it more than advisory for the majority of organizations in the nation. The HSAS applies directly to all federal government agencies, except for the Department of Defense, which has its own threat warning system (Force Protection Condition), based on much of the same intelligence that the HSAS is, but which does not share the same threat levels, terminology or protective response measures (Allen, 2004, p. 4). In a recent GAO report, 42 of 43 states reporting indicated they followed the HSAS or had an equivalent system, or both, but in many cases actions specified in response to each threat level are more regional, local and specific (GAO, 2004c, pp. 43, 44). There appears to be no attempt to make each state and locality system and response plan consistent (GAO, 2004c, p. 44). Just as the HSAS is advisory for state and local governments, it is also advisory to the private business sector through the Business Roundtable's Critical Emergency Operations Communications Link – CEOCOMLINK (GAO, 2004b, p. 6). Finally, threat level changes are communicated to the public via public announcements and media coverage, but rarely have the established emergency warning systems been used.[2]

What are the Goals of the HSAS?

As indicated in all official pronouncements concerning the HSAS, the objective of the system is to translate intelligence from diverse sources into a warning about the risk of terrorist activity. Much of the intelligence information is confidential, and passing it on to the public could pose a serious security risk by itself. However as seen in the latest two threat level inflations, when more specific geographical or economic targets are identified, the HSAS announcement will contain or refer to that information. Hitherto, potential terrorist activity seems aimed at three main targets: national icons or symbols, infrastructure and human life. Infrastructure can be broadly classified as physical or electronic. The transport system of air, road, rail and shipping is an obvious physical target, as are water and power supplies. Communications networks have become so important in everyday life in the US, from telephones to financial transactions, as well as all Internet-based activities, that cyber-threats have become their own entity separate from other 'security threats'.[3] Approximately 85 per cent of US infrastructure is in private hands (9/11 Commission, 2004). This means that the effectiveness of a threat warning system is critically dependent on the voluntary participation of many businesses and individuals, to contribute information necessary to interpret intelligence information into risk assessment and advice for the appropriate actions to mitigate against, prepare for and respond to threats.

Through both the HSAS level descriptions and the announcements of threat level changes, the emphasis is on the appropriate actions to take in response to the new threat. Reflecting on the vast research literature on risk perception and communication, Tierney and Clark (2003) state that warnings should be understandable, personal and actionable to individuals. In its review of the HSAS, the GAO identifies the following requirements for effective risk assessment:

1. Specific information including:
    a. the nature of the threat
    b. when and where it is likely to occur, and
    c. over what period
2. Guidance on actions to be taken. (GAO, 2004b, p. 9)

One major problem with the current HSAS and associated announcements remains that the threat is poorly specified, such that even if responsive actions are indicated, agencies, businesses and the public will not take any action because they do not know exactly what threat they are reacting to. Yet the objective of the HSAS is to create not a nation in perpetual fear, but one that is vigilant, aware and responsive, something that many critics currently believe is unattainable with the current system (Ridge, 2004).

What are the Criticisms of the HSAS?

The most cynical criticism of the HSAS is that threat level changes are primarily symbolic (Pena, 2002). For example in Secretary Ridge's most recent announcement of a geographically specific increase in threat level to orange, he stated:

> Rest assured, rest assured that the most talented security professionals and law enforcement professionals around this country are working hard every single day to protect all regions of the country and all sectors of our economy.
>
> There is much we can each do to remain vigilant, to be on watch, to be aware of unusual patterns or vehicles, and to report suspicious activities. And so this afternoon, I ask our citizens for their watchful eyes as we continue to monitor the situation. (Ridge, 2004)

In testimony before the House of Representatives Subcommittee on National Security, Emerging Threats and International Relations Committee on Government Reform, Kenneth Allen, representing the Partnership for Public Warning (PPW), commented that the HSAS is a 'threat assessment system' not a complete warning system. He states, 'the HSAS is America's mood ring'. Reporting on invited public comment in November 2003, Mr Allen identifies the following criticisms of the system:

(a) The system is too vague, such that the nature of the threat remains unknown, and appropriate response is indeterminate.
(b) One color across the nation is too general.
(c) The HSAS is inconsistent with other existing warning systems, which can cause confusion.
(d) The system relies too heavily on media reporting of announcements, rather than on the established and traditional warning systems and networks.

In its review of the HSAS, the GAO responds to the lack of specificity in the threat announcements with the recommendation that the DHS document its communication protocols regarding threat level changes including the methods, timing and content of guidance and threat information to be shared (GAO, 2004c, p. 39). Similarly, in reference to the amount of specific information conveyed by the HSAS, the Gilmore Commission reported:

> The Homeland Security Advisory System has become largely marginalized. This may be attributed to a lack of understanding of its intended use as well as the absence of a well-orchestrated plan to guide its implementation at all levels of government. The Governor of Hawaii chose to maintain a blue level in February 2003 when the Federal government raised the level to orange, and the Governor of Arizona announced that his State might do the same based on the particular threat or lack thereof to Arizona. (Gilmore, 2003)

Referring to the limitations of the HSAS, the GAO (2004c) report suggests that federal agencies varied their responses little when the threat level changed from yellow to orange. This was due to the high level of security that has now become the default level at these agencies and locations. Yet these are the organizations for which the advisory is binding. In contrast, the state and local governments, private businesses and the public for whom the HSAS is advisory vary their response to threat level changes (GAO, 2004c, p. 24). However much less is known as to how these organizations respond to threat level changes, or especially among the public, whether they alter their behavior at all.

Due to lack of specific information, preparation and response can be inappropriate in terms of type, level and timing. This ultimately means the misallocation of valuable resources to the activity of national security.[4] The country has developed an impressive organization to cope with natural hazards, which is employed throughout the year mitigating against, preparing for, responding to and recovering from hurricanes, floods, earthquakes, high winds, fires and even man-made disasters. Many critics have called for the integration of the HSAS into an all-hazards warning system in recognition of the infrastructure that currently exists (Allen, 2004).

The experiments developed in our research program are designed to investigate many of the issues and criticisms identified above. We consider the design elements of a terrorist alert system, as well as the behavioral response to system alternatives under varying threats, all in a decision environment where warnings and responses have real economic costs and benefits. The experimental design is described in the next section.

THE EXPERIMENTS

Vernon Smith has identified the study of choice under uncertainty as one of the two primary roles played by experimental economics. Moreover experiments require the following five conditions to hold to be valid: nonsatiation, saliency, dominance, privacy and parallelism (Smith, 1987, p. 7). In designing our experiments we have attempted to satisfy all of these criteria to create a decision environment from which observed behavior is relevant in making policy statements about the HSAS, or any other alternative alert system.

Our first goal has been to design a situation that contains the essential elements of the current system, recognizing that a major criticism of the current system is the very limited information it conveys concerning the nature of the terrorist threat. To this end, the experiment subjects can purchase improved threat information, in the form of more spatially detailed threat level code maps, and then choose a corresponding response of the kind suggested by DHS and the Red Cross. Subjects earn money as they progress through the experiment, which they can spend on purchasing detailed threat maps, and which they can possibly lose if actual threats are realized during the experiment. We are using an innovative web-based survey and interactive data-gathering instrument that we have used successfully in prior research (Bernknopf et al., 2003).

The first application is a pilot study to gather preliminary data and test the methodology with student subjects recruited in UNM fall session classes. Student subjects are invited to access the experiment website hosted by UNM and register to participate. Participation is voluntary and subjects are compensated for their time and efforts based on the outcomes of their decisions. The experiment takes approximately 20 minutes to complete and participants earned an average of $9. Once registered, subjects complete two web-based components, a survey and a main game. The first section requiring subject response is the short survey of six questions, three addressing awareness of the threat level advisory system and three asking demographic questions of the subject. Upon completing the survey, the subject is shown the main experiment introduction page. The experiment interface page provides all the information on experimental parameters, what decisions must be made and how to proceed. The subject must make two decisions to precede through the experiment each round: to buy the detailed map or not, and to choose an appropriate response to the threat. The subject may exit the experiment website at any time, and return to complete the experiment at any time. Upon completing all game rounds, subjects print a claim check which can be used to obtain payment in real currency.

The threat warning is provided in the form of a map, initially showing four cells, each colored using the same colors as the HSAS (we use the three highest levels: yellow, orange and red). The probability of a terrorist attack is given and fixed, but the spatial distribution of the threat level varies as a treatment between rounds. This model was chosen to reflect the actual nature of terrorist threats to date: some areas or sectors are considered more at risk from a particular attack, while others would remain relatively unaffected by the same event. The more spatially detailed threat map provides subjects with more specific spatial threat information, upon which they can make their desired response.

DATA, ANALYSIS AND RESULTS

The experiment website was developed and tested, then opened to general use by subjects during a three-week period in October 2004. During this time 53 subjects registered and completed the experiment and generated over 500 observations for inclusion in this analysis. The data are of a panel nature, with each subject generating an average of ten observations over a subset of treatments that includes different threat maps and varying detailed map costs. Subject decision variables include map purchase and threat response. In addition to the experimental data, each subject is required to complete a short survey covering their knowledge and experience of the HSAS and some basic demographics. The data allow us to test the following hypotheses:

H1: More spatially detailed threat information has value as expressed by a positive willingness to pay.
H2: The demand for more spatially detailed threat warnings is cost-sensitive.
H3: Costly response actions are more likely at higher threat levels.
H4: People are not subject to the 'Cry Wolf' syndrome postulated by Gruntfest and Carsell (2000).
H5: Responses match threat levels better for those people with higher HSAS awareness.

In these experiments, each subject acts independently, attempting to maximize the earnings from the experiment as a return on the investment of time and effort at the website. With each round the subject earns an income in tokens, that is threatened by terrorist activity, information about which is provided via the threat level map. While the probability of an attack is fixed, given the subject's location, the threat level and associated loss is randomly chosen each round. Initially, the subject sees the very coarse, four-sector map, where the threat level color is determined by the modal color of the nine segments within that sector. By buying the detailed map which reveals all 36 segments to the subject, he or she is buying more information about the probability distribution of loss which theoretically makes the calculation of expected loss and choice of appropriate response easier. The decision to purchase the detailed map is therefore based on the potential benefits a subject expects from greater information about the spatial

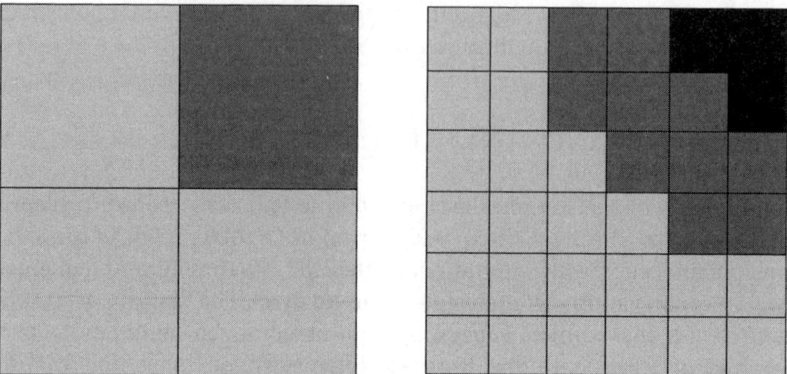

Figure 8.1 Coarse and detailed threat maps

distribution of loss amounts and location within that space. The subject will compare the cost of purchasing the map with the benefits of a potentially more accurate calculation of expected losses from the hazard. Figure 8.1 shows sample coarse and detailed threat level maps as used in the experiment: the location is chosen randomly and shown to the subject on the map.

The subjects are also asked to choose their most preferred response to the threat they perceive at their location on the map. The response is gathered via asking the following question:

What would you expect to do under this terrorist threat level?

1. do nothing different;
2. be more alert at work and in public places;
3. stay home from work and tune into the radio or TV for news; or
4. gather my family and evacuate to a safer place.

Each of these responses involves an increasing amount of effort and implicit cost to the subject. The subject should choose a higher cost response the higher the expected value of the perceived loss from the terrorist threat.

The empirical model entails two equations, one to explain the decision to purchase a map, the other the preferred response to the threat. What is the proper way to model the interaction between these two decisions? If they are alternatives, then a random utility model (RUM) framework would seem appropriate. But they are essentially complementary rather than substitute decisions. The more detailed map aids in making the response decision. The decisions are not independent, but they are not

Table 8.1 Definitions and summary statistics for variables used in analysis

Variable name	Variable description	mean[1]	std dev[2]
ID	subject identifier (53 subjects, 515 observations)		
Current level	subject correctly knows current threat level	0.377	
Unaware	subject is unaware of current threat level	0.421	
Response	subject knows recommended response to current threat level	0.400	
Female	proportion of sample female	0.412	
Age	proportion of sample over 21 years old	0.469	
FT student	proportion of sample full time student	0.874	
FT worker	proportion of sample working full time	0.089	
Mapcost	cost of purchasing detailed map (tokens)	55	33
Totalbalance	balance of account (tokens)	5234	51.7
Lossamt	potential loss at location	513	367
Outcome	terrorist attack occurred	0	
Lossprob	probability of attack fixed	0.001	
Boughtmap	1 = yes	0.317	0.466
React	subject chose some action in response to threat	0.796	

Notes:
1. Mean not provided for ID type variables.
2. Standard deviation not given for binary variables.

alternatives, hence modeling them as simultaneous equations with possibly correlated errors seems more appropriate. Each decision is modeled as a function of the variables specifying the cost of the decision, the expected loss from the hazard, demographics and subject knowledge, and a measure of the wealth of the subject at the time of the decision. The empirical model allows us to test all the hypotheses, either directly or indirectly.

Table 8.1 provides the variables used in the empirical analysis and gives definitions for these variables. The first set of variables gives some descriptive statistics for the sample of subjects participating in the experiment. Under half were female (41 per cent) and nearly half were over 21 years old (47 per cent) About one-third of the sample subjects were aware of

Table 8.2 Sample responses to threat levels, all rounds

Detailed map	Threat Level at location						Marginal totals
	Yellow		Orange		Red		
	buy	not	buy	not	buy	not	
Response:							
Do nothing	10	44	1	42	0	8	105
Be more alert	24	77	60	62	4	8	135
Stay at home, await news	4	9	15	39	8	14	89
Evacuate	2	15	12	28	23	6	86
Marginal totals	40	145	88	171	35	36	515

the current threat level and correctly identified it as yellow (38 per cent) while 42 per cent were completely unaware of the current threat level.[5] About 40 per cent of subjects were able to identify the appropriate response to a given threat level, as recommended by the DHS and the Red Cross.

Table 8.1 also gives other statistics for the experiment. A terrorist attack never occurred during the experiment which, given the very low probability of such an event, is not unexpected. Table 8.2 summarizes how the 515 decisions were categorized by threat level, response to threat and the decision to buy a map. On only 32 per cent of occasions did subjects buy the detailed map, but purchase was more likely if the subject was in a higher threat zone. For example the detailed map was bought 24 per cent of the time under a yellow threat level, 34 per cent of the time under orange and 49 per cent of the time under red. On only 20 per cent of occasions did subjects claim they would not respond to the threat, and generally the willingness of subjects to respond with greater effort increased as the threat level increased. In about two-thirds of cases under yellow and orange threats subjects said they would be more alert, but under red threats subjects stated they would evacuate to a safer location two-thirds of the time. More can be said about the relationship between threat levels, more detailed spatial information and subject response using a regression framework that controls for many factors. We turn to that analysis and discussion now.

As discussed above, a bivariate probit model was chosen to model the decision to purchase the detailed map and to choose a response to the threat. The results of this estimation appear in Table 8.3. There are two basic specifications of the bivariate probit model: one named Cluster, the

Table 8.3 Bivariate probit analysis of decision to buy detailed map and respond to threat with action (simultaneous estimations)[1]

Equation Variable	Buy Detailed Threat Information		Respond to Threat Level	
	Cluster[2]	No Cluster	Cluster	No Cluster
	(1)	(2)	(3)	(4)
Constant	**8.03**[3] (5.19)	**8.03** (5.27)	**3.64** (2.55)	**3.64** (2.30)
Map cost	**−0.011** (−4.80)	**−0.011** (−4.83)	−0.002 (−1.27)	−0.002 (−1.21)
Threat level	**0.440** (4.05)	**0.440** (4.29)	**0.446** (4.28)	**0.446** (4.18)
Log (loss amount)	**0.193** (2.58)	**0.193** (2.66)	0.043 (0.66)	0.043 (0.62)
Log (total a/c balance)	**−1.86** (−6.94)	**−1.86** (−6.79)	**−0.498** (−2.11)	−0.498 (−1.80)
Experience	**0.419** (6.41)	**0.419** (5.86)	**0.139** (2.47)	0.139 (1.95)
Buy map last game	**0.982** (4.32)	**0.982** (6.76)	0.218 (1.15)	0.218 (1.32)
Female	−0.183 (−0.90)	−0.183 (−1.25)	−0.184 (−0.64)	−0.184 (−1.27)
Over 21	**−0.437** (−2.05)	**−0.437** (−2.87)	**−0.646** (−2.30)	**−0.646** (−4.37)
FT student	−0.413 (−1.41)	−0.413 (−1.90)	−0.659 (−1.95)	**−0.659** (−2.83)
Know threat level	0.321 (1.26)	0.321 (1.59)	0.293 (0.87)	0.293 (1.46)
Unaware threat level	0.511 (1.90)	**0.511** (2.56)	−0.038 (−0.11)	−0.038 (−0.19)
Correctly assess threat	**0.511** (2.74)	**0.511** (3.40)	−0.508 (−0.54)	**−0.508** (−3.26)
Rho			**0.461**	**0.461**
Wald test for *rho* = 0			**15.27**	**18.76**
Sample size			515	515
Wald test for eqn.			**253.0**	**187.9**

Notes:
1. Estimates are full information maximum likelihood.
2. Clustering allows for correlated errors within observations from the same subject, but none across subjects.
3. Coefficients in bold are significantly different from zero at 95% confidence level.

other No Cluster. Since each subject generates more than one observation for the analysis, there is potential for non-independent observations and correlated errors. This potential is explicitly modeled in the Cluster specification, where the parameter values do not differ, but the standard errors are estimated more efficiently.

For most coefficients in both tables the standard errors are smaller for the Cluster estimates. This suggests that explicitly modeling the within-subject error correlations results in more efficient estimates of the coefficients. Estimates for *rho*, the correlation of errors between the two equations, are provided in the tables. For the model presented, with and without correction for panel data, there is a statistically significant correlation between the errors of the map purchase and threat response decision. While the model specification is quite consistent with the proposition that threat response is dependent in part on map purchase, the presence of a significant correlation between factors influencing the two decisions is explained not by the factors included as explanatory variables in the two equations but rather by unobserved factors for which data were not available.

Columns (2) and (4) of Table 8.3 show estimates of a Bivariate Probit model for the two decisions estimated simultaneously using the full information maximum likelihood method. Columns (1) and (3) show the same model specification corrected for the panel nature of the data gathering process. The relatively rich specification includes variables related to the expected value of the loss, the threat advisory level, a variable indicating past decisions by subjects, and some demographic variables. Map cost is important in determining whether a subject purchases the map, and the sign of the coefficient is consistent with expectations. The level of threat, as indicated by the advisory color code, is statistically significant and has the expected positive effect on the probability of buying a more detailed map. The amount of potential loss is also significant and a positive factor in increasing the likelihood that the subject will buy additional threat information. Subjects display habitual behavior in that they are more likely to buy a map if they purchased one previously. Neither age nor gender appears to be a factor in obtaining more detailed threat information.

The coefficient on the wealth variable (the natural log of accumulated experiment wealth) is negative and statistically significant. This result could be interpreted as evidence for less need of map information as subjects get wealthier, perhaps because of subjects self-insuring. However it is difficult to imagine how anyone can effectively self-insure against terrorist attacks in the same way as they self-insure against property damage or ill-health. Wealth could be acting as a proxy for experience with the game, since for most subjects in this experiment wealth increases as the game progresses, but not linearly depending on their map purchases. To test for repeated exposure to the risk, a variable was explicitly included in the models. For both the map purchase and the threat response the effect of repeated exposure is positive and statistically significant. This suggests that the negative wealth effect is not a proxy for experience, but has another explanation. It could be that as subjects get wealthier, and experience no losses, they become less risk-averse because of underestimates of the probability of loss.

While many variables have the same sign effect on map purchase and threat response, the magnitude of these impacts differs. Significantly, the cost of the map affects the purchase decision but not the anticipated response to the threat. A similar result is found for the size of the loss, having a significant positive impact on the need for more detailed information, but no statistically significant impact on threat response. A relatively small set of variables are found to be significant determinants of threat response, limited to threat level, wealth and experience and age. Older subjects are less willing to consider costly responses to threats.

The result found for experience in the threat response equation allows us to test the 'Cry Wolf' hypothesis. We find that repeated exposure to the threat warnings without actual terrorist attacks occurring do not reduce the perceived value of better threat information, nor the willingness to undertake costly actions in response to the threat. While this does not constitute a direct test of the hypothesis, the result is consistent with observations of the willingness of people living in the United States to take the threat of terrorist attacks seriously, and incur significant and prolonged expense in the name of mitigation and preparedness.

Using equations (1) and (3) for both map purchase and threat response, Table 8.4 gives estimates of the marginal effects of each variable on the joint probabilities of buying more detailed threat information and responding to the threat information. The average probabilities show that the most likely course of action is to not buy the detailed information, but to consider some response to the threat. The least likely action is to buy the detailed map but take no action in response to the threat – which is very good news for policy makers supporting the dissemination of threat advisories. The largest marginal impact comes from wealth, with a negative effect on undertaking both decisions, but a positive effect on responding with only the original threat advisory information. Subjects are also relatively insensitive to the cost of more detailed information, another positive sign for policy makers seeking to improve the threat advisory system.

In summary, the empirical results provide evidence of rational behavior by subjects consistent with the expected utility theory. Subjects are less likely to purchase additional threat information (the map) the more it costs, but are more likely to purchase more detailed information at higher initial threat levels. This suggests that more serious threats require more detailed information to be provided to the population – a finding consistent with sociological research recognizing that people do not simply respond to commands from authority, but rather need credible and trustworthy information to support their own conclusions. Experiment subjects were more likely to buy the detailed map if they had bought one previously, which is a positive indication that they perceived the map to be of value in

Table 8.4 Marginal effect of explanatory variables on joint probabilities

Variable	Impact on joint probability			
	(1)	(2)	(3)	(4)
	buy map and respond to threat	buy map, do not respond	do not buy map, respond	neither buy map nor respond
Average probability	0.234	0.011	0.597	0.158
Map cost	**−0.003**[2]	**−0.000**[1]	**0.003**	0.001
Threat level	**0.139**	**−0.001**	−0.027	**−0.112**
Log (loss amount)	**0.057**	**0.003**	**−0.046**	−0.014
Log (total a/c balance)	**−0.554**	−0.031	**0.429**	**0.157**
Experience	**0.125**	0.006	**−0.090**	**−0.041**
Buy map last game	**0.315**	0.021	**−0.263**	−0.074
Female	−0.057	0.000	0.010	0.047
Over 21	**−0.141**	0.006	−0.025	**0.160**
FT student	−0.149	0.006	0.021	**0.122**
Know threat level	0.103	−0.000	−0.032	−0.071
Unaware threat level	0.149	0.014	−0.159	−0.005
Correctly assess threat	**0.131**	**0.034**	**−0.266**	0.101

Notes:
1. Values less than 0.0005 are reported as 0.000.
2. Coefficients in bold are significantly different from zero at 95% confidence level.

assessing the threat and deciding how to respond. There was no evidence from the experiments that subjects tired of repeated warnings. The only factor that discouraged subjects from valuing more information and responding accordingly was wealth. As subjects became wealthier they were less likely to want more detailed information, and this effect was stronger relative to the impact of wealth on the decision to respond to the threat information. This is a purely empirical finding, with no guidance from theory as to why this effect should emerge. The usual explanation of self-insurance for the wealthier does not seem plausible for terrorist-like risks unless people believe they can mitigate and protect themselves with costly expenditures.

There is evidence presented here that supports the claim that more geographically detailed threat warnings are valuable, and that resources should be expended to provide such information. What is less clear is the optimal level of this information, since the experiments also show that in only a third of cases was the detailed threat map bought, and that subjects were less likely to want the map if it was relatively more costly. Since the cost of such public information is implicit in the national tax system, and seemingly provided 'free' to all citizens and residents, making the cost explicit in the experiments may make subjects more sensitive to price than they would be otherwise.

FURTHER DEVELOPMENTS

At present the experiment does not explicitly recognize the cost of responding to threat warnings, or to changes in threat level. The GAO report on raising the HSAS threat level from yellow to orange suggests costs of this change in threat level could range from $3000 to $100 million per week, but warns that cost estimates are particularly speculative (GAO, 2004c, p. 38). Of course these GAO estimates do not contain any estimates of private business or general public costs of increasing the threat level. Anecdotal evidence from information sources such as the DHS, the Red Cross or the government-sponsored information web Ready.gov would suggest that response costs are certainly not negligible. Development of our experiments will involve treatments where subjects face costs of improved threat information and explicit costs of response to allow us to observe the expected trade-off between the uncertainty that accompanies specific warnings and the costs of response. It is only reasonable to expect, given the current state of intelligence, more specific warnings will be associated with greater uncertainty regarding the risk to any individual, organization or geographical area.

Another development of the current instrument will include an investigation of alternative warning systems, and methods of communicating threat information. At present, some federal and state agencies report hearing about terrorist threats and changes in the HSAS level from the media before being notified by DHS (GAO, 2004c, p. 17). At the same time, DHS has not chosen to use the existing multi-hazard and natural hazard warning systems already in place. We can investigate subject responses to these alternatives using our experimental design.

Currently, our experiment does not contain a time element, so warnings and responses are essentially real-time to the subject. Even though one of the advantages of web-based experiments over other data-gathering methods is the element of real time, it may limit our ability to observe behavior when the threat information is time-sensitive. Of course, just as experiments can compress time to make decisions, it also has the potential to compress the temporal relevance of information, so long as parallelism is established and maintained. Finally, we envision using our experiments to place the HSAS and other terrorist threat information systems in a wider hazard context, and to consider the trade-off and relative priorities of allocating resources to terrorist security versus more general natural hazard mitigation, preparedness and response.

NOTES

* Funding for this research was provided in part by the US Geological Survey, and the Maria E. Granone Foundation for support of economic research.

1. The system was established in March 2002 and was initially set at level yellow (mid level of 5 possible levels.) Since then it has been raised to orange on 10 September 2002 for 14 days, 7 February 2003 for 20 days. 17 March 2003 for 30 days, 20 May 2003 for 10 days and 21 December 2003 for 20 days (GAO, 2004b, p. 4).
2. For example the Emergency Alert System (EAS) was not used on 11 September 2001, nor for any terrorist related alert since then.
3. There is a National Strategy to Secure Cyberspace, which led to the creation of the National Cyber Security Division (NCSD) which in turn has created the National Cyber Alert System, which appears to be separate from the HSAS. (See DHS website, 2004.)
4. Quoting Wermuth (2004): 'State and local jurisdictions have, in recent months, complained that raising the national alert level caused them to expend inordinate additional resources for law enforcement overtime and other increased security measures. Given the lack of more comprehensive or focused threat information, it is easy to understand how such a reaction may be viewed as a political necessity – the public will not understand, absent better explanations, why their own State or locality does not do something "more" when the national alert level goes from Yellow to Orange.'
5. There were subjects who incorrectly stated the current threat level.

BIBLIOGRAPHY

Allen, Kenneth and the Partnership for Public Warning (2004), 'The Homeland Security Advisory System: threat codes and public responses', testimony before the House of Representatives Subcommittee on National Security, Emerging Threats and International Relations, Committee on Government Reform, 16 March.

Bernknopf, R.L., D.S. Brookshire and P.T. Ganderton (2003), 'The role of geoscience information in reducing catastrophic loss using a web-based economics experiment', USGS Professional Paper 1683, USGS, Reston Virginia.

Bush, George W. (2003), 'Homeland Security Presidential Directive – 3' US Government Whitehouse, Washington, DC, March.

Carafano, James J. (2004), 'Homeland security: alerting the nation', testimony delivered to the House Subcomittee on National Security, Emerging Threats, and International Threats, 18 March.

Gilmore, Governor James (2003), 'Forging America's new normalcy: securing our homeland, preserving our liberty', 5th Annual Report to the President and the Congress, 15 December.

Government Accounting Office (GAO) (2004a), 'Homeland Security Advisory System: preliminary observations regarding threat level increases from yellow to orange', GAO-04–453R, 26 February.

Government Accounting Office (GAO) (2004b), 'Homeland security: risk communication principles may assist in refinement of the Homeland Security Advisory System' GAO-04–538T, 16 March.

Government Accounting Office (GAO) (2004c), 'Homeland security: communication protocols and risk communication principles may assist in refining the Homeland Security Advisory System', GAO-04–682, June.

Gruntfest, Eve and Kim Carsell (2000), 'The warning process: toward an understanding of false alarms', Department of Geography and Environmental Studies UC Colorado Springs, September.

Herring, Lee (2003), 'How would sociologists design a Homeland Security Alert System?' American Sociological Association website, Footnotes, April, http://www.asanet.org/footnotes/apr03/fn8.html

Lichtblau, Eric (2004), 'Report questions value of color-coded warnings', New York Times/NYTimes.com, 13 July.

The National Commission on Terrorist Attacks Upon the United States (the 9/11 Commission), 22 July 2004.

O'Meara, Kelly Patricia (2003), 'Alert system's deafening silence', *Insight on the News,* 25 November.

Pena, Charles V. (2002), 'Homeland Security Alert System: why bother?' Cato Institute 31 October, http://www.cato.org/cgi-bin/scripts/printtech.cgi/dailys/10–31–02.html

Purdum, Todd S. (2004), 'What, us worry? The new state of disbelief' *New York Times*, 8 August, section 4, p. 1.

Ridge, Thomas (2004), 'Remarks regarding recent threat reports', US Department of Homeland Security, Office of the Press Secretary, 1 August.

Smith, Vernon (1987), 'Experimental methods in economics', J. Eatwell, M. Milgate and P. Newman (eds), in *The New Palgrave: A Dictionary of Economic Theory and Doctrine*, New York: Macmillan Press.

Tierney, Kathleen and Lee B. Clarke (2003), 'Risk and disaster research: preparation, communication, and response', paper prepared for White House Office of Science and Technology Policy, April.

Wermuth, Michael (2004), 'Improving terrorism warnings: the Homeland Security System', testimony presented to the House Committee on Government Reform, Subcommittee on National Security, Emerging Threats, and International Relations on 16 March, Rand Corporation.

9. Land markets and terrorism: uncovering perceptions of risk by examining land price changes following 9/11

Christian L. Redfearn

INTRODUCTION

On 1 August 2004, the Department of Homeland Security (DHS) issued a heightened security alert for financial institutions in the greater New York City area and Washington, DC. It was the first time that specific targets had been identified in a DHS security advisory. Previously, the department had issued broad warnings regarding the level of risk from attacks on domestic targets without guidance as to where, when or what type of attack might be expected. Yet even when advisories are non-specific regarding location, it is implicitly clear that not all locales within the US are equally exposed to the risk of attack. This chapter exploits spatial variation in presumed risk to measure the public's assessment of actual risk from terrorism in the wake of the attacks of 9/11.

At issue are behavioral – rather than rhetorical – responses to terrorism. From the reorganization of the federal government's counter-terror activities to the media's coverage of the 'war on terror', consumers have had ample reason to reconsider their actions in light of the attacks and subsequent revelations about terrorist activities. Is consumer behavior consistent with consumer opinion about terror? One recent study (Lerner et al., 2003) reported that two months after the attacks on New York City and Washington, DC survey respondents placed the probability of their being hurt in a terrorist attack at 10 per cent, while the probability that an 'average American' would be hurt by a terrorist attack was deemed to be 50 per cent. Presumably this risk was not a general risk, but one concentrated on those living in areas that were likely targets of attack. If consumer behavior followed such sentiments, the cost of the attacks on 9/11 may be far greater than is generally calculated: the value of urban property may diminish substantially if consumers seek to avoid dense, 'target-rich' environments.

In the extreme, aversion to density could alter the basic shape of cities.[1] We might expect flatter, more dispersed cities as a long-term outcome, since city shapes are well established and the built environment is difficult and expensive to alter. However it is precisely these inherent features of real estate that make it an ideal subject for the analysis of consumer sentiment regarding changes in expectations. Because the quantity of housing supply is fixed in the short term, changes in demand will be seen in dwelling prices and/or transaction volumes. The attacks on 9/11 created a setting for studying changes in the perceived risk of terrorism. If the attacks signaled a change in the probability of attack, proximity to potential targets would be seen as more dangerous. Not only could an attack result in physical harm in the vicinity of the target, but it could also damage a dwelling or the elements of a neighborhood that make a dwelling valuable. Because of its long life and immobility, real estate values are necessarily tied to expectations about the future – both that of the structure and its neighborhood. Changes in these expectations should be capitalized in real estate prices.

This chapter looks to land-rent gradients around potential targets for evidence that consumers' perception of risk from terrorism changed after the attacks on New York City and Washington, DC on 11 September 2001. Specifically, housing markets in the vicinity of Los Angeles International Airport (LAX), the ports of Long Beach and Los Angeles, and the prominent skyscrapers in the downtown area are examined in the periods before and after 9/11. If individuals do in fact perceive a change in the threat from terror, they should pay a premium for land further from potential sites – or alternatively, demand a discount for land proximal to locations more likely to be impacted by a terrorist attack. Thus the gradient surrounding potential terrorist targets should increase in the months that follow the 9/11 attacks.[2] If the probability of terrorism is perceived to be permanently higher, the change in the gradient should also be permanent. If, on the other hand, the initial shock and caution regarding properties in the shadow of potential targets fades, the price gradient should first increase and then return to pre-attack levels. In fact, no significant change – temporary or permanent – is found.

The price gradients surrounding the three potential targets examined vary over time in a manner that is roughly consistent with the hypothesis that consumers perceived no change in the threat from terrorism. No impact is found in either local indexes of house prices and sales volume, or in the implicit price of proximity to potential targets of terrorism. The lack of findings in transaction data stands in marked contrast with the survey that found respondents anticipating a one-in-ten chance of personal injury, and with evidence of sophisticated consumer pricing of small-probability risk in other housing markets. Several competing stories could explain the observed market outcomes, but one that cannot hold is that consumers have voted with their feet. They have not – in statistically significant numbers – perceived a large enough risk of personal and/or property loss to change significantly how much prices declined around sites at higher risk of terrorist attack.

The remainder of the chapter is divided as follows. The next section develops a model of terrorism and land prices that follows from a broad literature on externalities and housing markets. The third section introduces and highlights the data used in the research. Results are reported and discussed in the following section. The chapter closes with a brief discussion of the conclusions and the planned extensions.

TERRORISM AND MODELS OF EXTERNALITIES

Risk from property loss due to terrorist attacks can be modeled as a special case of a more general spatial externality. In the presence of a spatial externality, otherwise identical dwellings will have market values that vary as a function of their proximity to the source of the externality – in this case, the risk of collateral damage due to a terrorist attack. If consumers require a discount to live near a potential target, the closer of these two dwellings will be valued lower, reflecting the penalty associated with the risk of attack and the resulting damage. The literature on spatial externalities is large, including research on both positive and negative externalities. Among the positive externalities are access to work and consumption – the central variables on which much of the urban-form literature is based; among the research on negative externalities is the study of the impact of exposure to noise (Wilhelmsson, 2000), smog (Kahn, 2000) and environmental hazards such as Superfund sites (Greenberg and Hughes, 1992), among many others.

The standard approach to measuring the value of individual attributes of bundled goods is to estimate a hedonic price equation. In the standard application of hedonic pricing to housing, observed value is a function of quality flow – the services provided by the dwelling's physical characteristics and locational amenities and disamenities – and the unit price of quality. That is,

$$V_{it} = P_t Q_{it}, \tag{9.1}$$

where V_{it} is property value, P_t is the unit price of quality, and Q_{it} is the quality flow; i and t index parcel and time, respectively. To arrive at the familiar hedonic pricing equation, take the natural log of both sides of the equation and reparameterize the log of quality, lnQ_{it}, as a linear function of attributes, $X_{it}\beta$:

$$lnV_{it} = lnP_t + X_{it}\beta. \tag{9.2}$$

The vector X_{it} consists of all attributes which contribute to the market price of the parcel.

To make clear the role of spatial externalities consider the following variation of equation (9.2). In it, environmental variables – in contrast to the physical characteristics of the dwelling itself – have been separated from the general matrix of dwelling attributes, X_{it}^D:

$$lnV_{it} = lnP_t + X_{it}^D\beta + \beta^N Noise_{it} + \beta^S SchoolQuality + \beta^C Commute + \ldots. \tag{9.3}$$

The list of environmental variables imparting spatially differing impacts on the value of dwellings is exceedingly long. In principle, estimating this regression would recover the contributions of both physical and spatial characteristics on dwelling values. In practice, the data required for its estimation are not generally available. As a proxy for the spatial variables, distances (or functions of distances) to point sources are occasionally used. (Although it is not uncommon to see aspatial hedonic pricing of housing.) If V_{it} is the value of periodic services for dwelling i in period t, an alternative definition of its sale price today – the dwelling's present value – is:

$$PV_{i0} = V_{i0} + \frac{V_{i1}}{1+r_1} + \frac{V_{i2}}{(1+r_1)(1+r_2)} + \ldots + \frac{V_{iN}}{(1+r_1)(1+r_2)\cdots(1+r_N)}, \tag{9.4}$$

where V_t is the value of the net service flow to the owner during time period t and PV_{i0} is the present value of the series of cash flows.

The future values of the service flows from the dwelling are not known with certainty. They are expected values, embedding expectations about the integrity of the structure, the future quality of the local schools, crime in the neighborhood, employment in the metropolitan area, interest rates, and among many others, the risk of terrorism. In order to make explicit the role of terrorism risk on house prices, equation (9.4) can be rewritten to include a basic parameterization that includes both the expected probability of an attack and the expected impact of an attack on the service flow from the dwelling. If p_t is the probability of attack in period t and d_t is the impact of the attack on the flow of services ($d=0$ indicates no change, $d=1$ indicates complete loss), equation 9.4 becomes

$$PV_{i0} = V_i0 + \frac{(1-p_1)(1-d_1)V_{i1}}{1+r_1} + \frac{(1-p_2)(1-d_2)V_{i2}}{(1+r_1)(1+r_2)} + \ldots + \frac{(1-p_N)(1-d_N)V_{iN}}{(1+r_1)(1+r_2)\cdots(1+r_N)} \tag{9.5}$$

Any non-zero probability of attack leads to lower home prices than would have resulted in the absence of terrorism risk. More generally, any change in the expectation of the probability of attack or its severity will cause a change in the value of homes. Specifically,

$$\partial PV/\partial p_k < 0, \quad \partial PV/\partial d_k < 0 \tag{9.6}$$

Of course, it is likely that changes in probability and loss are correlated as are changes in probabilities and losses in adjacent periods – destruction of a property in period t will lead to losses in service flow from the property for many subsequent periods.[3]

The two relevant questions for this approach are first, do consumers respond to changes in the perceived risk of terrorism or other small probability events? And second, is this approach capable of capturing risk pricing along a single dimension of an asset whose observed price is the capitalization of so many location-specific factors? On the matter of consumer responsiveness to terrorism, there is evidence that tourists are sensitive to attacks (Enders et al., 1992; Pizam and Smith, 2000; Sloboda, 2003). However tourism destinations are relatively fungible and easily adjusted, and these studies may not be applicable to durable goods markets like housing.

There is some support however for the hypothesis that consumers are sophisticated regarding their assessment of risk in the context of a larger and more permanent investment in a dwelling. In an examination of housing market behavior before and after an explosion of a local chemical plant, and after the subsequent announcement that the plant would be relocated, Carroll et al. (1996) find that after the relocation announcement, 'property values rebounded to reflect the reduction in the number of [local] hazardous plants'. Also, in a study of pricing of houses in the San Francisco Bay area after the Loma Prieta earthquake in 1991, Murdoch et al. (1993) find significant price differences by soil type. This reflects a remarkable sophistication on the part of consumers to assess and price risk. In this case, home buyers recognized that different soil types imply distinct distributions of damage in the event of an earthquake and warrant differential pricing.

Empirical Strategy

The central empirical challenge in measuring the impact of spatial externalities is controlling for other influences on real estate prices that vary by location. It may be for instance that ports are likely targets of terror. However it is also likely that land prices near ports are impacted by noise, truck traffic and pollution. A simple hedonic regression that includes dwelling characteristics and the distance to the port as explanatory variables may find that proximity to the port is in fact a significant and negative impact of housing values. Attributing this to terrorism risk would be inappropriate as the coefficient simply measures the influence of distance, commingling the influence of port noise, traffic and pollution as well as the exposure to fallout from an attack on the port.

The attacks on 11 September 2001 offer an opportunity to identify the idiosyncratic influence of perceived risk from terrorism. The attacks offer the opportunity to perform a natural experiment to assess home prices before and after the events in order to isolate price changes due to changes in expectations about future attacks and their impacts on housing values. In general the spatial variables mentioned above are slow-changing variables – noise, traffic and pollution are all relatively fixed in the short term. In the wake of the attacks on New York and Washington, DC, none of the other environmental variables should change significantly. As a result, changes in house prices around potential terrorist targets can be attributed to consumer responses to the attacks themselves. The hypothesis that consumers have altered their valuation of risk should be testable by examining the price gradient around these targets – prices closer to sites of greater perceived risk should become relatively less valuable.

There are several margins of variation across the data that will allow for identification of the penalty of terrorist risk. The first is spatial: the potential targets are spread throughout the metropolitan area. It will be possible to pool housing sales around several targets to look for systematic changes in the cost of proximity. The second is temporal. Ostensibly the risk of terrorism has been non-zero since well before the 9/11 attacks. But the attacks made the reality of that risk far more palpable and presumably made actors previously ignorant of terrorism more aware. Finally, there is variation in targets themselves, which are perceived to be differentially at risk.

These margins motivate two basic empirical approaches. The first is to consider proximity as discrete; dwellings are 'adjacent', 'near', or 'far' from the potential targets and face differential risk at each discrete location. Based on this conception of terrorism risk, the appropriate test of differential pricing of proximity – evidence of changes in perceived risk 'near' targets – would be based on differences in aggregate prices over the pre- and post-9/11 attacks. The second approach is to conceive of risk from terrorism as a continuous variable, declining with distance from potential targets. Here, distance from the target in question is included in the pricing regression. Again the inference of changes in consumer perception of risk would be apparent in changes in the coefficient on distance – that is, changes in the price gradient.

The aggregate index approach requires the estimation of price indexes for each of the subsamples – 'adjacent,' 'near,' and 'far.' This is undertaken by estimating a variant of equation (9.2):

$$lnV_{it} = lnP_t + X_{it}^D\beta + \sum \delta_k D_{ik} \qquad (9.7)$$

where k indexes quarters. D_k is an dummy variable, indicating whether or not dwelling i was sold in quarter k. exp(δ) is then the price level in quarter k. The hypothesis that proximity to potential targets became more penalized after 11 September 2001 would be examined by testing whether or not the indexes were significantly different before and after the attacks. This test may have little power against alternative hypotheses that some other factor coincident with the attacks led to changes. This is discussed further in the results section.

It is also possible that the aggregate indexes may not indicate any change in behavior despite a genuine increase in the discount required to live near a potential target. Consider a basic model of buyer and seller interaction. In the immediate post-attack housing market near a potential target, buyers have not yet lowered their reservation prices, but sellers have reduced their offer prices. Given the idiosyncracies of buyers and sellers and the distributions of their valuations of dwellings, transactions will still occur at similar prices, but fewer will occur in aggregate. In this setting, the impact of changes in perceived risk may first be apparent in sales volume, but not in prices. Both aggregate prices and sales volumes are reported below.

The second approach to assessing price changes is to conceive of risk as a continuous variable that varies with distance from the target. In this case, the basic hedonic equation is specified as follows:

$$\begin{aligned} lnV_{it} = lnP_t + X_{it}^D\beta + \beta^T \mathit{Terrorism\ Risk}_{it} \\ + \sum \beta^O \mathit{Other\ Locational\ Amenities}_{it} \end{aligned} \qquad (9.8)$$

Assuming that the other locational amenities and disamenities are not responsive to the attack on 9/11, they are fixed over our sample period and equation (9.8) becomes:

$$lnV_{it} = lnP_t + X_{it}^D\beta + \beta^T f(dist_i) \qquad (9.9)$$

Here, $f(dist_i)$ is one of several different functional forms used to examine changes in the price of proximity before and after 9/11.

The simplest functional form is an interaction with a dummy variable indicating whether the sale occurred before or after the attacks. If the change in perceptions – and pricing – is permanent, then this is the correct specification. If, on the other hand, consumer response varies over time after the attacks, it would be more appropriate to use a series of interaction dummies to pick up the evolution of pricing in the wake of the attacks.

DATA

Three types of variables from housing markets are required to make possible a measurement of changes in perceived terrorism risk. As discussed in the previous section, evidence of consumer responses will be looked for in housing market outcomes. It is then necessary to have transactional data: both sale price and sale date. These data are fairly easily obtained, but are by themselves inadequate to make a credible assessment of risk pricing. Housing varies substantially from dwelling to dwelling. In order to recover the parameters on interacted distance variables it will be necessary to control for physical heterogeneity. This implies that data on dwelling physical characteristics are also needed. Finally, locational information is essential.

All three types of data are gathered on an ongoing basis by DataQuick, a real estate market information firm. For this study, DataQuick data on dwelling transactions and characteristics for single family residences in the central and southern parts of Los Angeles county are employed. The data include sales price and date, a number of physical characteristics, and are identified by their census tract.

The geographic scope of the data was defined to include three prominent potential targets of terrorism and their surrounding housing markets; these include Los Angeles International Airport (LAX), the ports of Long Beach and Los Angeles, and the central business district (CBD) of downtown Los Angeles. Certainly there are other candidates for attack. Discussions in the media have identified water and power facilities as potential targets, as well as cultural institutions associated with the projection of America abroad (Hollywood), but none are as prominent as the three employed in this research.

Figure 9.1 shows the US Census centroids for the southern portion of Los Angeles county as well as the three locales being examined. For each of the three – the central business district (CBD), the ports of Los Angeles and Long Beach (the ports), and Los Angeles International Airport (LAX) – the figure also shows three concentric rings indicating the

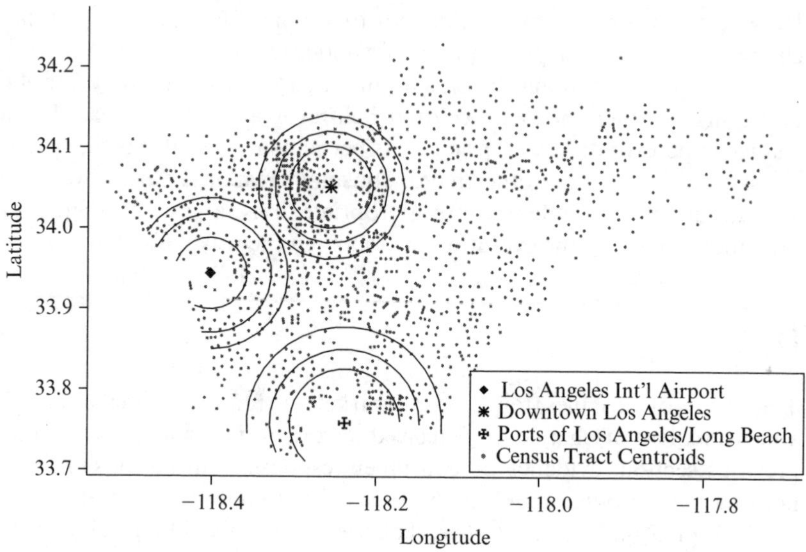

Figure 9.1 Potential targets and their environs

boundaries of the discrete regions introduced in the previous section. These regions – 'adjacent', 'near', and 'far' – are chosen to include roughly the same number of observations on housing sales. Note that the rings around the ports are bigger. The ports are comprised of large areas in which there are no dwellings and hence no sales. Therefore the rings have been extended.

Table 9.1 reports average characteristics for the dwelling sales used in this analysis. It makes clear the need to control for physical heterogeneity and suggests that while there are systematic differences across the types of dwelling within each of the discrete categories of proximity, the differences are far greater across the submarkets defined by the neighborhoods around each potential target. For example dwellings sold in the region adjacent to the potential targets are systematically smaller and lower quality, and sell for less. However there is essentially no difference in the average age by proximity, whereas the vintage of the housing stock appears to be drastically different across the three locational submarkets.

RESULTS

The models introduced above suggest that any measurable impact of changes in the perceived risk of terrorism should appear in either dwelling

Table 9.1 Sample means by proximity and locale (standard deviation in parentheses)

	Sales by Proximity			Sales by Locale		
	'Adjacent' Sales	'Near' Sales	'Far' Sales	LAX Sales	CBD Sales	Ports Sales
Observations	6342	11728	17696	12902	11464	11956
Sale Price	261	336	326	369	282	291
(000s of dollars)	(175)	(280)	(240)	(274)	(238)	(206)
Interior area	1297	1514	1486	1504	1432	1432
(sqft)	(607)	(762)	(707)	(697)	(755)	(677)
Baths	1.74	1.95	1.93	2.02	1.69	1.95
(number)	(0.76)	(0.94)	(0.92)	(0.95)	(0.87)	(0.84)
Bedrooms	2.43	2.70	2.68	2.70	2.55	2.67
(number)	(1.00)	(0.96)	(0.92)	(0.89)	(1.01)	(0.94)
Fireplace	0.24	0.34	0.36	0.32	0.42	0.28
(per cent)	(0.43)	(0.47)	(0.48)	(0.47)	(0.49)	(0.45)
Garage	0.42	0.53	0.57	0.55	0.50	0.54
(per cent)	(0.49)	(0.50)	(0.49)	(0.50)	(0.50)	(0.50)
Dwelling age	45.2	47.7	46.6	41.8	62.1	38.5
(years)	(29.4)	(27.6)	(25.3)	(23.7)	(27.6)	(23.2)
Renter occupied	0.12	0.10	0.10	0.10	0.11	0.10
(per cent)	(0.32)	(0.30)	(0.30)	(0.30)	(0.31)	(0.30)
Pool	0.02	0.04	0.05	0.04	0.04	0.06
(per cent)	(0.15)	(0.20)	(0.22)	(0.19)	(0.19)	(0.23)
View	0.02	0.06	0.05	0.03	0.09	0.03
(per cent)	(0.16)	(0.25)	(0.22)	(0.17)	(0.29)	(0.17)

prices or in aggregate sales volume. Aggregate price and sales volume are presented first. These models use discrete regions of proximity to potential targets to partition sales according to presumed exposure to risk. The results for the continuous models of risk – those that include linear distance to potential targets – are presented second.

The results of the aggregate price indexes are inconclusive. The indexes are shown in Figure 9.2. If consumer valuations of dwellings proximal to potential targets had indeed declined in response to their higher perceived risk, the aggregate index measuring prices in the adjacent regions should have shown a decline relative to the other two regions in the neighborhood of the potential targets. In fact it is the region furthest – ostensibly the region at least risk – that is the only one to show an absolute decline in the point estimates of price levels. Further conclusions cannot be drawn between the differences in the indexes because the 95 per cent confidence interval for each includes the other indexes.

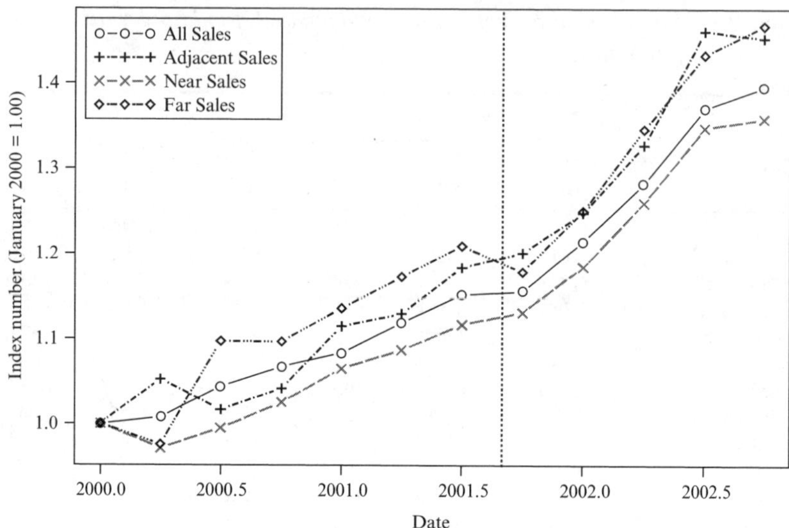

Figure 9.2 Aggregate house price indexes by proximity to potential targets

The same lack of any evidence of changes in housing markets resulting from the 9/11 attacks appears in Figure 9.3. It shows sales volume for the same three discrete regions within the neighborhood of the potential targets: 'adjacent', 'near', and 'far'. According to the results presented in the figure, there is no adverse market reaction to proximity. Quite the opposite: transaction volume in the areas adjacent to the three potential targets was relatively higher in the two-month period after the attack than in the two-month period preceding it. Transaction data are noisy and frequently reported with some lag – sale dates are the date of closing rather than the date of the agreement to sell. That said, there is no pronounced relative decline in the adjacent regions at any point in the sample period.

Both of the sets of results presented in Figures 9.2 and 9.3 are dependent on the delineation of what constitutes 'near'. Numerous radii were used, but none yielded evidence of systematic impact on housing markets as a result of the attack. Despite this robustness, it may be possible that using discrete regions and pooling sales across potential targets is masking marginal effects that vary across the sites.

To address this concern, the basic hedonic regression, equation (9.2), was modified to include a continuous measure of proximity. Also, housing sales around the three potential targets examined were not pooled. Testing for changes in the pricing of proximity is conducted by interacting the

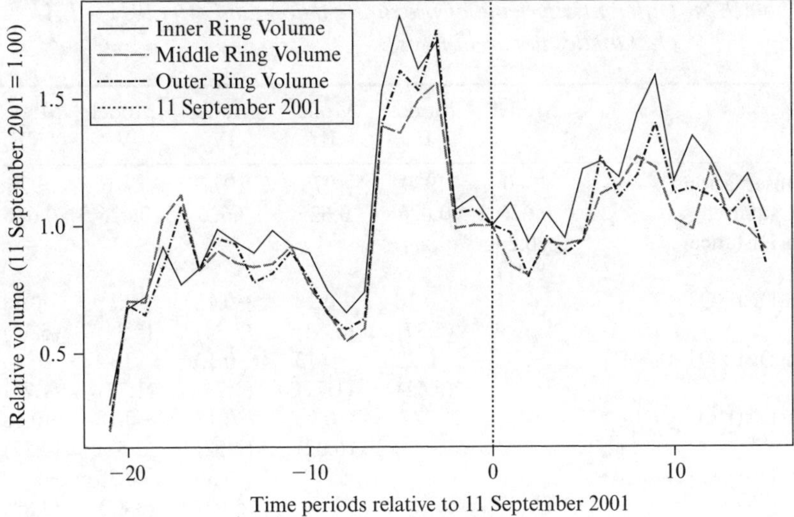

Figure 9.3 Aggregate house sales by proximity to potential targets

distance variable with several different specifications of time dummies. The base case is the simplest model: house price is a function of a dwelling's physical characteristics, its distance from the potential target and the price level during the quarter of sale.[4] The physical characteristics included in the regression include dwelling size (interior), number of baths, number of bedrooms, the age of the dwelling at time of sale (and its square), and a series of dummy variables indicating the presence of a fireplace, garage, central heating, central air conditioning, a pool, and whether or not it has a view and is occupied by the owner.[5]

Tables 9.2, 9.3 and 9.4 report the distance coefficients for regressions using dwelling sales from the neighborhoods of the Los Angeles International Airport, the central business district, and the ports of Los Angeles and Long Beach, respectively. For each submarket, the subsample of dwellings was selected from the cumulative discrete regions used in aggregate analysis above – using r-squared as the criteria for selection. That is, three regressions were executed for each of the potential targets. The first included only those dwellings from the 'adjacent' region, the second from the pooled 'adjacent' and 'near' regions, and the third included all sales from the three regions.

Each of the tables reports the base model (Model I) as well as five additional models. Each of the additional models allows more flexibility regarding the temporal variation in the price gradient around the targets.

Table 9.2 Differential pricing of proximity before and after 9/11 – LAX (t-statistics in parentheses)

	Model I	Model II	Model III	Model IV	Model V	Model VI
Observations	1980	1979	1978	1977	1976	1975
R-squared	0.626	0.626	0.625	0.626	0.626	0.626
ln(Distance)	−0.20	–	–	–	–	–
	(8.31)					
ln(Dist)*QTR7−	–	−0.18	−0.18	−0.18	−0.18	−0.18
		(5.37)	(5.33)	(5.34)	(5.34)	(5.34)
ln(Dist)*QTR8/8+	–	−0.22	−0.13	−0.13	−0.14	−0.14
		(6.52)	(1.72)	(1.73)	(1.73)	(1.74)
ln(Dist)*QTR9/9+	–	–	−0.26	−0.18	−0.18	−0.18
			(6.02)	(2.52)	(2.52)	(2.52)
ln(Dist)*QTR10/10+	–	–	–	−0.30	−0.38	−0.38
				(5.62)	(3.82)	(3.82)
ln(Dist)*QTR11/11+	–	–	–	–	−0.26	−0.21
					(4.27)	(2.48)
ln(Dist)*QTR12	–	–	–	–	–	−0.32
						(3.60)

Table 9.3 Differential pricing of proximity before and after 9/11 – CBD (t-statistics in parentheses)

	Model I	Model II	Model III	Model IV	Model V	Model VI
Observations	11 439	11 438	11 437	11 436	11 435	11 434
R-squared	0.589	0.589	0.589	0.589	0.589	0.589
ln(Distance)	−0.10	–	–	–	–	–
	(7.52)					
ln(Dist)*QTR7−	–	−0.12	−0.12	−0.12	−0.12	−0.12
		(6.24)	(6.22)	(6.22)	(6.21)	(6.21)
ln(Dist)*QTR8/8+	–	−0.08	−0.15	−0.15	−0.15	−0.15
		(4.70)	(3.08)	(3.08)	(3.08)	(3.08)
ln(Dist)*QTR9/9+	–	–	−0.07	−0.08	−0.08	−0.08
			(3.75)	(1.94)	(1.94)	(1.94)
ln(Dist)*QTR10/10+	–	–	–	−0.07	0.00	0.00
				(3.24)	(0.01)	(0.01)
ln(Dist)*QTR11/11+	–	–	–	–	−0.11	−0.10
					(3.99)	(2.65)
ln(Dist)*QTR12	–	–	–	–	–	−0.12
						(3.03)

Table 9.4 Differential pricing of proximity before and after 9/11 – ports (t-statistics in parentheses)

	Model I	Model II	Model III	Model IV	Model V	Model VI
Observations	11931	11930	11929	11928	11927	11926
R-squared	0.621	0.621	0.619	0.619	0.619	0.619
ln(Distance)	0.24	–	–	–	–	–
	(20.8)					
ln(Dist)*QTR7–	–	0.24	0.24	0.24	0.24	0.24
		(14.4)	(14.2)	(14.2)	(14.2)	(14.2)
ln(Dist)*QTR8/8+	–	0.25	0.18	0.18	0.18	0.18
		(15.9)	(4.67)	(4.67)	(4.67)	(4.67)
ln(Dist)*QTR9/9+	–	–	0.25	0.25	0.25	0.25
			(13.6)	(6.59)	(6.59)	(6.59)
ln(Dist)*QTR10/10+	–	–	–	0.25	0.22	0.22
				(12.0)	(6.11)	(6.11)
ln(Dist)*QTR11/11+	–	–	–	–	0.27	0.25
					(10.6)	(6.48)
ln(Dist)*QTR12	–	–	–	–	–	0.30
						(8.46)

A significant response on the part of home buyers to demand a discount in order to live near the potential targets would be reflected in the gradient becoming more positive. Note that the gradient can be either negative – if land closer to the site is in higher demand – or positive – if the opposite is true. In either case, a change in the perception of risk from terrorism and the resulting drop in relative demand near the site would have the effect of making either positive or negative gradients more positive.

Table 9.2 is typical of the three tables reporting the time and distance interactions. The table shows that very little additional explanatory power is gained by adding the interaction terms. Moreover there is no perceptible trend towards a more positive gradient. In the models with three or more interaction terms, the point estimate of the price gradient in the quarter following the attacks is greater. However the hypothesis that it is more negative cannot be rejected. Furthermore the greater the number of interaction terms, the more the trend appears to be towards a more negative gradient. This would imply the curious result that, in the wake of the attacks on 11 September 2001, consumers responded by bidding up dwellings closer to potential targets.

Table 9.3 repeats the same basic story as revealed in the previous table. The sample size is much larger for the CBD regressions, as the fit of the model was best using all three of the discrete surrounding regions. The explanatory power of the model is roughly equivalent as that using the LAX data. So too are the trends in the coefficients on the time–distance interactions. Once more, the immediate response in the quarter following the attacks appears to be that proximity is more valued, not less. Like the 'trends' in the LAX neighborhood, the absence of pattern is the most notable feature of this table.

Finally, Table 9.4 reports the interaction coefficients for the regressions using data from the environs of the ports of Los Angeles and Long Beach. As in the case of the CBD, the best statistical fit of the continuous model employed the full subsample comprised of all sales from the three discrete regions around the ports.

The notable difference in the ports regressions is that the price gradient is positive – implying that buyers already demanded a discount to be nearer the ports. However like the other potential targets, the immediate response of markets was to demand less of a discount – directly opposite of a collective move to avoid any perceived risk from living in the shadow of the ports.

Overall the regressions using distance as a continuous variable leave little impression that housing markets in the areas surrounding highly visible targets responded at all, let alone in a manner consistent with risk-averse individuals requiring compensation for bearing additional risk.

Of course there are a number of possible explanations for these collective results that are more in concert with the survey results reported in the introduction – that respondents felt they faced 10 per cent probability of personally being injured by a terrorist attack. They are all methodological. The most obvious is that the level of aggregation is too coarse. Indeed the distance variable that is so crucial to this analysis is measured not at the dwelling level, but at the Census block group level. This is possible, but with an average of approximately 158 different centroids for each of the three potential targets, there is ample variation to identify systematic trends in prices. In fact, if prices were to respond on the same scale as was enunciated in the survey, price trends in housing should be visible at a broader level of aggregation than the Census tract.

Alternatively, the wrong targets have been chosen to study. There are in fact over 100 sites in California considered at elevated risk of attack. Further research could address others on the list, but the three included in this list are consistently the most prominently discussed. (LAX was the intended target of a terrorist intercepted at the Canadian–American border.) Other potential targets might include Disneyland, or the other regional airports. That said, it is unlikely that the perceived risk is systematically higher at any other site. It is therefore difficult to believe that a stronger behavioral response can be found when none was found in the neighborhoods around LAX, the ports and the CBD.

An alternative hypothesis that could explain these findings is that individuals respond to surveys in a manner that is inconsistent with their actual behavior. While this is not directly tested, it is consistent with the results.

CONCLUSIONS AND EXTENSIONS

Since the attacks of 11 September 2001, the threat of terrorism has been viewed by the American public as sufficiently great to provide broad support for the invasion of two countries, to add an additional Cabinet post and create the Department of Homeland Security, and even cause the reorganization of the intelligence communities at the highest levels of government. In the private sector, commercial real estate markets have been hit with doubling of terrorism insurance premiums – where it remains available at all. Voters felt terrorism was a major issue in the presidential elections. The question addressed in this research is, do individuals act the same way when they buy houses as they do when they answer surveys?

The results presented in this chapter suggest that they do not. In fact, the results are consistent with the hypothesis that homebuyers' perception of risk is unchanged in the wake of the attacks of 9/11. No significant change was measured in prices or sales volume in neighborhoods of prominent potential targets of terrorist attack.

There is striking evidence of the ability of markets to price small probability risks – the type of soil, and its underlying performance during earthquakes, is shown to be priced in one study. This example of markets 'discovering' pricing indicates that the lack of any significant response is not likely the result of market participants being ignorant of the effect of even small changes in the likelihood of damage from terrorism. It is more likely that consumers simply do not believe that a second attack of the scale of the attacks on New York and Washington, DC will occur.

The apparent conflict between the survey discussed above, the inordinate media coverage of terrorism, and the absence of any manifest pricing of additional risk is best viewed as reason to use market-based transaction data. This capitalization of expectations represents an advantage over polls or surveys in ascertaining consumer beliefs, because transactions are costly whereas survey responses are not.

NOTES

1. Glaeser and Shapiro (2002) argue, however, that there is little evidence that armed conflict has ever undone the rationale for urbanization. Rossi-Hansberg (2004) and Harrigan and Martin (2002) suggest that terrorism will have only a mild effect on urban form.

2. 'Increase' should not be confused with 'steepen'. Because the pre-9/11 gradients can be either positive or negative, changes in supply and/or demand that penalize sites closer to the target will result in increasing gradients: negative gradients becoming less negative – or even positive – and positive gradients becoming more positive.
3. The underlying utility function of a representative consumer is simplified here. A risk-seeking individual may be willing to pay more for the opportunity to experience a wider range of outcomes and the signs on the partial derivatives in equation 9.6 would be reversed. It is also possible that an individual whose income is positively correlated with terrorism risk could find dwellings near target maximizing in a portfolio sense. While both are possible, the kind of aggregate effects we are examining are not likely to be influenced by these exceptions.
4. It should be noted in the results presented here, distance is not to the dwelling itself but rather to the centroid of the census block group in which the dwelling is located. This loses some of the individual variation in distance, but there remains substantial locational variation across block groups. Moreover, in trial tests using dwelling specific distances, there was no disagreement with the results presented in this chapter.
5. The coefficients on these variables are not included due to space constraints. They are available from the author. They behave as expected with view and pool as the most valuable of the indicator variables; interior size is highly valued; and age diminishes house price, but at a declining rate. All but the heating/cooling variables are consistently significant.

BIBLIOGRAPHY

Abadie, Alberto and Javier Gardeazabal (2003), 'The economic costs of conflict: a case study of the Basque Country', *American Economic Review*, **93** (1), 113–32.

Anderson, Dan R. and Maurice Weinrobe (1986), 'Mortgage default risks and the 1971 San Fernando earthquake', *American Real Estate and Urban Economics Association Journal*, **14** (1), 110–35.

Bleich, Donald (2003), 'The reaction of multifamily capitalization rates to natural disasters', *Journal of Real Estate Research*, **25** (2), 133–44.

Carroll, Thomas M., Terrence M. Clauretie, Jeff Jensen and Margaret Waddoups (1996), 'The economic impact of a transient hazard on property values: the 1988 Pepcon explosion in Henderson, Nevada', *Journal of Real Estate Finance and Economics*, **13** (2).

Enders, Walter, Todd Sandler and Gerald F. Parise (1992), 'An econometric analysis of the impact of terrorism on tourism', *Kyklos*, **45** (4), 531–54.

Glaeser, Edward L. and Jesse M. Shapiro (2002), 'Cities and warfare: the impact of terrorism on urban form', *Journal of Urban Economics*, **51** (2), 205–24.

Greenberg, M. and J. Hughes (1992), 'The impact of hazardous waste superfund sites on the value of houses sold in New Jersey', *Annals of Regional Science*, **26** (2), 147–53.

Harrigan, James and Philippe Martin (2002), 'Terrorism and the resilience of cities', *Federal Reserve Bank of New York Economic Policy Review*, **8** (2), 97–116.

Johnson, James H. and John D. Kasarda (2003), '9/11 and the economic prospects of major US cities', *Planning and Markets*, **6** (1).

Kahn, Matthew E. (2000), 'Smog reductions impact on California county growth', *Journal of Regional Science*, **40** (3), 565–82.

Klein, Lawrence R. and Suleyman Ozmucur (2002), 'Consumer behavior under the influence of terrorism within the United States', *Journal of Entrepreneurial Finance and Business Ventures*, **7** (3), 1–15.

Lerner, J.S., R.M. Gonzalez, D.A. Small and B. Fischhoff (2003), 'Effects of fear and anger on perceived risks of terrorism: a national field experiment', *Psychological Science*, **14** (2), 144–50.

Mills, Edwin S. (2002), 'Terrorism and US real estate', *Journal of Urban Economics*, **51** (2), 198–204.

Murdoch, James C., Harinder Singh and Mark Thayer (1993), 'The impact of natural hazards on housing values: the Loma Prieta earthquake', *American Real Estate and Urban Economics Association Journal*, **21** (2), 167–84.

Pizam, Abraham and Ginger Smith (2000), 'Tourism and terrorism: a quantitative analysis of major terrorist acts and their impact on tourism destinations', *Tourism Economics*, **6** (2), 123–38.

Rossi-Hansberg, Esteban (2004), 'Cities under stress', unpublished manuscript, February.

Sloboda, Brian W. (2003), 'Assessing the effects of terrorism on tourism by use of time series methods', *Tourism Economics*, **9** (2), 179–90.

Wildasin, David E. (2002), 'Local public finance in the aftermath of September 11', *Journal of Urban Economics*, **51** (2), 225–37.

Wilhelmsson, Mats (2000), 'The impact of traffic noise on the values of single-family houses', *Journal of Environmental Planning and Management*, **43** (6), 799–815.

10. Designing benefit–cost analyses for homeland security policies

V. Kerry Smith and Daniel G. Hallstrom*

INTRODUCTION

The purpose of this chapter is to outline the methodological and empirical issues associated with developing benefit–cost analyses for homeland security policies. The 9/11 attack on the United States transformed domestic and international perceptions of the ability of the public sector in developed economies to provide a secure environment for daily living. Security at this very general level affects nearly every aspect of life, including of course those individual behaviors that influence market outcomes. When one includes the scope of the impact on non-market behaviors that are motivated by fear and anxiety, it is difficult to imagine how current policy initiatives can restore earlier perceptions about our security.[1] For practical purposes, the change in the background environment for all private and public choices is probably best treated as irreversible. As a result, we argue that the task of measuring the net benefits provided by homeland security policies should not be treated as an effort to restore a pre-9/11 baseline.

Homeland security policy can reduce risk and/or reduce consequences from terrorist activities. Because there is no single physical measure that allows the diverse possible terrorist events to be reduced to a single loss metric, the task of specifying the connection between policies and risk reductions is likely to be complex.[2] Equally important, risk reduction can arise through public protection, self-protection or some combination of these two activities. The value of a public initiative to an individual depends on what is at risk; the ability to insure against bad outcomes; the ability to mitigate the risk on one's own (that is, the level of self-protection and prospects for self-insurance); and the potential for adaptation to the consequences of a bad outcome.

The current information base on the results of homeland security policies for these types of outcomes is inadequate. As a result, we suggest using people's responses to risk-related information about large-scale natural hazards as a gauge of how they might respond to changes in some dimensions of the risks to homeland security. This opportunity seems especially relevant for activities that affect an individual's living environment.[3]

The next section summarizes the rationale for using an efficiency criterion for security policy and discusses the particular complexities in defining it. After that we summarize the basic ideas underlying revealed and stated preference methods for measuring the economic value of policies that reduce risk or enhance other goods and services available outside markets. We then describe how the lessons from benefit transfer relate to adapting information on the trade-offs people are willing to make to reduce risk, to use them in evaluating homeland security policies. Our analysis then summarizes how studies of natural hazards may help to provide information that could be used to measure the value of avoiding large-scale disruptions to conditions of daily living. It summarizes the results for a more detailed set of research reported in Hallstrom and Smith (2005) using home sales that bracket Hurricane Andrew in Lee County, Florida to estimate how new information about the risk of severe storms is capitalized in housing prices for areas recognized to have potential for damage. In the case of Andrew, the hurricane missed Lee County. Thus residents of flood hazard areas with significant risk of damage from future storms received new information about the severity of these storms, but no actual damage.[4] The last section of the chapter will discuss implications of the example and next steps in developing the capacity to perform benefit analyses for homeland security policies.

BENEFIT–COST ANALYSIS FOR HOMELAND SECURITY POLICIES

Background

Benefit–cost analysis is usually described as a practical basis for judging whether a change in a benchmark resource allocation offers a potential Pareto improvement. A Pareto improving change would allow, in principle, for those gaining to compensate the losers and retain some positive increment as a result of the change in how resources are used. The framework takes as given the conditions defining the baseline resource allocation, including assignments of property rights to those resources. Moreover it does not claim that the evaluation of net gains would be invariant to these initial conditions (see Bradford, 1970, and Smith, 2004a).

To discuss some of the complexities associated with the definition of benefit concepts for security related policy, we adapt a framework introduced by Ehrlich and Becker (1972) to describe how self-protection and self-insurance might be represented in a model of individual decision-making under uncertainty. Lakdawalla and Zanjani (2004) have recently adapted it as an economic analysis of terrorism. Our description extends theirs so it is compatible with the empirical example discussed below.[5] A homeowner's expected utility, V, given opportunities to select a location, undertake some actions that involve self-protection (for example reduce risks of an event that causes harm) and insure (with a given information set) is represented in equation (10.1):

$$V = \pi\,(p\,(r, I), s) \cdot U_H\,(r, h, m - s - R\,(r, h, i_0, p\,(r, I)) - L\,(r, h, i_0,)) \\ + [1 - \pi\,(p\,(r, I), s)] \cdot U_{NH}(r, h, m - s - R\,(r, h, i_0, p\,(r, I))) \quad (10.1)$$

where:

$m =$ income (or wealth) less any hazard insurance
$h =$ housing characteristics
$r =$ site attributes for home that can relate to hazard attributes, amenities and local public good
$s =$ expenditures on self-protection
$R\,(\cdot) =$ hedonic price function (measured as an annual rent if m is annual income)
$i_0 =$ insurance rate per dollar of coverage
$p\,(r, I) =$ household's subjective probability of hazard at a given location and information set, I (factors that could be observed in a market)
$\pi\,(p, s) =$ household subjective probability of hazard with self-protection (s) $\pi(p, 0) = p$; if locational attributes are average substitutes for self-protection expenditures $\pi\,(p, s) = p\,(r, I) - g\,(s)$
$L\,(\cdot) =$ monetary loss due to hazard net of insurance coverage
$U_j\,(\cdot) =$ utility in state j ($H =$ harmful event, $NH =$ no harmful event).

Within this setting we can define a number of policy alternatives based on how they affect the parameters influencing this representation of individual well-being as captured with the expected utility.

Protection Policies

This structure allows distinctions in *ex ante* protection that is privately undertaken as well as protection that arises through public activities. Private protection increases the value of s, which we assume reduces the probability of the harmful event $\partial\pi/\partial s < 0$. Public protection affects more than one individual simultaneously. Policies that provide such increments are comparable to local public goods. If s is assumed to be due to public actions, we might hypothesize that individuals do not recognize they will ultimately have to pay for it. Alternatively, we could include a budget-balancing condition where an individual's perceived share of the cost of public activities is removed from the income argument in the U_H and U_{NH}.

Private protection would lead to reduced income and presumably would reduce the risk experienced by the individual undertaking it. Examples of these activities are avoiding public places thought to be threatening, and developing independent water sources (to protect from contamination of public supplies). Some forms of private (and public) protection create negative externalities. Assuming those engaged in terrorist activity allocate resources to achieve objectives efficiently, they will reallocate efforts away from more secure targets to less secure. Thus if public protection is done at the state level, then improvements in security in some states will increase the risks for others who live in less secure areas. At the individual level, when high-profile citizens who might be targets (for example politicians, significant public features or even entertainers) undertake averting behaviors that make them difficult targets, this process may increase the risks for others in this category who do not undertake the averting behavior. For ordinary citizens these external negative effects are hard to envisage, but they could entail other types of externalities (for example removing trees around a home to assure unobstructed views for protection reduces the neighborhood amenities provided by the trees).[6]

For analytical purposes three attributes of the protection policies are important: (1) they are assumed to affect probabilities of the harmful event and thus are *ex ante* (before an outcome); (2) they may influence other people positively or negatively (depending on whether they are public and whether they have external effects); and (3) they may or may not be 'visible' to external observers (including terrorists). If they are visible, then terrorists are likely to take them into account, and so might markets in judging the safety of a location (our specification in equation (10.1) assumes they are not noticeable or not relevant to the price of a location). All of these actions can also be included as forms of *ex ante* mitigation.

Insurance Policies

Equation (10.1) includes the effects of insurance in three ways – through the price term, i_0, implicitly through the loss net of insurance coverage (L) and similarly through income net of insurance premiums (m). Homeland security policy can take the form of subsidies to private insurance (or even establishing public insurance markets where private markets do not exist).[7] Lakdawalla and Zanjani (2004) discuss the interactions between insurance subsidies and self-protection, concluding it is reasonable to expect (given moral hazard together with the assumption that insurance and self-protection can be treated as substitutes) that subsidized insurance reduces self-protection. We take the insurance framework as a given in our benchmark.

Other Types of Policy

Public protection and insurance are not the only types of policy options. Equation (10.1) specifically identifies information as something that influences subjective risk perceptions. Public warning systems (or programs to describe private protection options independent of a specific threat) can be modeled as changing the information regime. As several authors have noted, these approaches must take account of the important and separate influence of the media in influencing the perceived value of any public information program.[8] Woo (2002) for example notes that Margaret Thatcher specifically identified the important role of the media as an 'oxygen of publicity' for terrorists. Thus models must consider the role of information for the receptors of terrorist actions as well as for the terrorists to evaluate its overall effectiveness.

Defining the Option Price for a Differentiated Policy

For our purposes it is important to recognize that pre-existing insurance markets will affect benefit measures developed for policies primarily directed at protection. We can see the logic underlying this conclusion by simply subtracting a term, OP, from m in both U_H and U_{NH} and adjusting the other arguments to reflect the dimensions we wish to use in characterizing a specific policy (for example public expenditures for protection, σ; subsidies to insurance rates, τ; an information program providing warnings, ΔI; m^* to reflect new net income, and so on) as in equation (10.2). OP is implicitly defined as the value that would assure, given a specific policy, that the resulting expected utility is exactly equal to the expected utility attained under the baseline condition (for example without the policy; this is designated here as V^0).

$$\begin{aligned}\pi\,(p(r, I+\Delta I), s+\sigma)\cdot U_H\,(r, h, m^* - s - R\,(r, h, i_0, -\tau, p\,(r, I+\Delta I))\\ - L\,(r, h, i_0) + \Delta \mathrm{L} - OP) + (1-\pi\,(p\,(r, I+\Delta I), s+\sigma))\cdot\\ U_{NH}(r, h, m^* - s - R\,(r, h, i_0, -\tau, p\,(r, I+\Delta I)) - OP) = V^0 \qquad (10.2)\end{aligned}$$

As a result, OP is a function of all the parameters describing the policy as well as the baseline condition.[9]

Three implications follow from this simplified description of how homeland policies might be included within a model of individual choice.

First, the evaluation of a policy must recognize the baseline conditions defining the choice being considered, as well as all the opportunities available for individual adjustment independent of the policy. Second, security-related outcomes are the result of both public action and the composite of all private actions. Our focus has been on one individual. To the extent that there are positive or negative effects of one agent on others, the nature of the information available about others' actions in response to that action and the concept of the equilibrium (such as the Nash equilibrium) needs to be considered to evaluate the overall effect of the policy.[10] These judgements will influence how we define the benefit measure as well. Finally, the externalities generated by public and private actions implicitly assume a model of terrorist behavior, and with it terrorists' responses to new policies.

All of these complexities make the task of policy evaluation seem hopeless. It is not. There are different, but equally daunting, issues that are present with the evaluation of any large, complex policy. We raise them here simply to establish background for our discussion of strategies for measuring how homeland security policies could affect behavior and to motivate our arguments for using 'parallel outcomes' to measure incremental benefits for specific aspects of a policy (for example a risk reduction).

INFORMATION AND METHODS OF EVALUATION

Homeland security policies share the evaluation challenge faced by any policy that impacts non-market services. That is, the outcomes relate to goods and services available outside markets. There is no routine basis for observing how people would acquire them in the absence of public provision. Moreover the institutions overseeing these activities usually do not collect information that can be used to understand how the policy affects people's choices. By contrast, for goods provided on markets the process of exchange itself provides information.

The primary focus of this section is on describing methods for measuring the economic benefits associated with policies that provide increments to non-market goods or lead to risk reductions for events that would reduce well-being. All measures for the economic value of a change in 'something' are derived from trade-offs that an individual's choices imply. Thus if a person purchases a home, the analyst knows that everything conveyed to the individual (for example the attributes of the structure, the associated land and the characteristics associated with its location) was worth at least as much as the purchase price. Otherwise the individual would not have agreed to the purchase. All of these features could be worth much more.

The single choice does not answer this issue. It reveals only a lower bound on what a person would pay.

Similarly, when a person is offered a house and chooses not to purchase it, the analyst knows all the characteristics of that house are not worth the price. In this case, price is an upper bound. Several conditions are important to how these choices are interpreted: the definition of the object of choice; the specification of the circumstances of choice; and the assumed decision-making unit.[11] All three are relevant to revealed and stated preference methods. In the first class of techniques (that is, revealed preference methods), the analyst has available (or collects information) about choices that have taken place. The challenge is to provide answers to these three sets of issues. These answers reconstruct the implicit decision process that led to the choice. In contrast, using stated preference methods the analyst is designing a potential hypothetical choice, and the challenge is to replicate as closely as possible the real-world choice.

Revealed Preference Methods

Most applications of revealed preference (RP) methods to estimate the demand for or economic value of (changes in) a non-market good assume that each person alters the amount consumed through the choices made for some other observable private good that has an identifiable (explicit or implicit) price. Using this logic requires an analyst to specify how the private good conveys different amounts of the non-market good to each person. Some examples may help to make the logic more tangible.

Hedonic models

Hedonic models rely on the existence of a set of differentiated objects of choice with identifiable attributes and prices – houses, jobs, automobiles and so forth. People are often assumed to buy one type of the good in the time frame hypothesized to capture the important elements in people's choices. The model assumes that knowledge of the alternatives and access to a wide array of types will lead to an equilibrium schedule of prices, where buyers and sellers would have no incentive to change their decisions. This schedule can be represented with a function that describes how the prices of the types relate to each alternative's attributes.[12] In the case of housing prices, this formulation implies that the house's price should differ by the important (to people) features of the location. Moreover the marginal price 'reveals' the incremental value to buyers (and sellers) of a small change in each attribute. It does not isolate (or allow the identification of) the schedule of marginal values.[13]

Demand models

In environmental applications, the most common application in this area is a recreation demand model for trips to one or more recreation sites (for example parks, lakes, beaches).[14] Recovering a measure of the demand for one or more aspects of a good's quality attributes (or values of changes in one of them) requires additional assumptions about how that quality feature contributes to individual well-being. These preference restrictions limit the way the attribute is hypothesized to affect each individual. These assumptions, in turn, generally allow a change in that attribute to be described as equivalent to a price change.

In the context of homeland security policy, suppose the policy reduces the risk of terrorist events at amusement parks or large sporting events (for example football games). A weak complementarity restriction would require that this risk reduction would only be valued if a person went to the parks or the games.

Other strategies that may well be closely related to homeland security could entail demands for averting goods. Private households might for example stockpile food and water as a precaution against terrorist contamination of typical sources. Changes in these demands with varying levels of threats would, under another set of assumptions (for example perfect substitution of a food stockpile with a reduction in the probability of harm due to contamination, see Smith, 1991), provide the information required to estimate the economic value of the threat reduction.

The distinction between demand and hedonic models arises from the information provided by the related good. In the hedonic case analysts are usually assuming the home location (or the job) is the only source of the attribute relevant to the person. By contrast, the demand relationship can only reveal whether an attribute is important to a person's choices. Demand and/or valuation (even marginal values) measures require the added restrictions on preferences.

Random utility models

The hedonic model can be considered as a strategy to avoid the conceptual issues raised by corner solutions. That is, when an individual selects one type of good from a diverse array of goods (in the housing case, one type of house and not any of the other alternatives available), that decision implies he or she has zero consumption of all other types. Conventional analysis underlying the demand functions just discussed assumes people select mixes of goods that imply positive levels of consumption for all goods. With more resolution in the types of goods available and efforts to model their demands, this maintained assumption is less likely to hold. Random utility models (that is, economic descriptions for a choice of one item from a set of k alternatives) were specified to respond to these conditions (McFadden, 1974). These models describe the possibility that a choice would be made, assuming it is motivated by preference functions with observable (indirect utility functions conditional on the specific choice) and unobservable (random) components. It is important to acknowledge that these models require significant assumptions for consistent welfare measures.[15]

Natural experiments

A natural experiment exploits an event outside the individual decision maker's control to provide a 'transparent exogenous source of variation' in the explanatory variable of interest. Repeat sales analyses are examples of this approach for housing markets. These studies examine price changes for the same set of homes before and after an event that is assumed to provide the variation in the relevant explanatory variables. One of the most common examples involves risk and information. This strategy is especially important to homeland security, where most policy alternatives seem likely to have important information and risk-reduction attributes.

Stated Preference Methods

All stated preference (SP) methods request hypothetical decisions from individuals. They vary in how the information is presented and what type of response is requested. To recover measures for economic trade-offs, the attributes of what is presented must be varied (either for a single individual or across different people).

Contingent valuation

Contingent valuation[16] (CV) questions generally ask for choices. They require the collection of primary data. This process necessarily requires selection of a population to be sampled, a method for sampling and a method for interviewing (see Champ et al., 2003 for a detailed discussion of these issues). The object of choice is a change in something from a well-defined baseline condition to a new level. Most CV surveys describe how the change would take place. The goal of the description is to convince those interviewed that it will work. However it is important to acknowledge that the choice they are making is about the plan described as the means to assure the change (see Smith, 1997). In addition, the question must specify the resources each respondent will be required to give up; it must describe how a decision is made; and how the resources will be collected.[17] For example in a discrete response (yes/no) question a price or cost to the individual is stated and the individual is asked what she would do. In most cases, the object of choice is sufficiently different from a private good that a purchase decision is not feasible. As a result, the statement is often a vote. This specified decision process must be accompanied with a description of how everyone else's statements will affect provision. Usually labeled the provision point, this aspect of the question describes how decisions are made and what happens to any excess of the sum of the resources collected over total costs (if there is uncertainty associated with cost). Variation in the stated cost across individuals allows analysts to use stated choices for different costs, together with an assumption that the decisions follow conventional economic models – akin to equations (1) and (2) – to estimate respondents' willingness to pay.

Three lessons emerge from this research. First, questions must be designed and evaluated to assure respondents understand them and that they appear consequential. Potentially as important, respondents need to be convinced that they would ultimately pay the amount proposed. Finally, the results will be affected by the models and estimators used to represent the decisions, so the estimates need to be interpreted as reflecting both types of information.

At first this method might seem the most viable for homeland security policies. However describing the object of choice provided by these policies and convincing respondents that their answers would be consequential seem especially important constraints. The experience to date in describing choices involving low-probability events has not been as successful with other non-market goods. Many of the issues identified in the risk-assessment literature concerning people's subjective probabilities for unfamiliar, dreaded and involuntary outcomes are certainly relevant.

Conjoint surveys

The primary difference between conjoint and contingent valuation methods is that a change in some object of choice is assumed to be capable of being decomposed into changes in a set of attributes. This assumption allows a variety of different types of questions – choice of one among several alternatives, ranking of a set of alternatives, adjustment in one attribute to define equivalent options and scoring of alternatives using Likert scales. Not all of these alternatives are directly compatible with an economic model that allows measurement of economic values.

Designing the variation in combinations of values of each attribute across individuals as well as the variations elicited from a single respondent is also another source of complexity that increases with the number of attributes and the extent of variation in each one (see Louviere et al., 2000 and Kanninen, 2002).

Several overall observations can be made about conjoint methods. They have been popular for applied research because they collect more information from each respondent. To accomplish this task and use the results, they largely assume responses are independent across the questions asked.[18] As with contingent valuation, they rely on a formal model of the decision-making process to interpret the responses. Finally, to develop valuation measures there must be a well-defined baseline for the situation where respondents do not select any of the alternatives presented.

Joint estimation of RP and SP models

Revealed and stated preference information can describe choices motivated by changes in the same non-market good. Cameron (1992a) first proposed joint estimation.[19] That is, it is possible to collect information from a common set of individuals about both the actual use of goods linked to non-market resources and the hypothesized choices they would make if changes were made in the resource. Both sources of information are used to estimate individual preferences. It requires a consistent description of the relationship between what is observed and the model describing individual behavior. As a rule, it assumes actual and hypothetical behavior stem from the same behavioral process.[20] Cameron (1992b) has suggested that joint estimation serves to impose a 'budget discipline' on the stated preference responses. In principle, it is also possible to extend this logic to combine RP and SP data for different individuals, following the logic of matching (see Heckman and Navarro-Lozana, 2004), and use the cross-model restrictions to link the responses.[21] These strategies are most effective where the object of choice has well-defined attributes and the analysts can be confident as to how to introduce them into a behavioral model. The reason is direct. The analysis relies on a priori restrictions to link the models.

Impact Analysis

Impact analyses have no direct role when the objective is an evaluation of policy alternatives based on efficiency criteria. These assessments consider what their name implies – the reallocation in resources that would be associated with an exogenous change in demands for a specific set of goods and services. Many of these types of analyses rely on a description of the input requirements per unit of output (for example an input–output matrix). These changes in demand are then translated into their implications for the other goods and services required to meet the specified demands.

Comparisons of impact multipliers have also been used to identify the potential for bottlenecks in meeting increased production. One significant issue with this strategy stems from the model itself. The input requirement coefficients are treated as constants, which implies the model does not allow for substitution. For very short-run assessments, the results are more likely to be relevant than for those where adaptation and adjustment is possible.

Other approaches for evaluating impacts involve using market models. These approaches are usually more aggregate than the preferred scope for impact analysis. They tend to focus on price and output effects rather than a detailed accounting of input responses. The two most commonly used are equilibrium displacement and computable general equilibrium models. The equilibrium displacement model for one or more industries is a set of comparative static equations describing responses to exogenous shocks (see Alston et al., 1995). These equations are usually expressed in terms of elasticities and expenditure and cost shares. Exogenous shifts – expressed as proportional changes in price or quantity – are specified and the model solved to describe a consistent overall response.

Computable general equilibrium models can be used in a similar format. However they include important distinctions. First, these models usually describe the full structure of preferences (and production). The preference function along with constraints to choice define the commodity demands and supplies. They also define factor supplies and the link to income. As a result, expenditures must balance with payments. Second, the models are comprehensive, representing a complete (often aggregated) description of goods and services. They tend to rely on competitive market conditions and generally use one single preference function to describe all households and one production relationship per sector for all firms in that sector.

Neither approach includes spatial detail (except as it might be linked to a reason for a demand or supply difference in the first case or a price wedge in the second). Equilibrium and smooth adjustment (or simple departures from these conditions) are important simplifying assumptions. Finally, all of these approaches require complete information on all the parameters to calibrate the models. This requirement has been a direct limitation on their ability to reflect non-market effects.

GETTING STARTED – HOMELAND SECURITY AND BENEFIT TRANSFER

Most uses of benefit–cost analysis involve some adaptation of existing economic measures of the benefits provided by market and non-market goods. The process of adapting estimates of the willingness to pay for changes in non-market goods and services (or risk) to meet the needs of specific policy analyses is often labeled 'benefit transfer'.

Benefit Transfer

Navrud [2004] describes two main approaches to benefit transfer.

1. Unit value transfer:
   - simple;
   - adjusting for income.
2. Function transfer:
   - benefit function from an individual study;
   - meta analysis of benefits across studies.

The simple approach treats a consumer surplus per unit of a change in the object of choice as if it is a constant. We can acknowledge in advance this is wrong – but information is often so limited that there have been few alternatives.[22]

Adjustments for income differences are sometimes undertaken because the unit benefit measure is recognized to be constrained by income. The typical strategy is simple (and not necessarily consistent with the theory underlying the definition of the benefit measures). It is represented in equation (10.3):

$$\hat{\beta}_P = \hat{\beta}_S \cdot \left(\frac{m_P}{m_s}\right)^{\eta} \tag{10.3}$$

where $\hat{\beta}_j$ = unit benefit measure in either the study ($j = S$) or the policy ($j = P$) application

m_j = average household income in either study ($j = S$) or the policy ($j = P$) application

η = income elasticity of willingness to pay for the environmental service yielding the unit benefit.[23]

A function transfer uses a multivariate functional relationship taken from an original study that can be used to describe how unit benefits change with characteristics of the individuals (or households) involved. This approach is distinguished from what he labels a meta-analysis in that the latter uses a function to describe estimates from multiple studies. Meta-analyses often include the features of the resources and the assumptions made in each study as potential determinants of estimates. It is important to acknowledge that methods are approximations and do not meet conditions to be consistent with the definition of the underlying benefit concepts.[24]

Navrud's suggestions for future areas where research could improve matters highlights the need for consistency in the object of choice between the studies available and the policies to be evaluated. He also notes the composite nature of most policies and the need to separate components consistently.[25] This objective seems especially relevant for homeland security policy.

Natural Hazards as Parallel Events

While some authors (notably Lakdawalla and Zanjani, 2004) have questioned the parallel between terrorist events and natural hazards, we believe these events offer the potential to connect the record of *ex ante* policies (for example information, insurance) and *ex post* public responses to the behavior of economic agents. Moreover our outline for the implicit definition of the option price as a benefit measure in equation (10.2) is compatible with using changes in property values as signals for these incremental values.

Natural disasters and 'near-miss natural disasters' provide an analogy, at least in the scale of destruction associated with large-scale terrorist attacks on infrastructure. These events may also serve to parallel the type of risk information on which decisions must be made. Nine of the world's ten largest catastrophes ranked by insured loss are natural disasters. As we noted, the largest is the terrorist attacks on 9/11. Robert Hartwig, senior vice-president and chief economist of the Insurance Information Institute, used this characterization in comparing the impacts of Hurricane Andrew and 9/11:

> Hurricane Andrew, until September 11, 2001, was the global insurance industry's event of record. For nearly a decade it was the disaster against which all other disasters worldwide were compared. Andrew struck Florida in August 1992 with 140 mile-per-hour winds and produced insured losses of $15.5 billion – about $20 billion in current (2001) dollars . . . Andrew's reign as the most expensive insurance disaster in history ended, of course, with the terrorist attack of September 11, 2001. (Hartwig, 2002, pp.1–2)

At a minimum the destruction of the World Trade Center cost more than three times Hurricane Andrew. The enormity of the losses on 9/11 has tended to overshadow the threat of natural disasters. However catastrophe models predict that if an earthquake or mega hurricane hit a major city it would produce as much or more damage (Insurance Information Institute, 2004). The next section illustrates the parallel hazard strategy for the case of Hurricane Andrew in Florida. This event is routinely cited as a parallel to 9/11.

ILLUSTRATING THE USE OF NATURAL HAZARDS AS NATURAL EXPERIMENTS – HURRICANE ANDREW IN FLORIDA

Natural hazards offer an opportunity to study the economic responses to a catastrophic risk. They have at least two types of effects on property values.

First, properties may lose value because of physical damage to their structural attributes. Beyond the property owners themselves, damages of this type are of special interest to insurance companies as they represent potential insurance claims. Second, there is a pure information effect. This effect is the loss in value due to an increase in the subjective risk of the future coastal hazards at the home's location. Information can reduce asset values even when there is no physical damage in situations where there is a permanent shift in demand away from a given location. Much of the economics literature on hazard mitigation assumes that property owners will incorporate the risk of a hazard into their decision processes, without explicitly testing this assumption (see Cordes and Yezer, 1998 for coastal analyses).

Hurricane Andrew offers a unique opportunity to study these types of effects of risk on asset values. This hurricane hit the Bahamas and south Dade County on 23–24 August 1992, and then moved across the Gulf of Mexico to strike Louisiana. Originally classified as a Class 4 storm, based on continuing study of the record Andrew has recently been upgraded to a Class 5. Peak wind gusts of almost 200 miles per hour destroyed entire communities. Total damages from Andrew were estimated at $20 billion, insurance claims $15.5 billion, with 25 000 homes destroyed, another 100 000 damaged and approximately 14 per cent of Dade County's economy was affected. All of the Homestead Air Force Base was destroyed.

Properties located near the eye of a Class 3 or higher hurricane will suffer structural damages. As we suggest, indirect effects on property values arise for properties that are not physically damaged when equilibrium housing prices respond to the new information on hurricane risk. In other words, if residents of a coastal community use hurricane events to learn and update their risk perceptions about the extent of risks of damage from coastal storms in specific locations, then there may be a shift in demand away from what are perceived to be high-risk areas to safer locations in relative terms. This prospect is especially relevant to situations when there has been a recent history of few storms.[26]

We propose measuring the information treatment by selecting locations that are generally at risk, but not directly affected by a severe storm. This argument maintains that individuals suffering a 'near miss' serve to identify a group who should have heightened awareness of the full effects of hurricanes. They may not, depending on past history in relation to their location choices, have accurate perceptions of the probabilities of storms. Under these circumstances, a storm that is 'noticed' but that does not directly affect them provides information.

Our evaluation of homeowners' responses to Andrew uses a composite of information for Lee County, Florida. This Gulf Coast county was narrowly missed by the hurricane. Such a 'near miss' situation serves two roles. First, it provides a means to evaluate the potential to isolate a pure information effect of the storm.

Second, Lee County results may well be of independent interest precisely because they illustrate information effects through a 'near miss'. This situation is similar to a failed terrorist attack. Woo (2002) notes that the task of characterizing the tail of a terrorism loss distribution is assisted by using events that narrowly fail to be significant disasters. The same reasoning holds true for studying behavioral responses. That is, it seems reasonable to suggest that the *ex ante* response to information about a hazard that could have taken place (except for the 'near miss') provides an approximate lower bound measure for the incremental value of avoiding the event.

Our data include records of all residential home sales (including repeat sales) in Lee County between 1983 and 2000 purchased from a commercial vendor (First American Real Estate Solutions). These data include detailed information on the characteristics of properties at the time of sale, the date of each sale (year, month and day), the sales price, the latitude and longitude coordinates and a variety of other variables describing the properties.[27] The housing sales data for our analysis were cleaned to remove several types of transactions, including: properties that sold for less than $100; properties that were bought and sold within a period of several months and had a price difference exceeding $500 000; and properties where the first sale was for land only and the second sale included land and a structure. Finally, the National Flood Insurance Program includes special provisions for properties built before 1974, making them eligible for subsidized insurance. In addition, substantial changes in the insurance rates along with notification requirements to reveal property locations on FEMA maps in the Coastal Barrier Resource Act of 1982 introduced likely changes in construction patterns and housing characteristics in the interval 1974 to 1982. As a result, we limited our attention to properties built after 1982.

The precise identification of location for each property allowed each to be merged with a geo-coded record of what would be known to potential homebuyers about the flood and hazard risks for each county (the Federal Emergency Management Agency's G3 flood map). Information about the Special Flood Hazard Area (SFHA) is in the public domain and a part of the considerations involved in setting hazard insurance rates. It is reasonable to assume homebuyers are aware of their property's location in relation to

TIMING OF SALES	LOCATION	
	IN SPECIAL FLOOD HAZARD AREA	OUTSIDE SPECIAL FLOOD HAZARD AREA
Bracket Andrew	**Hypothesized to Receive Information Treatment**	*Spatial Control* experience event but no differential hazard
Does Not Bracket Andrew	*Temporal Control* no different information regime for the two sales	*Joint Spatial Temporal Control* no difference in information and no differential risk

Figure 10.1 Information and experience in the Hurricane Andrew flood hazard are compared

these zones. We hypothesize that homebuyers and sellers recognize whether their home is inside or outside the SFHA zone.[28] As our formal model outlined below implies, the 'inside' and 'outside' distinction is hypothesized to convey different subjective risk beliefs (see Figure 10.1). When new information becomes available, these perceptions are assumed to be updated.

Availability of information on the sales prices for all the houses that sold at least twice between 1983 and 2000 allows the timing of these sales in relation to the hurricane and the location in relation to the SFHA to be used to isolate sales with the information treatment we attribute to Andrew. When there were no properties damaged by the hurricane (the situation in Lee County) a property would fall in one of four cells defined by these two dimensions.

A repeat sales model uses the logic of a hedonic property value model framework to consider how the spatial and temporally defined event influences the price changes for the same properties. The hedonic price equation that we begin with is given in equation (10.4).

$$\ln R_{it} = \sum_k c_k z_{ik} + F_i(b_t + \beta p_t + \eta_i + e_{it}) + (1 + F_i)(\gamma_t + \beta\phi_t + \eta_i + e_{it}) \tag{10.4}$$

where subscript i identifies the property and t the date of the sale. In equation (10.4), R_{it} is the sales price. The first term, $\Sigma_k c_k z_{ik}$, captures the effect of the housing characteristics. These attributes describe the features of the home and its lot. η_i is an idiosyncratic, time invariant effect due to unobserved heterogeneity. F_i is a qualitative variable identifying the location of properties inside (= 1) and outside (= 0) a Special Flood Hazard Area (SFHA). We assume there are different subjective probabilities of a hurricane strike causing major structural damage within an SFHA versus outside this area. They are p_t and ϕ_t, respectively. b_t and γ_t are the time effects for properties inside and outside an SFHA, respectively. e_{it} is assumed to be a well-behaved error (that is, independent and identically distributed).

The information provided by Andrew on the potential of major hurricane damage in the market area is hypothesized to cause households to update risk assessments from their baseline levels in each area. If we assume that sales before Andrew are based on an initial set of risk perceptions, for example $p_t = p_0$ and $\phi_t = \phi_0$, then after Andrew households have received the new information and adjust their risk assessments to $p_t = p_1$ and $\phi_t = \phi_1$. Defining $A_t = 1$ if Andrew occurred and $A_t = 0$ otherwise, p_t and ϕ_t can be defined recognizing this hypothesized discrete change in risks for the two locations by equations (10.4) and (10.5), respectively:

$$p_t = A_t p_1 + (1 - A_t) p_0 \tag{10.5}$$

$$\phi_t = A_t\phi_1 + (1 - A_t)\phi_0 \tag{10.6}$$

Substituting (10.5) and (10.6) into equation (10.3) yields equation (10.7).

$$\begin{aligned}\ln R_{it} = \sum_k c_k z_{ik} &+ F_i(b_t + \beta(A_t p_1 + (1 - A_t)p_0) + \eta_i + e_{it}) \\ &+ (1 - F_i)(\gamma_t + \beta(A_t\phi_1 + (1 - A_t)\phi_0) + \eta_i + e_{it})\end{aligned} \tag{10.7}$$

A repeat sales model measures the homeowner's responses to the change in the perceived risk of hurricanes through the changes in housing values due to the information treatment group. This effect is identified through the other controls provided by using the price changes for the same homes and by controlling for homes' locations and the timing of their sales.

Differencing equation (10.7) for the same property *i*, we have equation (10.8).

$$\begin{aligned} ln\left(\frac{R_{it}}{R_{is}}\right) &= (\gamma_t - \gamma_s) + F_i((b_t - b_s) - (\gamma_t - \gamma_s)) + \beta(\phi_1 - \phi_0)(A_t - A_s) \\ &+ \beta \cdot ((p_1 - p_0) - (\phi_1 - \phi_0))F_i \cdot (A_t - A_s) + (e_{it} - e_{is})\end{aligned} \tag{10.8}$$

To derive equation (10.8) we assumed that the structural characteristics remained constant and these terms will cancel. For this result to be plausible we must be able to control or exclude homes damaged by the storm.[29] This is the advantage of a 'near miss' – no homes are damaged. The interaction term indicating the sales bracketed Andrew and that a property is in an SFHA measures $\beta[(p_1 - p_0) - (\phi_1 - \phi_0)]$, the incremental option price scaled by the differential risk, for the areas with significant hazard compared to those without. The identifying restrictions required to estimate this pure information effect are that: (1) there are no significant changes in housing attributes between the two time periods (for example the z_k's remain the same); (2) the partial effects of structural attributes on the log of the sale prices are constant (the c_k's do not change); and (3) the unobserved heterogeneity is not differentially influenced by the event or the group.

Table 10.1 provides a summary of our estimates for the repeat sales model in equation (10.8) by the treatment of time.[30] Our primary interest is in the estimated effect of the risk information conveyed to homeowners living in publicly announced high-risk areas as a result of the hurricane. In all cases, these effects are significantly estimated. They confirm our a priori hypothesis in that the risk information attributed to Hurricane Andrew clearly reduces the property values for homes in the area prone to coastal hazards. The results for Lee County display consistently significant negative effects on property values. The measured effects of the information

Table 10.1 Modeling information effects of Andrew: the case of Lee County[a]

Effect of risk information	Treatment of timing of sales	
	No time effect	Time effect
	−0.198 (p-value = 0.00)	−0.194 (p-value = 0.001)
Andrew*SFHA	−0.187	−0.196
	(−2.69)	(−2.09)
Andrew	−0.012	−0.012
	(−0.26)	(−0.26)
SFHA	0.025	0.026
	(0.50)	(0.52)
Time between Sales (t-s)	0.003	0.003
	(4.87)	(4.87)
SFHA*(t-s)	0.005	0.005
	(4.10)	(4.06)
National Flood Insurance Change*SFHA	−0.260	−0.264
	(−5.75)	(−5.40)
Andrew*SFHA*time	–	0.002×10^{-1}
	–	(0.16)
Inverse Mills (Selection)[b]	−0.763	−0.763
	(−8.87)	(−8.86)
Intercept	0.962	0.962
	(9.96)	(9.95)
Sample Size	5212	5212
R^2	0.052	0.052

Notes:

[a] The numbers in parentheses refer to the ratio of the estimated parameter to the robust (Huber, 1967) estimate of the standard error. The estimated effect of the risk information for the 'no time' model sums the coefficient for Andrew and Andrew*SFHA. For the 'time' model it also includes Andrew*SFHA*time with time evaluated at the sample mean and treated as nonstochastic.

[b] This term is a correction for the potential selection effects associated with limiting the sample to properties with at least two sales. It is based on the computation of the inverse Mills ratio (see Heckman, 1979) derived from estimates of a probit model that assumes the outcome having at least two sales can be modeled as a function of the timing of the most recent sales using fixed effects for each year.

conveyed by Andrew imply about a 19 per cent reduction in the rate of change of the property values.

This example suggests a repeat sales model may well offer one means for estimating measures of the trade-offs required to evaluate some types of homeland security policies. These policies would involve changes in the perceived values of the risks associated with property damage and disruption to living conditions due to the potential for threats to security at a local level. These outcomes may well be more relevant than treating homeland security policies exclusively in terms of *ex ante* values of risks to life and *ex post* damages to structures. The incremental option price measure reflects the full consequences of avoiding large-scale disasters. Estimating how it behaves for different types of hazards, information and local conditions would allow greater insight into the effects of other dimensions of policy such as insurance markets and *ex post* damage mitigation.

SUMMARY AND IMPLICATIONS

Decisions among policy alternatives should be informed by economic analyses of the trade-offs people would make so that they would be able to experience the improved conditions implied by homeland security policies. This chapter has acknowledged the difficulty of measuring these trade-offs as benefits of such a policy. However we believe that the methods developed for evaluations of large-scale policies involving other non-market goods and services offer a starting point for these analyses. As a result, this chapter began with a brief summary of revealed and stated preference methods. It also discussed the concepts underlying benefit transfer methods because it seems likely analysts will have to use records of how people respond to risks and new risk information for large natural hazards as a starting point to characterize the trade-offs associated with avoiding disruptions to daily activities. Security-related events bundle risk to life, property and daily activities. They are not simply one more added risk to life. Rather, they alter the quality of life. No doubt one of these changes does involve increasing the risks to life. However efforts to secure large cities or to activities important to our political system (for example political conventions) will not be adequately described in this context.

There is an important issue that distinguishes security policy from other areas of non-market policy. The source of the externality (or risk) must be assumed to respond in ways that attempt to undo the policy. For environmental policy, coordination of private and public action has certainly been a large part of some policy discussions. Often this involves a 'backing out' of private action (or charitable contributions) when public action to reduce an external effect increases. However in these cases we do not argue that agents purposefully increase the externality. Rather, they are usually efforts to reduce one's own costs of controlling sources of externalities. These feedback effects are not necessarily important to benefit measurement at the individual level. They are relevant to aggregate benefit–cost analysis where what is 'delivered' by a policy must take account of these strategic feedbacks. As a result, the analysis of the aggregate benefits from policy needs to incorporate what is akin to a general equilibrium framework; the induced responses of the sources of the hazard in order to capture what might by termed the general equilibrium response to the policy. This feature is a significant difference from the context of all large-scale benefit–cost analyses to date and a clear area for new conceptual research.

NOTES

* Thanks are due to Alex Boutaud, Michael Darden and Jaren Pope for research assistance and help in assembling the data used in this analysis and to Susan Hinton and Alex Boutaud for preparing the manuscript.

1. Sunstein (2003) discuss the dimension of fear and anxiety that are related to the loss of security. Sunstein's focus is on the potential for individuals to ignore low probabilities and focus on extreme outcomes. Fischhoff et al. (2003) and Viscusi and Zeckhauser (2003) are among the first studies of subjective risk perceptions following 9/11. Additional research will be needed to identify how specific types of public mitigation relate to perceived risks.
2. Economic benefit measures can describe the monetary compensation an individual would require in lieu of the suite of changes to risk, severity of outcomes, personal freedom and so forth that are associated with a policy. As a result, they offer one consistent metric for this measurement. We return to this point below.
3. Lakdawalla and Zanjani (2004) suggest the use of natural hazards is not as appropriate as decisions involving other types of risk. Their reason seems to stem from interest in insurance as a policy instrument. Our focus is on measuring the *ex ante* incremental value of reducing risk. Here, we argue the parallel is more direct.
4. Andrew took place after a long lull in hurricane activity in Florida. Thus given the length of stay of most US households in a given area (about seven years) it would be reasonable to assume that residents of this county had not experienced a severe storm.
5. Our example is an extension of work reported in Hallstrom and Smith (2004).
6. It is also important to consider how security is produced. Arguments such as those developed by Hirshleifer (1983) for production of public goods could well apply in these cases as well.
7. We have structured the problem in this way because we do not consider insurance directly – only its effects as reflected in housing prices.
8. See Löfstedt (2004) for an interesting discussion of changes in the effectiveness of risk communication in Europe.
9. This assumes we wish an *ex ante* money metric interpretation. That is, the baseline parameters are what determine the V^0.
10. Nash equilibrium concepts could be accommodated within Graham's (1992) general description of the criteria for defining movements toward efficient resource allocations in the presence of uncertainty.
11. The object of choice simply represents what the individual believes she receives from a decision to do whatever is involved in the choice. The circumstances of choice relate to the terms (for example what must be given up and when); the property rights to the object of choice; the degree of certainty; any limitations on the individual's ability to make the choice (for example information, time, resources); and the full consequences of the choice. The last component relates to how such choices are made – by an individual, a household or a group of unrelated individuals (for example voting).
12. Tinbergen (1956) demonstrated analytically this relationship. Rosen (1974) is perhaps the most widely cited discussion of the economic relationship between what is

observed and the underlying behavioral model. Ekeland et al. (2004) offer a more modern description of the logic. Palmquist (2005a) provides the most comprehensive overview of the literature.

13. Different marginal values at different locations do not comprise the schedule because these are the values of different people (who selected those locations) and without more information the model does not explain all the reasons for the differences.
14. See Phaneuf and Smith (2005) for a review of these studies.
15. These structures also implicitly restrict the way attributes are assumed to contribute to preferences. See Morey (1999), Haab and McConnell (2002) and Phaneuf and Smith (2005) for discussion.
16. See Smith (2004a) for a more detailed review of the literature.
17. There are a variety of ways contingent valuation questions are asked, including:

    a. discrete choice: a person is asked a yes/no question after the object of choice and a stated payment required to have the object of choice is described.
    b. open-ended: a person is asked to state a maximum payment he or she would be willing to make for the object of choice.
    c. payment: a person is asked to select a maximum amount from a list of amounts for an object of choice card.

    There are also repeated discrete choice questions with varying amounts that adjust (or do not adjust) in response to amounts and other variations on the questions asked. For example, if more than one unit could be purchased (such as vaccines to prevent disease for family members) this type of question leads to another type of response.
18. This is an issue that has been questioned with CV applications.
19. Even when they relate to different aspects of the same resource there are advantages in using the two data sources in joint estimation.
20. There are a wide array of different types of applications. Those most associated with conjoint sources of the SP data tend to use a random utility framework and assume the RP and SP data arise from a common preference function with different errors that reflect unobserved heterogeneity. The errors are allowed to have different variances so the ration of their scale factors is often interpreted as a calibration factor. See Louviere et al. (2000) for discussion.
21. See Smith (2004b) for a simple example.
22. Smith et al. (2002) have proposed one such alternative, but it requires restrictive *a priori* assumptions about preferences.
23. Navrud (2004) describes this parameter as the income elasticity of demand. It is not an income elasticity of demand, but rather an income elasticity for the marginal willingness to pay. Under some conditions, the income elasticity of marginal willingness to pay for a non-market service will equally the income elasticity of demand for a private good if it is a weak complement to the service and preferences are consistent with the Willig (1978) condition (see Palmquist, 2005b).
24. See Smith and Pattanayak (2002) for a discussion of the importance of consistency in the concepts summarized in these meta-analyses.
25. Preference calibration offers one way to impose this consistency. See Smith et al. (2002) for discussion of the methods and examples.
26. Hurricanes appear to run in cycles caused by factors such as the direction of equatorial stratosphere winds, Atlantic and Caribbean Sea pressure readings and the amount of rainfall in the Sahel region of West Africa. The 20 years prior to Andrew were a period of below normal hurricane activity (Goldenberg et al., 2001).
27. The extent to which each record offers complete data varies by county because the data are derived from county tax records on housing sales. Different counties devote more or less resources to maintaining the full characteristics of the properties involved in the transactions, and the data provided by the commercial vendors vary with these differences. No effort is made to assure uniformity.

28. We tested this hypothesis and could not reject a null hypothesis implying equal effects for the zones with adequate data on sales transactions that overlap the zones. Not all zones had transactions that were before and after the hurricane. For example we had no transaction in the highest risk zone.
29. In Smith et al. (2004) we test the model using a repeat sample for Dade County and the results confirm our a priori expectations.
30. More detail on this analysis is available in Hallstrom and Smith (2004).

REFERENCES

Alston, Julian M., George W. Norton and Philip G. Pardey (1995), *Science Under Scarcity*, Ithaca, NY: Cornell University Press.

Bradford, D. (1970), 'Benefit–cost analysis and demand curves for public goods', *Kyklos*, **23** (December), 1145–59.

Cameron, T.A. (1992a), 'Combining contingent valuation and travel cost data for the valuation of nonmarket goods', *Land Economics*, **68** (3), 302–17.

Cameron, T.A. (1992b), 'Nonuser resource values', *American Journal of Agricultural Economics*, **74** (5), 1133–7.

Champ, Patricia, Kevin J. Boyle and Thomas C. Brown (eds) (2003), *A Primer on Nonmarket Valuation*, Boston, MA: Kluwer Academic Publishers.

Cordes, J.J. and A.M.J. Yezer (1998), 'In harm's way: does federal spending on beach enhancement and protection induce excessive development in coastal areas?', *Land Economics*, **74** (1), 128–45.

Ehrlich, I. and G. Becker (1972), 'Market insurance, self-insurance and self-protection', *Journal of Political Economy*, **80**, 623–48.

Ekeland, I., J.J. Heckman and L. Nesheim (2004), 'Identification and estimation of hedonic models', *Journal of Political Economy*, **112** (February), Part 2, S60–S109.

Fischhoff, B., R.M. Gonzalez, D.A. Small and J.S. Lerner (2003), 'Judged terror risk and proximity to the World Trade Center', *Journal of Risk and Uncertainty*, **26** (2/3), 137–51.

Goldenberg, S.B., C.W. Landsea, A.M. Mestas-Nuñez and W.M. Gray (2001), 'The recent increase in Atlantic hurricane activity: causes and implications', *Science*, **293** (July), 475–9.

Graham, D.A. (1992), 'Public expenditure under uncertainty: the net benefit criteria', *Economic Review*, **82** (4), 822–6.

Haab, Timothy C. and Kenneth E. McConnell (2002), *Valuing Environmental and Natural Resources: The Econometrics of Non-Market Valuation*, Cheltenham, UK and Northampton, MA, USA: Edward Elgar.

Hallstrom, Daniel G. and V. Kerry Smith (2005), 'Market responses to hurricanes', *Journal of Environmental Economics and Management* (in press).

Hartwig, Robert P. (2002), 'Florida case study: economic impacts of business closures in hurricane prone counties', Working paper, Insurance Information Institute, June.

Heckman, J.J. (1979), 'Sample selection bias as a specification error', *Econometrica*, **47** (January), 153–61.

Heckman, J.J. and S. Navarro-Lozana (2004), 'Using matching instrumental variables and control functions to estimate economic choice models', *Review of Economics and Statistics*, **86** (February), 30–57.

Hirshleifer, J. (1983), 'From weakest-link to best-shot: the voluntary provision of public goods', *Public Choice*, **41**, 371–86.

Insurance Information Institute (2004), 'Hot topics and insurance issues', available at www.iii.org/media/hottopics/insurance.

Kanninen, B. (2002), 'Optimal design for multinomial choice experiments', *Journal of Marketing Research*, **39** (March), 214–27.

Lakdawalla, D. and G.H. Zanjani (2004), 'Insurance, self-protection, and the economics of terrorism', *Journal of Public Economics*, **X**.

Löfstedt, Ragnar (2004), 'Risk communication and management in the 21st century', AEI-Brookings Working paper 04-10, forthcoming in *International Public Management Journal*, (April).

Louviere, Jordan J., David A. Hensher and Joffre D. Swait (2000), *Stated Choice Methods: Analysis and Applications*, New York: Cambridge University Press.

McFadden, Daniel (1974), 'Conditional logit analysis of qualitative choice behavior', in Paul Zarembka (ed.), *Frontiers in Econometrics*, New York: Academic Press.

Morey, Edward R. (1999), 'TWO RUMS UNCLOAKED: a nested logit model of site choice, and nested logit models of participation and site choice', in Joseph A. Herriges and Catherine L. Kling (eds), *Valuing Recreation and the Environment*, Cheltenham, UK and Northampton, MA, USA: Edward Elgar.

Navrud, Ståle (2004), 'Value transfer and environmental policy', in T. Tietenberg and H. Folmer (eds), *International Yearbook of Environmental and Resource Economics*, Cheltenham, UK and Northampton, MA, USA : Edward Elgar.

Palmquist, Raymond (2005a), 'Property value models', in Karl G. Mäler and Jeffrey Vincent (eds), *Handbook of Environmental Economics*, Amsterdam: North Holland, in press.

Palmquist, Raymond (2005b), 'Weak complementarity, path independence, and the interaction of the Willig condition', *Journal of Environmental Economics and Management*, forthcoming.

Phaneuf, Daniel J. and V. Kerry Smith (2005), 'Recreation demand models', in K.G. Maler and J. Vincent (eds), *Handbook of Environmental Economics*, Amsterdam: North-Holland, forthcoming.

Rosen, S. (1974), 'Hedonic prices and implicit markets: product differentiation in perfect competition', *Journal of Political Economy*, **82** (February), 34–55.

Smith, V. Kerry (1991), 'Household production functions and environmental benefit estimation', in J.B. Braden and C.D. Kolstad (eds), *Measuring the Demand for Environmental Quality*, Amsterdam: North Holland.

Smith, V. Kerry (1997), 'Pricing what is priceless: a status report on non-market valuation of environmental resources', in Henk Folmer and Tom Tietenberg (eds), *The International Yearbook of Environmental and Resource Economics 2004/2005*, Cheltenham, UK and Northampton, MA, USA: Edward Elgar.

Smith, V. Kerry (2004a), 'Fifty years of contingent valuation', in Tom Tietenberg and Henk Folmer (eds), *The International Yearbook of Environmental and Resource Economics 2004/2005*, Cheltenham, UK and Northampton, MA, USA: Edward Elgar.

Smith, V. Kerry (2004b), 'Will cost-benefit analysis retain its place at the policy table?', in Jon Neil (ed.), *Upjohn Institution's Benefit–Cost Symposium*, forthcoming.

Smith, V. Kerry, Jared Carbone, Daniel Hallstrom, Jaren Pope and Michael Darden (2004), 'Market and non-market responses to risk information: "trying to reason with hurricane season"', working paper, North Carolina State University, December.

Smith, V.K. and S.K. Pattanayak (2002), 'Is meta-analysis a Noah's ark for non-market valuation?' *Environmental and Resource Economics*, **22** (June), 271–96.

Smith, V. Kerry, G. Van Houtven and S.K. Pattanayak (2002), 'Benefit transfer via preference calibration: "prudential algebra" for policy', *Land Economics*, **78** (1), 132–52.

Sunstein, C.R. (2003), 'Terrorism and probability neglect', *Journal of Risk and Uncertainty*, **26** (2/3), 121–36.

Tinbergen, J. (1956), 'On the theory of income distribution', *Weltwertshaftliches Archive*, **77**, 489–05.

Viscusi, W.K. and R.J. Zeckhauser (2003), 'Sacrificing civil liberties to reduce terrorism risks', *Journal of Risk and Uncertainty*, **26** (2/3), 99–120.

Willig, R.D. (1978), 'Incremental consumer's surplus and hedonic price adjustment', *Journal of Economic Theory*, **17** (February), 227–53.

Woo, Gordon (2002), 'Quantifying insurance terrorism risk', paper prepared for the National Bureau of Economic Research, Cambridge, MA, 1 February.

11. Analyzing terrorist threats to the economy: a computable general equilibrium approach*

Adam Rose

INTRODUCTION

Recent Osama bin Laden videotapes clearly suggest that the major objective of the al-Qaida terrorist network is to 'bankrupt the United States'. Although popular attention to conventional military and terrorist activity usually focuses on human lives, strategic assets, and troop and public morale, expert strategists have long appreciated the importance of the economy as a symbolic target or as the key support base of military action. Examples include Nikita Khrushchev's warning that the Soviet Union would 'bury' us with the production of goods and services, and the Second World War strategic bombing study to identify key economic sectors supplying the German war machine (US Strategic Bombing Survey, 1945; Baran and Galbraith, 1947).

The economic impact of terrorist attacks is not limited to the obvious physical destruction of property at the moment of maximum news exposure. It includes the lost production in gross terms (sales revenue) or net terms (income from wages/salaries, profits, rents and royalties) from these assets. It also includes potential turmoil in national markets, costs of increased risk, dampening of consumer and investor confidence, and social impacts (many of which translate into economic losses as well).

The challenge to estimate the economic threats of terrorism increases exponentially with the temporal and spatial distance from the point of attack. Property damage can readily be assessed in terms of simple accounting or cost-engineering considerations relating to purchase costs, or can be addressed by more sophisticated accounting stances of replacement cost, all at a given point in time. However production losses take place over an extended time, and are highly variable after the attack, depending on private and public policy decisions that affect response and recovery. Broader impacts are even more difficult to estimate because of their remoteness, pervasiveness and intangible nature.

To estimate the economic losses from terrorism, it is necessary to deploy a comprehensive and sophisticated model. We are faced with two alternative strategies. First, we could adapt existing models from related areas such as impact analysis and the economics of natural hazards. Second, we could begin from square one and develop an entirely new modeling approach for the purpose at hand. It is the opinion of this author that the best strategy would be to enhance the existing approach of computable general equilibrium (CGE) analysis, which has proven successful in recent applications to related areas. At the same time, there is an acknowledgement of limitations of the approach, though most of them are not insurmountable.

The purpose of this chapter is to assess the capability of CGE analysis to estimate the production-related losses of a terrorist attack. This assessment will include a discussion of advantages and disadvantages of CGE in general and in the context of the economics of terrorism. It will elaborate on recent advances by the author to overcome CGE model limitations with respect to disequilibria, parameter specifications and behavior. It will emphasize the ability of CGE modeling to address two aspects of loss estimation that have typically been neglected (at least quantitatively) in almost all studies of disasters, both man-made and natural. The first of these is the full range of indirect, or general equilibrium, impacts, which have the potential to increase substantially the size of loss estimates. The second is individual business and market resilience, or the inherent ability of businesses and markets to cushion themselves against shocks, which have the potential to lower these loss estimates.[1]

COMPUTABLE GENERAL EQUILIBRIUM MODELING

Basic Considerations

A layman's definition of CGE is: a model of the entire economy based on decisions by individual producers and consumers in response to price signals, within limits of available capital, labor and natural resources. As such, CGE is a comprehensive model with behavioral content, which mimics the workings of markets under explicit constraints (for example see Shoven and Whalley, 1992).[2]

CGE is the state of the art in regional economic impact analysis (Partridge and Rickman, 1998). It has been applied extensively to such topics as simulating the impacts of a change in sales tax rates, development of new oil or gas fields, industrial targeting, and air quality regulations. It also has a nearly 20-year history in fields closely related to the economic impacts of terrorism, such as natural hazards and climate change. A brief summary of some of the major contributions follows.

The first economy-wide modeling of related topics was a CGE analysis of climate change damages by Kokoski and Smith (1987), with a significant emphasis on the sensitivity of the results to the value of key parameters. Brookshire and McKee (1992) provided an overview of advantages and disadvantages of CGE modeling to the application of natural hazards, while Boisvert (1992) provided a simple example of a CGE model applied to a utility service disruption following an earthquake. His model used Cobb-Douglas production functions, which means that the elasticity of substitution between all factors of production is assumed to equal unity. Unfortunately this simple and early standard approach in CGE modeling, used in great part because data on parameters is lacking, yields an overly flexible response for short-run phenomena. Early simulations by Rose (1998) indicate that these Cobb-Douglas production functions would estimate that a regional economy suffering an outage of electricity of say 50 per cent might only suffer a reduction of output (totally apart from resilience other than input substitution) of only 2 or 3 per cent. Note however that the use of Cobb-Douglas elasticities is less of a problem when one examines long-term phenomena such as climate change damages or reconstruction following a terrorist attack, because of the longer period that the economy has to adjust to equilibrium.

An important contribution to the literature was the work by Cochrane et al. (1997) on the Federal Emergency Management Agency hazard loss estimation system, HAZUS (FEMA, 1997). The basis of the indirect economic loss module (IELM) of HAZUS is an input–output (I–O) model. However unlike the standard, linear and inflexible version of I–O, Cochrane's formulation allows for flexibility that equilibrates supply and demand imbalances through changes in imports and exports. This is similar to the handling of these trade flows in a CGE model. The major difference is that in the CGE framework, these changes are an explicit response to prices, while Cochrane's formulation is a more mechanical equilibrating mechanism in the absence of price signals.

Rose (1998) outlines some key modeling issues associated with the application of CGE analysis to natural hazards, including laying out specific needs for model improvement. One of these considerations, especially important in the context of terrorist attacks, is the fact that economic activity is not uniformly distributed throughout a region. Moreover the major feature that distinguishes terrorist attacks from natural hazards is the deliberate intent of the former, which rather than being random, is focused on targets that can generate the greatest direct and indirect damage. This leads to relatively greater concentrations of property damage and production disruption among economic sectors. Rose and Guha (2004) developed a methodology to differentiate disruptions of utility lifeline services across customers. Together with the use of more realistic elasticities of substitution, their model yielded reasonable results for a major earthquake simulation in the Memphis, Tennessee region.

Several major advances have been offered by Rose and Liao (2005), some of which are discussed at greater length below. These include operational definitions of resilience, ways of linking real-world resilience options to key parameters of economic production functions, an algorithm for recalibrating key parameters to empirical or simulation data, and a method for separating partial equilibrium from net general equilibrium impacts. These methodological refinements were successfully applied to an analysis of a water service disruption in Portland, Oregon in the aftermath of an hypothetical earthquake. Some of these refinements were also used in the analysis by Rose et al. (2004) of the rolling blackouts of electricity in Los Angeles in the summer of 2001, caused not by natural or man-made hazards but rather attributable to policy failures associated with deregulation. Major aspects of this study found economic losses to be minimal for a set of one-hour rolling blackouts because of resilience in general and especially production rescheduling, or the ability to make up lost output at a later date by overtime work (see also the application of this concept by Rose and Lim, 2002, to actual electricity outages during the Northridge earthquake).

Impact Analysis Considerations and CGE Models

To assess the worthiness of CGE for the analysis of terrorist threats to the economy, we identify specific impact considerations and how the modeling framework can address them. In the course of the discussion, we also compare CGE with the other two approaches typically used to analyze economic impacts of disasters – input–output and macroeconometric models. This provides a more focused assessment of relative advantages and disadvantages of CGE analysis.

Impact considerations include the following.

(1) *Specific targets*. This is a relative advantage of CGE models because the basic unit of analysis is an individual firm or household; moreover these are often grouped into sectors and socio-economic classes respectively. Other 'multi-sector' modeling approaches like I–O and even highly disaggregated econometric models are not specified below the 'meso' scale (sector groupings). Individual targets can be pinpointed in all these

modeling approaches through a GIS overlay, but their separate identity is easier to maintain in a CGE model (cf. French, 1998; Rose et al., 2004).

(2) *Individual behavior*. Here again, CGE has distinct advantages in the ability to model both normal behavior and the broader category often referred to as 'bounded rationality', which includes non-maximizing objectives, panic and more random reactions. I–O models lack any behavioral content, and the behavioral content of econometric models is typically limited to optimization.

(3) *Market behavior*. In CGE models, prices provide signals to allocate resources. Prices are absent in I–O models, and their role is more indirect in econometric models. The resilience of communities is greatly aided by the workings of markets but this has been an oft-neglected aspect of disaster studies.

(4) *Stock and flow losses*. CGE models can estimate the effects of terrorist attacks in terms of both property damage and business interruption. The former is especially relevant in the case of terrorism, where even a 'threat' can result in losses from business closure or population evacuation. Most I–O models lack the matrix of capital coefficients necessary to evaluate the former. CGE models are superior to econometric models in analysing the pattern of decisions to rebuild the capital stock and its ability to influence business interruption losses.

(5) *Non-market considerations*. Many terrorist attacks are intended to have a symbolic impact in addition to business impacts. Such targets would include environmental and iconic cases such as the Grand Canyon and the Statue of Liberty. Another example of non-market impacts would be infrastructure, including highways, electric and water utilities, and communication networks. These are obvious economic entities, but their provision of services is not often accomplished through the market, so prices must be inferred. Recent advances in CGE analysis have extended its capability to include non-market considerations (for example Oladosu, 2000). Non-market impacts have been incorporated into I–O models extensively (for example see Duchin and Lange, 1992), though not in relation to any surrogate markets that might influence changes in their value if they are damaged or if economic conditions change. Non-market values have been much less frequently incorporated into macroeconometric models.

(6) *Economic resilience to terrorist attacks*. Failure to incorporate individual business and market resilience is likely to lead to overestimation of negative impacts. Non-linearities and the ability to substitute inputs are major aspects of resilience that are inherent in CGE models but nearly impossible to incorporate in I–O models. They are also somewhat difficult to incorporate into econometric ones. However econometric models are superior in modeling the role of inventories.

(7) *Recovery processes*. Recovery from major terrorist attacks may take a long period of time, and there is a dynamic adjustment process that would ideally be modeled. CGE models can be extended to a dynamic form, including incorporation of changing conditions and adaptations, to trace the entire time path of adjustment. This is more difficult with I–O models. Though it is a somewhat standard feature of econometric models to trace a time path, it is relatively more difficult to incorporate changing conditions.

(8) *Economic disequilibria*. A shock to the system from a terrorist attack will cause the economy to be out of sync, and its return to equilibrium may take some time. As discussed at length below, CGE models can be adapted to take into account various disequilibria with respect to labor markets, government budgets, trade balances and input availabilities. I–O models by their very nature cannot accommodate disequilibria, and it is difficult to do so in econometric models as well.

(9) *Macroeconomic repercussions*. This would include the range of effects, beginning with more basic multiplier effects, then general equilibrium impacts, and then broader, less tangible macro effects, including synergies. I–O models can only include basic multiplier processes, while CGE can include a broader range of general equilibrium effects and some synergies, as can econometric models. However econometric models have an edge over CGE models in dealing with matters relating to interest rates and financial markets (I–O models are incapable of taking these factors into account at all). The reason for the advantage of econometric models may not however be due to inherent capabilities, but simply to their relatively longer existence and their much more prevalent application to these areas.

(10) *Distribution of impacts across socio-economic groups*. Economic losses are unlikely to be evenly distributed, and any equivalent loss will have a more adverse effect on low-income populations. All three modeling approaches (if we consider the social accounting matrix extension of I–O models) are adept at addressing these impacts. CGE and econometric models have the advantage of being able to incorporate differences in behavior across socio-economic groups.

(11) *Spatial diffusion of the economic impacts*. A terrorist attack in one location spreads throughout the economy of a region and often beyond to other regions and nations. Moreover, there is likely to be some feedback effect in the target region as well. I–O and econometric models are more advanced in terms of their inter-regional application, but again this is probably more a matter of modeling experience than any inherent inability of CGE models. It should however be noted that because of their complexity, it is relatively much more difficult conceptually to design and to obtain the data for an inter-regional CGE model.

(12) *Mitigation*. This is also an economic impact of potential terrorist activity. Mitigation activities are much easier to incorporate into CGE and I–O models than econometric models. The latter is typically based on time series data, which limits its ability to incorporate new technology or structural changes. Moreover CGE and I–O models are not estimated as simultaneous equations systems in the same way as econometric models, so that modifications for structural, as well as behavioral changes in the former, are easier to incorporate.

We should also evaluate modeling considerations as follows.

(13) *Operational (and in real time)*. This is important in facilitating an emergency response. I–O models are the easiest to use, in part because of their simplicity. Econometric models have become easier to use, in part because off-the-shelf versions have been developed (see, for example REMI, 2004). Admittedly CGE models are more difficult to utilize than the other two modeling approaches, though this may in part be due to their more recent development, more complex software[3] and lack of 'canned' versions.

(14) *Data availability*. One of the main disadvantages of econometric models is that they tend to extrapolate the past, and terrorist activity is intended to bring about major changes. I–O and CGE models can more readily accommodate engineering data that can reflect changes. From the standpoint of estimation, it is also easier to incorporate changes of data into I–O and CGE models than econometric models because of the simultaneous equation estimation of the latter.

(15) *Cost*. I–O models are very inexpensive (see for example, MIG, 2003), though the cost of developing a formidable I–O model with several important capabilities can lead to significant expense as well. Econometric models are generally expensive, though off-the-shelf versions have reduced the cost significantly. CGE models are possibly more costly, but this is not necessarily due to inherent disadvantage vis-à-vis econometric models, but rather fewer years of experience with the former.

(16) *Transparency*. Finally, it is important that the model not be a black box, so as to instill more confidence in the user, to be able to trace causation, and to facilitate checking the results. CGE and econometric models are much less transparent than I–O models, though recent advances in 'decomposition' analysis have closed this gap somewhat (Rose and Liao, 2005).

Although this summary has emphasized the superiority of CGE to its two major competitors, both of them deserve credit for facilitating the construction and enhancing the abilities of CGE models (see for example Rose, 1995). Nearly all CGE models have at their core the production of intermediate goods, the data for which almost always come from input–output tables, as do basic data on primary factors of production, and on government revenues and expenditures. Broader account balances relating to savings and investment, as well as imports and exports, are usually obtained from social accounting matrices. Econometric specification of CGE model parameters is considered to yield more accurate estimates than the standard practice of data transfer and calibration.[4] Also, both I–O and CGE models by themselves have no forecasting ability, so 'conjoining' them with econometric models is desirable for long-run analyses. Finally, the relatively lower complexity of I–O models makes it easier to conjoin them with other types of models in an integrated system (see for example Gordon et al., 2004; Sohn et al., 2004).

RESILIENCE TO TERRORISM AND OTHER DISASTERS

Basic Considerations

In general 'economic resilience' refers to the ability or capacity of a system to absorb or cushion against damage or loss (see for example Holling, 1973; Perrings, 2001). A more general definition that incorporates dynamic considerations, including stability, is the ability of a system to recover from a severe shock. We also distinguish two types of resilience in each context:

- Inherent: the ability under normal circumstances (for example the ability of individual firms to substitute other inputs for those curtailed by an external shock, or the ability of markets to reallocate resources in response to price signals).
- Adaptive: the ability in crisis situations due to ingenuity or extra effort (for example increasing input substitution possibilities in individual business operations, or strengthening the market by providing information to match suppliers without customers to customers without suppliers).

Resilience emanates both from internal motivation and from the stimulus of private or public policy decisions (Mileti, 1999). Also resilience, as defined in this chapter, refers to post-disaster conditions and response, which are distinguished from pre-disaster activities to reduce potential losses through mitigation.

The concept of resilience emanates from several sources. For example Holling (1973) and other ecologists, as well as Perrings (2001) and other ecological economists, have defined it in terms of the broader concept of sustainability as the capacity to absorb stress and shocks. Several ways to measure this property have been put forth including: stability, persistence, resistance, non-vulnerability, stochastic return time and resilience (Tinch, 1998). However Perrings (2001, p. 323) notes: 'The property that most closely connects with the idea of sustainability as conservation of opportunity is resilience.'

In disaster research, resilience has been emphasized most by Tierney (1997) in terms of business coping behavior and community response, by Comfort (1999) in terms of non-linear adaptive response of organizations (broadly defined to include both the public and private sectors), and by Petak (2002) in terms of system performance. Recently Bruneau et al. (2003, p. 3) have defined 'community earthquake resilience' as 'the ability of social units (e.g., organizations, communities) to mitigate hazards, contain the effects of disasters when they occur, and carry out recovery activities in ways that minimize social disruption and mitigate the effectors of further earthquakes'. Further, they divide resilience into three aspects, which correspond to the concepts defined above in an economic context. First is reduced failure probability, which we view as equivalent to mitigation in this chapter. Second is reduced consequences from failure, which corresponds to our basic static definition of resilience. Third is reduced time to recovery, which adds a temporal dimension to our basic definition.[5] In sum, Bruneau et al. (2003) have offered a very broad definition of resilience to cover all actions that reduce losses from hazards, including mitigation and more rapid recovery. These refer to how a community reduces the probability of structural or system failure, in the case of the former, and how quickly it returns to normal in the case of the latter. We have focused on the essence of resilience – the innate aspects of the economic system at all levels to cushion itself against losses in a given period.[6]

Resilience can take place at three levels:

- Microeconomic: individual behavior of firms, households or organizations.
- Mesoeconomic: economic sector, individual market or co-operative group.
- Macroeconomic: all individual units and markets combined, though the whole is not simply the sum of its parts, due to interactive effects of an economy.

Examples of individual resilience are well documented in the literature, as are examples of the operation of businesses and organizations

(Tierney, 1997; Comfort, 1999). What is often less appreciated by disaster researchers outside economics and closely related disciplines is the inherent resilience of markets. Prices act as the 'invisible hand' that can guide resources to their best allocation even in the aftermath of a disaster. Some pricing mechanisms have been established expressly to deal with such a situation, as in the case of non-interruptible service premia that enable customers to estimate the value of a continuous supply of electricity and to pay in advance for receiving priority service during an outage (Chao and Wilson, 1987).[7]

The price mechanism is a relatively costless way of redirecting goods and services. Price increases, though often viewed as 'gouging', serve a useful purpose of reflecting highest-value use, even in the broader social setting. Moreover if the allocation does violate principles of equity (fairness), the market allocations can be adjusted by income or material transfers to the needy.

Of course markets are likely to be shocked by disasters, in an analogous manner to buildings and humans. In this case, we have two alternatives for some or all of the economy: (1) substitute centralized decree or planning, though at a significantly higher cost of administration; (2) bolster the market, such as in improving information flows (for example the creation of an information clearing house to match customers without suppliers to suppliers without customers).[8]

Resilience in the Context of CGE Models

The production side of the CGE model developed by the author and his research team to analyze economic aspects of terrorism is composed of a standard, multi-layered, or multi-tiered, constant elasticity of substitution (CES) production function for each sector (see for example Rose et al., 2004; Rose and Liao, 2005). The production function is normally applied to aggregate categories of major inputs of capital, labor, energy and materials, with sub-aggregates possible for each (for example the energy aggregate is often decomposed by fuel type – electricity, oil, gas, and coal). This production function represents a type of hierarchical or sequential decision-making process. For a given level of output, the firm's manager first chooses the optimal combination of capital and energy. He or she next juxtaposes that combination to labor to determine the optimal choice of inputs in the third tier, and so on. In the top tier, input decisions are made regarding water in terms of the various ways it can be provided.

Inherent resilience is embodied in the basic production function for individual businesses and in the combination of producers, consumers and markets (including interaction effects) for the economy as a whole. Adaptive resilience is captured by changes in the parameters. For example an increase in the productivity term for water would reflect conservation, while an increase in the substitution elasticity would reflect increased substitution possibilities between utility water service and other inputs (such as bottled water). In the aftermath of a disaster, people behave in a more urgent manner and are more likely to call forth ingenuity. In the case of a disruption to water supplies for example, for short periods maintenance can be skipped, water fountains can be turned off, water can be reused and so on. Also, in general, inefficient practices can come to light and new opportunities can be initiated. There is an extensive literature suggesting that managers can become more clever in emergency situations. There is additional literature, now very prominent in the energy and environmental fields, indicating a much greater range of conservation opportunities when one looks at the production process from a holistic standpoint (see for example Porter and van der Linde, 1995).

Empirical Specification of Resilience

CGE models used for hazard analysis are likely to yield estimates of business disruptions for some if not all sectors of an economy that differ significantly from the direct loss estimates provided by empirical studies. This is because production function parameters are not typically based on solid data, or even where they are, the data stem from ordinary operating experience (inherent resilience only) rather than from emergency situations. Hence, it is necessary to explicitly incorporate adaptive resilience responses into the analysis.

Rose and Liao (2005) have recently developed a methodology for altering the behavioral parameters in the sectoral production functions of the CGE model based on an optimizing routine and solutions utilizing both analytical and numerical methods. Empirical or simulation model estimates of direct output changes, emanating from an input supply disruption, are used to recalibrate productivity and substitution elasticity parameters of the CES production function. When the initial parameters are accurate for business-as-usual contexts, we say they embody 'inherent' resilience. The difference between these original and the recalibrated parameters would then reflect 'adaptive' resilience. Unfortunately, accurate initial parameters are rarely available, so that in such cases, while the recalibration encompasses both types of resilience, the overall effect cannot yet be accurately decomposed into its two components. Still, the method is sufficiently general to be able to do so when better parameter data become available.

GENERAL EQUILIBRIUM EFFECTS

General equilibrium effects refer to broader impacts generated through both the price and quantity interactions of markets. We will illustrate them and their distinction from partial equilibrium (individual business or individual market) effects by summarizing modeling approaches used to estimate the costs of electricity outages. Partial equilibrium (or direct) effects of outages manifest themselves in four major ways: lost sales, equipment damage or restart costs, spoilage of variable inputs and idle labor costs. In addition, costs are incurred to reduce potential losses through the purchase of back-up generators, permanent changes in production schedules, and utility capacity expansion to promote flexibility (Munasinghe and Gellerson, 1979). At the margin, the cost of outages should be equal to the cost of these adaptive responses. Hence the most popular way of measuring electricity outage losses has been tabulating expenditures on back-up generation rather than measuring damages directly (Bental and Ravid, 1986; Beenstock et al., 1997). Still, measurement of just a single coping tactic, or type of damage, is likely to understate the direct dollar loss.

Estimates of direct losses of electricity shortages range from $1.00 to $5.00/kwh in the US (see for example Caves et al., 1992). Many regions of the US suffer outages of as many as ten to 30 hours per year due to ordinary circumstances of engineering failures and severe storms. The voltage disturbance blackouts of 1996 for example are estimated to have cost California more than $1 billion (Douglas, 2000).

We recommend the use of economic output losses (which can be adjusted to net, or value-added terms and consequently translated into welfare measures) as a common denominator for both partial and general equilibrium effects. This facilitates the inclusion of some capital and productivity costs into the measurement. General equilibrium effects thus consist of:

1. Output loss to downstream customers of a disrupted firm through its inability to provide crucial inputs. This sets off a chain reaction beyond the first line of customers of firms who have had their electric power curtailed.
2. Output loss to upstream suppliers of disrupted firms through the cancellation of orders for inputs. Again, this is transmitted through several rounds but on the supplier side.
3. Output loss to all firms from decreased consumer spending associated with a decreased wage bill in firms directly affected by the electricity outage, as well as all other firms suffering negative general equilibrium effects.

4. Output loss to all firms from decreased investment associated with decreased profits of firms suffering the electricity outage and other firms negatively impacted by general equilibrium effects.
5. Output loss to all firms from cost (and price increases) from damaged equipment and other dislocations (including uncertainty) that result in productivity decreases in firms directly impacted.

The direct and indirect costs of electricity outages thus do not just take place during the period in which power is curtailed. Back-up generators are purchased in anticipation of outages, and the carrying cost of increased inventories of critical materials are incurred over a longer period as well. Equipment damage, spoilage and idle labor costs may translate into an immediate loss in profits, but they may not be passed through in the form of price increases until a later date. The same is true of electric utility cost and price increases that lag, even in a deregulated market. The three time periods, which we designate as preparatory, crisis and recovery, will vary in length depending on the context. For estimation purposes however, they may all be simulated simultaneously in cases where there are no significant dynamic (that is, time-related) effects.

Note also that not all general equilibrium effects are negative. Some firms may benefit from the decreased prices associated with a shift in demand by other firms for various products. Several analyses indicate the existence of this possibility for several sectors, though the positive general equilibrium effects do not more than offset the negative ones. For many years, I–O models have been used to estimate the cost of utility service disruptions. These models reduce general equilibrium effects to quantity interdependencies and are typically unidirectional (for example there are no offsetting effects through price reductions). It is not unusual for I–O models to yield multiplier effects that more than double the direct loss. General equilibrium models incorporate a broader range of interactions in the economy and more accurately measure regional economic impacts.

ECONOMY-WIDE RESPONSES AND DISEQUILIBRIA

As noted above, the market system is inherently resilient to shocks and can be bolstered by various policies. All of this can best be modeled in a CGE framework. However an inherent shortcoming of CGE is its equilibrium emphasis. Following a major disaster, a sustained period of disequilibrium is likely to ensue. Fortunately, several refinements of CGE modeling by the author and others have moved to overcome this limitation. These disequilibria are typically related to 'closure rules', or account balance conditions.

It is now possible to operate a CGE model in situations where demand need not always equal supply in the following cases:

1. The labor market, which allows for unemployment.
2. The government budget, which allow for deficit spending.
3. Trade, which allows for import/export imbalances.
4. Goods and services, which allows for explicit shortages.

The last of these advances bears some elaboration. Ordinarily, any gap between supply and demand is resolved by a change in price. However it is possible in CGE modeling to fix the price of a commodity and have the supply constrained, so that potential demand exceeds actual demand. This refinement is facilitated by the development of software that uses a complementarity programming solution approach, thereby allowing for some 'slack' in the system, and hence disequilibrium. For example Rose and Liao (2005) were able to limit the supply of water to each sector, and on a differential basis. Ordinarily this would increase the price of water, but this is unrealistic given the fact that water is not priced in an ordinary market but rather under the administrative authority of a public service agency. Therefore price of water was fixed, essentially modeling it as a disequilibrium market. The slack is taken up by a reduction in the profit margin in the water sector. Rose and Guha (2004) performed a similar analysis for electricity under both fixed and flexible pricing.

Closely related are the ad hoc adjustments and temporary equilibria that ensue after a disaster, many of which can be incorporated through further refinement of the CGE model. Examples identified by West and Lenze (1994) include additions to the labor market in the form of outside government and NGO volunteers, examples identified by Cochrane (1997) include households dipping deep into savings or increasing their borrowing to fund repairs, and those identified by Rose and Lim (2002) include businesses recapturing lost production through overtime work at a later date.

EMPIRICAL INSIGHTS

Will an *x* per cent loss of electricity result in an *x* per cent direct loss in economic activity for a given firm? The answer is definitely 'no' given the presence of economic resilience. For the purpose at hand, we use as our measure of direct resilience, the deviation from the linear proportional relation between the percentage utility disruption and the percentage reduction in customer output (see Rose, 2004b). One of the most obvious resilience options for input supply interruptions in general is reliance on inventories.

This has long made electricity outages especially problematic, since this product cannot typically be stored. However the increasing severity of the problem has inspired ingenuity, such as the use of non-interruptible power supplies (capacitors) in computers (Douglas, 2000). Other resilience measures include back-up generation, conservation, input substitution, and rescheduling of lost production. In many business enterprises, these measures are adequate to cushion the firm against some losses of a rather short or moderate duration.

Will a *y* per cent loss in direct output yield much larger general equilibrium losses? Here both market-related adjustments suggest some muting of general equilibrium effects, if we measure market or net general equilibrium, resilience as the deviation from the linear multiplier effect that would be generated from a simple input–output analysis of the outage (Rose, 2004a). Adjustments for lost output of goods and services other than electricity include inventories, conservation, input substitution, import substitution and production rescheduling at the level of the individual firm, and the rationing feature of pricing at the level of the market.

Table 11.1 summarizes loss estimates from utility service disruptions. The number of studies is rather sparse, because we have limited inclusion to those studies that used customer lost output as the unit of measure and that have also included indirect (either ordinary multiplier or general equilibrium) effects. The first study noted in Table 11.1 is that of Tierney (1997), who received responses to a survey questionnaire from more than 1000 firms following the Northridge earthquake. Note that maximum electricity service disruption following this event was 8.3 per cent and that nearly all electricity service was restored within 24 hours. Tierney survey results indicated that direct output losses amounted to only 1.9 per cent of a single day's output in Los Angeles County. A study by Rose and Lim (2002) used a simple simulation model of three resilience options to estimate adjusted direct losses at 0.42 per cent and used an I–O model to estimate total region-wide losses of 0.55 per cent. Although this study did not include the full range of resilience tactics as was inherent in the Tierney study, it is also likely that in the Tierney study the effects of production rescheduling would be underreported. A CGE analysis by Rose and Guha (2004) of the impacts of a hypothetical New Madrid earthquake on the Memphis, Tennessee economy indicated that a 44.8 per cent loss of utility services would result in only a 2.3 per cent loss of regional output; however it should be noted that this model did not explicitly include resilience measures and was constrained from reducing major parameters, such as elasticities of substitution, to levels that truly reflected a very short-run crisis situation. A study by Rose and Liao (2005) for a hypothetical earthquake in Portland, Oregon, and for water rather than electricity utilities, incorporated engineering simulation estimates of direct

Table 11.1 Summary of loss estimates from utility service disruptions

Study	Location/ Event	Utility/ Duration	Method or model	Loss of utility services (%)	Direct output loss (%)	Total output loss from adjusted direct (%)	Direct Q loss/ loss of utility services (%)	Individual business resilience (%)	Total Q loss/ direct Q loss (%)	Market resilience (%)
Tierney (1997)	Los Angeles/ Northridge	Electricity/ 36 hrs	Survey	8.3	1.9	1.9[b]	22.9[b]	77.1	–	–
Rose–Lim (2002)	Los Angeles/ Northridge	Electricity/ 36 hrs	I–O	8.3	0.42[c]	0.55	5	95	131	79.3
Rose–Guha (2004)	Memphis/ Hypothetical	Electricity/ First week	CGE	44.8	–	2.3[d]	5.1[e]	94.9	–	–
Rose–Liao (2005)	Portland/ Hypothetical	Water/ First week	CGE	50.5	5.7[f, g, h]	7	11.3	88.7	122	75.6
Rose–Liao (2004)	Portland/ Hypothetical	Water/ First week	CGE	31	3.5[f, g, i]	5	11.4	88.6	143	52.2

Notes:

a. Survey response incorporates direct resilience practices.
b. Includes only direct effects.
c. Resilience adjustments limited to time-of-day use, importance factor, and production rescheduling.
d. Model not able to incorporate very short-run elasticities; hence, flexibility of response is exaggerated.
e. Numerator is total output loss, since direct and indirect output losses could not be distinguished in this model.
f. Production rescheduling (recapture) factors from Rose and Lim (2002) were applied to study results.
g. Resilience adjustments limited to conservation and inputs substitution for water.
h. Prior to any mitigation.
i. After mitigation.

output losses into a CGE model. The first simulation, which represented a business-as-usual scenario, indicated that a 50.5 per cent loss of utility services would result in a 33.7 per cent direct output loss, factoring in some resiliency measures. Further adjustment for production rescheduling reduces this to 5.7 per cent. A second simulation, representing the case of $200 million capital expenditure initiative of replacing cast-iron pipes with modern materials, indicated that a 31 per cent loss of utility services would result in a 3.5 per cent loss of direct output in the region. Note that direct resilience declined following mitigation (direct output losses as a proportion of utility outage levels increased), because mitigation reduces initial loss of service and hence ironically narrows the range of resilience options that can be brought into play.

Individual business, or direct, resilience is presented in column 9 of Table 11.1. This measure is simply the complement of the figure in column 8 (the column 8 figure subtracted from 100 per cent). The results of the several studies, using several alternative methods, indicate that individual business resilience is quite high and that results of analyses that included this factor would be between 77 per cent and 95 per cent lower than for analyses that neglected it (for example a purely linear model).

General equilibrium effects are presented in column 10 and indicate a moderate increase over direct (partial equilibrium) effects, ranging from 122 per cent to 143 per cent. The I–O model of the Rose and Lim (2002) study did not allow for ordinary multiplier effects, because of assumed adequacy of inventories for goods other than electricity for the 36-hour outage period, and thus considered only 'bottleneck effects' (see also Cochrane et al., 1997). Interestingly the first simulation by Rose and Liao (2005) yielded general equilibrium effects of the order of 22 per cent of direct effects, and the second simulation yielded general equilibrium effects 43 per cent as great as direct effects. This means that mitigation not only lowered direct business resilience but also made the regional economy as a whole less resilient, thus offsetting some of this strategy's benefits.

Thus in this group of studies direct resilience is a stronger force on the downside than are general equilibrium effects on the upside.[9] These two sets of effects do not cancel each other out, and a study that omitted both is still likely to significantly overestimate the effect that a terrorist attack on a utility lifeline has on the overall economy.

While we have assessed the implications of omitting general equilibrium effects, it is equally likely that they might be overestimated, especially if a linear model is used. The extent of this problem can better be appreciated by examining market resilience, or the percentage deviation between an analysis that takes the workings of the market into account and one that does not. Market resilience can, however, be taken into account in a linear model like I–O analysis, as in the work of Cochrane et al. (1997), Rose et al. (1997) and Rose and Lim (2002). In the former case, the solution algorithm allows for market resilience by changing the pattern of imports and exports, while the latter includes an assumption that customers without suppliers will find new suppliers without customers in a type of 're-contracting' arrangement. Indirect effects in both of these approaches are thus limited to 'bottleneck' effects, where one sector is so extensively disrupted that it limits the 'smoothing' effects on supply and demand throughout the economy. Otherwise if the standard I–O formulation is used, multiplier effects (as a proxy for general equilibrium effects) can be quite large. In the studies listed in Table 11.1, the LA County multiplier is 2.5 and the Portland Metropolitan area multiplier is 1.9. Column 10 represents a measure of market (net general equilibrium) resilience as a percentage deviation from the purely linear result. However even with the overestimation resulting from a standard I–O model, direct resilience appears to be the more dominant of the two effects.[10]

CONCLUSION

This chapter has summarized the current capabilities of computable general equilibrium (CGE) models designed to analyse and estimate the economic impacts of a terrorist attack. The CGE approach is a formidable one. It performs well in terms of nearly all of the modeling considerations applicable to the task, and is superior to its major modeling competitors in most respects. CGE is especially adept at modeling two major aspects of the economic losses in this context – resilience and general equilibrium effects. It should be noted that the formulation and application of most CGE models to date has been in respect of the economic impacts of disruptions to individual utility lifelines. Additional refinements are necessary to model the ramifications of more complex cases with widespread devastation of property stemming from large bombs or typical natural hazards. In these cases, it should be emphasized that the sum of the indirect damage stemming from simultaneous damage to several individual targets is greater than the actual damage because of redundancy, that is, one must avoid counting lost production in a factory from both its own destruction and its inability to produce because of the unavailability of several lifeline services (see for example Chang et al., 1996). Most terrorist attacks however are likely to be relatively more targeted, in which cases further adjustments are not needed.

Future research on CGE modeling of terrorism should focus on important aspects of the issue, as well as limitations of CGE modeling in addressing them. This combination includes improving the ability of CGE models to incorporate financial variables, technological change and cumulative adaptive behavior, short-term adjustments to equilibrium and long-term effects on economic growth.

NOTES

* The research in this chapter is supported by funding from the DHS Center for Risk and Economic Analysis of Terrorist Events and by several grants from the NSF Multidiscipilinary Center for Earthquake Engineering Research.

1. This is distinct from partial equilibrium (firm- or industry-specific models) or tools that emphasize forecasting, such as econometric models.
2. CGE models are operational versions of Walrasian general (multi-market) equilibrium analysis. The first CGE models were developed around 1960, but they were primarily small-scale versions for the purposes of illustration. Advances in solution algorithms for solving large-scale models were soon forthcoming to the point today that there is virtually no limit in the number of sectors or economic units that can be incorporated into a CGE model.
3. The major software to run CGE models is GAMS (Brooke et al., 1988) and MPSGE (Rutherford, 1995).
4. Unfortunately, the detailed time series data for this are rarely available, such that there are only a handful of CGE models in existence that are based primarily on econometric estimation.
5. Note that in the infancy of conceptual and especially empirical analysis of economic resilience, we believe it is prudent to pin down fundamental considerations first. Dynamic aspects of resilience, including intertemporal tradeoffs, system 'flipping', irreversibilities, and extreme non-linearities, are beyond the scope of this chapter.
6. We briefly note the relationship between resilience and two other concepts. Preparedness refers to steps taken before a disaster to subsequently reduce losses. Some of these actions, such as the building up of inventories, improve the capacity of inherent resilience, while others, such as the establishment of an improved communication network, increasing adaptive resilience capacity. Preparedness typically focuses on ways of enhancing resilience before the event, while resilience emphasizes the reduction of economic losses due to an earthquake during and after the ground-shaking (that is, the benefits of reduced losses). Moreover, not all preparedness affects inherent resilience (for example that portion of preparedness that is pure mitigation), and not all resilience stems from preparedness (for example innate human ingenuity and the natural self-adjusting feature of markets). Note also that resilience differs from the concept of adaptation. Adaptation consists of two components: an active effect to reduce losses after an event has taken place (for example migration) and a passive absorption ('suffering') of the loss. Our concept of adaptive resilience overlaps with the first component.
7. Rose and Benavides (1999) have identified a potential flaw in non-interruptible service premia in a general equilibrium context because a given firm considers only its own benefits from continued service and not the benefits to its suppliers and customers (see also Rose and Guha, 2004).
8. In fact, emergency management officials in Los Angeles, California are investigating prospects for establishing an information clearing house to help expedite such adjustments.
9. It should be noted that the various studies listed in Table 11.1 are not entirely independent. For example, Rose and Liao used some of the Tierney survey findings on resilience to recalibrate their production function parameters. In addition the same recapture factors used in the Rose and Lim study were applied to the study results by Rose and

Liao. It should be kept in mind, however, that these are only a few of several considerations that influence the numerical value of the results.

10. This is reinforced mathematically by the fact that business resilience is applied to the direct effect, which serves as the base for the market effect. That is, a 90 per cent decrease in direct economic impacts due to resilience also reduces the general equilibrium impacts in absolute (though not in percentage) terms. However, a reduction in general equilibrium effects does not reduce individual business resilience.

REFERENCES

Baran, P. and J.K. Galbraith (1947), 'Professor Despres on "The effects of strategic bombing on the German war economy"', *Review of Economics and Statistics*, **29**, 132–4.

Beenstock, M., E. Goldin and Y. Haitobsky (1997), 'The cost of power outages in the business and public sectors in Israel: revealed preference vs. subject evaluation', *Energy Journal*, **18**, 39–61.

Bental, B. and S.A. Ravid (1986), 'A simple method for evaluating the marginal cost of unsupplied electricity', *Bell Journal of Economics*, **13**, 249–53.

Boisvert, R. (1992), 'Indirect losses from a catastrophic earthquake and the local, regional, and national interest', in *Indirect Economic Consequences of a Catastrophic Earthquake*, Washington, DC: FEMA.

Bram, J., J. Orr and C. Rappaport (2002), 'The impact of the world trade center attack on New York City: where do we stand?' New York: Federal Reserve Bank of New York.

Brooke, A., D. Kendrick and A. Meeraus (1988), *GAMS: A User's Guide*, San Francisco, CA: Scientific Press.

Brookshire, D. and M. McKee (1992), 'Other indirect costs and losses from earthquakes: issues and estimation', in *Indirect Economic Consequences of a Catastrophic Earthquake*, Washington, DC: FEMA.

Bruneau, M., S. Chang, R. Eguchi, G. Lee, T. O'Rourke, A. Reinhorn, M. Shinozuka, K. Tierney, W. Wallace, and D. von Winterfelt (2003), 'A framework to quantitatively assess and enhance seismic resilience of communities', *Earthquake Spectra*, **19**, 733–52.

Caves, D., J. Harriges and R. Windle (1992), 'The cost of electric power interruptions in the industrial sector: estimates derived from interruptible service programs', *Land Economics*, **68**, 49–61.

Chang, S., H. Seligson and R. Eguchi (1996), *Estimation of the Economic Impact of Multiple Lifeline Disruption: Memphis Light, Gas, and Water Case Study*, Buffalo, NY: National Center for Earthquake Engineering Research.

Chao, H.P. and R. Wilson (1987), 'Priority service: pricing, investment and market organization', *American Economic Review*, **77**, 899–916.

Cochrane, H., S. Chang and A.Rose (1997), 'Indirect economic losses', in FEMA (1997) *Development of Standardized Earthquake Loss Estimation Methodology Vol. II*, Menlo Park, CA: RMS.

Comfort, L. (1999), *Shared Risk: Complex Seismic Response*, New York: Pergamon.

Douglas, J. (2000), 'Power for a digital society', *EPRI Journal*, **25**, 18–25.

Duchin, F. and G. Lange (2002), *The Future of the Environment*, New York: Oxford.

FEMA (1997), *Earthquake Loss Estimation Methodology (HAZUS)*, Volume 3, Chapter 16, Washington, DC: National Institute of Building Sciences and Federal Emergency Management Agency.

French, S. (1998), 'Spatial analysis techniques for linking physical damage to economic functions', in M. Shinozuka, A. Rose and R. Eguchi (eds), *Engineering and Socioeconomic Impacts of Earthquakes: An Analysis of Electricity Lifeline Disruptions in the New Madrid Area*, Buffalo, NY: MCEER.

Gordon, P., J. Moore II, H. Richardson, M. Shinozuka, D. An and S. Cho (2004), 'Earthquake disaster mitigation for urban transportation systems', in Y. Okuyama and S. Chang (eds), *Modeling Spatial and Economics Impacts of Disasters*, Heidelberg: Springer.

Holling, C. (1973), 'Resilience and stability of ecological systems', *Annual Review of Ecology and Systematics*, **4**, 1–23.

Kokoski, M. and V. Smith (1987), 'A general equilibrium analysis of partial equilibrium welfare measures: the case of climate change', *American Economic Renew*, **77** (3), June, 331–41.

MIG – Minnesota IMPLAN Group (2003), *Impact Analysis for Planning System* (*IMPLAN*), Stillwater, MN.

Mileti, D. (1999), *Disasters by Design: A Reassessment of Natural Hazards in the United States*, Washington, DC: Joseph Henry Press.

Munasinghe, M. and M. Gellerson (1979), 'Economic criteria for optimizing power system reliability levels,' *Bell Journal of Economics*, **10**, 353–65.

Oladosu, G. (2000), 'A non-market computable general equilibrium model for economic analysis of climate change in the Susquehanna river basin', unpublished Ph.d. dissertation, Department of Energy, Environmental, and Mineral Economics, The Pennsylvania State University.

Partridge, M. and D. Rickman (1998), 'Regional computable general equilibrium modeling: a survey and critical appraisal', *International Regional Science Review*, **21**, 205–48.

Perrings, C. (2001), 'Resilience and sustainability', in H. Folmer, H.L. Gabel, S. Gerking and A. Rose (eds), *Frontiers of Environmental Economics*, Cheltenham, UK and Northampton, MA, USA: Edward Elgar.

Petak, W. (2002), 'Earthquake resilience through mitigation: a system approach', paper presented at the International Institute for Applied Systems Analysis, Laxenburg, Austria.

Porter, M., and C. van der Linde (1995), 'Towards a new conception of the environment–competitiveness relationship', *Journal of Economic Perspectives*, **9**, 97–118.

REMI – Regional Economic Models Incorporated (2004), www.remi.com, Amherst, MA.

Rose, A. (1995), 'Input–output economics and computable general equilibrium models', *Structural Change and Economic Dynamics*, **6**, 295–304.

Rose, A. (1998), 'Computable general equilibrium analysis of economic losses from earthquakes', in *Proceedings of the Structural Engineers World Congress*, New York: Elsevier.

Rose, A. (2004a), 'Economic principles, issues, and research priorities of natural hazard loss estimation', in Y. Okuyama and S. Chang (eds), *Modeling of Spatial Economic Impacts of Natural Hazards*, Heidelberg: Springer, pp. 13–36.

Rose, A. (2004b), 'Defining and measuring economic resilience to disasters', *Disaster Prevention and Management*, **13**, 307–14.

Rose, A. and J. Benavides (1999), 'Optimal allocation of electricity after major earthquakes: market mechanisms versus rationing', in K. Lawrence (ed.), *Advances in Mathematical Programming and Financial Planning*, Greenwich, CT: JAI Press.

Rose, A., J. Benavides, S. Chang, P. Szczesniak, and D. Lim (1997), 'The regional economic impact of an earthquake: direct and indirect effects of electricity lifeline disruptions', *Journal of Regional Science*, **37**, 437–58.

Rose, A. and G. Guha (2004), 'Computable general equilibrium modeling of electric utility lifeline losses from earthquakes', in Y. Okuyama and S. Chang (eds), *Modeling the Spatial Economic Impacts of Natural Hazards*, Heidelberg: Springer, pp. 119–42.

Rose, A. and S. Liao (2005), 'Modeling resilience to disasters: computable general equilibrium analysis of a water service disruption', *Journal of Regional Science*, **45**, 75–112.

Rose, A. and D. Lim (2002), 'Business interruption losses from natural hazards: conceptual and methodological issues in the case of the Northridge Earthquake', *Global Environmental Change B: Environmental Hazards*, **4**, 1–14.

Rose, A., G. Oladosu and D. Salvino (2004), 'Regional economic impacts of electricity outages in Los Angeles: a computable general equilibrium analysis', in M. Crew and M. Spiegel (eds), *Obtaining the Best from Regulation and Competition*, Dordrecht: Kluwer, pp. 179–210.

Rutherford, T. (1995), 'Computable general equilibrium modeling with MPSGE as a GAMS subsystem: an overview of the modeling framework and syntax', available at http://www.gams.com/solbers/mpsge/syntax.htm

Shoven, J. and J. Whalley (1992), *Applying General Equilibrium*, New York: Cambridge University Press.

Sohn, J., G. Hewings, T.J. Kim, J.S. Lee and S. Jang (2004), 'Analysis of economic impacts of an earthquake on a transportation network', in Y. Okuyama and S. Chang (eds), *Modeling Spatial and Economic Impacts of Disasters*, Berlin: Springer.

Tierney, K. (1997), 'Impacts of recent disasters on businesses: the 1993 midwest floods and the 1994 Northridge Earthquake', in B. Jones (ed.), *Economic Consequences of Earthquakes: Preparing for the Unexpected*, Buffalo, NY: National Center for Earthquake Engineering Research, pp. 189–222.

Tinch, R. (1998), 'Resilience and resource management under risk', School of Environmental Science, University of East Anglia.

United States Strategic Bombing Survey (1945), *Summary Report (European War)*, Washington, DC: US GPO.

West, C. and D. Lenze (1994), 'Modeling the regional impact of natural disaster and recovery', *International Regional Science Review*, **17**, 121–50.

12. Evaluating the viability of 100 per cent container inspection at America's ports

Susan E. Martonosi, David S. Ortiz and Henry H. Willis

INTRODUCTION

The US and the global economy are wholly dependent on overseas trade and the integrated transportation system that moves cargo around the world and throughout the US. Six million cargo containers, equivalent to over 11 million 20-foot equivalent units (TEUs),[1] of goods arrive at United States seaports (Maritime Administration, 2002; Bureau of Transportation Statistics, 2003). Approximately 90 per cent of global trade, including 75 per cent by value of non-North American trade to and from the US, is shipped via cargo container (Stana, 2004; Willis and Ortiz, 2004). The multi-modal structure of the containerized supply chain permits containers entering via a seaport to exploit the US road and rail network to penetrate deeply into the country.

Any disruption to the steady flow of containers into and out of the United States can have a devastating economic impact. Estimations of the costs from a ten-day West Coast port lock-out ranged from $500 million to as high as $19 billion (Crist, 2003), and a simulation conducted by the consulting firm Booz-Allen-Hamilton estimated that the discovery of proposed attacks on selected ports could lead to nationwide shutdown of ports carrying economic effects up to $58 billion (Gerencser et al., 2003). Though these estimates are highly dependent upon underlying assumptions and subject to debate, the fact remains that there are many port disruption scenarios that would result in billions of dollars in damages.

The volume of containers and the pervasiveness of the delivery system reveal two distinct vulnerabilities: an attack on a port could carry a devastating economic impact and also the system itself could be used to deliver a weapon to any location in the country. These vulnerabilities are not new. The efficiency and anonymity of the containerized supply chain have also made it a useful target of smugglers and vulnerable to theft. Stephen Flynn of the Council on Foreign Relations has long warned that the vulnerability of this system and consequences of attacks on it, or using it, make the containerized shipping system an attractive terrorist target (Flynn, 2000, 2002, 2004).

Prior to the terrorist attacks of 11 September 2001, the primary focus of port security was to prevent theft and to ensure that illegal or undeclared goods were not brought into the United States. The United States and international responses to the terrorist threat has expanded the focus of port security. Within the Department of Homeland Security (DHS), Customs Service and Border Patrol functions were merged to become US Customs and Border Protection (CBP). The International Maritime Organization updated the Convention for the Safety of Life at Sea and issued the International Ship and Port Facility Code. The United States passed the Maritime Transportation Security Act of 2002, instituting new protocols for the declaration of cargo, and has stationed customs inspectors at overseas ports. The private sector is now encouraged to participate in voluntary programs for securing their supply chains through the Customs–Trade Partnership Against Terrorism (Crist, 2003). The Smart and Secure Tradelanes consortium funds pilot projects to demonstrate new technology to make the supply chain more transparent ('SST Phase One Report', 2003). Despite this extensive response, there is little evidence that enough has been done to secure US ports or that what has already been done is effective.

We argue that the goal of transportation security initiatives, focused on the ports of entry for cargo containers, is to balance the costs of providing increased security with the reduction of risks from the unintended use of the container supply system. While unintended uses include the movement of any dangerous or illegal goods, we focus on the reduction of risks from terrorist attacks at a port or deriving from cargo arriving at a port. To this end, we propose that cost–benefit analysis be used to assess security initiatives directed at preventing terrorist attacks. This chapter provides a case study for a specific proposal: 100 per cent scanning of containers at US ports. Container scanning and inspection are essential steps in the process of ensuring a secure containerized shipping system. These processes may reduce the risk of an attack on the port itself through deterrence or by increasing the likelihood that terrorist weapons will be detected.[2]

Previous work by the authors has developed a framework for assessing and evaluating the security of the containerized supply chain (Willis and Ortiz, 2004). Here we present an extension of that work focused on technological requirements for implementing the specific policy of inspecting all incoming containers via scanners.

We begin by defining some terms. Homeland Security Presidential Directive HSPD-11 defines 'terrorist-related screening' in a general context as 'the collection, analysis, dissemination, and use of information related to people, cargo, conveyances, and other entities and objects that pose a threat to homeland security' (Bush, 2004). Accordingly we call 'screening' the initial assessment of the risk of a container based on manifest, shipper, carrier, consignee and other information associated with the shipment. 'Primary inspection' or 'scanning' is the radiographical scanning of a container via an X-ray or a gamma-ray scanner to identify its contents. 'Secondary inspection' is the hand-inspection of the contents of a container by a team of CBP inspectors.[3]

The small fraction of containers that currently undergo primary inspection has motivated calls for complete scanning: US House of Representatives minority leader Nancy Pelosi called for complete inspection of containers in the Democratic response to the 2004 State of the Union address (Pelosi and Daschle, 2004). At the 2004 Democratic National Convention in Boston, former president Bill Clinton highlighted the need for dramatically increased scanning at our nation's ports (Clinton, 2004). Stephen Flynn proposes electronic scanning of containers at departure and arrival, comparing images to verify security (Flynn, 2004). A recent study (Wein et al., 2003) examined potential container inspection policies against nuclear materials from a game-theoretic standpoint, where the government would like to choose an inspection scheme that falls within budgetary constraints and maximizes detection probabilities over a range of possible terrorist responses. In this chapter, we perform a cost–benefit analysis of implementing a policy of scanning 100 per cent of incoming containers at US ports, exploring issues of technological cost and performance, and we examine the minimum threat required to justify the costs of particular inspection proposals.

In this context, we present three questions:

1. Given current technological effectiveness, how does changing the percentage of containers selected for scanning alter the cost and effectiveness of the containerized supply chain? In particular, under what situations is 100 per cent scanning cost-effective?
2. What are the implications of policy decisions for small versus large ports?
3. What technological improvements would be required to make increased scanning of incoming ocean containers effective?

The remainder of the chapter is organized as follows. We follow the introduction with an overview of proposals for increasing container inspection processes and associated technology issues. We then describe a cost–benefit approach for assessing the viability of increased inspections of containers using a queuing model to simulate the inspection process. Limitations because of simplifications in the model and estimates of parameters are discussed. We conclude by presenting results from this modeling approach and the implications of these results on policy efforts to secure US ports.

CONTAINER INSPECTION PROCESSES AND TECHNOLOGY ISSUES

Overview of Container Screening, Scanning and Inspection Process

A container arriving at a US port is subjected to several checks. The 24-hour advanced manifest rule requires carriers to submit manifest information 24 hours before cargo is loaded onto a US-bound vessel. In this time, CBP performs a background screen on the manifest, carrier and shipper to determine if the shipment poses a risk to the United States. In some cases, the container is denied permission to be loaded on the vessel. CBP performs additional manifest screening prior to shipment arrival via a computerized targeting system. Currently, approximately 5 per cent of incoming containers from the sea are selected for additional scrutiny, which consists of a two-stage inspection process. Primary inspection consists of scanning via an X-ray or a gamma-ray scanner. Gamma-ray scanners tend to be less expensive and faster than X-ray scanners; gamma-ray scanners however operate at lower power and therefore have difficulty producing clear images of densely packed containers. Scanning occurs by passing a container through a fixed scanner, or by moving the scanner over a fixed container. Inspectors examine the scanned image for discrepancies with the manifest and other signs of risk.

In some cases, actual physical inspection is required. Of these already suspicious containers, it is estimated that roughly 5 per cent show irregularities in the image, or are so densely packed that the image is not clear; these containers require a hand-search in which the container is opened and its contents removed and examined (Schiesel, 2003, Krikorian, 2004). This is a time-consuming process involving as long as four hours using 15 to 20 inspectors (Bowser and Husemann, 2004) or three days for five agents (Johnson, 2004). Neither of these estimates has been statistically studied.

Proposed Policies for Increased Scanning and Inspection of Containers

Any proposed policy change requiring increased primary inspection of containers raises several issues. Additional scanning equipment would need to be purchased, operated and maintained. Competing technologies have different costs and performance, measured by detection capability and scanning rate. Increased scanning of containers would also require more teams of inspectors to complete secondary inspections by hand. These factors form the basis of alternative policies for increased inspection of containers, described below. The alternative policies are compared against a 'base policy', which is modeled on the current scanning regime.

- *Base policy, 'current' scanning processes*: The base policy randomly[4] selects 5 per cent of incoming containers to be scanned via deployed X-ray scanners. Of these containers, 5 per cent require additional inspection by hand. The costs for this policy are annual operations and maintenance costs for the scanning equipment and salaries for the inspectors.

To assess the viability of 100 per cent inspection of containers at US ports, we present three alternative policies (see also Table 12.1).

- *Policy 1 – 100 per cent inspection using current technology*: This policy mandates the scanning of 100 per cent of arriving containers with current technology. More scanning machines are required than for the base policy. The costs of this policy include capital, operations, maintenance and inspection costs.
- *Policy 2 – 100 per cent inspection using faster and cheaper technology*: This policy requires the scanning of 100 per cent of arriving containers, but with improved equipment. The new scanning technology is assumed to be gamma-ray based, but improved from currently available gamma-ray equipment. The improved scanning equipment is characterized by a faster scanning rate and lower equipment costs than the current technologies in the base policy and Policy 1, but carries the same 5 per cent false positive rate. Additionally, we assume a faster hand-inspection rate, because of improved training for inspectors or improved signaling from the scanning equipment as to the region of the container requiring scrutiny.
- *Policy 3 – 100 per cent inspection with greater accuracy*: This case improves on Policy 2 by reducing the false positive rate to 1 per cent.

APPLYING COST–BENEFIT ANALYSIS TO CONTAINER INSPECTION POLICIES

The goal of increasing container inspection is to reduce the risks from terrorist attacks on or using the containerized shipping system. Any

Table 12.1 The three policies considered in the case study of 100 per cent scanning of incoming containers are each characterized by 11 parameters. These parameters are based on assessments of current technology and possible performance characteristics of future technology. The three alternative cases are based on a simplification of the current policy

Parameter	Base policy	100% scanning same technology (Policy 1)	100% scanning slightly improved technology (Policy 2)	100% scanning greatly improved technology (Policy 3)
Fraction containers screened	0.05	1.00	1.00	1.00
Targeting method	Random	N/A	N/A	N/A
Detection rate	0.95	0.95	0.95	0.95
Scanning rat (TEU/hr)	20	20	30	30
False positive rate	0.05	0.05	0.05	0.01
Equipment unit cost ($M)	$4.5	$4.5	$1.0	$1.0
Annual maintenance costs ($)	$200 000	$200 000	$90 000	$90 000
Operators per scanner	4	4	4	4
Hand searching rate (containers per day)	1	1	4.8	4.8
Number of inspectors per team	5	5	5	5
Annual operator/inspector salary ($)	$50 000	$50 000	$50 000	$50 000

proposals for increasing container inspection must be compared to current policies. Cost–benefit analysis provides a normative approach to evaluate proposals for increased container scanning. Using this approach, a new policy should be adopted if the marginal costs the policy achieves are less than the expected marginal decrease in risk due to terrorist attacks.

A cost–benefit analysis requires defining the scope of costs and benefits considered. We have defined the direct benefits of the policy to be associated with stopping the damage of a terrorist attack, both to the port and to the economy in general. These benefits are a result of deterrent effects of scanning and the potential to detect and remove or disarm a weapon before it is used. The indirect benefits of a policy are more difficult to determine; for example 100 per cent scanning might allow CBP to more readily intercept misrepresented cargo and thus collect additional tariff revenue. The direct costs that we will consider are the equipment and personnel costs associated with 100 per cent scanning. There are also indirect costs associated with increased scanning, delays being the most important. We do not estimate other indirect costs associated with allocation of real estate at the port for inspections, nor expenses associated with inspector training.

It is important to account for uncertainty in parameters of the model for container inspections. For costs, this uncertainty can be reduced through surveys of relevant data and sensitivity analysis of results to this uncertainty. There is greater uncertainty about benefits, since the benefits of container inspection depend upon the probability that attacks would be stopped if they were attempted, the consequences of such an attack, and also the probability that a terrorist attack might be attempted in the first place. The last issue introduces a high level of uncertainty. Terrorist motivations and capabilities can be studied and understood through intelligence gathering, though at some level, this uncertainty is irreducible. Nevertheless, cost–benefit analysis is a useful framework for this decision context.

For each policy, a threshold attack probability defines conditions for adoption of the policy to be cost-effective. Calculating the threshold probability of attack provides bounds that can inform comparisons of competing policy alternatives. The methodology is similar to that used by Barnett and Martonosi (2003) to evaluate aviation security policies. The threshold annual probability of an attack on the United States on or using a cargo container may be derived as:

$$P(\text{Attack}) = \frac{(\text{Cost of Proposed Policy}) - (\text{Cost of Baseline Policy})}{\text{Attack Cost}\begin{pmatrix} P(\text{Proposed Policy Prevents Attack}) - \\ P(\text{Baseline Prevents Attack}) \end{pmatrix}}$$

The difference in costs and detection capabilities between the base and proposed policies can be both positive and negative. This creates several cases to consider, two of which are degenerate since they would produce negative threshold probabilities. First, note that when the denominator is positive, the new policy improves detection capability, and when it is negative, it degrades the detection capability. The first degenerate case occurs when the new policies improve detection capability and decrease costs; then it is always beneficial to switch to the new policy. The second degenerate case occurs when the detection capability decreases and the costs rise; then it is never beneficial to switch to the new policy.

For other cases, the decision to switch policies is more interesting. If the new policy improves detection capability but increases costs, it makes sense to switch if the threat is sufficiently high to justify the increased costs. In this case, the threshold probability is a lower bound: the proposed policy is cost-effective if the perceived probability of a terrorist attack is greater than this threshold. However if in decreasing detection capability, costs also decrease, then it might still be beneficial to switch to the new policy if the probability of a terrorist attack is believed to be sufficiently low.

Finally, there are two trivial cases to consider. If the policies have the same detection performance, the function is undefined as the denominator equals zero and switching depends only on relative costs, so the cheaper policy is better. If policies have the same costs, the numerator equals zero and the decision to adopt depends only on the relative detection probabilities, so the higher-performing policy is better.

CALCULATING COSTS AND BENEFITS OF CONTAINER INSPECTION

We develop a queuing model to estimate the cost and performance of each policy. The model takes into account scanning equipment technology, performance, acquisition requirements, depreciation and operation. The number of scanning machines and hand-inspection stations required is calculated as a function of the container arrival, scanning and inspection rates. We also consider incurred costs due to cargo delays. The benefit of any policy is the averted financial damages due to a terrorist attack on the system. All parameters are based on estimates from publicly available literature, though considerable uncertainty remains with respect to the advancement of scanning technology, the variability in arrival and service rate and the estimation of costs.

Cost and Performance of Container Inspection

Our base technology scenarios assume the technology most widely available and applicable currently is X-ray scanning. The X-ray scanners in use today cost approximately $4.5 million with estimated annual operating costs of approximately $200 000 (Frankle, 2004). We converted fixed equipment costs into annual costs by amortizing evenly over ten years. For the case of X-ray scanners, the total annual equipment costs are $650 000. We assume that X-ray scanners are 95 per cent effective at detecting dangerous materials, though this value is a function of both the technology and the operator. It is estimated that approximately 5 per cent of scanned containers require additional inspection and that few carry dangerous materials (Schiesel, 2003); hence we estimate the false positive rate to be equal to the total positive rate, 5 per cent.

Estimates for scanning rates vary. X-ray scanners can scan a 20-foot container in 30 seconds (ARACOR, 2004). But an operator may take up to 15 minutes to review the image. Having more operators per machine would reduce the average time a container spends being scanned. For simplicity, we have assumed that each machine requires four inspectors – one to operate the machine and three to examine the images – and that the total inspection rate is 20 TEUs per hour, or equivalently three minutes for scanning and reviewing the image of each container.

Though gamma-ray scanners are currently being used at some ports, we choose it to model policies employing improved technology. Operational concerns regarding gamma-ray scanners remain: their ability to scan densely packed containers is less than that of X-ray devices, which could cause them to have a high false positive rate; and truck drivers have expressed concerns about gamma-ray scanners because of potential radiation exposure. Gamma-ray scanners such as SAIC's Vehicle and Cargo Inspection System (VACIS) cost approximately $1 million, again amortized over ten years, and require $90 000 in annual maintenance costs, including the cost of replacing the radioisotopes once every five years (McDaniel, 2004; Schiesel, 2003). VACIS literature estimates a total inspection time of one to three minutes per TEU – an average of 30 TEU per hour – and we again assume a team of four inspectors per scanner.[5] We assume a 95 per cent rate of detection.

There are also parameters that do not rely on the type of scanning equipment used. The annual salary of a port inspector is assumed to be $50 000, based on an estimate by the Bureau of Labor Statistics (Bureau of Labor Statistics, 2004). Times for hand-inspections vary, ranging from four hours using 15 to 20 inspectors (Bowser and Husemann, 2004) to as high as three days for five agents (Johnson, 2004). We have thus chosen a value of one container per day for a team of five agents for the current case. For the cases considering improved technology, we reduced the search time to roughly five hours per container, or 4.8 containers per day, for a team of five people. While this reduction is not necessarily associated with improvements in technology, new technology might provide the inspectors with more information regarding the exact location of the material instigating a search.

Container Arrivals, Scanning and Hand-Inspection Service Rates

The model for container arrival, scanning and hand-inspection is that of a tandem queue. We assume that containers arrive at the port according to a Poisson process with rate λ containers per hour, which is easily calculated for any particular port.[6] The average arrival rate for the United States is 1 474 TEUs/hour over 157 ports, and arrival rates for prototypical large (for example Los Angeles)[7] and small ports (for example Miami) are 365 TEUs/hour and 50 TEUs/hour, respectively. The containers that arrive at a port are selected for scanning according to a Bernoulli random process with parameter p. For the base case, p will be 0.05, or 5 per cent of containers; for the case of 100 per cent scanning, p will be 1. A certain percentage of containers that are machine scanned will be selected for secondary inspection by hand; we assume that this selection process follows a Bernoulli process with parameter f representing the false-positive rate associated with the scanning technology. We assume that the scanning time per machine is exponentially distributed with parameter μ_S containers (TEU) per hour and that the rate for hand scanning is μ_H containers (TEU) per hour.[8] We assume that a port has M_S scanning machines and M_H hand-inspection stations, which are chosen to be the minimum number guaranteeing that the queue of containers to be scanned remains finite. This value is given by constraining the arrival rates ($p\lambda$ and $pf\lambda$ for primary and secondary inspection, respectively) to be strictly less than the total service rates ($M_S\mu_S$ and $M_H\mu_H$, respectively).[9]

Inspection Costs: Equipment and Man Hours

The costs of scanning are equivalent to equipment purchase, maintenance and operation costs. Therefore if C_S is the purchase price of each primary scanning machine, and A is the period over which the cost of the machine will be amortized, then the purchase price per year is C_S/A assuming straight-line depreciation. Furthermore each machine will require maintenance and repairs, R_S, per year. Lastly, each machine will require N_S operators at any time, and we assume that these operators earn a salary, S, per year and work in three shifts per day. Thus the annual cost for primary (machine) scanning per port is $M_S(C_S/A + R_S + 3N_SS)$. Because not all ports operate three full shifts a day, this assumption will underestimate somewhat the machine and staffing requirements per shift, yielding conservative estimates.

For hand inspection, the calculation is similar. Let M_H be the number of hand-inspection teams required at a port as calculated above. Since each hand-inspection team consists of N_H workers, again requiring a salary S and working in three different shifts daily, the total cost associated with hand inspections is $M_H(3N_HS)$.

Thus each port contributes a total of $M_S(C_S/A+R_S+3N_SS)+M_H(3N_HS)$ to the total equipment and labor costs of the scanning and inspection policy. We have calculated this value exactly for the top 30 ports representing 99.5 per cent of container imports based on data from the Maritime Administration. We apportion the remaining costs equally among the 127 remaining seaports.

Delay Costs per Container

Increased delays for containerized freight are cited as one of the principal concerns associated with increased scanning. For any given container, the delay time is probabilistically distributed based on the arrival and service processes (see Burke, 1968, 1972; Bertsekas and Gallager, 1972; and Larson and Odoni, 1981, among others). Therefore with knowledge of the delay costs per container per hour of delay, it would be a straightforward calculation to determine the total delay costs. Unfortunately the costs per hour of delay are exceptionally difficult to estimate.

The sensitivity of a shipment to a delay varies according to the contents. Short delays – from minutes to hours – most likely have little economic effect so long as delivery falls within a prescribed window. Delays of perishable items, such as fresh fruit, might incur no cost for a delay of several hours, but may incur a total loss if the delay is several days. Items critical to manufacturing supply chains might incur large costs almost immediately, and induce exponentially growing costs as assembly lines close due to lack of parts. The cost per hour of delay is certainly a non-linear function. Some scholars have attempted to estimate the costs of supply chain delays: Spencer (2004) for example cites a Fortune 100 estimate that a delay of one day adds 0.5 per cent of the product value to its cost, implying a linear relationship between delay time and incurred cost.

Rather than propose an estimate of the distribution of delay costs, we have chosen to use in our analysis several values for the costs of the delay: \$0, \$6 and \$60 per TEU-hour. In these scenarios, \$0 per TEU-hour represents the delay costs of time-insensitive cargoes, \$6 per TEU-hour represents 0.5 per cent value per day costs of a \$30 000/TEU shipment using Spencer's estimate, and $60 per TEU-hour represents extremely time-sensitive cargo – for example 5 per cent loss of value per day.

Direct and Indirect Attack Costs

Estimates of the cost of a terrorist attack vary widely. We are concerned with an attack on a port, nearby infrastructure, or a remote destination facilitated by using a shipping container. The cost of the attack includes loss of life, infrastructure damage and residual repercussions through the economy. We are assuming that increased scanning could eliminate the costs of an attack by allowing authorities to isolate the container from port facilities and other areas in which it may cause damage. We consider a range of attack costs from $1 billion to $1 trillion.

It is possible to place these figures into the context of other terrorist attacks and natural disasters. The 1993 attack on the World Trade Center was estimated to inflict a cost of $510 million, and the bombing of the Murrah Federal Building in Oklahoma City in 1995 was estimated to inflict a cost of $125 million (CNNMoney, 2004). The Booz–Allen–Hamilton simulation estimated the total cost of sequential port shutdowns at $58 billion. Estimates for the costs of the attacks of 11 September 2001 begin at $100 billion (Looney, 2002). Natural disasters, too, carry large price tags: Hurricane Andrew caused damages in the range of $100 billion (Looney, 2002), initial estimates for damages to Florida from Hurricane Ivan are $50 billion (Treaster, 2004), and an economic analysis of a hypothetical magnitude 7.1 earthquake on the Elysian Park Fault estimated costs up to $94 billion (Cho et al., 2001). The cost of a terrorist nuclear attack on the United States could begin at approximately $600 billion (Abt, 2003). Therefore our estimates for the costs of an attack via a container fit into the range of costs related to other attacks and natural disasters.

Expected Benefits of Policy

The expected benefit of increasing scanning at the nation's ports is the expected averted cost of attack. No scanning protocol is perfect: if only a fraction p of the containers are scanned, then if any of the $1-p$ per cent of containers that are not scanned is dangerous – for example contains a weapon of mass destruction – it will enter the country. Furthermore the scanning systems do not have perfect detection rates. If d is the probability of detection, then the probability that a dangerous container is prevented from entering the country is the product of the probability of scanning and the probability of detection: pd. We assume that hand-searching has a 100 per cent detection rate. The expected benefit therefore is the product of the probability that a container is dangerous, the probability of detection and the cost of an attack: $P(\text{Attack})*(pd)*C_A$.

Case Parameters

The parameters for the base policy and the three alternative policies were listed earlier. The scanning equipment and staffing requirements were determined as follows. For each of the top 30 incoming ports, we calculated average container arrival rates to determine equipment and staffing requirements (Maritime Administration, 2002). For the remaining 127 ports that handle container traffic – 0.5 per cent of the annual total – we allocated container traffic equally over all of these ports, determined equipment and staffing requirements for a single port, and replicated it 127 times to estimate nationwide requirements.

RESULTS

The decision to switch to a new scanning and inspection policy is based on the probability of an attack within a year and the costs of delay, attack, equipment acquisition and labor. Figure 12.1 illustrates how the threshold probability of attack depends on delay and attack costs. Looking first at the policy using current technology and the curve corresponding to a \$1 billion attack, we see that as delay costs increase from \$0 per TEU-hour to \$60 per TEU-hour, the estimated annual probability of attack required to switch to 100 per cent scanning varies from 80 per cent to almost 100 per cent. Thus unless an attack of that magnitude is very likely to occur within a year, it is not cost-effective to switch to 100 per cent screening using current technology. For an attack costing up to \$10 billion, the switching probability varies from 15 to 45 per cent. For attacks inflicting costs from \$100 billion to over \$1 trillion, the switching threshold probability is less than 10 per cent. The graphs for the other policies show that when technology is improved, the switching probability declines precipitously. For an attack inflicting \$1 billion of costs, the probability of attack required to make 100 per cent scanning beneficial varies from 23 per cent for \$0-per-hour delays, to 60 per cent for \$60-per-hour delays. For \$10 billion in inflicted costs, the probability of attack required to switch varies from approximately 3 per cent to approximately 10 per cent. Therefore the use of improved technology in scanning reduces the threshold probability of attack by an order of magnitude. New technology offers performance gains causing the decision to switch to 100 per cent scanning to be beneficial even when the estimated probability of attack is very low.

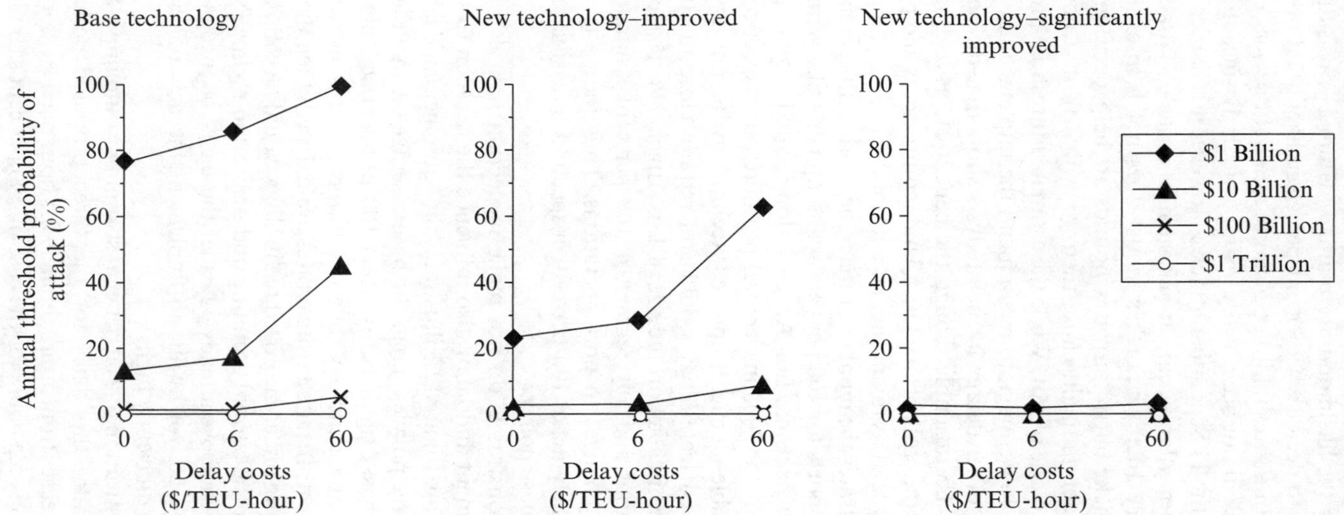

Figure 12.1 The threshold probability of attack required to switch to a new scanning policy for a range of attack costs

While estimating the likelihood of an attack within a year is difficult, it is somewhat easier to decide whether our perceived likelihood of attack is higher or lower than a threshold. For instance we might be very confident a $1 billion attack will not occur every year, particularly since it has been several years since the 11 September attacks. However it is harder to determine whether or not a large-scale attack such as a nuclear attack would occur roughly every 1000 years. This model does not help estimate the probability of attack, but it provides bounds to help decision makers understand what factors might cause them to switch from a position of adopting a policy to one of not. While the estimated threshold probability of attack might be low enough to recommend the implementation of 100 per cent scanning, other details in the analysis show that the decision is more complicated. For example though the benefit of preventing a large attack might offset the costs of machines, land requirements and personnel considerations may lead us to another conclusion.

Figure 12.2 illustrates the number of machines and hand-search stations required at typical ports for 100 per cent scanning per shift. With current technology, a large port like Los Angeles alone would require over 400 hand-search stations (or 2000 inspectors) per shift[10] to inspect containers to maintain a stable queue. Improved technology is not necessarily a panacea: improved technology would still require close to 100 hand-search stations per shift at a port the size of Los Angeles. Port space is optimized for throughput and any regime of 100 per cent scanning would require significant changes to port operations. Thus the costs excluded from our model likely make 100 per cent inspection infeasible using the technology of the base policy.

Even if space constraints do not make inspection policies infeasible, the costs of equipment and labor also influence the decision to switch to 100 per cent scanning. Figure 12.3 illustrates the equipment and labor costs per TEU for the three policies versus the base case. We see that the average cost per TEU increases significantly when 100 per cent scanning is performed with current technology, but that improvements in technology can decrease this cost. If false positive rates are reduced, then the costs of 100 per cent scanning under improved technology would be comparable to those estimated for the current scanning and inspection regime. Note that the thresholds shown above already consider these cost changes, and indicate that it can still be worthwhile to implement the new policies if the threat of attack is sufficiently high.

Of course the institution of 100 per cent scanning would impose a delay. Figure 12.4 illustrates this delay for the three proposed policies. The expected delay increases from approximately 0.5 hour per TEU for the base case to approximately 5.5 hours for the case of 100 per cent scanning using

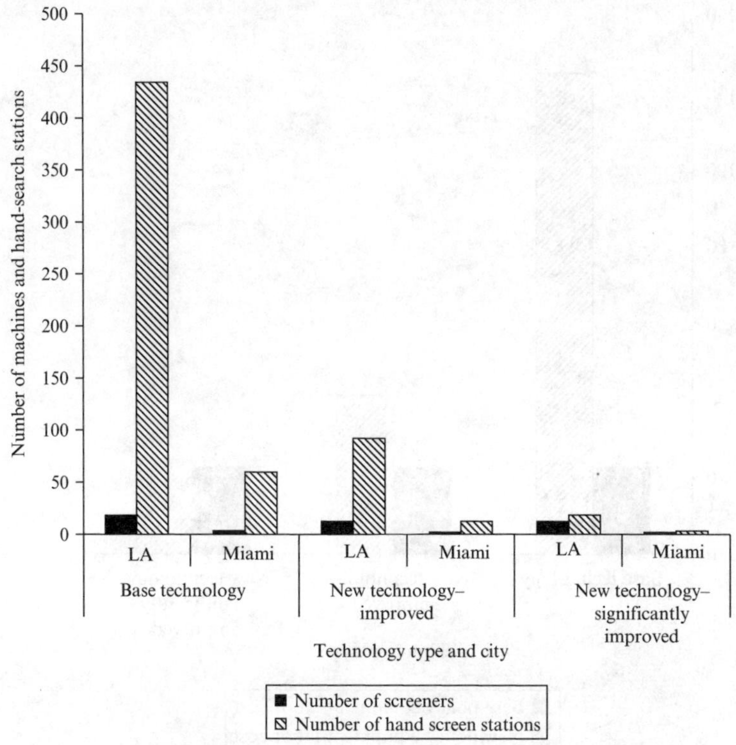

Figure 12.2 The number of scanning machines and hand-search stations required at prototypical ports per shift for 100 per cent scanning versus the base case for different levels of technology

current technology. This is the worst-case scenario, which could be tolerated with appropriate coordination among land-based carriers and shippers. Improved technology reduces this delay to approximately an hour, and greatly improved technology, offering a low false positive rate, has an inspection-induced delay comparable to that of the current 5 per cent scanning regime. Because the majority of a container's inspection time comes from the very long hand-searches, reducing the fraction of containers needing to be hand-searched causes a steep reduction in the average inspection time over all containers.

In summary, with currently available technology, 100 per cent scanning of arriving containers at US seaports may be cost-effective, but only if the land and personnel constraints prove feasible. To justify the switch to such a regime from a cost–benefit perspective would require at least a minimum

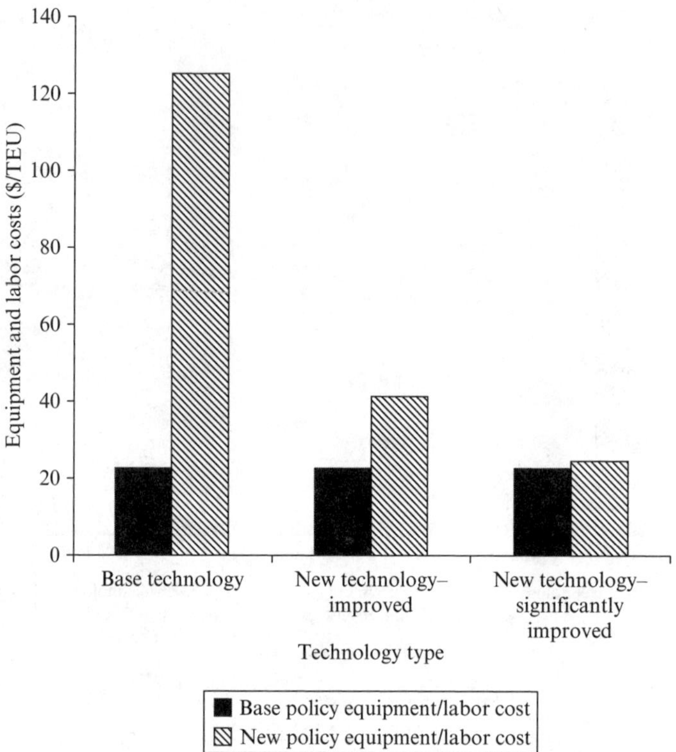

Figure 12.3 Equipment and labor costs per TEU for 100 per cent scanning versus the base case for different levels of technology

of a 14 per cent chance of an attack with consequences of $10 billion within a year, or a minimum of 80 per cent for an attack with consequences of $1 billion. However at high-traffic ports 100 per cent inspections may demand personnel increases of more than an order of magnitude beyond current staffing levels. Most of the inspection-related delays and labor costs stem from the vast number of containers that would require hand-searches. If advances can be made toward less-expensive and faster technologies with a lower false positive rate, then costs of inspection would not rise if 100 per cent scanning were employed and could make 100 per cent scanning a viable option at all ports. Nonetheless if our threat of attack is sufficiently high, then 100 per cent scanning could be justified with current technology.

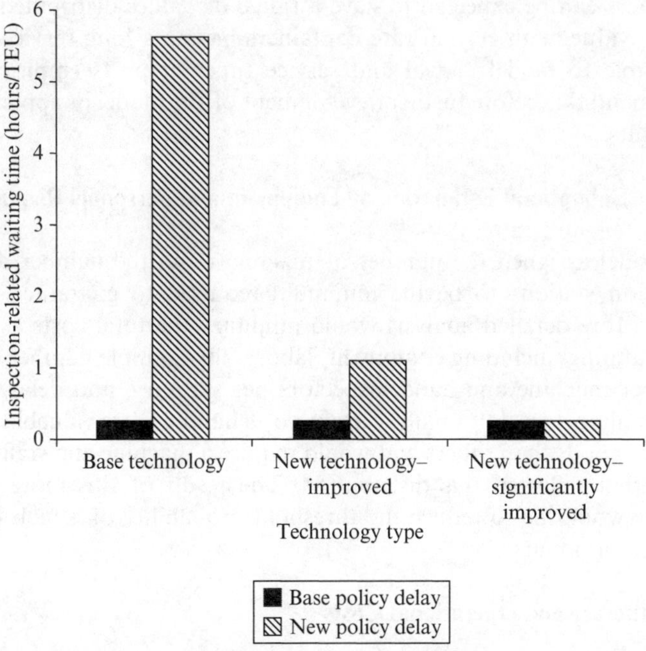

Figure 12.4 The expected delay because of inspection per TEU compared to the base case

LIMITATIONS

The results presented in this chapter are subject to model and data assumptions. This section discusses the limitations of our analysis stemming from the idealized queuing model, the algorithm for assigning machines and inspection teams to ports, and excluded costs and benefits.

Limitations of the Queuing Model

This model employed a tandem queue with Poisson arrivals and exponential service times. The inter-arrival times are independent and memoryless: the probability at any instant that an arrival occurs is independent of how long it has been since the last arrival. The assumption allows a closed-form solution for the distribution of waiting times in the queue, but overlooks the reality that container arrivals are coordinated with ship arrivals, which would tend to bunch container arrivals in batches. The assumption of exponential service times is justifiable, because scanning and inspection of containers can be expected to have a range of values distributed around a mean value, with certain rare containers having a long service time. It is possible to model arrival and service times at ports empirically; we recommend this before further development of the model or application of the results.

Possible Suboptimal Estimation of Equipment and Personnel Requirements

The model assigned the number of machines and the number of hand-inspection stations to be the minimum required to guarantee a stable queue. More detailed analysis would minimize the total costs associated with scanning, including equipment, labor – for example number of operators per machine and hand inspectors per station – and delay costs at individual ports. Additionally, certain ports handle more valuable or time-sensitive goods than others and would require a machine and staffing allocation that reflected this distribution. The result of this more detailed analysis would be to reduce the threshold probability of attack by some unknown amount.

Infrastructure and Operational Costs

As discussed above, the model did not consider infrastructure and operational costs that would be incurred to provide space for drayage, scanning and additional personnel. Additionally, we excluded scanning machine failure rates and the possibility that many small ports would need at least two scanners: one for normal operations and one to be used when the primary scanner fails or is undergoing maintenance. Inclusion of such costs would make 100 per cent scanning even less desirable than what was estimated in this analysis.

Marginal Analysis

In this chapter, we compared the total costs of implementing 100 per cent screening at all ports to the total benefits of such screening. Another strategy would have been to conduct this analysis incrementally, on a port-by-port basis. Starting with those ports that offer the greatest benefit of screening on a 'per dollar spent' basis, implement 100 per cent screening at those ports, and continue adding ports until the marginal costs of the next best port outweigh the marginal benefits. We have chosen not to use this method however because such analysis would require estimating the threat of attack on each port separately. While we may have some idea of the general level of threat facing our nation, the implementation of

100 per cent screening on a dynamic basis could very well shift the target away from those ports conducting the screening to those ports that do not screen, causing the results to vary at each increment. Furthermore if we believe those ports that are most desirable to attack are the very large ports, then our analysis has shown that these are the same ports for which 100 per cent screening is not currently feasible. Another problem is the potential political repercussions of choosing some ports for 100 per cent screening while ignoring others. Our study chooses to focus on the feasibility of a policy affecting all ports rather than on the incremental decision of which ports to protect before others. In addition, our research acknowledges marginal analysis in two other ways: considering alternative probabilities of an attack and mentioning, if not modeling, screening rates intermediate between the 5 per cent base case and 100 per cent screening.

CONCLUSIONS AND RESEARCH DIRECTIONS

This chapter has presented a cost–benefit analysis of 100 per cent scanning of incoming sea containers at US ports. The model uses cost estimates associated with equipment acquisition, operations and maintenance, inspector pay and the delay in delivery of goods. The benefits of the policy are the expected averted costs due to prevention of a terrorist attack. The analysis does not consider the costs of allocating space for the scanning equipment and inspection stations at ports, nor the benefits due to increased interception of illegal or misrepresented goods likely to occur from the imposition of 100 per cent scanning. We draw the following conclusions:

- Adopting a policy of 100 per cent scanning with current technology is not viable because of restrictions on land and personnel. If port land and personnel considerations are negligible – an unlikely case – then scanning 100 per cent of all incoming containers is cost-effective for attacks with direct and indirect consequences greater than \$10 billion. For an attack inflicting a cost of \$1 billion, the minimum annual probability of attack to switch to a policy of 100 per cent scanning is close to 0.80. However the threshold probability of attack is considerably smaller when attacks inflicting costs of \$10 billion or more are considered. When slightly improved scanning technology is deployed, personnel and land area requirements remain significant at high-volume ports when 100 per cent scanning is imposed. If these improvements manifest themselves as a reduction in the false positive rate, reduced land costs would make adoption of a 100 per cent scanning policy cost effective and could prompt a policy discussion regarding risk tolerance at America's ports. Technology developers should seek to reduce the false positive rate of their technology as they improve scanning rate, reliability and other performance characteristics.

- An area ripe for future study is the impact of 100 per cent scanning on deterrence. Complete scanning and subsequent inspection of containers at ports would most likely deter terrorists and smugglers under particular circumstances. A sufficiently high detection rate would render irrational an attempt to employ a container in an attack on an interior target, since it would have little chance of reaching the desired location. Of course the ability to attack a port via a container would remain. There are different ways to model deterrence. For example Martonosi and Barnett (2004) assign a threshold probability of success below which a terrorist will decide not to attack; the probability of a successful attack in their model is a function of the security measures in place and the deterrence threshold. Such a deterrence threshold could be incorporated in our model; however since there is little empirical evidence regarding successful deterrence of terrorists, any policy decision would require making assumptions regarding terrorist behavior. Incorporating deterrence into our model would embolden the case for 100 per cent scanning, because it would reduce the likelihood of an attack.
- The base policy assumed that 5 per cent of incoming containers were selected at random for scanning. However there is a broad range of scan rates between 5 and 100 per cent that may be employed to a certain degree of success, especially if such a policy mitigates needs for large parcels of land at ports. Any policy scanning less than 100 per cent of incoming containers would likely employ a targeting algorithm to increase the rate of detection. GAO concluded that there was no empirical evidence that US Customs and Border Protection's Automatic Targeting System identified dangerous cargo more readily than random scanning (Stana, 2004). Therefore to implement a policy scanning less than 100 per cent of containers, empirical demonstration of the ability of automatic targeting algorithms to detect dangerous cargo would be required.
- We found that port area for scanning and inspection was a critical driver of a policy's viability. The same issues in the case of air cargo may not be as serious: air cargo pallets are smaller than standard intermodal containers, are more readily scanned and inspected, and airport operations already require ferrying cargo around an airfield. A similar analysis could be applied directly to airfreight to evaluate policies requiring increased scanning of air cargo.

NOTES

1. The standard container is a 20 ft equivalent unit, which is a sturdy steel box measuring $20 \times 8 \times 8$ ft, although containers are often 40 ft long and can come in various configurations to support different kinds of cargo.
2. Further protection of US ports as targets would require detection prior to port arrival.
3. CBP 'screens' 100 per cent of incoming containers. Manifest information for US-bound containers must be communicated electronically to CBP 24 hours before being loaded on a US-bound vessel. Ninety-six hours prior to arrival at a US port, a vessel must declare crew and manifest information. Based on this information, CBP operates an automated targeting system to assess the risk each container may pose, and select some – roughly 5 per cent (Wasem et al., 2004) – to be radiographically scanned and/or hand-inspected.
4. Currently, containers are selected for targeting based on an automated targeting algorithm. The US General Accounting Office (Stana, 2004) determined that the Automated Targeting System (ATS) used by Customs and Border Protection has not undergone the rigorous testing that have similar systems. Furthermore, the GAO reported that industry experts believe that the data used by ATS to identify suspicious containers, including manifest declarations, are often unreliable and do not provide a sound basis for targeting. Hence it is unclear if the ATS performs better than random selection. It is also possible that terrorists could outwit the targeting system (Chakrabarti and Strauss, 2002).
5. It should be noted however that current scanning rates reported by those ports already using VACIS are approximately 8–10 per hour because of unfamiliarity with the technology (Schiesel, 2003).
6. A Poisson process is a stochastic counting process often used to simulate arrivals at a service queue such as a bank teller or bus stop. It has several characteristics that make it attractive for modeling such systems: the times between successive arrivals are independent and exponentially distributed with parameter λ; if two Poisson processes are combined, the resulting process is also Poisson; if a Poisson process is split into two processes by assigning a probability, p, to each arrival, then the resulting two processes are Poisson with rates λp and $\lambda(1-p)$ respectively (Bertsekas and Gallager, 1992). Poisson processes are considered good approximations for aggregate arrival processes, but might not be so well suited to the batch-like characteristics of a ship discharging cargo. As such, our use of a Poisson process will serve as a lower bound on the required equipment to achieve a certain level of container scanning.
7. All references in this chapter to the Port of Los Angeles consider this port individually and do not combine its traffic with that of the adjacent port of Long Beach.
8. It is traditional to assume that the service times of a queuing system follow an exponential distribution. This assumption and that of a Poisson arrival process guarantee that the scanning and hand inspection queues are $M/M/M_s$ and $M/M/M_H$ queues, for which probability distributions for the queuing delays are well understood (Bertsekas and Gallager, 1992). Future research may entail empirical estimation of the arrival and service processes at ports.
9. By choosing the smallest number of screeners satisfying this requirement, we minimize the equipment and labor cost, but perhaps do not minimize the total cost, which includes the inspection-related delay a container experiences at the port. Optimizing the number of machines with respect to total costs could alter somewhat the results of the analysis.
10. As a point of reference, the total CBP personnel at the Ports of Los Angeles and Long Beach increased to a total of about 500 after 9/11 (Fleming, 2004). Inspectors make up a portion of this staff.

REFERENCES

Abt, C.C. (2003), 'The economic impact of nuclear terrorist attacks on the freight transport systems in an age of seaport vulnerability', Cambridge, MA: Volpe National Transportation Center.

ARACOR (2004), 'ARACOR Eagle Product Information', Sunnyvale, CA: ARACOR, Inc.

Barnett, A.I. and S.E. Martonosi (2003), 'A cost–benefit risk analysis of three airport security measures', working paper, Cambridge, MA: Massachusetts Institute of Technology.

Bertsekas, D. and R. Gallager (1992), *Data Neworks*, 2nd edn, Englewood Cliffs, NJ: Prentice Hall.

Bowser, G.F. and R.C. Husemann (2004), 'Full cargo inspection possible through recent technology advances', Port Technology International, http://www.porttechnology.org/journals/ed11/downloads/pt11_69-72.pdf, 27 September.

Bureau of Labor Statistics (2004), 'Occupational employment and wages, May 2003: 53-6051 transportation inspectors', US Department of Labor, http://www.bls.gov/oes/2003/may/oes536051.htm, 5 October.

Bureau of Transportation Statistics (2003), 'US international trade and freight transportation statistics', BTS03-02, Washington, District of Columbia: US Department of Transportation.

Burke, P.J. (1968), 'The output process of a stationary M/M/s queuing system', *Annals of Mathematical Statistics*, **399**, 1144–52.

Burke, P.J. (1972), 'Output processes and tandem queues', *Proceedings of the Symposium on Computer-Communications, Networks, and Teletraffic*.

Bush, G.W. (2004), 'Comprehensive terrorist-related screening procedures', Homeland Security Presidential Directive/HSPD-11, 27 August.

Chakrabarti, S. and A. Strauss (2002), 'Carnival booth: an algorithm for defeating the computer-assisted passenger screening system', *First Monday*, **7** (10).

Cho, S., P. Gordon, H.W. Richardson, M. Shinozuka and S.E. Chang (2001), 'Integrating transportation network and regional economic models to estimate the costs of a large urban earthquake', *Journal of Regional Science*, **41**, 39–65.

Clinton, W.J. (2004), 'Text of former president Clinton's Remarks to the Democratic National Convention', *Washington Post*, http://www.washingtonpost.com/wp-dyn/articles/A16929-2004Jul26.html, 4 October.

CNNMoney (2004), 'Insurance claims to reach billions: the WTC attack could be the costliest manmade disaster', CNN, http://money.cnn.com/2001/09/12/worldbiz/ins/index.htm, 9 August.

Crist, P. (2003), 'Security in maritime transport: risk factors and economic impact', Paris: OECD Directorate for Science, Technology and Industry, Maritime Transport Committe.

Federal Highway Administration (2004), 'FHWA freight management and operations: Los Angeles Port', US Department of Transportation, http://ops.fhwa.dot.gov/freight/freight_analysis/state_info/california/pb_lax.htm, 27 September.

Fleming, M. (2004), Public Affairs Officer, Port of Long Beach, personal correspondence, 17 December 2004.

Flynn, S.E. (2000), 'Beyond border control', *Foreign Affairs*, **79** (6), 57.

Flynn, S.E. (2002), 'America the vulnerable', *Foreign Affairs*, **81** (1), 60.

Flynn, S.E. (2004), *America the Vulnerable: How Our Government is Failing to Protect Us from Terrorism*, New York: Harper Collins Publishers.

Frankle, R.S. (2004), 'Discussion regarding ARACOR products, services and costs', Arlington, VA, July.

Gerencser, M., J. Weinberg and D. Vincent (2003), 'Port security war game: implications for US supply chains', McLean, VA: Booz Allen Hamilton.

Johnson, E. (2004), 'Cargo is reviewed several times', *Long Beach Press Telegram*, 11 July.

Krikorian, G. (2004), 'Ports called "enormous target": about 12 000 containers arrive daily in LA. On average, 43 of them are inspected by hand under the "layered" system of Homeland Security', *L.A. Times*, 26 November.

Larson, R.C. and A.R. Odoni (1981), *Urban Operations Research*, New York: Prentice-Hall.

Looney, R. (2002), 'Economic costs to the United States stemming from the 9/11 attacks', Center for Contemporary Conflict, National Security Affairs Department, Naval Postgraduate School.

Maritime Administration (2002), 'US waterborne foreign trade: containerized cargo, Top 30 US ports, calendar year 2002', Washington, District of Columbia: US Department of Transportation.

Martonosi, S.E. and A.I. Barnett (2004), 'How effective might security profiling of airline passengers be?', Cambridge, MA: Massachusetts Institute of Technology, submitted for publication.

McDaniel, B. (2004), 'SAIC's vehicle and cargo inspection system cost and performance', Arlington, VA, July.

Pelosi, N. and T. Daschle (2004), 'Pelosi and Daschle deliver pre-buttal to State of the Union Address', United States Senate, Office of the Democratic Leader, http://democrats.senate.gov/~dpc/releases/2004116B38.html, 4 October.

Schiesel, S. (2003), 'Their mission: intercepting deadly cargo', *New York Times*, 20 March, G1.

SST Phase One Report (2003), 'Smart and secure tradelanes Phase One report. Network visibility: leveraging security and efficiency in today's global supply chains', SST Initiative.

Spencer, C. (2004), 'International supply chain security regulatory programs' presented at McComb School of Business, University of Texas at Austin, 16 October 2003, IMS Worldwide, http://mba.mccombs.utexas.edu/plus/Academies/BAB/CurtisSpencer.ppt, 17 August.

Stana, R.M. (2004), 'Homeland security: summary of challenges faced in targeting oceangoing cargo containers for inspection', testimony before the Subcommittee on Oversight and Investigations, Committee on Energy and Commerce, House of Representatives, GAO-04-557T, Washington, District of Columbia: General Accounting Office.

Treaster, J.B. (2004), 'After being bounced around Florida is bouncing back', *New York Times*, 18 September.

Wasem, E., J. Lake, L. Seghetti, J. Monke and S. Viña (2004), 'Border security: inspections practices, policies, and issues', Washington, District of Columbia: Congressional Research Service, Library of Congress.

Wein, L.M., A.H. Wilkins, M. Baveja and S.E. Flynn (2003), 'Preventing the importation of illicit nuclear materials in shipping containers', submitted for publication.

Willis, H. and D. Ortiz (2004), 'A framework for evaluating the security of the global containerized supply chain', TR-214-RC, Santa Monica, CA: RAND Corporation.

13. An overview of US port security programs

Jon D. Haveman, Howard J. Shatz and Ernesto I. Vilchis*

INTRODUCTION

Since the 11 September 2001 terrorist attacks on the World Trade Center in New York City and the Pentagon in Washington, DC, concerns over safety and the prevention of similar attacks have became paramount both on the US national political scene and in the daily lives of Americans. Policy makers initially focused on air passenger traffic, increasing passenger screening and restricting cockpit access. As the debate broadened however, the issue of goods movement moved to the fore. US ports, and seaports in particular, include two security vulnerabilities. Terrorists can attack a port, making it a target. Or they can use international supply routes to ship materiel, making a port a conduit.

The first security vulnerability aims to disrupt economic activity. In the aftermath of 9/11, policy makers closed down the nation's aviation system until they could assess the scope of the threat. A waterborne attack could similarly result in the temporary closing of all ports around the country.

The second security vulnerability encompasses a number of possibilities. An explosive device could arrive on US shores in a container and be successfully transported inland. As an alternative, terrorists themselves could arrive in a container and travel undetected throughout the United States.

Containers, once loaded, are rarely opened or otherwise inspected before their arrival in the United States. Once in the United States, a container can be loaded onto the back of a truck and make its way inland to a target quite independent of the port. The task of inspecting all containers is currently infeasible, and the current inspection rate is startlingly low. As late as May 2002, only 2 per cent of all containers unloaded at US ports were subject to any sort of inspection.[1]

These vulnerabilities pose the following challenge: How does the United States realize the gains of international trade when opening its ports to foreign goods poses substantial security risks? As Flynn (2002) notes,

'Ultimately, getting homeland security right is not about constructing barricades to fend off terrorists. It is, or should be, about identifying and taking the steps necessary to allow the United States to remain an open, prosperous, free, and globally engaged society.' Just how to strike a balance between the provision of protection from an attack and the normal pursuit of economic activity is a puzzle that will plague policy makers for some time.

Despite this unresolved challenge, policy makers are implementing measures that are likely to enhance the safety of maritime shipping. These policies fall into five related classes. First, they plan for protection, response and recovery. Second, they harden ports as targets. Third, they seal gaps in international supply chains, points where terrorist materiel could enter shipping channels. Fourth, they push US borders out, so that security weaknesses are discovered and solved away from the United States. Fifth, they include technology upgrading to accomplish the first four tasks.

The Maritime Transportation Security Act of 2002 (MTSA), supplemented by the Coast Guard and Maritime Transportation Act of 2004, dominates the effort to secure the maritime supply chain.[2] MTSA sets out broad guidelines for securing US ports and related intermodal facilities. Tasked with implementing many of the MTSA measures, the US Coast Guard (USCG) plays a vital role in providing for the security of waterborne cargo. The USCG is also responsible for overseeing the implementation of the International Ship and Port Facility Security Code (ISPS), measures developed by the International Maritime Organization (IMO).

Additionally, US Customs and Border Protection (CBP) has launched a pair of initiatives aimed at sealing weak points in global supply chains and moving efforts to secure the US port facilities beyond the US border. These initiatives are the Customs–Trade Partnership Against Terrorism (C-TPAT) and the Container Security Initiative (CSI). The C-TPAT encourages shippers and carriers to implement security plans and measures to promote greater security at all points along the supply chain. The CSI facilitates the screening of containers for hazardous materials at the foreign port of origin, long before the containers reach US shores.

This chapter paints the landscape of current US port security efforts. The next section defines the issue of port security, and then the following section gives more details about each of the port-security efforts. The section after that evaluates these initiatives. A final section concludes.

THE ISSUE OF PORT SECURITY

The 361 US seaports make an immense contribution to US trade and the US economy. They move about 80 per cent of all US international trade by weight, and about 95 per cent of all US overseas trade, excluding trade with Mexico and Canada. By value, $807 billion worth of goods flowed through the seaports in 2003, about 41 per cent of all US international goods trade.

The need to secure ports and their extended intermodal structures stems from two concerns. First, ports in and of themselves present attractive targets for terrorists. Ports are a significant choke point for an enormous amount of economic activity. Even temporarily shutting down a major US port will likely impose significant economic costs throughout not only the United States, but also the world economy. Second, transporting something from one place to another, the very activity that the ports facilitate, is an important activity for terrorists. There is a substantial risk that a port could be used as a conduit through which terrorists build their arsenal within the nation's borders.

The container, a large metal box widely used in ocean shipping, presents the most obvious threat to the maritime transportation system. Each day, tens of thousands of containers flow through US ports, largely undisturbed in their trip from one part of the world to another. In general, containers are loaded and sealed, perhaps only closed, well inland of a port. They are then transferred by truck, or truck and train, to a seaport where they are loaded onto a ship. Following the sea journey, they are transferred to another truck and perhaps another train for a further journey over land to the ultimate destination.

Each container trip to the United States has on average 17 intermediate points at which the container is temporarily stopped.[3] The adage 'goods at rest are goods at risk' readily applies to the terrorist threat. At any point in the journey that involves a modal change for the container, the container will be at rest. While at rest, the container is vulnerable to thieves and terrorists alike. Providing port security therefore involves not only closely scrutinizing activities at the port, but at points all along the shipping chain.

Perhaps the greatest barrier to securing the ports is the extent to which port security of any sort was, until recently, neglected. Security at America's ports in the fall of 2000 was labeled as generally poor to fair.[4] At the time, the difficulty in securing a port was widely acknowledged. These difficulties stem primarily from the following: volume, intermodality, jurisdictional issues, number of stakeholders, the global nature of the industry, time sensitivity and the involvement of both private and public entities. Any attempt at securing the ports must take into account each of these issues.

In the wake of 9/11, the federal government moved with surprising speed to address the vulnerability of US ports. On 25 November 2002, President Bush signed the Maritime Transportation Security Act of 2002, the backbone of US port security measures. It was possible to produce this legislation quickly only because much of the legwork was already in process.

Indeed in the late 1990s the US government initiated several efforts regarding protection of the ports, mostly focusing on crime however.

An early attempt came in 1997, when the Department of Transportation produced 'Port Security: A National Planning Guide.'[5] This report provided an overview of security issues and other challenges facing US ports and discussed many of the essential ideas that were to become the core of the current US strategy on port security. Another contributor to the effort was the Marine Transportation System (MTS) Initiative, which started in 1998 and incorporated a large number of agencies connected with overseeing activities at the ports and in the US waterway system. Although port security was not the exclusive focus of the MTS Initiative, it was a core element.

Late in 1998, Congress directed the creation of an MTS Task Force to 'assess the adequacy of the Nation's marine transportation system . . . to operate in a safe, efficient, secure, and environmentally sound manner'.[6] The Task Force's report, issued in September 1999, recognized that rogue states and transnational terrorists could target US critical infrastructure, including seaports.

Reinforcing the efforts of Congress, President Clinton in April 1999 established a commission to undertake a comprehensive study of crime in US seaports and to examine the potential threats posed by terrorists and others to the people and critical infrastructures of seaport cities. Aside from its own investigations, this commission received recommendations from the MTS Task Force. The result, in 2000, was the publication of the *Report of the Interagency Commission on Crime and Security in US Seaports*. At the time that the report was published, the FBI considered the threat of terrorism directed at any US seaports to be low, but also considered the vulnerability of ports to be high, and the commission expressed the belief that an attack had the potential to cause significant damage.

These various efforts culminated in US Senate Bill 1214, introduced by Senator Ernest F. Hollings on 20 July 2001 and co-sponsored by Senator Bob Graham. This bill formed the heart of MTSA, signed in November 2002.

POST-9/11 PORT SECURITY MEASURES

Current federal policy initiatives appear to have two aims. The first is to institute a port security system, including plans, personnel and equipment to stave off or recover from a port security incident. The second is to strike a balance between safety and commercial efficiency. MTSA is key to the first and contains elements for the second. Its overall thrust is to reduce the probability of a transportation security incident, whether terrorist-related or otherwise. The Container Security Initiative (CSI) and the Customs–Trade Partnership Against Terrorism (C-TPAT) are key to the second. CSI places US customs officials at foreign ports and has reporting requirements for cargo bound by ship for the United States. It is intended to interdict explosive devices and other threats before they arrive at US ports. C-TPAT is designed to more closely control the movement of goods between their foreign source and final US destination. Other important elements of US port security measures include a program to test new technologies (Operation Safe Commerce) and a federal grant program aimed at providing an incentive to facilitate spending by ports and the private sector. An additional effort is taking place at the international level: the implementation of a new International Ship and Port Facility Security Code, adopted in December 2002. Although we do not describe these international measures, we touch on their USCG implementation.

Maritime Transportation Security Act of 2002

The majority of these post-9/11 laws, rules, regulations and programs have their origin in MTSA. Among other steps, the act requires:

- The creation of national, area, facility and vessel security plans.
- The identification by federal authorities of vessels and US facilities at risk.
- The creation of vessel and facility response plans.
- The roll-out of transportation security cards for people who have access to vessels and facilities and of crew-member identification cards.
- The creation of rapid-response maritime safety and security teams.
- An assessment of antiterrorism efforts at foreign ports.
- The placement of automatic identification systems on vessels in US waters.
- A new grant program (to be described in a subsequent section).

This comprehensive new law has a high estimated price tag and even higher estimated benefits (Table 13.1). The USCG estimates that implementation and continued fulfillment of the rules will cost between \$7.3 and \$13.9 billion in 2003 dollars, depending on the threat level. Benefits, estimated to be on the order of \$10 trillion, seem implausibly high given that they roughly equal annual US GDP. However, they may well be close to accurate if some type of highly catastrophic event were likely – such as a multiple detonation of nuclear devices at US ports – and if MTSA measures had a high probability of stopping the event.

Table 13.1 Estimated costs and benefits of MTSA measures ($ millions)

	Vessel Security	Facility Security	OCS Facility Security	AMS Plans	AIS	Total
First-year cost	218	1125	3	120	30	1496
First-year benefit	781 285	473 659	13 288	135 202	1422	1 404 856
10-year present value cost	1368	5399	37	477	26	7307
10-year present value benefit	5 871 540	3 559 655	99 863	1 016 074	10 687	10 557 819

Notes: OCS is outer continental shelf. AMS is area maritime security. AIS is automatic identification systems, the technology ships must install so they can be identified. Costs are based on the lowest maritime security level.

Source: Federal Register, *Implementation of National Maritime Security Initiatives, Final Rule*, Table 2. First-Year and 10-Year Present Value Cost and Benefit of the Final Rules, Vol. 68, No. 204, 22 October 2003, p. 60467.

Security plans

Mandatory security planning for deterring and responding to a transportation security incident forms the core of MTSA. At the heart of the national plan are the assignment of duties and responsibilities among federal agencies and the coordination of their efforts with state and local agencies. The national plan delineates a system of surveillance and notice to ensure the timely dissemination of information to the appropriate agencies whenever an incident occurs or is likely to occur. It also defines localities requiring area maritime transportation security plans.

The USCG has developed 43 area maritime security plans, assisted by area maritime security committees comprising government officials and industry and labor officials connected with maritime transportation.[7] These plans describe the area and infrastructure covered, and how that infrastructure is integrated with the plans for other areas.

A third level of security planning requires owners and operators of vessels and facilities to submit independent plans with a focus on deterring a security incident. An estimated 12 350 plans were filed by the deadline of 1 July 2004, when they were to go into effect. These included 3150 facility plans and 9200 vessel plans. In a measure of quality control, the USCG was then to complete on-site inspections of facility plans by 1 January 2005 and of vessel plans by 1 July 2005.[8]

On 1 July 2004, the USCG was immediately faced with overseeing

Table 13.2 US Coast Guard enforcement actions through 6 July 2004

ISPS enforcement	
Foreign vessel port calls	1600
Security examinations	442
Denied entry	9
Expelled from port	10
Detained, or operations restricted	30
MTSA enforcement	
Facilities restricted or suspended	18
Vessels restricted or suspended	33

Source: US Coast Guard (2004c).

compliance with two broad sets of plans. First, all domestic facility and vessel plans went into effect. Second, all international vessel and facility plans, required by the IMO, went into effect. Inspections of domestic facilities and vessels started then. At the same time, the USCG intended to board every foreign vessel on its first visit to a US port unless there had already been a verification examination. In addition, officials from a new USCG International Port Security Program started visiting foreign ports. The immediate implantation resulted in vessel and facility restrictions (Table 13.2). However by September the USCG has focused its inspections in two ways. First, it issued a list of countries whose vessels were to receive increased boardings because of poor compliance; and second, it issued a list of 17 countries whose ports were not reported to be in compliance and announced the targeting of vessels that had visited these countries during their last five port calls.[9]

Transportation Worker Identification Credential (TWIC)

Identification cards, now known as the Transportation Worker Identification Credential (TWIC), have followed a phased introduction. The cards are meant for all transportation workers requiring unescorted access in secure areas of seaports, airports and other transit facilities. The Transportation Security Administration (TSA) started planning in 2002.

In August 2004, the TSA announced that a new ID card would be tested for seven months at four locations in the Northeast, at the ports of Los Angeles and Long Beach, and at 14 major port facilities in Florida.[10] Participation in this test was to be voluntary, and the actual use of the prototype card started in November, with the Long Beach container terminal the first site. After a further review, the TSA is to make the card available for a nationwide roll-out.

Updates to MTSA, and the technology wish-list

MTSA received its first major update in summer 2004 with the Coast Guard and Maritime Transportation Act of 2004, signed as Public Law 108–293 on 9 August. The law adds more reporting requirements, including a requirement for a plan within 90 days for creating a maritime intelligence system. The system had been specified in MTSA, but without a deadline. Recognizing coastline vulnerabilities aside from ports, it also requires a vulnerability assessment of nuclear facilities near US coasts. Aside from several other changes, the new law changes a research and development grant program specified by MTSA and lengthens the list of types of technology that policy makers now want.

The Container Security Initiative

Whereas the USCG is the lead agency with MTSA, CBP has taken the lead on CSI and C-TPAT. The concept for the CSI was first presented on 17 January 2002 by CBP Commissioner Robert C. Bonner in a speech at the Center for Strategic and International Studies. CSI is based on the idea of expanding US borders and intercepting dangerous cargo before it arrives in the United States. CSI consists of four core elements:

- Using intelligence and automated information to identify and target high-risk containers.
- Pre-screening containers identified as high risk, at the point of departure.
- Using detection technology to quickly pre-screen high-risk containers.
- Using smarter, tamper-evident containers.

It is best known for screening containers at foreign ports. As of December 2002, all ocean carriers had to notify CBP of the contents of their cargo 24 hours before it was loaded on a ship. Under the CSI, CBP personnel stationed at foreign ports screen the manifest submitted for the ship and assess the potential threat that is implied by the contents or the identity of the shipper. Threatening containers are to be inspected at the foreign port and are not to reach US shores unless they pass muster.

The CSI has been implemented in two stages. In the first stage, arrangements were made with 23 ports – three Canadian ports and then the 20 largest overseas source ports for maritime trade with the United States – to implement the inspection process. These ports, listed in the first column of Table 13.3, are the source of 68 per cent of all container traffic into the

Table 13.3 Foreign ports participating in the CSI

Phase I Ports	*Phase II Ports*
Algeciras, Spain	Barcelona, Spain
Antwerp, Belgium	Colombo, Sri Lanka
Bremerhaven, Germany	Durban, South Africa
Felixstowe, UK	Fos, France
Genoa, Italy	Gioia Tauro, Italy
Halifax, Canada	Gothenborg, Sweden
Hamburg, Germany	Liverpool, UK
Hong Kong	Livorno, Italy
Kaohsiung, Taiwan	Marseilles, France
Kobe, Japan	Naples, Italy
La Spezia, Italy	Osaka, Japan
Laem Chabang, Thailand	Port Kelang, Malaysia
Le Havre, France	Southampton, UK
Montreal, Canada	Tanjung Pelepas, Malaysia
Nagoya, Japan	Thamesport, UK
Pusan, Korea	Tilbury, UK
Rotterdam, The Netherlands	Valencia, Spain
Shanghai, China	Zeebrugge, Belgium
Shenzhen, China	
Singapore	*Other Ports*
Tokyo, Japan	Piraeus, Greece
Vancouver, Canada	
Yokohama, Japan	

Source: Flanagan (2003) and US CBP (2004b).

United States. All but three were operational as CSI ports as of November 2004. A second phase of negotiations resulted in the addition of the ports in the second column, increasing coverage to 80 per cent of all container traffic into the United States. All but six of those were operational as CSI ports as of November 2004, and Piraeus, Greece, not designated in either phase one or phase two, had become operational as well, bringing the total to 32 ports. Phase three of the CSI will focus on capacity building at higher-risk ports.[11]

The eligibility of entry into the CSI program for foreign ports is subject to the following criteria:[12]

- A country's customs administration must be able to inspect cargo originating or being transshipped through a country.

- The seaport must have or be in the process of acquiring non-intrusive inspection equipment – large X-ray-type systems – and radiation detection equipment in order to conduct security.
- The seaport must have regular, direct and substantial container traffic to ports in the United States.
- The seaport must commit to establishing a risk management system and to sharing intelligence with CBP.
- The seaport must conduct a thorough port assessment to find and resolve vulnerabilities.

These are fairly onerous conditions, making it unlikely that complete coverage of all sources of containers is achievable. In fact, the third point appears to rule out the notion of complete coverage altogether. There are some 2600 commercial ports in the world, of which 575 handle significant numbers of containers.[13]

The Customs–Trade Partnership Against Terrorism

C-TPAT is a joint government–business initiative to build cooperative relationships that strengthen overall supply chain and border security. Through this partnership, started in November 2001, the US government is asking businesses to develop security procedures designed to maintain the integrity of their shipments and to have these procedures certified by the government.

Businesses must apply to participate in C-TPAT and in so doing, commit to the following actions:

- Conduct a comprehensive self-assessment of supply chain security using the C-TPAT security guidelines.
- Submit a supply chain security profile questionnaire to CBP.
- Develop and implement a program to enhance security throughout the supply chain in accordance with C-TPAT guidelines.
- Communicate C-TPAT guidelines to other companies in the supply chain and work toward building the guidelines into relationships with these companies.

The first phase of C-TPAT welcomed participation by major importers. The next opened the program to global transportation companies and the third opened the program to brokers, freight forwarders and non-vessel owning common carriers. By September 2004 it had 7000 members covering greater than 50 per cent by value of maritime cargo. Members benefit from reduced inspections and therefore reduced border wait times.

Participation in C-TPAT also produces positive spillovers primarily associated with the better tracking of containers. Shippers acknowledge that this will reduce theft and other losses of containers, thereby lowering costs. It has been reported that from 6 to 10 per cent of the containers in yards of some US West Coast terminals are in the 'unable to locate' category.[14] Presumably, the closer supervision over the loading, unloading and transporting of containers by shippers will reduce this figure, reducing costs.

Federal Port Security Grants

As noted previously, estimates for implementing new port security measures placed costs in the billions of dollars. In order to defray some of these costs, the federal government instituted port security grants even before MTSA. They were then written into MTSA.

As of September 2004, the Department of Homeland Security (DHS) has awarded $623 million in port security grants.[15] Most have been distributed through the TSA, with $75 million distributed through the DHS Office of Domestic Preparedness (ODP).

TSA port security grants

Authority for TSA's port security grant program was established in early 2002. These grants were intended to assist critical national seaports in financing the costs of facility and operational security enhancements. Public and private ports, terminals or US-inspected passenger vessels, state and local governments, and consortiums of local stakeholder groups could apply for a grant as long as they met the eligibility criteria. To qualify, applicants had to be:

- A 'strategic port', as designated by the US Maritime Administration (MARAD) and the Military Traffic Management Command (MTMC).
- Ports with access controls for vessels from certain countries due to national security concerns.
- A port or terminal of national importance responsible for a large volume of cargo movement, or movement of products vital to US economic interests.
- Ports, terminals, commuter vessels or ferry service vessels responsible for a high number of passengers.
- Port or terminals responsible for the movement of hazardous cargo.

Originally, grants were awarded for one of three broad categories: (1) to conduct security assessments and develop mitigation strategies; (2) to enhance facility and operational security; and (3) to finance proof-of-concept demonstration projects. Ultimately however, grants have primarily been awarded under category (2).

In selecting grantees, preference has been given to single terminal- or facility-specific rather than port-wide projects.[16] However projects that enhance intermodal transportation security within the footprint of the port have also been given preference. TSA prefers projects that address access, command, control, coordination and communication and physical security (for example lighting, fencing and cameras). There is also an emphasis on prevention, deterrence and detection rather than consequence management.

The first round of grants, announced 17 June 2002, included 77 awards to 51 ports, ranging from $8000 to $6.8 million for a total of the $92.3 million. A second round of grants was awarded in July 2003, with $169 million given to 199 state and local governments and private companies for projects such as surveillance equipment at roads and facilities, construction of new command and control facilities, and new patrol boats in harbors.

The third round awarded $179 million to 235 entities to finance 442 projects in 326 locations. Grants ranged from $2860 to $3 million. The fourth round awarded $49.4 million to 144 projects in amounts ranging from $650 to $3.3 million. The US Congress set aside $150 million for port security grants in fiscal year 2005 for a fifth round.[17]

Operation Safe Commerce

Operation Safe Commerce (OSC) funds pilot programs that are meant to enhance and complement other security initiatives, such as C-TPAT and CSI, by testing technologies and business processes that protect commercial shipments from tampering along the supply chain, from point of origin to point of destination. In order for a project to be funded, it must accomplish one or more of the following:

- Validate security at the point of origin, to include the security of the shipment itself and the information that describes it.
- Secure the supply chain from the point of origin to its final destination and all the points in between.
- Monitor the movement and integrity of the cargo while in transit using available technology.

OSC started with a pilot program called Operation Safe Commerce–North East (OSC-NE), launched in May 2002.[18] In OSC-NE, state and federal agencies joined with private companies to develop effective security models for international shipping systems.[19] The goal was to improve security practices by using point-of-origin security, in-transit tracking and monitoring, and data query capabilities to facilitate commerce while improving security. In implementing the OSC-NE, officials chose commercially available technology to track and monitor an individual container with 400 000 tail lamps as it made its way from Slovakia to Hillsborough, NH.

After this experiment, the TSA instituted OSC proper for the three largest container-load centers – the port complexes of Los Angeles and Long Beach, Seattle and Tacoma, and New York and New Jersey. In June 2003, TSA awarded the first round of these grants, with ten grants ranging from $1.1 to $3.8 million for a total of $28.3 million.[20] An additional $30 million of funding was appropriated by Congress on 20 February 2003.[21] These funds were distributed on 18 July 2003.

ODP port security grants

The US Office for Domestic Preparedness (ODP) provides training, money and other assistance to state and local governments, and launched the Urban Areas Security Initiative (UASI) in 2003 to provide financial assistance to large urban areas. Early that year Congress appropriated $700 million for discretionary grants under UASI. In selecting projects for funding, Congress instructed ODP 'to take into consideration credible threat, vulnerability, the presence of infrastructure of national importance, population, and identified needs of public agencies'.[22] Consequently, one component of the UASI was a port security program, for which ODP set aside $75 million.

The guidelines for selecting projects for the UASI port security program were the same as those for TSA's port security grants, and grantees for this program were selected from a pool of applicants that had previously applied for TSA grants. ODP awarded the UASI port security grants in May 2003, funding 85 projects ranging in cost from $10 000 to $3.5 million at 15 ports.

R&D grants

Aside from the more general port security grants, MTSA instituted research and development grants aimed mostly at technologies. The bill authorized $15 million for each fiscal year from 2003 through 2008. The money was aimed at the development of:

- targeting and inspection methods;
- equipment to detect explosives, chemical or biological agents and nuclear materials;
- container tags, seals and tracking sensors;

- tools to mitigate the consequences of a terrorist act at a port; and
- ways of applying existing technologies to port security.

The Coast Guard and Maritime Transportation Act of 2004 broadened the scope of activities these grants could fund. In particular it requested the development of technologies to track activities in marine areas, known as maritime domain awareness, and to improve container design, including blast-resistant containers; and methods (rather than new technologies) to improve the security and sustainability of ports in case of a terrorist incident. The money authorized for this was raised to $35 million annually from 2005 to 2009.

EVALUATING PORT SECURITY POLICIES

Four significant issues emerge in evaluating existing port security measures. First is the question of balance. Are the measures instituted appropriate, in the sense of getting the most security for their cost and directing assets optimally? Second is the issue of compliance and efficacy. Will thousands of ship owners, facility executives, and managers comply with the various security plans and will these plans actually work? Third is the issue of financing. Who is meant to pay for this? Finally, regarding transportation workers, is the issue of civil liberties and individual freedoms. What kinds of information will dock workers, truckers and other transportation employees have to cede in order to continue their jobs?

Balance is perhaps the most difficult, because to be perfectly answered it requires a fully informed understanding of the threats, the probabilities of those threats occurring or a range of probabilities of them occurring, the benefits of stopping such events, and the costs of stopping them. Complicating this is the fact that port security is but one piece of homeland security, and hardening the ports and the maritime transportation system makes another target, such as sports events or shopping malls, even more inviting.

The maritime security strategy includes numerous initiatives – more than those described above – under the broad headings of awareness, prevention, protection, response and recovery.[23] In the absence of full information, and given that much of the implementation of the strategy is voluntary on the part of private businesses in global supply chains, it is likely that resources are being allocated non-optimally. This is not to say that they are being poorly allocated – relying on the instincts and imperfect analysis of experienced security specialists can go a long way, especially if programs must be expedited as in the case of US homeland security. It is only to say that a concrete goal of US homeland security policy should be to create an analytic framework that takes account of costs, benefits and uncertainties in order to better allocate resources going forward.

More concretely, such a framework could better inform the level of funding to be provided to the USCG, the lead agency in port security. The Coast Guard's budget has increased since 9/11, but it is not clear that it has increased enough to adequately cover the new duties enumerated in MTSA along with the legacy duties of rescue, safety and other tasks.

A number of points regarding compliance and efficacy can be highlighted. MTSA demands an enormous amount of paperwork in the form of thousands of vessel and facility security plans. Although these plans are to be reviewed, there is no guarantee that anyone will have enough time to review them adequately. Nor are they in a common electronic format, so that comparing them across regions is difficult. As of the 1 July 2004 deadline for turning in approved plans, approximately 5900 were self-certified, including 5700 vessel plans and 200 facility plans. Of the 6400 plans that had gone through USCG review processes, every one needed revision before approval.[24]

C-TPAT compliance also raises monitoring issues. Thousands of companies have applied for the program but await verification. Once verified, it is unclear whether there are measures in place to make sure participants remain in compliance. It is also unclear whether security will be adversely affected by the fact that some companies decline to sign up for C-TPAT, a voluntary program. These are generally smaller companies.[25]

The issues of plans and C-TPAT show that port security depends on the actions of private carriers, shippers, terminal operators and others. Indications were that even as the deadline for compliance approached, many were not yet satisfied with their own security provisions. Responding to a survey that took place from February to May 2004, only 35 per cent of maritime firms interviewed reported that they had fully implemented their security strategies. However nearly all of them (89 per cent) indicated that homeland security would be a high priority for executives over the next 12 months.[26]

Allocation issues may go beyond monitoring and verification and the activities of the private sector. CSI presents a number of challenges. CBP is now stationing inspectors not only at US ports, but also at foreign ports; but it is not clear yet whether the bureau has hit upon the right mix of locations – foreign versus foreign and foreign versus domestic – or the right overall level of inspectors.

CBP is playing a non-cooperative game with terrorists. The government must select ports from which dangerous materials are likely to come, given that potential terrorists know that the government will be selecting ports from which dangerous materials are likely to come. Starting with the 20 largest might have been an easy decision, but it made it more likely that other ports would be used, something which the CBP may and should be taking into account in its risk assessment strategies.

As noted previously, complete coverage is nearly impossible, and only a very small proportion of containers coming into the United States is inspected. How much coverage is enough? Inspections have costs. There is evidence that the CSI program has increased the variability of lead times for US shippers by raising the probability of missing a sailing, and therefore has caused them to increase buffer inventories. Since sailings to a specific port can be infrequent, a delay caused by inspection overseas can be much longer than a delay caused by inspection at the US port of clearance. However the costs of the detonation of a smuggled nuclear weapon could be so catastrophic as to make the costs of screening every container using at least non-invasive screening techniques, such as radiation detection, seem trivial.

It should also be noted that CBP disputes the meaningfulness of a low rate of physical inspections.[27] CBP says it screens data and information for all of the containers arriving in the United States, estimated at 5.7 million at the time of the CBP document, and that it then more closely scrutinizes those containers identified as high risk. Identification of such high-risk containers comes through C-TPAT participation, an Automated Targeting System, and then identification of anomalies by targeting teams. The CBP is likely correct that setting an arbitrary goal of screening a specific proportion of containers is not meaningful, in the absence of a risk assessment system. However it is certainly not clear whether the systems in place adequately safeguard against terrorism events, and more importantly whether there are ways for terrorists to get around the systems, such as by inserting dangerous weapons into low-risk cargo from a long-established and trusted importer.[28]

The third major issue in evaluating current US port security programs is funding: specifically, who pays? It was immediately clear with the passage of MTSA that the federal government would not be allocating enough money to cover the costs of MTSA implementation, especially since the section covering port security grants said they could fund up to 75 per cent of a project, rather than the entire project. This became abundantly clearer when the USCG published the interim rule for MTSA on 1 July 2003. Costs far outweighed estimated appropriations. The Coast Guard and Maritime Transportation Act of 2004 sealed the requirement for non-governmental participation with a new report request. Within three months following its passage, the secretary of DHS was to report to Congress on funding and include a recommendation on 'matching requirements to ensure that Federal funds provide an incentive to grantees for the investment of their own funds in the improvements financed in part by Federal funds provided under this program'.[29]

The new law also foreshadows possible solutions to the debate of who pays. Different members of the California congressional delegation alone have proposed at least three methods. These include general fund allocations, a diversion of customs duties, and user fees at the ports. The new reporting requirements ask for estimates of the cost of inspecting vessels in one year, the per-vessel cost, the total cost of inspecting containers in one year, and the per-container costs of these inspections. With these costs in hand, it may be much easier to move to a user-fee system of financing.

Although many of the remaining gaps point towards issues of compliance of businesses and the allocation of government resources, labor relations constitute an important fourth area where US port security programs may be lacking. As of early 2004, US West Coast dockworkers had expressed great concern about the types of background checks that might be needed for maritime industry identification cards. Certainly, without dockworker cooperation, global supply chains could remain vulnerable to terrorist contraband.

CONCLUSION

In the years since 11 September 2001, the US government has seized upon the notion that securing the nation's seaports is an important element of a broader homeland security agenda. Indeed the speed with which broad federal legislation on port security was introduced and passed was remarkable. These laws and regulations present an important backdrop against which specific port security initiatives can be developed and implemented.

What was lacking in the MTSA legislation was a treatment of the broader issue of the maritime transportation supply chain. Recognizing this shortcoming, CBP developed companion programs. These programs move the securing of containers to foreign shores, lessening the danger posed to US ports and the United States itself, and encourage participants in the maritime shipping network to develop security plans of their own.

Although these regulations and programs appear to provide broad security coverage for waterborne trade, significant shortcomings remain. There is still much progress to be made in evaluating the costs and benefits of different initiatives and focusing resources on where they might best be spent. In particular, the resources are not yet available to either fully implement or inspect the implementation of federally mandated security measures. There are also significant gaps in coverage provided by some programs. The CSI leaves many foreign ports without inspectors, and many supply chain security plans created under the C-TPAT remain unverified as to their efficacy or actual implementation. Even after verification, continuing implementation will have to be monitored.

The securing of the US maritime transportation network is clearly of vital importance to providing more general protection to the nation from terrorist activity. Much has been done. However, without greater conviction on the part of those providing resources and without continued focus on the highest benefit tasks, the network will remain vulnerable to a terrorist event and unable to respond appropriately should an event occur.

NOTES

* The authors thank Greg Wright for research assistance, and participants at a conference on Economic Costs and Consequences of a Terrorism Attack, held 20–21 August 2004 at the University of Southern California Center for Risk and Economic Analysis of Terrorism Events, in particular Clark Abt, Panha Chheng, Howard Kunreuther, Larry Samuelson and Chip White. All errors remain the responsibility of the authors.

1. Nacht (2002). As will be described later, US Customs and Border Protection disputes that this is a meaningful number.
2. MTSA is US Public Law 107–295, and the Coast Guard and Maritime Transportation Act of 2004 is US Public Law 108–293.
3. Flynn (2004), p. 89.
4. Interagency Commission on Crime and Security in US Seaports (2000).
5. US Department of Transportation (1997).
6. Marine Transportation System Task Force (1999).
7. Hereth (2004).
8. US GAO (2004).
9. USCG (2004a and 2004b).
10. US DHS, TSA (2004).
11. US Office of Management and Budget (2004).
12. US CBP (2004a).
13. See www.lloydsports.com.
14. Nacht (2002).
15. $92.3 million were awarded in June 2002 (before the existence of DHS).
16. An example is a project that focuses on increasing security at a particular terminal, as opposed to a project to construct a new fence around the whole port.
17. US Public Law 108–334, 18 October 2004.
18. A very detailed timeline of the project is available from the NI2 Center for Infrastructure Enterprise at http://www.ni2cie.org/SecureCargo/DevelopmentalOutline.htm
19. The following agencies and companies were involved in the project: Immigration and Naturalization Service (Border Patrol, now part of CBP), US Marshals Service, US Attorney Offices in New Hampshire and Vermont, USCG, US Customs Service, (now part of CBP) and US Department of Transportation. Participants from the private sector included Osram Sylvania, BDP International, and C.P. Ships. The Port of Montreal and the New Hampshire International Trade Association were also involved in the project (Osram Sylvania news releases, http://www.sylvania.com/press/06142002.html).
20. A detailed breakdown of the grants is available from the TSA at http://www.tsa.gov/interweb/assetlibrary/OSCGrantInfo.doc
21. Consolidated Appropriations Resolution, 2003, Public Law 108–7, 20 February 2003.
22. Conference report (H Rept 108–76) for US Public Law 108–11, 16 April 2003, pp. 82–3.

23. Hereth and Sloan (2004).
24. US GAO (2004).
25. Deloitte & Touche (2004).
26. Deloitte & Touche (2004).
27. US CBP (n.d.).
28. Flynn (2004) presents one such scenario in Chapter 2, 'The Next Attack'.
29. US Public Law 108–293, Section 804(d)(4).

REFERENCES

Deloitte & Touche USA LLP (2004), *The Unfinished Agenda: Transportation Security Survey*.

Federal Register (2002), 'Notices: Operation Safe Commerce', 67 (224), 20 November, 70110.

Federal Register (2003), *Implementation of National Maritime Security Initiatives, Final Rule*, Washington, DC: US Government Printing Office.

Flanagan, William (2003), 'CSI Operations and Overview', presentation to Fifth International Conference on Export Controls, Budapest, 17 September.

Flynn, Stephen E. (2002), 'America the Vulnerable', *Foreign Affairs,* January/February.

Flynn, Stephen (2004), *America the Vulnerable: How Our Government is Failing to Protect Us from Terrorism,* New York: HarperCollins Publishers.

Hereth, Larry (2004), 'Statement of Rear Admiral Larry Hereth on Maritime Transportation Security Act Implementation Before the Subcommittee on Coast Guard and Maritime Transportation, Committee on Transportation and Infrastructure, US House of Representatives', Washington, DC, Department of Homeland Security, US Coast Guard, 9 June.

Hereth, Larry and James F. Sloan (2004), 'Statement of Rear Admiral Larry Hereth and Mr James F. Sloan on The 9/11 Commission Report and Maritime Transportation Security Before the Subcommittee on Coast Guard and Maritime Transportation, Committee on Transportation and Infrastructure, US House of Representatives', Washington, DC, Department of Homeland Security, US Coast Guard, 25 August.

Interagency Commission on Crime and Security in US Seaports (2000), *Report of the Interagency Commission on Crime and Security in US Seaports,* Washington, DC, Fall.

Marine Transportation System Task Force (1999), *An Assessment of the US Marine Transportation System: A Report to Congress*, Washington, DC, September.

Nacht, Michael (2002), 'A call for closer guarding of coasts: upgrades required for safety, economy', *San Jose Mercury News*, 5 May.

US Coast Guard (2004a), 'Coast Guard targets vessels from countries for increased boardings', Washington, DC, 10 September.

US Coast Guard (2004b), 'Coast Guard issues list of countries that have not reported full compliance with new international port security requirements', Washington, DC, 10 September.

US Coast Guard (2004c), 'Coast Guard concludes first week enforcing new security requirements', press release, 8 July, available at http://www.uscg.mil/news/Headquarters/Release, MTSA July 8 doc.

US CBP – US Customs and Border Protection (n.d.), 'The 2% myth', Washington, DC.

US CBP – US Customs and Border Protection (2004a), 'Container security initiative fact sheet', Washington, DC, 1 November.

US CBP – US Customs and Border Protection (2004b), 'Global milestone reached with 32 operational CSI ports', Washington, DC, 12 November.

US DHS, TSA – US Department of Homeland Security, Transportation Security Administration (2004), 'TSA to test new ID card for transportation workers', press release, 10 August.

US Department of Transportation (1997), *Port Security: A National Planning Guide,* Washington, DC: US Department of Transportation.

US GAO – US Government Accountability Office (2004), *Maritime Security: Substantial Work Remains to Translate New Planning Requirements into Effective Port Security,* Washington, DC, June.

US Office of Management and Budget (2004), 'Department of Homeland Security', in *The President's 2005 Budget*, Washington, DC, 2 February.

14. The economic impact of a terrorist attack on the twin ports of Los Angeles–Long Beach

Peter Gordon, James E. Moore II, Harry W. Richardson and Qisheng Pan

INTRODUCTION

The Los Angeles metropolitan region is (because of its size, visibility and diversity) a prime target for a terrorist attack. There are many specific targets: the Los Angeles International Airport (LAX), downtown high rises (with the highest skyscraper – the US Bank Tower[1] – west of the Mississippi), its theme parks (for example Disneyland, Universal Studios), its freeways (some of the interchanges have the highest traffic densities in the United States), and its ports, among many. We have developed a spatially disaggregated economic impact model that can evaluate all of these and any other plausible attacks. As a representative example, in this research we consider moderate radiological bomb (so-called 'dirty bomb') attacks at the twin ports of Los Angeles and Long Beach. Because these two ports handle almost half of the United States seaborne international trade, any disruption of their trade is likely to have major economic impacts. However this kind of attack is not the most dangerous imaginable, because it would involve minimal destruction of infrastructure. Many of its impacts would be more psychological, and much would depend on the length of time before the authorities thought it safe to reopen the ports. Accordingly our scenarios also include simultaneous attacks on freeway access to the ports that would magnify the adverse economic impacts. These would not only delay the emergency response but would also stretch out the disruption period because it would take a longer time to rebuild destroyed bridges (or construct temporary bridges), and alternative routes (in the port access region) are few and would be highly congested.

THE PORTS AND THE LOCAL ECONOMY

Tables 14.1 and 14.2 provide some basic data about the ports' role in the local economy. In a metropolitan region of 16.4 million people, the twin ports of Los Angeles and Long Beach account for 103 million tons of seaborne trade, the fifth-largest port complex in the world (Hong Kong and Singapore rank first and second) and catching up fast. Directly and indirectly, the ports employ over half a million workers, accounting for almost 7 per cent of the region's labor force. In terms of containerized traffic, the two ports ranks first and second nationally. To put it in perspective, its combined trade (imports and exports) of almost $200 billion. Reflecting the national economy, imports are much more important than exports ($165 billion compared with $34 billion), and a substantial majority of both the imports and the exports are to and from outside the region. In other words, the ports fulfill a national even more than a regional function. Thus the port of Los Angeles and the port of Long Beach are of central importance to the regional economy, and the loss of transshipment capabilities at these sites has profound impacts. We assume that both export and import flows currently using seaport facilities would terminate for as long as the ports were out of service (the issue of port diversion is addressed below).

Table 14.1 Basic data for the Los Angeles metro area, 2000

Population	Housing units	Civilian labor force	Median household income (1999)	Total seaborne trade (short tons)
16 373 645	5 678 148	7 458 249	$45 903	LA: 42 267 055 LB: 60 882 795

Table 14.2 Dimensions of port activity

	Long Beach	Los Angeles	Total
Imports ($b.)	77.98	86.76	164.74
Exports ($b.)	16.72	17.44	34.15
Port-related jobs ('000)	265.80	235.40	501.20

'DIRTY BOMB' ATTACKS

It is well known that the ports have been highly vulnerable since 9/11 because of the infrequency of container checks. On 1 July 2004, new rules were introduced to increase the degree of protection. The measures include replacing hand-held radiation detectors with stationary radiation screening devices analogous to the X-ray screening of passenger luggage at airports and efforts to screen all containers (estimated at 11 million per annum through the twin ports). However these more advanced measures will not be in place until later[2], and their effectiveness has yet to be tested (see Chapters 12 and 13). Also, although the details of the testing procedures are not fully known, it may be easier to plant simultaneous radiological bombs (assuming that terrorists have access to radiological material in the United States) on outbound rather than inbound freight, especially because the effects may not be very different if the bombs are set off at the perimeter (prior to passing through security) rather in the heart of the port terminals.

The extent of disruption may depend on the size of the bombs. As social scientists we have minimal knowledge of the technical aspects of radiation contamination and exposure, and our sole concern is with how these translate into a period of closure of the ports. Thus the rest of this paragraph draws on the external technical literature. Hypothetically, we assume the explosion of two small RDDs (radiological dispersal devices), each of them containing 5 lb of high explosive, more or less simultaneously at the two ports. Blast damage would be quite limited, with deaths and serious injuries within a range of about 15 meters and with very limited damage to physical infrastructure. The evacuation zone would include all areas with exposure $>$ 1 REM, probably within the 5–10 km^2 range, but this depends on weather conditions (wind speed, direction, precipitation, and so on). In any event, this would require the closure of both ports on health even more than on security grounds. The early phase of exposure lasts about four days (EPA guidelines); the time frame for intermediate and later phases is variable and subjective (weeks, months, even years). We ignore the plume beyond the port, which might extend several miles in one of a number of directions; however it would be a very short-term event.

When the ports would be reopened would be a policy rather than a technical decision. For the purposes of our economic impact analysis, we assume two alternative closure times (the 'bookends' of our analysis): 15 days and 120 days. The 15-day closure assumes no mitigating adjustments (for example major diversions to other ports and transport modes), while the 120-day closure also involves road access disruptions and might involve adjustments in behavior (for example exploring other sources for inputs and other transshipment points for sales). These closure periods are chosen for illustrative purposes; they seem reasonable, but it is easy to substitute alternative closure periods and make new impact estimates based upon them. We examine two different types of impact. The first and most obvious but the lesser type is the primarily local effects of the cessation of port activities (that is, the effects of a decline in final demand for port services). The second type is the economic consequences of the interruption of trade flows, both imports and exports. These affect the economic activities of all firms directly or indirectly involved in international trade throughout the region and beyond. These impacts, in terms of both output and jobs, are much larger than the local effects.

PRECEDENT

To our knowledge, there has been no detailed prior study of the economic impacts of port disruption because of a terrorist attack. At first sight, the port strike (more precisely, lock-out) of 2002 might offer some relevant information. However the strike was confined to Los Angeles; Long Beach was unaffected. More important, the strike was anticipated for at least six months so that measures were already in place to mitigate its impacts; the timing of a terrorist attack, on the other hand, is unpredictable. Thus what happened then is of very limited significance in evaluating the consequences of an unanticipated terrorist attack. Also, as the passing reference to the strike in Chapter 7 suggests, most estimates of the costs were grossly inflated. Media reports at the time of the 2002 ports strike widely quoted cost estimates of $1 billion per day. The origins of this estimate are unknown, but it is much too high. Over 120 days, it would amount to about 15 per cent of gross regional product. Accordingly, it is a reference base of limited value. Nevertheless studying what happened before and during the strike may be helpful in the design of anticipatory and prevention strategies.

THE BRIDGES

In this study, we consider supplementing radiological bomb attacks on the ports with the destruction of access bridges. We modeled the destruction of two major access bridges (on I-10 and I-710 south of the I-405 freeway) and the Vincent Thomas Bridge linking the two ports. The last of these is important because it would deny access to both Terminal Island and the Alameda Corridor (see below) from the west and would break the link between the two ports.

THE SOUTHERN CALIFORNIA PLANNING MODEL (SCPM)

Inter-industry models are among the most widely used models to measure regional economic impacts. They attempt to trace all the impacts, including those of intra- and inter-regional shipments, usually at a high level of sectoral disaggregation. Being demand driven, they account primarily for losses via backward linkages.

The first Southern California Planning Model Version 1 (SCPM1) was developed for the five-county Los Angeles metropolitan region, and has the unique capability to allocate all impacts, in terms of jobs or the dollar value of output, to 308 sub-regional zones, mainly individual municipalities. This is the result of an integrated modeling approach that incorporates two fundamental components: input–output and spatial allocation. The approach allows the representation of estimated spatial and sectoral impacts corresponding to any vector of changes in final demand. Exogenous shocks treated as changes in final demand are fed through an input–output model to generate sectoral impacts that are then introduced into the spatial allocation model.

The first model component is now built upon the Minnesota Planning Group's well-known IMPLAN input–output model which has a high degree of sectoral disaggregation (509 sectors). The second basic model component is used for allocating sectoral impacts across 308 geographic zones in Southern California. The key is to adapt a Garin-Lowry style model for spatially allocating the induced impacts generated by the input–output model. The building blocks of the SCPM1 are the metropolitan input–output model, a journey-to-work matrix, and a journey-to-nonwork-destinations matrix. This is a journey-to-services matrix that is more restrictively described as a 'journey-to-shop' matrix in the Garin-Lowry model.

The journey-to-services matrix includes any trip associated with a home-based transaction other than the sale of labor to an employer. This includes retail trips and other transaction trips, but excludes non-transaction-based trips such as trips to visit friends and relatives. Data for the journey-to-services matrix include all trips classified by the Southern California Association of Governments as home-to-shop trips, and a subset of the trips classified as home-to-other and other-to-other trips.

The key innovation associated with SCPM1 is to incorporate the full range of multipliers obtained via input–output techniques to obtain detailed economic impacts by sector and by submetropolitan zone. SCPM1 follows the principles of the Garin-Lowry model by allocating sectoral output (or employment) to zones via a loop that relies on the trip matrices.

Induced consumption expenditures are traced back from the workplace to the residential site via a journey-to-work matrix and from the residential site to the place of purchase and/or consumption via a journey-to-services matrix (see Richardson et al., 1993) for a further summary of SCPM1.

Incorporating the Garin-Lowry approach into spatial allocation makes the transportation flows in SCPM1 exogenous. These flows are also relatively aggregated compared with transportation models, defined primarily at the level of political jurisdictions (most transportation models use Traffic Analysis Zones [TAZs] which are much smaller). However with no explicit representation of the transportation network, SCPM1 has no means to account for the economic impact of changes in transportation supply. Terrorist attacks are likely to induce such changes, including capacity losses that will contribute to reductions in network level service and increases in travel delays. SCPM1 does not account for such changes in transportation costs, underestimating the costs of any exogenous shock.

In this study we use a more refined version of SCPM that endogenizes traffic flows by including an explicit representation of the transportation network. We call this SCPM2 (see Figure 14.1). Models of this type are based on data from a variety of different sources. Consequently updating and reconciling data resources is an ongoing activity. Currently, we are also developing a much more sophisticated model that:

- revisits and re-evaluates many of the fundamental assumptions of SCPM2;
- accounts for non-highway access to the ports;
- involves a much more detailed sectoral–spatial allocation of economic activity within the Southern California five-county region (Gordon et al., 2004); and
- also integrates this updated SCPM2 with an interstate freight model (the National Interstate Economic Model, NIEMO).

We call the full model SCPM2004. This latter model is still in the course of development, and the current analysis will be re-estimated when the new version of the model is available. Hence it should be emphasized that the results reported here are very provisional and incomplete.

SCPM2 results are computed at the level of the Southern California Association of Governments (SCAG) 1527 traffic analysis zones, and could then be aggregated (if desired) to the level of the 308 political jurisdictions (cities and different types of unincorporated areas) defined for SCPM1. These jurisdictional boundaries routinely cross traffic analysis zones. Results for traffic analysis zones that cross jurisdictional boundaries are allocated in proportion to area. Like SCPM1, SCPM2 aggregates to 17

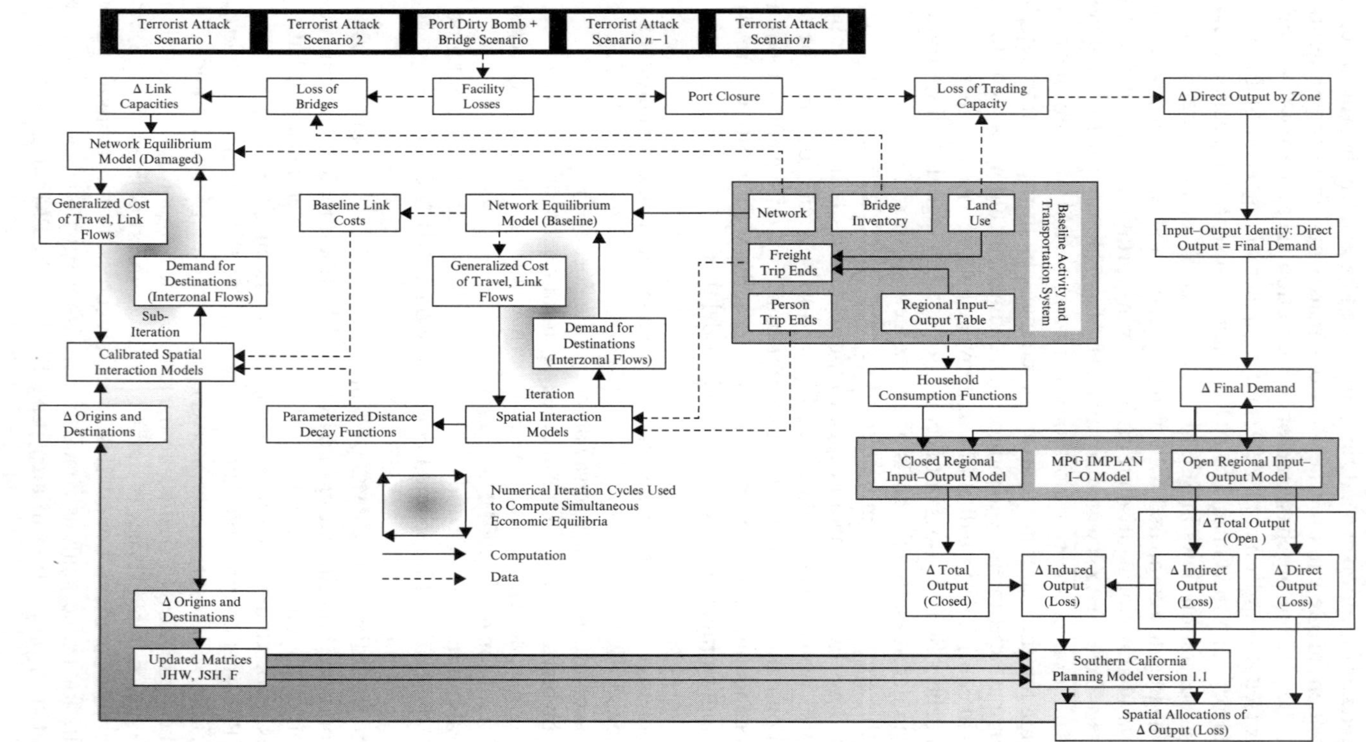

Figure 14.1 SCPM data flow

at the local level the 509 sectors represented in the IMPLAN I–O model. Treating the transportation network explicitly endogenizes otherwise exogenous Garin-Lowry style matrices describing the travel behavior of households, achieving consistency across network costs and origin–destination requirements. The model also accounts for intra-regional freight flows. SCPM2 makes distance decay and congestion functions explicit. This allows us to determine the geographical location of indirect and induced economic losses by endogenizing choices of route and destination. This better allocates indirect and induced economic losses over zones in response to direct port-related losses (wherever these losses may occur) in trade, employment and transportation accessibility (see Cho et al., 2001, for a further summary of SCPM2).

BUSINESS INTERRUPTION

The major impact of port closure (especially from a radiological bomb that does little physical damage) is its effects on businesses. The traditional way to estimate business interruption is via an *ex post* survey of individual firms (for example Gordon et al., 1998). This method has its problems: the representativeness of the sample (especially in a large metropolitan area), and the need to undertake the survey after the event. The approach adopted here is much simpler, although by necessity it focuses on economic sectors rather than individual firms. Also, it has the advantage of an *ex ante* estimate that is very important to measure the resources that might need to be allocated to prevention, mitigation and restoration. Very simply, we shut off exports to and imports from the ports via our freight model and the sectors affected suffer a decline in final demand of sales and/or indirect supplies.

QUANTIFYING THE ECONOMIC EFFECTS OF A TERRORIST 'DIRTY BOMB' ATTACK ON THE TWIN PORTS AND PORT-RELATED TRANSPORTATION ACCESS

This research applies SCPM2 to quantify the potential economic impact of a terrorist attack (more specifically, moderate-sized radiological bombs) on the twin ports of Los Angeles and Long Beach, California, and on nearby transportation infrastructure affecting freeway access to the ports. The duration of the disruption determines the length of time for which firms throughout the region will be non-operational or operating below normal levels of service. This allows the calculation of exogenously prompted reductions in demand by these businesses. These are introduced into the inter-industry model as declines in final demand. The I–O model translates this production shock into direct, indirect and induced costs. The indirect and induced costs are spatially allocated in terms consistent with the endogenous transportation behavior of firms and households. Thus interrupted trade at the ports is converted into lost economic output and employment, and the effects are modeled zone by zone over the Southern California region as a whole. The results of the modeling show that distributed losses related to these events in Southern California and beyond could exceed $34 billion, and cost more than 212 000 jobs (measured in person-years of employment).

The spatial economic impact model is able to calculate direct losses within an impact area as well as the distributed economic effects of these losses throughout the regional economy. The model also calculates the geographical economic impacts of disruption to the transportation network. Direct losses arise from lost opportunities to produce goods and services and, in the case of the ports, the capacity to ship goods. Indirect and induced losses arise as people and businesses in the impacted areas become unable to work or generate income as a result of the event. Indirect losses are the losses to suppliers whose products and services are no longer purchased by directly impacted firms and households. Induced losses are losses in secondary consumption as direct and indirect workers are laid off.

For this study, the ports are assumed be closed for 15 days in the 'no bridge damage' scenarios. If a port attack is combined with destroying access bridges, we assume that the impacts extend over 120 days. The 120-days assumption is based on the experience with the La Cienega Boulevard bridge on the I-10 Santa Monica Freeway after the Northridge earthquake of 1994 which took 4.5 months to rebuild, despite substantial incentives to the construction company. The port could reopen in the reconstruction phase of the bridge damage cases, but trade would be very severely disrupted. In terms of economic impacts, we assume that the differences in bridge damage and no damage scenarios for the same time period are primarily reflected in network performance results. These assumptions are for illustrative purposes, but they are easy to adjust. Longer or shorter interruption periods can be scaled proportionately and/or a period of partial operation could be introduced to account for the facilities' gradual return to service. In other words, our results are illustrative rather than definitive.

Potential damage to the transportation infrastructure in Southern California implies additional impacts over and above the effects of the radiological bombs. For the purpose of this study, freeway segments close to the destroyed bridges were assumed to be closed. The SCPM2 representation of the transportation network includes freeways, state highways and high-design arterials. Small surface streets are not included in the model.

Some degree of trade activity could be possible despite port closures because some trade can be shifted to other ports and some purchases can be diverted to domestic suppliers. However these changes are unlikely to occur in the short run. We analyzed six basic scenarios (with subsets: 'local' impacts and total impacts), but in the interests of space we will report only three cases here: the local effects with both ports closed down for 15 and 120 days without bridge damage, and the total impacts of both ports closed for 120 days with bridge damage:

- Scenarios 1 and 2: The Port of Los Angeles is closed for a period of 15 days (no bridge damage) or 120 days (key bridges destroyed), and all import and export trade is interrupted.
- Scenarios 3 and 4: The Port of Long Beach is closed for a period of 15 days (no bridge damage) or 120 days (key bridges destroyed).
- Scenarios 5 and 6: Both ports are closed for a period of 15 days (no bridge damage) or 120 days (key bridges destroyed).

Tables 14.3 and 14.4 show the 'local' impacts in the most affected zones in both ports over 15 days and 120 days. Many of these impacts are located close to the ports. The 'local' direct losses accrue only in the port and nearby zones (TAZs), but indirect and induced losses can accumulate throughout the region. When both ports are closed down, the direct job loss in the port TAZs is 687 over 15 days and 5495 over 120 days. The total job loss (including the indirect and induced losses, and the jobs lost outside the region) is 1258 over 15 days and 10 061 over 120 days, of which more than two-thirds occur within the region, primarily in Los Angeles County. In terms of output, the total impacts are \$138.5 million and \$1107.6 million, with more than half in Los Angeles County.

However these impacts are relatively small compared to the business interruption effects of the cessation of international trade, which affects exporters in terms of the loss of sales and importers, especially in the form of intermediate inputs (for example petroleum). Table 14.5 examines the full range of impacts for both ports. Destroying the bridges severely complicates the problems for the ports. The ports could reopen and shippers could resort to congested surface streets, but at an extreme efficiency cost. The key result combining the impacts on the two ports with the bridges down scenario over 120 days represents the maximum impact scenario. The economic losses amount to more than \$34 billion of lost output and 212 165 person-years of employment. In this case, not much more than one-third of the impacts occur within the region, of which about two-thirds

Table 14.3 'Local' output and employment losses of 15-day port closure, ports of Los Angeles and Long Beach – no bridge damage

	GRP ($1000s)				Jobs			
	Direct	Indirect	Induced	Total*	Direct	Indirect	Induced	Total
City of Los Angeles	13 965	5262	5068	24 295	125	48	57	230
City of Long Beach	37 058	548	521	38 127	362	5	6	373
County of Los Angeles	51 024	11 966	12 277	75 267	488	106	138	732
County of Orange	0	3432	3479	6911	0	31	39	70
County of Ventura	0	763	907	1671	0	7	10	17
County of Riverside	0	763	992	1755	0	7	11	18
County of San Bernardino	0	1058	1259	2317	0	10	15	24
Sum of five counties	51 024	17 983	18 915	87 921	488	161	213	861
Regional leakages	30 286	11 194	9052	50 529	199	95	102	396
Regional total	81 310	29 176	27 967	138 453	687	256	315	1258

Table 14.4 'Local' output and employment losses of 120-day port closure, ports of Los Angeles and Long Beach – no bridge damage

	GRP ($1000s)				Jobs			
	Direct	Indirect	Induced	Total*	Direct	Indirect	Induced	Total
City of Los Angeles	111 723	42 098	40 536	194 356	1003	381	454	1838
City of Long Beach	296 467	4384	4172	305 023	2900	37	47	2984
County of Los Angeles	408 190	95 728	98 216	602 134	3902	850	1102	5854
County of Orange	0	27 454	27 836	55 289	0	248	312	561
County of Ventura	0	6108	7258	13 366	0	54	82	136
County of Riverside	0	6103	7932	14 035	0	56	92	148
County of San Bernardino	0	8467	10 075	18 542	0	77	116	193
Sum of five counties	408 190	143 860	151 317	703 367	3902	1285	1704	6891
Regional leakages	242 290	89 552	72 419	404 229	1593	760	816	3170
Regional total	650 480	233 412	223 736	1 107 596	5495	2045	2520	10 061

Table 14.5 Total output and employment losses of 120-day port closure, ports of Los Angeles and Long Beach – bridge damage

	GRP ($1000s)				Jobs			
	Direct	Indirect	Induced	Total*	Direct	Indirect	Induced	Total
City of Los Angeles	2 112 863	752 657	519 864	3 385 384	9492	5788	5831	21 111
City of Long Beach	553 600	93 227	53 484	700 310	4008	640	601	5249
County of Los Angeles	5 252 325	1 759 341	1 259 721	8 271 386	24 722	13 233	14 142	52 097
County of Orange	1 246 977	495 913	357 140	2 100 029	5502	3841	4009	13 352
County of Ventura	344 904	142 855	93 101	580 860	1459	971	1052	3482
County of Riverside	296 139	114 810	101 748	512 697	1306	890	1175	3371
County of San Bernardino	424 042	161 191	129 281	714 515	1842	1218	1487	4548
Sum of five counties	7 564 387	2 674 110	1 940 991	12 179 488	34 831	20 154	21 865	76 850
Regional leakages	14 255 919	4 116 421	3 519 554	21 891 893	64 401	31 259	39 655	135 316
Regional total	21 820 306	6 790 530	5 460 545	34 071 381	99 232	51 413	61 520	212 165

of the local impacts are within Los Angeles County. These numbers underline two key points: the closure of the ports can have major economic consequences and the ripple effects are national, not merely regional.

We developed several maps to show the spatial consequences of each scenario; however, we show only one (Map 14.1 displays the higher 'bookend', that is, maximum impact). The important point shown in the map is that in the trade interruption cases the output losses are widely diffused throughout the region. The closure of the ports is not a local event. However it is not even a regional event. It is a national event and an international event. This explains why the ports are such a significant target.

There are mitigation strategies that could be put in place (these include shipments to and from other ports, transfer of supplies of intermediate goods to domestic sources involving a modal shift from the ports to truck or rail, traffic management measures to get around the destroyed bridges). However these mitigation measures cannot be included in the model; hence their effects are discussed in general terms.

TRANSPORTATION IMPACTS

The impacts on the transportation network are of two kinds, each offsetting the other. If the ports are closed there are obviously many fewer freight trips to and from the port which will reduce the traffic load on the region. On the other hand, with these critical bridges down, congestion increases on the network. The net effect is not predictable *ex ante*. Transportation delays are measured in terms of passenger car unit (PCU) hours and millions of dollars. The number of freight trips declines in each scenario. However the methodology assumes that the lower level of service resulting from destroyed bridges has no additional trip deterrence effect. Also the model assumes that the number of auto trips remains constant. These results are shown in Table 14.6. The monetary value of the transportation impacts are found in Table 14.7. Negative values represent reductions in delay relative to the baseline. These reductions in delay are because of the container trucks that can no longer access the ports. However there is an improved level of service for other trip makers because of this, but being forced from the freeways to the surface streets increases congestion costs. We have no information on the income distribution of automobile drivers so we assume two values, \$6.50 and \$13.00, for travel time, with the true value perhaps somewhere in between. For the purpose of elaboration, we focus on the higher values of Scenario 6 (the 120-day closure of both ports with the bridge interruptions). They suggest that the traffic congestion adds almost \$648 million of delay costs, all of them because of the

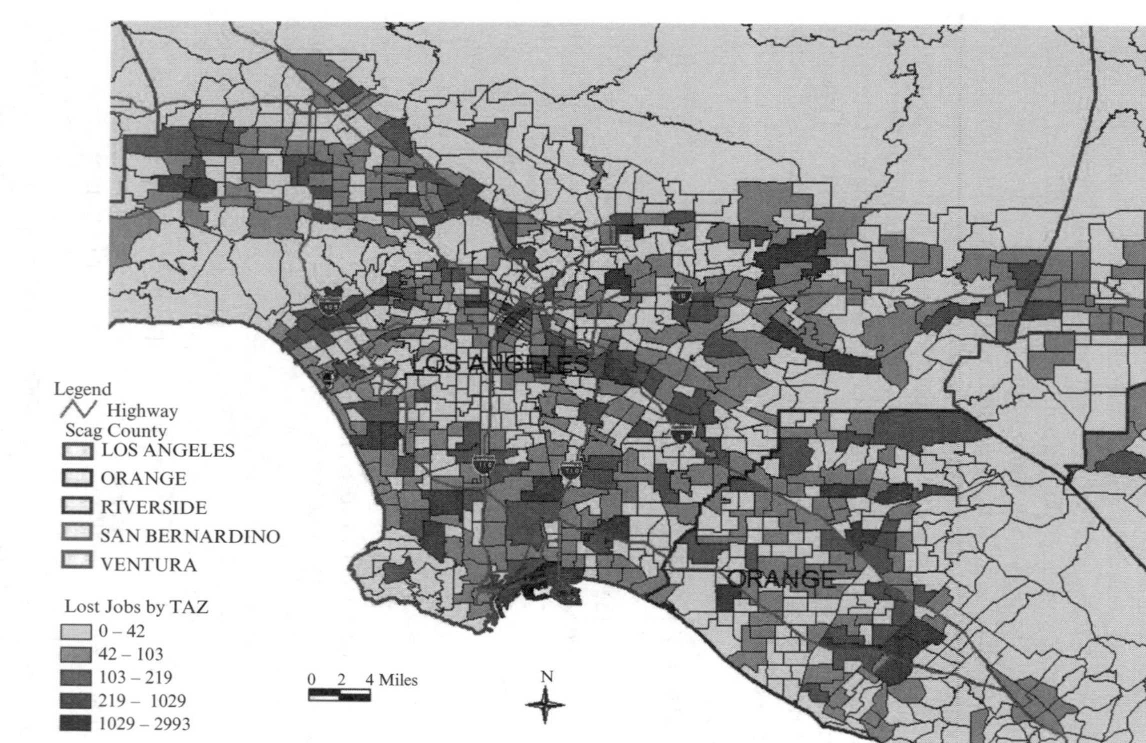

Map 14.1 Spatial distribution of job losses by 120-day port closure, port of Long Beach and port of Los Angeles, bridge damage (Scenario 6)

Table 14.6 Comparison of network performance in peak hours, multiple impact scenarios: freight and personal trips with time costs measured in PCE-minutes

	Freight trips	Personal trips	Total trips	% of freight trips	Freight travel cost	Personal travel cost	Total travel cost	% freight/ total travel costs
Baseline	120 011	5 249 246	5 369 257	2.2352	17 338 612	221 730 845	239 069 458	7.2525
Scenario 1	118 268	5 249 246	5 367 515	2.2034	17 306 258	223 911 512	241 217 770	7.1745
Scenario 2	118 268	5 249 246	5 367 515	2.2034	17 283 293	223 554 346	240 837 639	7.1763
Scenario 3	117 791	5 249 246	5 367 037	2.1947	17 154 239	221 457 684	238 611 924	7.1892
Scenario 4	117 791	5 249 246	5 367 037	2.1947	17 220 699	223 830 140	241 050 839	7.1440
Scenario 5	116 050	5 249 246	5 365 296	2.1630	17 115 162	223 324 249	240 439 410	7.1183
Scenario 6	116 050	5 249 246	5 365 296	2.1630	17 241 634	225 822 085	243 063 719	7.0935

Table 14.7 Comparison of network performance over 120 days, multiple impact scenarios: $ million

	Freight travel costs[1]	Personal travel costs[2]	Total costs	% of freight travel costs	Freight travel costs[1]	Personal travel costs[3]	Total costs	% freight/ total travel costs
Baseline	7896.43	18753.73	26650.16	29.6299	7896.43	37507.46	45403.89	17.3915
Scenario 1	−14.73	184.44	169.70	−0.2424	−14.73	368.88	354.14	−0.1668
Scenario 2	−25.19	154.23	129.04	−0.2369	−25.19	308.46	283.27	−0.1630
Scenario 3	−83.97	−23.10	−107.07	−0.1968	−83.97	−46.21	−130.18	−0.1355
Scenario 4	−53.70	177.56	123.86	−0.3376	−53.70	355.11	301.41	−0.2322
Scenario 5	−101.76	134.77	33.00	−0.4180	−101.76	269.54	167.77	−0.2873
Scenario 6	−44.17	346.03	301.87	−0.4957	−44.17	692.06	647.90	−0.3406

Notes:
1. Freight trip cost is assumed as $35 per PCE per hour.
2. Personal trip cost is assumed as $6.50 per PCE per hour.
3. Personal trip cost is assumed as $13 per PCE per hour.

Source: Authors' calculation by dividing by peak-hour ratio (0.1537028) and translating the time period to 120 days.

additional costs to automobile drivers. Freight travel costs are consistently reduced in all scenarios because of canceled freight trips.

From the results above, it is clear that the costs associated with even a moderate radiological bomb at the ports and associated freeway access disruptions result in substantial direct, indirect and induced costs flowing from lost economic opportunities. This dollar amount over a period of 120 days could be more than $34 billion, primarily because of the interruptions to export and import flows at the ports. The greatest increase in transportation delays would occur in cases where port trade flows are diverted to other ports and to other modes (for example bringing in intermediate inputs from outside the region may add to traffic congestion because of the possibility of longer intra-metropolitan freight trips). These effects are not modeled.

As a comparison to the results reported here, Cho et al., (2001) used a similar methodology to calculate the economic losses associated with a hypothetical magnitude 7.1 earthquake on the Elysian Park blind thrust fault under downtown Los Angeles. They calculated that an earthquake of this type could produce as much as $135 billion in total costs, with a median amount of $102 billion. The scenarios defined here amount to as much as 24.2 per cent of their maximum estimate (or 73 per cent if converted to dollars per year; the earthquake has even more long-lasting effects). This enables a comparison to be made between the economic impacts of a terrorist attack and those of a plausible natural catastrophe.

A STRATEGIC QUESTION

Our study shows that a simultaneous terrorist attack on the ports and major access routes would be much more damaging to the economy than an attack on the port alone, primarily because it takes much longer to rebuild the bridges than to reopen the ports. Also, to our knowledge, these attacks would be relatively easy: two radioactive bombs on the perimeter of both ports and three explosionary devices at relatively unprotected bridges. Is it desirable to make this knowledge public on the ground of 'aiding the enemy?' First, this is an obvious rather than a counterintuitive finding (so there is no disclosure of important security information); the issue is not that there is an additional negative impact, but rather how large it is. Second, even if potential terrorists are aware of this, the fact that US counterterrorism authorities also know it implies that the level of protection would be higher, and this in itself could be a deterrent. Third, quantifying the potential scale of the impact is very important in determining how much to spend on prevention.

A TECHNICAL QUESTION

A recurrent problem with transportation network models is how quickly they converge. The appendix shows how convergence was measured while Appendix figure 14.1 gives an example for one of our scenarios. It shows a very rapid convergence after four to five runs. Accordingly, we ran all the network scenarios for six iterations.

QUALIFICATIONS

There are a few important qualifications to this current research, and we should stress the preliminary nature of the results. Perhaps the most important omission is the potential influence of the Alameda Corridor, a $2.9 billion 20-mile grade-separated rail corridor from the ports to the marshaling yards north of downtown that opened in April 2002. Our model is currently based on the highway network. The Alameda Corridor currently takes about 13 per cent of the ports' trade, but has the capacity to take much more. By 2025, the objective is to carry 45 000 containers per day out of 90 000 (or almost 33 million per year). The Corridor is currently grossly underutilized, with 35–40 trains per day compared to a capacity of 150 per day. The primary reason is that many distributors find it more convenient to ship goods by truck to the Riverside and San Bernardino County distribution hubs, for example Ontario (for repackaging and distribution either by truck or rail). Only the simplest loads use the corridor. An additional 12 per cent of trade (2400 containers per day) is trucked to a facility in Carson, then loaded on to the Corridor. One argument in favor of promoting the rail corridor is the alleviation of air pollution from trucks (the potential air pollution risks are in the region of 2000 cases of cancer per million population compared with policy objectives ranging between one and 100 cases per million).

Alternatives include building one or more truckways, which are even more expensive than the rail corridor. One would run on the I-710 freeway, costing between $4 billion and $10 billion (depending upon the number of truck lanes and additional car lanes); another would make SR47 a freeway from the port complex to Alameda Street (costing about $450 million); while the third, the most expensive and most ambitious, would extend the truckway as far as Barstow, a city 120 miles away. These are unlikely to be built in the foreseeable future, given the transportation cutbacks in the California State budget.

Another idea is to run more trains from the northern terminus (near downtown) to the San Bernardino and Riverside hubs, but the tracks are already congested and it would cost $100–$200 million to build new unloading and storage facilities at the distribution yards. Also, there are no train lines that run directly to the inland hubs. Furthermore it is more expensive (by about $100 per container) to ship by rail rather than by truck to the inland hubs. In addition, trade may triple over the next 20 years, and the infrastructure to cope with this expansion is not yet there.

Of course we could have modeled a bomb attack on the Corridor itself, but surmise that a sub-grade rail line could be repaired within a few days.

The 120-day bridge reconstruction period may be optimistic. It would be somewhat faster than the rate achieved after the 1994 Northridge earthquake. Also, if an attack on the Vincent Thomas Bridge brought it down, its rebuilding would be a multi-year rather than a multi-month project. We have not investigated in detail the bridge reconstruction costs, but based on our previous earthquake-related research the two freeway bridges would probably cost about $50 million each. The Vincent Thomas Bridge is a different scale of magnitude and would be difficult and very expensive to replace (perhaps $5 billion); however a single bomb might require only a modest repair. We have not estimated the costs of mortality and radiation-related illness. An attack on this scale would have very moderate human-related costs (except for psychological costs) compared to the massive economic impacts. It is understandable why the public may be more concerned about terrorist events that threaten persons rather than property, but it would be a policy failure to pay too little attention to those events that primarily incur economic rather than human damages.

A chronic problem is the expected doubling of freight traffic on the I-710 and other port access freeways by 2025. In the context of a potential terrorist attack, the rail access adds a degree of redundancy into the port-related transportation system. While it is true that an attack on Terminal Island could take down the Badger Rail Bridge, it could be replaced by a temporary structure relatively quickly (see below), while the effects of a bomb on the Alameda Corridor could be remedied even faster. However rail access exists only to some of the terminals, and the others will not receive such access in the foreseeable future.

Although attention should be paid to the potential diversion of trade to other ports, the medium-term prospects are not promising. Trade might go to other West Coast ports such as Oakland and Seattle-Tacoma, or move through the Panama Canal to Savannah or Jacksonville, or even take an eastern route from Asia via the Suez Canal. However the other West Coast ports have limited capacity (for example Oakland port has not kept up with its dredging schedule while Seattle is beginning to convert port facilities to other waterfront uses), the Panama Canal is operating close to capacity and it would take a decade or more to widen the channel to accommodate the new, larger ships, and shipping from Asia via the Suez Canal would be very expensive. Analysis of port diversion is complicated because of capacity constraints and ship sizes, but obviously diversion is a mitigating factor. However the consensus among maritime specialists is that the potential for trade diversion, especially within a 120-day time frame, is minimal.

Another issue is whether short-term economic losses would be made up via more deliveries later. In other words, is the problem merely deferred demand rather than lost demand? Also, there may be medium-term substantial substitution possibilities, such as goods from Europe to the East Coast, goods shipped into Canada and Mexico and then via truck into the United States, or diversion to domestic suppliers (for example automobile sales). All these options suggest that our estimates are upper-bound estimates. Our assessment however is that these palliatives would have a modest effect.

FUTURE RESEARCH

This remains a research project in its early stage. Our economic impact model can easily measure the consequences of days of port closure and degrees of closure. The key problem from our perspective (given our limited knowledge of ports, the shipping industry and supply logistics) is how to come up with these parameters. Our future research will focus on alternative scenarios, the degree of trade diversion, and on whether lost production and deliveries are merely delays that will be made up later. We will rely heavily on port, shipping and logistics specialists to refine our scenarios.

One scenario that we are definitely investigating is the isolation of Terminal Island, an island located between the two ports that handles approximately 55 per cent of the combined port trade and has the most up-to-date loading and unloading facilities. This would be a very cost-effective attack because it would require taking out only three highway bridges and one rail bridge. A temporary trellis rail bridge to put the Alameda Corridor back in service plus restoring highway access might be built in less than 120 days (but at some cost in terms of the blockage of shipping lanes), but it would take years to rebuild the bridges (especially the wide spans of the Vincent Thomas and the Jerry Desmond Bridges). Provisional estimates of the economic losses amount to $45 billion of output and 280 000 person-years of employment per year (because this is a linear model these numbers can be scaled up or down according to different estimates of the period that the Island cannot be used).

MITIGATION AND PREVENTION

The parameters of these impacts give some idea of the resource expenditures that might be justified to attempt to avoid these attacks. Video surveillance of the major bridges and overpasses would appear to be a very cost-effective option (and may even be in place). Attempts to improve the screening of containers in and out of the ports is currently being implemented (see Chapters 12 and 13), but a radiological bomb attack just outside the perimeter would be almost as dangerous and almost risk-free.

CONCLUSIONS

The examples presented here illustrates a methodology for calculating the economic impacts of a plausible terrorist attack in Southern California. The examples used are a radiological bomb attack on one or both ports (Los Angeles and Long Beach), in some scenarios supplemented by the destruction of key access freeway bridges. However the methodology is easily applicable to a wide variety of different types of terrorist attacks. The model distributes the total economic impacts of a terrorist disruption to households and businesses throughout the metropolitan economy and, indeed, to the rest of the country (but in the latter case not in any spatial detail, at least until our national model [NIEMO] is developed and integrated with SCPM). Not all post-event economic behavior is knowable, but this approach makes it possible to calculate the economic impacts associated with a variety of scenarios, including changes in import and export chains and (potentially) transshipment modes.

The local impacts (that is, the effects of the closure of the port on labor and other port services) of a radiological bomb attack at the two ports are modest but significant: about $1.108 billion of lost output and 10061 person-years of employment (about two-thirds of these impacts occurring within the region, with about 85 per cent of these within Los Angeles County). However the results of this preliminary study with respect to the disruption of international trade (both exports and imports), when the bomb attack is combined with a pinpointed disruption of transportation access to the ports, implies much more damage: up to $34 billion worth of direct, indirect and induced costs, 212000 person-years of employment losses, and up to $648 million imputed time costs of transportation-related delays.

The other implication is that a radiological bomb attack at the ports would have to be large to have a major economic rather than a primarily psychological impact. Interrupting access to the ports by bringing down key bridges would be much more damaging and, unfortunately, easier to carry out. This is merely one example among hundreds of the difficulties that the Department of Homeland Security faces in how to allocate scarce resources among competing options.

APPENDIX: CONVERGENCE

The objective function of the assignment follows the formula developed by Sheffi (1985) for Wardrop's (1952) first principle to minimize travel costs as follows:

$$\text{Min} \sum_a \int_0^{x_a} C_a(x)dx \tag{14.1}$$

subject to

$$x_a = \sum_o \sum_d \sum_p \delta_{a,p}^{od} h_p^{od} \quad \forall a \tag{14.2}$$

$$\sum_p h_p^{od} = T_{od} \quad \forall o,d \tag{14.3}$$

$$h_p^{od} \geq 0 \quad \forall p,o,d \tag{14.4}$$

where x_a is the total flow on link a, including both personal and freight trips.

$C_a(t)$ is the cost-flow function to calculate average travel cost on link a,
$\delta_{a,p}^{od}$ is a link-path incidence variable; equal to one if link a belongs to path p connecting OD pair o and d,
h_p^{od} is the flow on path p connecting OD pair o and d,
T_{od} represents total trips between origin node o and destination node d, and
p is a network path, with o and d being the two end nodes on the network.

As Sheffi (1985) stated, this objective function is the sum of the integrals of the link cost-flow or link performance functions. The cost-flow function in this simulation model (SCPM 2) follows the one published by Bureau of Public Roads (BPR, 1964), and is applied to represent the relationships between link flow and travel time, shown as follows:

$$C_a = C_a(0)\left[1 + \alpha\left(\frac{x_a}{D_a}\right)^{\beta}\right] \tag{14.5}$$

where $C_a(t)$ is the cost-flow function to calculate average travel cost on link a, and $C_a(0)$ is the free-flow travel cost on link a,

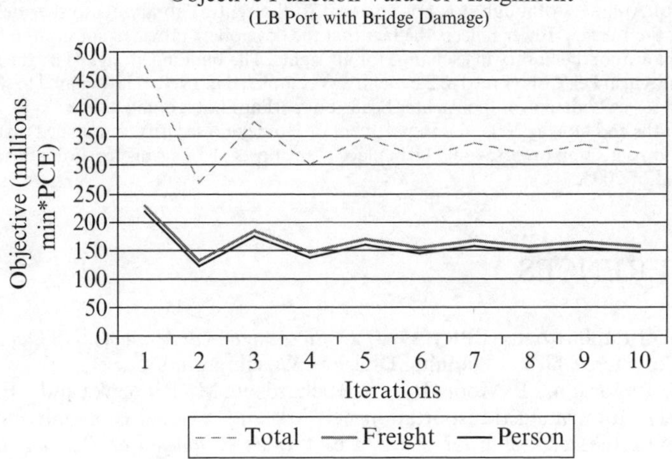

Appendix figure 14.1 The rate of convergence

x_a is the total flow on link *a*, including both personal and freight trips,
D_a is the capacity of link a, and
α and β are parameters, while 1 + α is the ratio of travel time per unit distance at practical capacity D_a to that at free flow. Both α and β are estimated from empirical data. In this study, α is assigned a value of 0.15 and β is assigned a value of 4.

The regional impact simulation model was run over multiple iterations to reach an optimal point minimizing travel costs, as described in formula (14.1). Scenario 4 (the closure of the port of Long Beach and the bridges) is used as an illustrative case to test how quickly the model converges. Appendix figure 14.1 shows that the objective value of the sum of freight and personal trips approaches a convergence point after four or five iterations. Given this evidence, we ran six iterations of the simulation model for each scenario.

NOTES

1. It is the tallest building in Los Angeles County, formerly known as the Library Tower. It is located in downtown Los Angeles at 633 West Fifth Street. With 73 floors, it stands at 1018 feet in height. It is the tallest building between Chicago (the nation's tallest building is the Sears Tower with 110 floors at 1450 feet) and Southeast Asia (the Petronas Towers in Kuala Lumpur, Malaysia has 88 floors and is 1483 feet tall). The building is

the 7th tallest building in the United States and the tallest outside of Chicago, New York, and Atlanta. Although it is not adjacent to the central library, its former description as the Library Tower reflects the fact that the developers provided substantial funds for renovating the library in exchange for air rights. The building, designed by the architectural firm Pei, Cobb Freed & Partners, was completed in 1990. It is designed to withstand an 8.3 earthquake on the Richter Scale, but perhaps not a bomb attack.

2. At the end of May 2005, the Department of Homeland security announced that 90 radiation detection towers would be in place at the ports of Los Angeles–Long Beach by the end of 2005.

REFERENCES

Bureau of Public Roads (BPR) (1964) *Traffic Assignment Manuals*, US Department of Commerce, Urban Planning Division, Washington, DC.

Cho, S., P. Gordon, J.E. Moore II, H.W. Richardson, M. Shinozuka and S.E. Chang (2001), 'Integrating transportation network and regional economic models to estimate the costs of a large urban earthquake', *Journal of Regional Science*, **41** (1): 39–65.

Gordon, Peter, James E. Moore II, Harry Richardson, Masanobu Shinozuka, Donghwan An and Sungbin Cho (2004), 'Earthquake disaster mitigation for urban transportation systems: an integrated methodology that builds on the Kobe and Northridge experiences', in Yasuhide Okuyama and Stephanie E. Chang (eds), *Spatial and Economic Impacts of Natural Disasters*, New York: Springer Verlag, pp. 205–32.

Gordon, Peter, Harry W. Richardson and Bill Davis (1998), 'Transport related impacts of the Northridge earthquake', *Journal of Transportation and Statistics*, **1** (2), 21–36.

Richardson, Harry W., Peter Gordon, Myung-Jin Jun and Moon-Hyun Kim (1993), 'PRIDE and prejudice: the regional and racial impacts of local growth controls', *Environment and Planning A*, **25**.

Sheffi, Y. (1985), *Urban Transportation Networks: Equilibrium Analysis with Mathematical Programming Methods*, Englewood, NJ: Prentice Hall.

Wardrop, J.G. (1952), 'Some theoretical aspects of road traffic research', *Proceedings of the Institution of Civil Engineers*, Part II, Vol 1, 325–62.

15. The transportation implications of a terrorist attack on Seattle's highway network

Chang-Hee Christine Bae, Larry Blain and Alon Bassok

INTRODUCTION

The range of potential terrorist attacks on targets in the United States is very wide, and predictability by location and type is even less than for natural disasters. Many, if not most, potential attacks can be divided into three categories: symbolic targets, infrastructure destruction, and anti-personnel. Some attacks would include all three, such as 9/11 itself. This chapter examines an infrastructure attack in the Seattle metropolitan region (more specifically, the four counties – King, Pierce, Snohomish and Kitsap – covered by the Puget Sound Regional Council, Seattle's Metropolitan Planning Organization). An obvious symbolic attack would be to bring down the Space Needle, the 520-foot tower built as part of the 1962 World Fair. However the direct economic impact of such an attack would be very small, although there might be indirect economic effects in the form of deterred investment.

A pinpointed attack on infrastructure, especially transportation infrastructure, on the other hand, could have devastating consequences. Primary reasons are the characteristics of Seattle's topography, the current state of the transportation network, and the fact that the road network is already very congested, especially in peak hours. The Puget Sound metropolitan region has great natural beauty, but its lakes, forests, hills and nearby mountains interfere with the smooth flow of transportation. To make matters worse, the State of Washington has, over many decades, underinvested in highways as a matter of public policy. Among large metropolitan areas, the Puget Sound Region has an average amount of freeway capacity, but there is little redundancy in the road network. Furthermore, according to the Texas Transportation Institute's annual road congestion index, Seattle has been one of the most consistently congested metropolitan regions in the United States (it was second only to Los Angeles in 2002, which has sufficient redundancy that the informed driver can switch to several alternative surface streets if appropriate), but improved to rank #13 in 2003 because of a change in methodology (dropping the criterion of daily traffic per lane-mile which penalizes metropolitan areas that keep traffic moving instead of stop-and-go).[1]

RESEARCH OBJECTIVES

Knowledgeable terrorists would have little difficulty in identifying the weakest points in the transportation network – the two bridges across Lake Washington, on the I-90 and the SR520 roads. Given that both are floating bridges, the most efficient way to destroy these links would be to attack the approaches (or to cut down their key suspension wires). If both bridges were brought down simultaneously, travelers would have little choice: either abandon their cross-bridge trips, or take circuitous, relatively narrow and already congested roads around the lake. This would be highly disruptive because the two bridges are the main links between downtown Seattle and the rapidly expanding Eastside (including the suburban city Bellevue, Redmond, the home of Microsoft, and other high-income residential communities, such as Kirkland and Issaquah). There is no significant contraflow because traffic in both directions is of similar magnitude in both the morning and afternoon peaks.

Another research issue is the length of the disruption, because the damage to the regional economy would last until the bridges were operational. Accordingly this chapter includes some suggestions about the bridge reconstruction period (and their costs). A related issue to the imputed costs of additional travel time is the business interruption impacts (disruption and the extra cost of supply deliveries and freight shipments, inability of workers to get to their jobs, and so on). We currently have no model to measure these, but we have been able to address the issue in a general way by comparing this event with other studies of business interruption resulting from earthquakes and other natural disasters.

In addition, we explore the impact of disrupting traffic flows on the key North–South link, the I-5 freeway. This route is very important because it accommodates much of the through freight traffic between Canada and the western coastal states in the US. Some of the traffic can be diverted to the ring freeway (the I-405), but this will be overburdened by the lack of the cross-lake bridges. On the other hand, the traffic disruption consequences downtown would be somewhat more manageable than the effects of the lost bridges because of the multiplicity of alternative (if already congested) routes around the blocked covered section and the fact that it would much faster to clear the freeway than to rebuild the bridges.

The primary aim of this research is to assess the trip-making adjustments to the infrastructure destruction, with specific attention to changes in travel times. The number of trips would also change in the real world (many discretionary trips will be abandoned or, at least, shifted to alternative destinations on the residential sides of the lake), but we cannot model these changes with the current model that holds the number of trips constant. We examine three basic scenarios: baseline, destruction of the SR520 and the I-90 bridges (Scenario 1), and destruction of both bridges plus blocking the I-5 freeway (Scenario 2). We evaluate these scenarios for the morning and afternoon peaks and for off-peak hours. We are also interested in policy mitigations, such as measures to induce modal shifts and traffic management schemes to keep traffic moving on arterials and other roads.

PRECURSOR TO THIS RESEARCH

There is an important antecedent to this research, the analysis of a Puget Sound earthquake by Chang (2003). She employed two case studies – one of the catastrophic earthquake in Kobe, Japan in 1995, the other of a hypothetical large earthquake in the Seattle region. Obviously the latter is more relevant to this research. Of course earthquakes are very different from terrorist attacks. Both types of event are unpredictable. However the bridges most vulnerable to terrorist attacks (in the sense of those that disrupt the most traffic rather than in terms of degree of protection) can be identified, whereas those affected by an earthquake are less predictable, depending on the location of the epicenter, the type of earthquake, the extent and incidence of seismic retrofitting, and other factors. Nevertheless the characteristics of the two types of event are similar enough that they can be analyzed with the same kind of model.

In fact this research uses an updated (2000) version of the same model used by Chang (the 1998 Puget Sound Region Transportation Model) and a co-author of this chapter (Blain) participated in the earlier research. The former work differs in that it is concerned primarily with how an earthquake would directly affect accessibility. This approach is justified by the more dispersed pattern of infrastructure damage that can affect access to many locations. In this research, where the damage is pinpointed and very localized, our emphasis is on additional travel times and on the conversion of these effects to economic costs. Accessibility at many locations would not be significantly affected because of their distance from the damaged sites. The two approaches are related however because 'a post-disaster accessibility measure should be based on a model of travel time changes in the damaged network' (Chang, 2003, p. 1061).

The 1998 PSRC transportation model had 6187 nodes and 16 769 links (compared with 7908 nodes and 19 019 links in the 2000 model). The spatial units used consisted of 832 traffic analysis zones (TAZs) with an average population of 3300 (the 2000 model has 938 TAZs with an average population of 3294). Travel times were based on TAZ centroids. The PSRC model is the standard type of four-step model (trip generation, trip distribution, mode choice and network assignment). The first analysis was restricted to the last step, implying that the earthquake did not change the number of trips, the time of travel or the mode of travel (our research relaxes some of these assumptions, albeit in a heuristic manner). The method involved comparison of a baseline network equilibrium with post-earthquake flows after the network adjusts to the absence of the damaged links. A major difference between Chang's research and ours is the number of links damaged; in her research 106 out of 1137 bridges are damaged (although they are heavily concentrated in the North–South I-5 and I-405 loop corridors), in ours only the two most important bridges in the region and one covered freeway section are damaged. Hence her research is more complex in that the probability of bridge failure had to be assigned on the basis of distance from the fault, liquefaction of the underlying soil and age of the bridge, then converted in a deterministic scenario via adopting a Monte Carlo simulation model. In addition she chose to evaluate two alternative restoration states; in our research, we assume that the bridges are reconstructed simultaneously and within the same time frame. While her research suggests that the Eastside communities would lose the most accessibility (as obviously is the case in our research), her analysis shows that the preferred restoration strategy would nevertheless focus on rebuilding the damaged bridges on the I-5 corridor because the number of travelers benefiting is greater than in alternative strategies. Although congestion effects are embedded in increases in travel time, the estimates are underbounded because traffic back-ups and imperfections in driver information are not taken into account.

Although this research builds heavily on Chang's work (after all, it uses an updated version of the same model and shares personnel), it is different in several respects. It is more narrowly focused: by examining a feasible, in the sense of a manageable, terrorist strike, the research is able to isolate its direct impacts unlike the more amorphous earthquake scenarios. It also goes beyond trip assignment. The research begins to consider trips deterred, the economic cost of additional travel times, the extent of the modal shift to buses, traffic management and other mitigating policy measures, business interruption impacts and infrastructure restoration costs.

The ultimate aim is to come up with a 'ballpark' estimate of the full economic impacts of a terrorist attack of this kind, a goal not attained in this chapter. The emphasis on 'ballpark' is important because some of our estimates rely upon specific assumptions, or extrapolations from studies elsewhere rather than as outputs of our model.

TRIP DIVERSION AND COSTS BY ROUTE

Trip diversion is a natural response to substantially increased road congestion. The most important type of diversion in this case, where major highway links are removed, is to change the route. With the two cross-lake bridges down, travelers have no choice but to go around the lake, either via northern routes – I-405 North to either I-5 South or shorter (in distance terms) routes on arterial roads (for example Lake Washington Blvd. – Juanita Drive – NE Bothell Way – Lake City Way) or the southern route (I-405 South to I-5 North). Whether trip makers choose the northern or the southern route obviously depends on their origins and/or destinations. Also there will be ripple effects along the alternative routes as some other trip makers at intermediate locations change their routes as their usual ones become much more congested. With the I-5 Tunnel (under the Convention Center at University St. and 8th Avenue)[2] blocked, there are many alternative surface streets. Downtown Seattle is a grid system with alternative one-way streets. Downloading the traffic from I-5 is feasible, but there are few entry and exit ramps and the surface streets are already congested. A major focus of this research is the additional trip times involved in these route diversions.

As expected, the increase in travel times associated with the damaged highway infrastructure is concentrated in the already peak commuting periods. Table 15.1 shows the total minutes of travel by time of day, mode and scenario. The three scenarios are: the baseline (normal traffic in the absence of a terrorist attack); Scenario 1 (the situation with both bridges down); and Scenario 2 (both bridges down plus the I-5 blocked at the Convention Center). The peaks are nominally 6–9 a.m. and 3–6 p.m., evening is 6 p.m. to midnight, and night is midnight to 6 a.m. These peaks are a standard if not universal convention, but may be subject to some questioning as a result of 'peak-lengthening'. Some credence for this is given by the high 'Midday' numbers. About a half of the trips take place in the 'Midday' period. This seems quite high, although the 'Midday' is six hours long (as opposed to three hours in the peaks), lunchtime traffic is notoriously heavy, and many schools finish before 3 p.m. Peak lengthening or peak adjusting might be appropriate, but we have not followed this step here.

Table 15.1 *Aggregate daily travel times by mode, time of day, and scenario (hours)*

	SOV	CP2	CP3+	Van	L Truck	M Truck	H Truck	Total TT/Day
Night	112 478.25	15 458.25	4257.65	–	8079.85	2148.63	1196.52	143 619.15
Night 1	121 020.33	16 609.27	4554.63	–	8407.32	2270.32	1282.82	154 144.68
Night 2	122 469.72	16 802.60	4603.13	–	8526.03	2307.78	1304.65	156 013.92
AM	268 987.17	39 119.68	13 593.43	378.42	22 322.20	10 452.83	6121.52	360 975.25
AM 1	295 756.43	42 342.60	14 381.60	416.88	24 441.38	11 754.12	7017.68	396 110.70
AM 2	349 768.30	52 572.03	18 581.53	416.68	26 698.83	11 710.70	7050.97	466 799.05
Midday	394 249.70	112 194.17	34 983.62	–	42 490.48	24 556.78	14 587.83	623 062.58
Midday 1	433 382.08	122 595.17	37 808.03	–	45 855.42	27 071.87	16 403.07	683 115.63
Midday 2	438 954.13	124 178.53	38 281.05	–	46 577.93	27 562.53	16 711.10	692 265.28
PM	504 966.08	119 423.13	40 695.72	485.05	32 922.37	14 150.05	8155.48	720 797.88
PM 1	578 418.22	135 131.13	45 401.48	548.67	37 336.17	16 455.27	9684.88	822 975.82
PM 2	592 389.00	138 149.33	46 329.00	562.70	38 485.03	16 989.05	10 011.63	842 915.75
Evening	176 265.78	58 491.32	20 477.95	–	13 324.90	3089.63	1396.75	273 046.33
Evening 1	188 470.32	62 354.18	21 756.17	–	14 137.98	3339.58	1535.25	291 593.48
Evening 2	190 328.52	62 950.92	21 953.85	–	14 331.52	3395.08	1563.62	294 523.50

A noteworthy feature of the data is the much denser flows in the afternoon than the morning peak, a common fact although the difference is very substantial, about double in the baseline comparison. On the other hand, the effects of the terrorist event impact the morning peak proportionately more (for example, in Scenario 2 travel times in the morning peak increase by 29.3 per cent over the baseline compared to 16.9 per cent in the afternoon peak).

Overwhelmingly, SOVs (single-occupant vehicles) dominate the traffic (accounting for about four-fifths of total travel time), although car-pooling is significant – perhaps facilitated by extensive car-pool lanes on the major freeways.

The baseline total travel time amounts to 2.122 million hours. Scenario 1 increases these by 226 200 hours (or by 10.7 per cent) while Scenario 2 increases travel time relative to the baseline by 330 800 (or by 15.6 per cent). These results suggest that the bridges are a more effective traffic-disrupting target (more than twice as effective) than blocking I-5. Of course there is no alternative to the bridges except very circuitous routes while North–South traffic flows can divert either to downtown surface streets or (with origins/destinations north and/or south of the I-5/I-405 interchanges) to I-405 rather than via I-5. Of course these are system-wide results, and the consequences for some specific individual routes are much more dramatic (see below).

Table 15.2 shows the regionwide average travel times (they are zonal averages rather than personal or vehicle travel times) for single-occupant vehicles by scenario and time of day (they are available for other modes, but their presentation would be tedious). The data show that, not surprisingly, average trip times increase in Scenario 1 and again in Scenario 2. The averages are consistently higher in the p.m. than in the a.m. peak (almost 27 per cent higher in the baseline), although the proportionate increase in the a.m. peak is much larger (especially in Scenario 2). As expected, the offpeak changes from scenario to scenario are much more modest. On the whole, average travel times are shorter than those suggested in other sources such as the 2000 Census (the Seattle CMSA auto commute is 25.2 minutes), but the Census data are on commuting and exclude nonwork trips that are often shorter. The high nighttime numbers are a little surprising; the answer may well be longer trip lengths.

An important component of the economic costs of a transportation-related terrorist attack is the monetary cost of the additional travel time incurred by individual travelers. There is a sizeable literature on the value of travel time with estimates that range between 20 per cent and 50 per cent of the wage rate. Not only does the wage rate vary among workers but also the percentage of that rate at which travel time is valued, not to mention

Table 15.2 SOV regionwide average travel times by time of day and scenario (mins)

	Night	AM	Midday	PM	Evening
Baseline	21.75	15.73	13.35	19.91	13.61
Scenario 1	23.40	17.30	14.67	22.81	14.55
Scenario 2	23.68	20.46	14.86	23.36	14.70

Table 15.3 Value of daily travel time for all modes (lower range: $)

	Night	AM	Midday	PM	Evening	Daily sum
Baseline	1 365 845	4 148 310	8 450 149	7 863 957	2 811 226	24 639 488
Scenario 1	1 462 836	4 588 000	9 299 245	9 009 926	3 006 635	27 366 641
Scenario 2	1 481 739	5 173 198	9 440 468	9 242 520	3 039 178	28 377 104

Table 15.4 Value of daily travel time for all modes (upper range: $)

	Night	AM	Midday	PM	Evening	Daily sum
Baseline	2 438 989	6 833 121	13 475 143	13 759 204	5 229 894	41 736 351
Scenario 1	2 614 772	7 518 877	14 794 433	15 713 385	5 586 721	46 228 188
Scenario 2	2 647 391	8 690 167	15 006 993	16 102 786	5 644 471	48 091 808

that the value of commuting time may vary from the value of time for non-work trips; ideally we would need to know the distribution of income of all travelers and the split between work and non-work trips to reach a precise estimate. Usually, as in this case, the required information is not available. Accordingly we adopt a common device, choosing a low average value of travel time (in this case $6.50 per hour) and comparing the results with a high value (assumed here to be $13.00 per hour). In practice the true average may be at some value between the lower and upper end of the range. We also use another conventional travel time assumption: $35 per PCE (passenger car equivalent) hour for a commercial vehicle (these travel time assumptions are the same as in Chapter 14). The results are shown in Tables 15.3 and 15.4. At the lower wage rate peak travel time losses are valued at $2.73 million per day in the 'no bridges' scenario and at $3.74 million if the blocked I-5 is added to the destroyed bridges. These costs increase to $4.49 million and $6.36 million respectively if the upper-end travel time estimate is chosen. These numbers can be expressed in a different way by comparing them to the baseline: Scenario 1 raises baseline travel costs by

Table 15.5 Comparison between lower and higher values of travel time

	Lower Value ($)		Higher Value ($)	
	Daily sum	Reconstruction period	Daily sum	Reconstruction period
Baseline	24 639 488	4 435 107 753	41 736 351	7 512 543 142
Scenario 1	27 366 641	4 925 995 338	46 228 188	8 321 073 824
Scenario 2	28 377 104	5 107 878 781	48 091 808	8 656 525 359

Table 15.6 Changes in commute times on selected disrupted routes (mins)

Scenario	AM			PM		
	Baseline	S. 1	S. 2	Baseline	S. 1	S. 2
Bellevue to Downtown	22.4	54.3	54.4	30.3	87.2	89.9
Downtown to Bellevue	22.1	51.0	51.2	31.6	86.5	90.6
Redmond to Downtown	30.6	58.0	60.4	39.8	90.3	94.5
Downtown to Redmond	29.9	57.7	59.8	39.9	90.3	94.5
Renton to Downtown	22.7	27.2	27.1	32.4	39.9	39.8
Downtown to Renton	21.3	22.8	32.6	33.7	47.3	49.0
UW to SeaTac Airport	26.4	27.6	34.2	41.6	47.6	56.7
SeaTac Airport to UW	27.5	29.9	33.5	48.8	53.0	63.7

11.1 per cent while Scenario 2 raises these costs by 15.2 per cent (lower-range values; the upper-range values are similar, 10.8 per cent and 15.2 per cent respectively).

To estimate the total value of travel time losses as a result of the event, we have to assume a restoration period for the bridges and the blocked I-5. We have decided on 180 days; the numbers can be adjusted if a different reconstruction period is considered more reliable. The 180-day period results in a lower range of the travel time losses under Scenario 1 of $490.9 million and of $672.8 million under Scenario 2 (lower range). The higher range values are $808.5 million and $1144.0 million respectively (based on data in Table 15.5).

Table 15.6 shows the changes in travel times of some representative trips that would be disrupted by these attacks. For example consider the commute between Downtown Bellevue and Downtown Seattle, trips that would be among the most disrupted because of the proximity of both the origin and destination to the SR520 bridge. Comparing Scenario 1 with the baseline shows that the one-way commute time increases by more than 140 per cent in the morning and by almost 175 per cent in the afternoon, resulting in inbound times of 54.3 minutes as opposed to 22.4 minutes in the morning, and outbound times of 87.2 minutes compared with 30.3 minutes. The trip time increments between locations affected by the I-5 block (for example Downtown Seattle–Redmond, University of Washington–Seatac Airport) were much smaller (in the 30 to 50 per cent range), presumably reflecting the availability of many alternative routes near Downtown Seattle.

OTHER ISSUES

Trip Diversion by Time

Nationally, about 77 per cent of all trips are non-work trips, and many of these take place during peak hours, especially in the afternoon peak. Many, but not all, of these non-work trips are discretionary and could be taken in off-peak hours, or (in some cases) not taken at all. In addition, via flextime programs adopted by either private or public employers, some worktrips could be diverted to off-peak hours. However an important limitation is the already heavy traffic flows in the 9 a.m. to 3 p.m. ('Midday') period. This implies that the most scope for time diversion would be to the evening and night-time periods; diverting freight traffic is one of the few feasible options available. The problem is how to estimate any potential time diversions and to incorporate their effects in the travel time cost estimates.

Trip Diversion by Mode

Apart from minimal rail services and the considerable ferry services across Puget Sound, public transport in the Puget Sound Region is by bus. King County Metro has 257 000 passenger trips per day but only 1000 rail trips (2002 data). These are equivalent to about 2.5 per cent of person trips by automobile. More relevant, it is approximately equal to the number of passengers crossing the bridges. To take an extreme and wholly unrealistic case, bus travel would have to be doubled to shift all the auto trip makers to buses. Although buses take up much more road space than cars, especially on the relatively narrow arterials around the north shore of Lake Washington, a full bus is much more economical of road space than if the equivalent number of bus passengers were solo drivers. Accordingly a modal shift in favor of buses can minimize some, but not all, of the travel time impacts of the disruptions. Modal shifts could be accommodated within the model, but the assumptions needed to do this precisely are very restrictive. How much congestion mitigation is attainable via shifts from single-occupant vehicles to buses and car-pools remains an open question.

We were not able within the time frame of the research to devise a bus strategy to accommodate the consequences of this attack. The issues are complex: frequency of service; alternative routes (very few); the availability of enough buses to expand (or switch) service, and if more buses are needed where they would come from; the congestion impacts of more buses on the low-capacity roads that would be used if the Lake Washington bridges were down; and the traffic management schemes that might be introduced to facilitate round-the-lake traffic flow. However we were able to perform a simulation by slowing down bus speeds. This simulation did not capture all the attributes of the modal shift involved, but it gave us a few generalized results. Regionwide, the impact on bus ridership was modest. However on certain routes the consequences were impressive. For example from the transit center in Downtown Bellevue to Downtown Seattle the bus share would increase from an already impressive 33 per cent to 57 per cent. The key point is that a plan to arrange a significant modal shift from automobiles to buses would be an important mitigating factor, although it is very difficult to quantify the extent of the mitigation.

With respect to car-pools, Table 15.7 provides some evidence for the carpool share (in terms of vehicles not person-trips). The peak shares are the most relevant; off-peak trips especially in the evening and at night are very likely to be non-solo vehicles. Also, the high middle-of-the-day car-pools reflect lunch groups, shopping, children being picked up from school and other non-work trips. The peak shares are 18.9 per cent in the morning and 24.9 per cent in the afternoon. These are somewhat high by national standards so that the prospect of raising them substantially, even for a relatively short time, is challenging.

Table 15.7 Carpool share by time of day

Time of day	Traffic volume				Carpool share
	SOV	CP2	CP3	LT	
Night	310 354	51 329	14 365	43 268	15.67%
AM	1 025 857	187 520	72 813	89 297	18.93%
Midday	1 772 317	545 765	171 600	159 262	27.08%
PM	1 521 798	401 970	139 431	110 471	24.91%
Evening	777 005	283 063	101 548	57 997	31.54%

Note: Vanpool traffic volumes are only available for peak periods, and are excluded.

Trip Deterrence

The trip disruptions associated with these terrorist events are so consequential that many trips, especially of the discretionary type, may not be taken at all. For example if you live on the Eastside, why bother taking the trip to a restaurant in Downtown Seattle? Why not stay home or perhaps eat out a local restaurant? (The latter would of course be a trip diverted rather than deterred.) The difficulty with trip deterrence is that it is so difficult to estimate *ex ante*. *Ex post* survey evidence might provide some details. Also monitored examples of what happened during past events are few. One of the few relevant examples is the 1984 Los Angeles Olympics where it was estimated that a significant proportion of the usual trips did not take place, and traffic counts were below normal despite the increase in the number of out-of-towners. However the Olympics lasted only a few weeks, whereas these disruptions will last at least several months.

WSDOT estimates of average daily traffic flows (2003 data) across the two bridges are 116 812 vehicles on I-90 and 101 840 vehicles on SR520. All of these trips would have to diverted (by route, some possibly by time) or deterred. We suspect that almost all of the deterred trips would be non-work trips because many non-work trips (except to family and friends) have substitutable destinations. Also although non-work trips account for a high share of total trips, many are short trips so that a smaller proportion of the total trips crossing the lake would be non-work trips. Any estimate of the trips deterred would be little more than a blind guess, but even 5 per cent of the former cross-lake trips would make a substantial difference to congestion levels on the alternative routes (the model can account for trips diverted to nearby destinations).

Restoration Period

We calculated the travel time losses on the assumption that the bridges and other infrastructure would not be back in use for 180 days. These could be scaled downwards or upwards as required. Any restoration period estimate is speculative because the damage is unknown. However there are also institutional and political considerations to be taken into account, for example obtaining the funds, hiring the contractors and so on. There are many war stories about the funding of transportation projects in Washington State, and these obstacles should not be taken lightly. A sound approach would be to have an emergency fund available in advance; a voter-approved bond issue would take too long, although going to capital markets might be an option.

Restoration Costs

Bridge restoration costs are sensitive to the nature of the damage and the characteristics of the bridge. To provide some perspective, in the Puget Sound Region there is a planned project for a new SR520 bridge. However a four-lane bridge would cost $2.9 billion and take seven years. Here, obviously, we are referring to reconstruction not new construction. One estimate that may have some relevance is by Gordon et al. (2004). A study of a hypothetical 7.1 earthquake on the Elysian Park fault in Los Angeles identified 233 damaged bridges, but only three collapsed. The mean repair estimate for these three was $47.274 million per bridge. The structure damage that might be involved with the Convention Center might be more costly than each bridge, but a starting point for an estimate of the reconstruction costs with the three events might be $200 million.

Freight Delays and Business Interruption Impacts

The freight delays are not as severe as might be expected, primarily because most of the freight traffic is North–South with modest amounts crossing the lake. Freight delays increase by 12.6 per cent in Scenario 1 over the baseline, and by an additional 2.1 per cent in Scenario 2 (based on the data in Table 15.8). The modest marginal increment in Scenario 2 compared with Scenario 1, given the fact of a North–South freight corridor, is explained by through the region traffic avoiding both obstacles (the bridges and downtown Seattle) by taking I-405 instead of I-5. Thus business interruption impacts are not as damaging as has been found in other disaster studies, for example earthquakes where the costs of business interruption can be similar to the costs of structure damage (Gordon et al., 2004). Congestion and longer trip times will raise business costs, but freight delay costs ($172.6 million in Scenario 1 plus an additional $28.2 million in Scenario 2 for a total of $200.8 million, less than 15 per cent more than the baseline total) are relatively small. There will be other additional costs, such as extra commuting costs, but these will largely be borne by workers rather than businesses. On the whole however this is a relatively modest business interruption event, at

Table 15.8 Total travel time for medium and heavy trucks (hours)

	Night	AM	Midday	PM	Evening	Daily sum
Baseline	3 345.15	16 574.35	39 144.62	22 305.53	4 486.38	85 856.03
Scenario 1	3 553.13	18 771.80	43 474.93	26 140.15	4 874.83	96 814.85
Scenario 2	3 612.43	18 761.67	44 273.63	27 000.68	4 958.70	98 607.12

least from the transportation perspective. There are other significant business interruption costs, of course, but these are not modeled.

Traffic Mitigation Measures

The consequences of this type of terrorist attack in an area with the topographical characteristics of the Seattle region would have dramatic impacts on travel patterns for a period of several months. Thus it makes sense to have a traffic mitigation plan in hand in case an event of this kind is likely to occur. The dollar costs of such a plan would be very small compared with the travel time delay costs that we have estimated, so the effort would be very worthwhile. There are several types of traffic mitigation. First, introduce traffic flow improvements on the undamaged routes. Second, promote more car-pool use via public education, incentives or even mandates. Third, induce more of a modal shift to buses by organizing new routes, increasing service frequency and perhaps free fares. New buses (especially for temporary use) could not be ordered and purchased within the time frame, but buses might be loaned from transit agencies outside the region. Fourth, achieve more trip diversion by time, especially for work trips by measures to facilitate more flextime and compressed work weeks.

CONCLUSIONS

This chapter has presented some preliminary results of the primarily transportation impacts of a potential and plausible terrorist attack on the transportation infrastructure of the Seattle metropolitan region. This would have major effects because of the topography and limited road redundancies of the region. The hypothetical event is a highly focused attack on the two bridges (I-5 and SR520) crossing Lake Washington with the possible addition of a third attack on the North–South I-5 corridor in downtown Seattle near the Convention Center. We use a standard transportation model to explore the effects of the disruption of these three major highway routes.

The characteristics of the model require us to focus primarily on route diversion, but we discuss other impacts (changes in time, modal shifts, trip deterrence, freight delays, bridge reconstruction and traffic mitigation) in more general terms. Total travel times increase by 10.7 per cent comparing Scenario 1 (bridges down) with the baseline and by 15.6 per cent comparing Scenario 2 (bridges down plus I-5 blocked) with the baseline. The increases were, as expected, greater in the peaks (especially the morning peak, although traffic volumes were much larger in the afternoon peak).

To estimate the economic costs of the traffic delays and added congestion, we needed travel time values and a restoration period before the infrastructure is back in place. To illustrate, we chose two alternative values for personal travel ($6.50 and $13 per hour), a commercial vehicle value of $35 per PCE hour, and a 180-day restoration period. This yielded an upper-end total cost of $808.5 million for Scenario 1 and $1144 million in Scenario 2. These values provide a guide to how much it might be worth spending on mitigation and prevention. The consequences are much more serious of course for individual trip makers (especially commuters) who live and work close to the bridges. As an extreme case, the trip times between downtown Bellevue (the largest suburban center on the Eastside) and downtown Seattle increase by 2.3 times in the morning peak and by three times in the afternoon, to 90 minutes. Turning to issues on which our answers are more uncertain, freight delays would add at least $200 million to business costs and infrastructure reconstruction might cost another $200 million. There are some opportunities for traffic mitigation, but contingency plans would need to be made well in advance of anticipated terrorist attacks. Also more research is needed on the effects of bridge and road closures. This is a preliminary research study to give some idea of the scale of the problem we might have to deal with in a metropolitan area as topographically vulnerable as Seattle.

NOTES

1. See http://mobility.tamu.edu/ums/report/
2. This is also part of the bus tunnel.

BIBLIOGRAPHY

Chang, S.E. (2003), 'Transportation planning for disasters: an accessibility approach', *Environment and Planning A*, **35**, 1051–72.

Cho, S., P. Gordon, J.E. Moore II, H.W. Richardson, M. Shinozuka and S.E. Chang (2001), 'Integrating transportation network and regional economic models to estimate the costs of a large urban earthquake', *Journal of Regional Science*, **41**, 39–65.

Gordon, P., J.E. Moore II, H.W. Richardson, M. Shinozuka, D. An and S. Cho (2004), 'Earthquake disaster mitigation for urban transportation systems: an integrated methodology that builds on the Kobe and Northridge experiences', in Y. Okuyama and S.E. Chang (eds), *Modeling Spatial and Economic Impacts of Disasters*, Heidelberg: Springer, pp. 205–32.

Gordon, P., H.W. Richardson and B. Davis (1998), 'Transport-related impacts of the Northridge earthquake,' *Journal of Transportation and Statistics*, **1** (2), 21–36.

Nojima, N. and M. Sugimoto (2000), 'Simulation and evaluation of post-earthquake function performance of transportation network', in *Proceedings of the 12th World Conference on Earthquake Engineering*, New Zealand Society for Earthquake Engineering, Upper Hutt, CD-ROM, Paper #1927.

Wakabayashi, H. and H. Kameda (1992), 'Network performance of highway systems under earthquake effects: a case study of the 1989 Loma Prieta earthquake', in *Proceedings of the US–Japan Workshop on Earthquake Disaster Prevention for Lifeline Systems*, Public Works Research Institute, Tsukuba Science City, pp. 215–32.

Wesemann, L., T. Hamilton, S. Tabaie and G. Bare (1996), 'Cost-of-delay studies for freeway closures by Northridge earthquake', *Transportation Research Record*, **#1559**, 67–75.

Index